Eco-Reformation

Eco-Reformation

Grace and Hope for a Planet in Peril

edited by
LISA E. DAHILL
& JAMES B. MARTIN-SCHRAMM

Foreword by Bill McKibben

CASCADE *Books* · Eugene, Oregon

ECO-REFORMATION
Grace and Hope for a Planet in Peril

Cascade Books
An Imprint of Wipf and Stock Publishers
199 W. 8th Ave., Suite 3
Eugene, OR 97401

www.wipfandstock.com

PAPERBACK ISBN: 978-1-4982-2546-5
HARDCOVER ISBN: 978-1-4982-2548-9
EBOOK ISBN: 978-1-4982-2547-2

Cataloguing-in-Publication data:

Names: Dahill, Lisa E. | Martin-Schramm, James B. | McKibben, Bill.

Title: Eco-reformation : grace and hope for a planet in peril / edited by Lisa E. Dahill and James B. Martin-Schramm ; foreword by Bill McKibben.

Description: Eugene, OR: Cascade Books, 2016. | Includes bibliographic data.

Identifiers: ISBN 978-1-4982-2546-5 (paperback) | ISBN 978-1-4982-2548-9 (hardcover) | ISBN 978-1-4982-2547-2 (ebook)

Subjects: LCSH: Ecotheology. | Human ecology—Religious aspects—Christianity. | Lutheran Church—Doctrines.

Classification: BT695.5 E2626 2016 (paperback). | BT695.5 (ebook).

Manufactured in the U.S.A.   10/06/16

*To future generations of reformers who love God's creation
and all God's creatures*

We need a new dialogue about how we are shaping the future of our planet ... a conversation that includes everyone, since the environmental challenge we are undergoing, and its human roots, concern and affect us all ... [This challenge requires] an ecological conversion.

POPE FRANCIS

The Word of God, whenever it comes, comes to change and renew the world.

MARTIN LUTHER

Contents

Foreword

WHEN A SYSTEM GETS stuck, change has to come from somewhere.

For the last half millennium, a template for that change has been Martin Luther and his theses, nailed to the door of the Wittenberg Castle Church. Those 95 charges and questions began a revolution that played out with world-shaking results; much of the modern spirit, and hence the modern world, derives from the consequences of that act. Some of the change was for the better, some perhaps for the worse; historians can argue the results, but not the importance.

We're in a somewhat similar place right now, not only theologically but economically and politically. The world is stuck in an orbit around its main power source—fossil fuel. Like the medieval Church, coal/oil/gas has defined most of what it means to be a modern human, from mobility to consumerism. And now it's killing us. Literally—the latest data shows that by 2030 one hundred million of our fellow souls may die from the direct effects of air pollution or the indirect effects of climate change, a number that will rise steadily for many generations to come.

Unless we can intervene now, powerfully, to switch from that world of centralized energy to a distributed model that depends on local sun and wind. It's not entirely different from the move from a central church to the localized autonomy of Protestantism.

Except, of course, that the politics has shifted. White American Protestants are the least likely people on earth to care about climate change. Pope Francis, by contrast, has emerged as a great champion. His 2015 encyclical, *Laudato Si'*, used our overwhelming climate crisis as the entry point for a sweeping and majestic critique of modernity, one that has opened many minds.

One hopes that these essays from theologians in the Lutheran tradition will do something similar. It is refreshing to see the power of argument and of organizing inherent in these words. For people of faith these questions could not be more real or timely: this year we're seeing the destruction of vast swaths of coral reef, unprecedented Arctic melt, and a disastrous cycle of flood and drought. Our ability as stewards, and our conviction that we are neighbor-lovers, has never been more deeply called into question. Thank heaven that, as the fever builds, the antibodies are coming into play!

Bill McKibben

August 2016

Preface

—LISA E. DAHILL & JAMES B. MARTIN-SCHRAMM

IN 1517, MARTIN LUTHER famously put hammer to nail, posting his outrage at the economic corruption of the church of his time. His 95 *Theses* brought together scriptural, pastoral, ethical, and theological arguments against the practice of the sale of indulgences: the linchpin of what quickly grew into a much larger critique of theological malfeasance and its damage to the faithful and to the faith. Arguing that "[e]very true Christian, whether living or dead, has part in all the blessings of Christ and the Church . . . [granted] by God, even without letters of pardon" (Thesis 37), Luther pointed to the open doors of grace in Jesus Christ, the Gospel of endless and redemptive divine mercy for all who trust in this love. In the years since, Christians in Europe and eventually around the world have found liberation, solace, dismay, aggravation, and inspiration in the Reformation Luther sparked; popular history through the centuries has granted his challenge to the medieval ecclesial structuring of European society iconic status—for better or worse—in giving rise to modernity.

In 2017 Christians around the world, and Lutherans in particular, mark the five hundredth anniversary of the Reformation. Worship services, conferences, festivals, and pronouncements of all kinds herald this anniversary with much fanfare and critical attention to the continuing significance of Luther's insights and legacy. In the midst of many appeals for reformation today, an overarching chorus is becoming audible in which human cries join with croaks and squawks and storms: the slowly suffocated or violently silenced voices of people, cultures, species, and ecosystems at risk. That is, a growing number of theologians, scholars, and activists around the world—including those gathered in this volume—believe that Reformation celebrations in 2017 and beyond need to focus now on the urgent need for an *Eco*-Reformation.

Indeed a great deal has changed since 1517. For one thing, this time the Pope isn't the enemy. In preparation for the 2015 United Nations Climate Change Conference in Paris, Pope Francis published a watershed encyclical, titled *Laudato Si': On Care for Our Common Home*, calling all people on Earth of every faith and culture to love, care for, and protect our planet. Perhaps here is a voice today like that of the 1517 Luther: "I urgently appeal, then, for a new dialogue about how we are shaping the future of our planet. We need a conversation which includes everyone, since the environmental challenge we are undergoing, and its human roots, concern and affect us all . . . All of us can cooperate as instruments of God for the care of creation, each according to his or her own culture, experience, involvements and talents."[1] Along with many other religious, scientific, and political leaders, Pope Francis points out that the rise of industrial, fossil-fuel-driven capitalism and the explosive growth in human population are endangering the fundamental planetary life-support systems in which life as we know it has evolved. In fact, the overwhelming impact of our species is leading many scientists to conclude that we have entered a new era of planetary history—the Anthropocene. Recent reports by the world's leading scientists make it clear that the twenty-first century will be increasingly marked by unprecedented climate change. The collective impact of human production, consumption, and reproduction is undermining the ecological systems that support human life on Earth. If human beings don't reform our relationship with God's creation, enormous suffering will befall many—especially the weakest and most vulnerable among all species.

The conviction at the heart of this collection of essays is that a gospel call for ecological justice thus belongs at the heart of the five hundredth anniversary observance of the Reformation in 2017 and as a—if not the—central dimension of Christian conversion, faith, and practice (in collaboration with others among the world's diversity of religious and spiritual traditions) into the foreseeable future. Luther protested the sale of indulgences, God's grace marketed to the desperate as a fund-raising tool; and Christians in many contexts have condemned the commodification of human life in countless forms of slavery, impoverishment, trafficking, and oppression, the deadly injustice of global economic systems.

1. Pope Francis, *Laudato Si': On Care for Our Common Home* (Rome: Libreria Editrice Vaticana, 2015), para. 14.

Now Christians along with many others are recognizing the even more catastrophic implications of the past millennium's shift from regarding the natural world as a living and beloved face of divine creation to treating it as a commodity to be exploited for profit. The Lutheran World Federation has brought together all three of these interwoven—indeed, inseparable—layers of economic idolatry in its theme for the global 2017 Reformation anniversary, a banner under which surely all those of good faith might unite today: "Salvation: Not for sale. Human beings: Not for sale. Creation: Not for sale."

This volume features essays by some of the world's leading Lutheran scholars who publish in English, offering resources for Christians to address the urgent need for Eco-Reformation. Like Luther's 95 *Theses*, it brings together critical biblical, pastoral, theological, historical, and ethical perspectives—attempting to pull forth resources from the Lutheran tradition in particular that constructively advance the vision of a socially and ecologically flourishing Earth.

David Rhoads begins the volume with an introduction that lays the foundations for an Eco-Reformation. As the Protestant Reformation addressed the most important issue of the day (human salvation), Rhoads argues the heirs of the Reformation must address the critical issue of our day (planetary well-being). Rhoads argues persuasively that the integrated social, economic, political, and environmental crises we face are at their root a spiritual crisis that can only be resolved by recovering and reorienting key biblical, theological, ethical, liturgical, and ecclesiastical insights. The presence of the Spirit of God in, with, and under all of life and the very grace present in Jesus Christ now to be discerned everywhere rest at the heart of this great work.

Larry Rasmussen connects this volume's focus on the need for an Eco-Reformation with one of the themes the Lutheran World Federation will emphasize during its commemoration of the five-hundredth anniversary of the Reformation: "Creation—Not for Sale." Rasmussen reviews fundamental modern assumptions that have fostered anthropocentrism and yielded an instrumentalist mindset that relentlessly commodifies nature. He contrasts this crass and empty materialism with an understanding of creation as priceless to recover the intrinsic value of all that God has made. The rest of his essay explores how the First Article of the Creed and a sacramental imagination can restore deeply personal relationships that have been torn asunder by a master-slave relationship between human beings and the rest of creation.

Cynthia Moe-Lobeda plows similar theological ground by reflecting on the sure promise of God's unconditional love and the opportunity and calling all Christians have to love the world as God does. This love compels us, however, to face the fact that the collective impact of human activities are not furthering Earth's life-generating capacity but harming it through structural sin made manifest in climate change and racism. She argues Christians must repent for these sins while exploring theological seeds of hope and moral power that can be found in Christian claims about the resurrection, the theology of the cross, and Martin Luther's sense of God indwelling all creation. Moe-Lobeda concludes by reflecting on the paradoxical nature of moral anthropology and by exploring a practical framework for expressing neighbor-love as ecological-economic vocation.

Wanda Deifelt further develops Lutheran insights related to care for creation and connects them at the outset to efforts within the World Council of Churches to promote justice, peace, and the integrity of creation. She draws on ecofeminist theologians, Ivone Gebara and Rosemary Radford Ruether, to explore interrelated systems of stratification that subjugate people and the planet. Similarly, she draws on Emmanuel Levinas and Enrique Dussel to explain how creation has been rendered an inferior "other" along with so many deemed less worthy by colonialist mindsets. To bridge these gaps and heal these wounds Deifelt explores Martin Luther's theological insights regarding creation as God's mask, the locus of God's work in the suffering in and of the world, and how the cross can become the tree of life without idealizing suffering. Deifelt emphasizes that God's saving action on the cross seeks to restore all of creation to its original dignity and beauty.

Paul Santmire strives to deepen the Lutheran accent on nature by exploring two voices revealed in scripture that emphasize the integrity and expressiveness of nature. He argues that God values nature for itself and thus it has intrinsic value for God apart from any human valuation of nature. Throughout the essay Santmire engages classical biblical texts, other theologians, and the works of scientists to demonstrate that God hears the destructibility of nature as the groaning of nature, but also that God hears the creativity of nature as nature's praise. Santmire believes a revised understanding of the integrity and expressiveness of nature properly expressed in the church's liturgical and spiritual practices is vital to counter the rampant anthropocentrism of our age.

Robert Saler's essay on the work of Joseph Sittler mirrors Santmire's essay insofar as he emphasizes that Sittler's theological style was more dialogical, less didactic, and more evocative. Saler demonstrates how Sittler drew on the fine arts (literature, film, and poetry) and not solely theology to reflect on the ambiguities of life in our postmodern era. He explains why Sittler insisted Christians need to rethink the relationship of nature and grace not only to proclaim the gospel but also to address the fact that human beings are transforming life on Earth in unprecedented ways. Saler demonstrates that care for the environment, creative imagination, and cultural analysis were invariably linked in Sittler's mind. For Saler Joseph Sittler modeled a much-needed type of fragmentary, provisional, post-Enlightenment theological reflection that connects the realms of science and aesthetics in vital ways.

James Martin-Schramm explores the contributions of another important Lutheran theologian of the twentieth century—Dietrich Bonhoeffer. He focuses on Bonhoeffer's provocative 1933 essay on "The Church and the Jewish Question" and draws parallels to climate change, which he argues is the most important issue facing the church today. Martin-Schramm is convinced Bonhoeffer would have grave concerns about the impacts of climate change on present and future generations and ponders how Bonhoeffer might challenge the feeble responses of both the state and church thus far. Martin-Schramm explains how Martin Luther's doctrine of the two kingdoms shaped Bonhoeffer's critique of the church and state in his day, and he explores how this key Lutheran insight might shape perceptions about how God is at work in the world today among all who are calling for climate justice.

Terence Fretheim turns the focus back to Scripture and explores texts in the Old Testament that reveal how God enables all of God's creatures to engage in creation. Focusing primarily on Genesis 1–2, Fretheim argues provocatively that God did not create the world alone but rather in an interdependent manner with all of God's creatures, requiring ongoing divine self-limitation. Furthermore, Fretheim views disorder in the world as a good thing and part of God's good creation. All of God's creatures must adapt to this good disorder and may even contribute to it. Like other creatures, God gives human beings a key role in the ongoing development and evaluation of creation. As a result, while the future is ultimately in God's hands, Fretheim argues much depends on how human beings exercise moral agency in terms of caring for creation.

Barbara Rossing's essay draws this attention to Scripture forward into preaching—specifically the power of preaching apocalyptic texts in the face of ecological crisis. Contra popular caricatures of the anti-Earth, "heavenist" bent of biblical apocalypses, Rossing asserts that apocalyptic texts, especially the book of Revelation, offer profound narrative and visual images of hope precisely in the midst of imperial powers and paralyzing fear. Her essay opens many features of an eco-reformation homiletic visible in Revelation: imagining ourselves into its storyline, preaching safe birth-space within chaos, witnessing to communal solidarity, and enacting public spectacles and activism. All of these dimensions point to eschatology as healing and hope, the flourishing of the Tree of Life, rather than eschatology as doom.

Benjamin Stewart considers the power of Christian baptism in enacting this eco-reformation healing for the flourishing of all life on Earth. His essay traces three root metaphors of baptism—the stream, the flood, and the spring—in their respective symbolic significance for Christian life and for the protection and honoring of the beleaguered literal waters of Earth. In its grace-full descent and flow, its ominous and nutrient-laden rising, its mysterious upwelling, all water is holy water, Stewart asserts; and attending to its life calls for our highest spiritual, political, and liturgical attention.

Lisa Dahill's work on "rewilding" Christian spirituality begins here in the water, with a return to the early-church practice of baptizing into local creeks, rivers, springs, or seas. Such baptism both demands attention to the health of a given watershed and immerses new Christians into the fullness of its life: becoming kin with the creatures of all kinds who depend on those waters. This larger interspecies kinship animates as well her additional proposals for learning again to attend to the Book of Nature—as a source alongside Scripture of divine revelation in living relationship with these creatures and the larger eco-systemic and climactic forces of the planet—and for the largest possible Eucharistic life, a ceaseless, divinely permeated eating and being eaten unfolding within cycles of predation, nourishment, and mutual belonging.

Ernest Simmons orients readers to the context of higher education—specifically religiously oriented colleges and universities—as he claims, with David Orr, that "all education is environmental education." In particular, he proposes that the Lutheran tradition of liberal arts higher education includes unique resources positioning it well as a site for forming critical, courageous citizens for global/climate and local ecological leadership in the twenty-first century. The dialectical nature of Luther's thought, its essential relationality, and its emphasis on vocation for the common good equip thinkers able to find their way in the endlessly "entangled" scientific/social complexities of our time.

Victor Thasiah moves to another geography altogether in his case study of a Rwandan Lutheran theologian, bishop, and community organizer whose work in forest restoration both mirrors and contributes to his compatriots' psychic healing from genocide. Although the larger Protestant Council of Churches of Rwanda had taken courageous leadership in responding to climate change and Christians' environmental responsibility, its emphases lacked attention to post-genocide contextual problems of power, healing, and poverty. Thasiah explores the life and leadership of John Rutsindintwarane, whose organizing of thousands of Rwandans has made possible large areas of reforestation as well as the emergence of strong voices for local democratic decision-making and sustainable rural and urban development: an on-the-ground eco-reformation and rebuilding of a world.

Aana Vigen continues the emphasis on healing through her analysis of climate injustice as illness: both in its reflecting of broader social/spiritual dis-ease (of which human beings, and especially over-privileged Westerners, are the "infection agents") and in quite literally contributing to the intensification of widespread human illness and suffering across the globe. Vigen frames her work through the liturgical metaphors of Advent and Lent, seeing in the hopeful, ascetic, and anticipatory dimensions of these seasons windows into the broader levels of healing that our planet and its most vulnerable inhabitants require. Through comprehensive global statistics, United Nations analyses, and the use of Luther's theological method, Vigen moves through sections titled "Hunger," "Thirst," and "Bugs" toward an Eco-Reformation whose "justice is never abstract."

Terra Rowe contributes the essay most clearly critical of a central aspect of the Reformation tradition, specifically the emphasis on grace as free gift. Drawing on Marcel Mauss's theory of gift-exchange, Rowe explores John Milbank's assertion of a connection between the rise of capitalism and the Reformation wedge—in the name of free grace—between gift and giver that allowed "resources" to be commodified into "capital." She shows how Luther himself exemplified a more complex understanding of grace than that which hardened into Reformation doctrine, using the Finnish school of Luther interpretation to demonstrate that for

Luther Christ is both gift and giver, a central aspect of the Reformer's fundamentally sacramental worldview and a window into a contemporary view of grace open to the divine permeation of all things.

Finally, Norman Habel brings together key aspects of all these essays' emphases into a culminating contribution: a new set of Ninety-Five Theses for an Eco-Reformation. These theses draw from Habel's expertise in ecological biblical hermeneutics but encompass theological, ethical, and liturgical dimensions as well of a renewed, re-formed Christian faith adequate to the fullest life of the world in our time.

With these essays, we are honored to publish what we hope will become a widely used appeal for the continuing power and liberating efficacy of the Christian tradition for the life of the world. We give special thanks to Bill McKibben, another Luther for our time, whose tireless organizing and compelling writing give voice to these urgent concerns perhaps more than anyone else alive today; we are so grateful for his engaging Foreword for this volume. Additional thanks go to Luther College student Hannah Sackett for her many hours of close reading and formatting of the manuscript.

Finally, where this volume ends, readers' own testimony begins: we look forward to taking part in expanding circles of Eco-Reformation, with new generations of reformers who insist that to be Christian today means nothing less than the repentance of privilege, immersion in the holy waters of Earth, and courageous costly witness against the economics of alienation. With people of all backgrounds, with creatures of all kinds, we give thanks for the relationships, beauty, and joy that make life on this planet so rich, all grace. Here we stand: we can do no other.

Contributors

Lisa E. Dahill, PhD, Associate Professor of Religion, California Lutheran University, Thousand Oaks, California

Wanda Deifelt, PhD, Professor of Religion, Luther College, Decorah, Iowa

Terence E. Fretheim, PhD, Elva B. Lovell Professor Emeritus of Old Testament, Luther Seminary, St. Paul, Minnesota

Norman C. Habel, PhD, Professorial Fellow at Flinders University of South Australia, Adelaide, Australia

James B. Martin-Schramm, PhD, Professor of Religion, Luther College, Decorah, Iowa

Bill McKibben, Schumann Distinguished Scholar at Middlebury College, Middlebury, Vermont

Cynthia D. Moe-Lobeda, PhD, Professor of Theological and Social Ethics, Pacific Lutheran Theological Seminary, Berkeley, California

Larry L. Rasmussen, PhD, Reinhold Niebuhr Professor Emeritus of Social Ethics, Union Theological Seminary, City of New York, New York

David M. Rhoads, PhD, Professor of New Testament Emeritus, Lutheran School of Theology at Chicago, Chicago, Illinois

Barbara R. Rossing, PhD, Professor of New Testament, Lutheran School of Theology at Chicago, Chicago, Illinois

Terra S. Rowe, PhD, Drew University, Madison, New Jersey

Robert C. Saler, PhD, Executive Director, Center for Pastoral Excellence, and Research Professor of Lutheran Studies, Christian Theological Seminary, Indianapolis, Indiana

H. Paul Santmire, PhD, Retired Chaplain and Lecturer in Religion and Biblical Studies, Wellesley College, Wellesley, Massachusetts

Ernest L. Simmons, Jr., PhD, Professor of Religion, Concordia College, Moorhead, Minnesota

Benjamin M. Stewart, PhD, Gordon A. Braatz Associate Professor of Worship, Lutheran School of Theology at Chicago, Chicago, Illinois

Victor Thasiah, PhD, Assistant Professor of Religion, California Lutheran University, Thousand Oaks, California

Aana Marie Vigen, PhD, Associate Professor of Christian Social Ethics, Loyola University of Chicago, Chicago, Illinois

Abbreviations

DBWE	*Dietrich Bonhoeffer Works in English*
ELCA	Evangelical Lutheran Church in America
ELW	*Evangelical Lutheran Worship*
EPA	Environmental Protection Agency
IPCC	Intergovernmental Panel on Climate Change
LRC	Lutherans Restoring Creation
LW	*Luther's Works*
LWF	Lutheran World Federation
UN	United Nations
WCC	World Council of Churches
WHO	World Health Organization

1

A Theology of Creation

Foundations for an Eco-Reformation

—DAVID M. RHOADS

AN ECO-REFORMATION PROPOSAL

LUTHERANS HAVE ALWAYS CONSIDERED "perpetual reformation" to be an important dimension of our ecclesial tradition.[1] It has been one of our great strengths that we have been able to re-form ourselves in times of great challenges through the centuries. The ongoing reformation we need now is something quite radical. We are facing unprecedented changes in our life on Earth. To address the ecological crises, a foundational transformation of the church needs to take place. Two decades ago, the ELCA social statement, "Caring for Creation," issued a warning for the church to respond to the looming ecological crises and the social justice issues related to them. Now it is time to meet the challenges presented by that document.[2] This is a clarion call for a new re-formation—an Eco-Reformation.

---

1. This essay is a revised and shortened version of "Reflections on a Lutheran Theology of Creation." I am grateful to *Seminary Ridge Review* for their permission to reprint a revised version in this volume. The ideas presented here are based on the theology and practices of my Lutheran tradition.

2. ELCA, "Caring for Creation: Vision, Hope, and Justice."

THE ECOZOIC AGE
AND THE GREAT WORK OF OUR TIME

In the first Reformation, the critical issue of the time was human salvation. Today, the critical issue of our time is the fate of the planet, including humankind. The list of crises we are facing as a planet is long and substantive. Global climate change is the most threatening, already resulting in unpredictable weather patterns, an increase in frequency and intensity of storms, drought, rampant wildfires, shifting agricultural conditions, and the rise of sea levels. In addition, we are experiencing the rapid destruction of rain forests, the loss of arable land to desert, deterioration in air quality, and the pollution of freshwater sources and oceans. All of these are causing an alarming loss of the species diversity that is so critical for adaptation and survival. In addition, human population growth along with the lifestyle demands of first world societies is putting stress on every eco-system. All of these are interrelated. And all of them are having horrific impacts on human life, particularly the most vulnerable people and societies.

Thomas Berry has said humanity is entering an *Ecozoic Age*—an Earth age in which ecological issues will dominate our society and our global life together. He argued that creating a sustainable life on the planet is the *great work* of our time.[3] It is a work in which all people and institutions can and must participate. It will involve systemic changes in our shared assumptions, in our laws and policies, and in our commitments to the common good. It will also involve transformations in our personal lifestyles, priorities, and daily habits. The environment is not a fad, not one more issue alongside others, not just for those who happen to be interested in this cause. Earth is our common home. The crises impact all living things. The great work involves everyone and all societies.

The Transformation of Society

In response to this situation, societies need to act now at national and global levels to address the challenges posed by these environmental crises. We desperately need a rapid transition to clean and renewable energy as well as massive reforestation projects with the replanting of native species everywhere. We will benefit from limitations on the use

---

3. Berry, *The Great Work*.

of pesticides and herbicides, prohibitions against clear-cutting of forests and strip-mining of land, protections of our parks and nature preserves from commercial development, and the preservation of wetlands and wilderness. We will need to become much more efficient and conservative in our use of energy and water. We will need to eat less meat and more local foods. The development and sharing of new technologies is certainly high on the order of importance. In other words, we need to rethink fundamentally how we manage the land and use the resources of nature. In so doing, we need an economic system that settles in and sustains life for everyone instead of an economy that depends on the fantasy of unlimited resources and unlimited growth.

Whether or not governments and corporations are making systemic changes, we as individuals, organizations, and local communities must begin to address these issues *now* on a voluntary and unilateral basis. Many actions and changes are already taking place, but we need a pervasive grassroots groundswell of action.

The institutions of the church can take leadership in these societal changes. In order to do that, the church will need to go through its own transformation. As humans, as Christians, as Lutherans, we need to rise to this great work and embrace personal and systemic changes for the sake of all Earth community—and for the sake of the God we confess to be the creator, redeemer, and preserver of Earth and the whole universe.

THE ECO-REFORMATION OF THE CHURCH

The ecclesiastical transformation we need must be radical and comprehensive. Care-for-creation activities, programs, and advocacy are happening in many Lutheran congregations and institutions. However, these actions are often isolated and sporadic. We need a comprehensive and systemic approach featuring collective and collaborative actions that will infuse creation-care and love of creation into our marrow.

All church organizations—denominational leadership, congregational life and mission, synods, educational institutions, social ministry organizations, camps, and individual members—need to be involved if we are to care for creation and contribute to our survival as a species. Lutherans have the traditions and the organizations needed to bring us into this new reformation dedicated to a sustainable world.[4] And in order to

---

4. See five mandates for mission in a new Reformation in Rhoads and Rossing, "A

have the greatest impact, we will continue to learn from and collaborate with other denominations and religions.

The Sixteenth-Century Reformation

What might a Lutheran Eco-Reformation look like? And how might it be similar to and different from the first Reformation? A Methodist historian, Phillip Watson, identified the sixteenth century Reformation as a "Copernican Revolution" in religion. Just as the perspective of the cosmos shifted dramatically from being Earth-centered to being sun-centered, so also the first Reformation shifted the conception of salvation from being human-centered to being God-centered, from human efforts as the source of salvation to God's actions of grace through Christ.[5]

This was a shift in basic perception that *changed everything* in relation to the dominant views and practices of the time. Lutheran churches embraced a theological image of God as a God who justifies people freely by grace. People were liberated from the bondage of needing to please God with religious actions and good works in order to be acceptable. They saw ethics as a grateful response to grace that is characterized as a vocation to love the neighbor, especially the poor and the hungry. They focused on a servant theology of the cross rather than a triumphalist theology of glory. They read the Bible with justification by faith as the internal canon of interpretation. They placed Scripture in the hands of the laity and reinvented church order around a priesthood of all believers. They worshipped in ways that focused on God's word and action in worship. They affirmed the goodness of creation.

A New Eco-Reformation

Without losing the foundational fruits of that revolutionary Reformation, and building on them to address our current context, we need a new Copernican revolution: from being human-centered to being creation-centered; from focusing on God's relationship with humans alone to focusing on God's relationship with all of creation; from fostering the extreme individualism of our culture to fostering the common good of the planet. We humans need to see ourselves embedded in the rest of

---

Beloved Earth Community."

5. Watson, *Let God Be God*.

nature and find our proper place and role in it—both our responsibilities and our limitations. We need to end the self-centeredness by which we are curved in upon ourselves and with which we have treated the rest of nature as an unlimited resource available for our unrestrained use and abuse. We need to find the commitment to care for the rest of nature as if our life depended on it, because it does! For most of us, such an Eco-Reformation is as mind-bending a change in perception as the first Reformation was for people of its time. It will require *metanoia* (repentance) in the true sense of the word, a mind change and a behavior change—both individually and collectively. To make this shift as a church, we need theologies and practices that are Earth-friendly and creation-centered.

Luther himself laid the groundwork for this foundational paradigm shift. In his fervent affirmation of the value of creation, he lifted up a traditional view of creation as the "Book of Nature" and called it the second Scripture, a complementary revelation of God. Just as Luther translated the Bible in order to put it into the hands of the laity, so we need to find ways to celebrate the Book of Nature so as to put it into the hearts and minds of laity and clergy alike. Both books (Scripture and Nature) can be the foundations for an Eco-Reformation.[6]

In this new Reformation, we are not in conflict with the rest of the Church. Rather, this reformation is a confessing movement *for the world* carried out along with the whole church of Christ. This is a reformation that unites rather than divides. As such, this reformation is ecumenical. For example, we join with Pope Francis and the Roman Catholic Church along with other Christian traditions in seeking justice for all Earth community.[7] And we join with other religions, for all have salient traditions and resources that contribute to an eco-ethics for Earth. Christians, Unitarian Universalists, Jews, Muslims, Buddhists, Hindus, Sikhs, Taoists, indigenous religions, and secular organizations together can find common ground (Earth!) in our collective calling to Earth-care.[8] We are all in this together, and it will take all of us working together to address our situation.

This new focus on the signal issue of our time will *change everything* for us. What follows are examples of the kind of transformations that

6. For more on this topic, see the essay by Lisa E. Dahill in this volume.

7. Francis, *Laudato Si'*.

8. For an in-depth analysis of different religions and their contribution to Earth-care, see the *Religions of the World and Ecology* series edited by Tucker and Grim. Visit the Forum on Religion and Ecology at www.emergingearthcommunity.org.

will benefit us—transformations in our reading of the Bible, our theologies, our understanding of our human role in creation, our ecclesial life together, our worship practices, our ethics, and our life in the Spirit.

READING THE BIBLE ANEW

If anything was critical to the first Reformation, it was a renewed interpretation of the Bible. We look to the Bible to show us who God is and how we are to live. If we have a distorted or limited view of the Bible, we will surely be limited in our understanding of God and God's will for humans.

In the first Reformation, Luther chose the biblical affirmation of justification by grace through faith as the lens—the canon within the canon—through which we are to interpret the Bible as a whole. Without relinquishing that principle, we now need an additional lens that points us to the restoration of creation throughout the Bible. Paul's statement that "creation has been groaning" and "waits with eager longing . . . [to] be set free from its bondage to decay" will serve as a starting point (Rom 8:19–21). Another passage is this statement in 2 Corinthians 5:17: "For if anyone is in Christ, there is new creation: everything old has passed away; see, everything has become new." There are many more such passages. While steadfastly upholding justification by grace through faith, we are called to have a new grasp of Scripture in light of this additional canon within the canon—and to bring out all the rich resources of Scripture about creation for the tasks before us.[9] We might refer to this correlative canon as "the fullness of creation" as a means to embrace the extent of creation beyond and including humanity but also the sweep of creation through time, encompassing the bondage, the renewal, and the consummation of creation.

We can use this lens to comprehend the integral role of all creation in the Bible as a whole—and we see it everywhere. The biblical materials reflect salvation history not as human history alone but as *creation history*. The first passage in the Bible is about God creating all things as good (Gen 1:1–25). God gave humans responsibility for caring for garden Earth (Gen 1:26–31). After the flood, God made a covenant with

9. This notion of a second canon within the canon appropriate to reading the Bible in our time was suggested to me by Paul Santmire. For more on the groaning and praise of creation, see Santmire's essay in this volume.

Noah and all the creatures of Earth (Gen 9:1–17). The laws of the land call humans to rest animals on the Sabbath (Deut 5:12–15) and to let the land lie fallow every seven years (Lev 25:1–7). The psalms celebrate creation and call for all creation to praise God. The prophets warn that injustice among humans will result in the land languishing (e.g., Isa 24:4–7). Hopeful prophecies about the future include the flourishing of the land (e.g., Joel 3:18).

Jesus' announcement of the arrival of the kingdom of God (Mark 1:14–15) encompassed a restoration of all creation—through healing and exorcism as well as by the calming of storms and the provision of bread in the desert. In John, Jesus declares that God "so loved the world" (John 3:16). Paul proclaims to gentiles that their "unknown god" is the "God who made the world and everything in it, he who is Lord of heaven and earth . . ." (Acts 17:24). Paul discerns the whole creation waiting for the "revealing of the children of God" who will care for creation (Rom 8:19). The author of Colossians claims that through Christ, "God was pleased to reconcile to himself all things, whether on earth or in heaven, by making peace through the blood of his cross" (Col 1:20). The prophet John shares a vision in which "I heard every creature in heaven and on earth and under the earth and in the sea, and all that is in them," singing praises to God (Rev 5:13). The final revelation of the Bible is the vision of a New Jerusalem, a city with enough free food and water for all and with God and the lamb in their midst (Rev 21:1—22:5). The whole of the New Testament imagines Jesus "coming back" to Earth, not destroying it (e. g. Mark 13:26).

Even in places in Scripture where nature is not explicitly mentioned, it is nevertheless everywhere assumed to be integral to the mighty acts of God. We need a creation lens in order to see it, to lift it up, and to allow it to reveal to us the God of all life and the call for humans to care for it.[10]

REORIENTING OUR VIEW OF GOD

If we are to have an Eco-Reformation, changing the way we think about God is critical. How we think determines how we relate and act. Foundationally, Lutherans have a very strong theology of creation rooted in an affirmation of the first article of the creed: "I believe in God . . . creator

---

10. A project working in this direction is the *Earth Bible* series. See, e.g., its first volume, *Readings from the Perspective of Earth*.

of heaven and earth."[11] However, in propounding the Trinity, Lutherans have tended to give greater emphasis to the second article of the creed, affirming the redemption of Christ in the cross. This emphasis has riveted our attention on God's salvation of *humanity* to the neglect of God's redemption of *creation as a whole*. Furthermore, this emphasis on the salvation of humans has reinforced a focus on the salvation of the individual apart from the context of community and apart from our place in nature. In an Eco-Reformation, we begin our theology with the first article of the creed, with creation as the foundation of God's work, and then we understand the second and third articles of the creed as redeeming and fulfilling all of creation, including humanity.

Furthermore, we have sometimes interpreted the three articles of the creed as *events* that happen sequentially in time rather than as continuous *realities*—creation, redemption, and sanctification/consummation. But the first article of the creed affirms a God involved in creation as a continuous activity, not as a single event in the past. The second article sees a continual effect of redemption through Christ that simultaneously renews and builds on creation. The third article affirms that the Holy Spirit continually works to sustain and consummate creation. As such, the whole sweep of salvation is the ongoing creative activity of God in multiple ways. This is a focus not just on the redemption and fulfillment of *humans* but on the redeeming and fulfilling of *all creation*. What a difference such a view can make!

God In, With, and Under All Creation

In the first Reformation, Luther articulated a view of God as a God of grace. This is hardly lost in a new Eco-Reformation. An Eco-Reformation sees the grace that redeems humans to be in continuity with the grace working *in creation as a whole*. This perspective represents a major shift that can change the way we relate to the world around us, how we act ethically, and how we worship.

As such, a gracious God works not only among humans but is present in all things. Of course, this is not new. However, in our time we need to recognize the power of this insight and embrace it in a new way. It

11. On this point see the essays in this volume by James B. Martin-Schramm and Ernest L. Simmons Jr.

was a conviction of Luther that God is present "in, with, and under" all things. Luther wrote:

> God is substantially present everywhere, in and through all creatures, in all their parts and places, so that the world is full of God and He [*sic*] fills all, but without His [*sic*] being encompassed and surrounded by it . . . How can reason tolerate it that the Divine Majesty is so small that it can be substantially present in a grain, on a grain, through a grain, within and without . . . His [*sic*] own divine essence can be in all creatures collectively and in each one individually more profoundly, more intimately, more present than the creature is in itself, yet it can be encompassed nowhere and by no one.[12]

To take with utter seriousness that God has been and always will be fully present in every creature and in every thing is a life-changing realization. If God is present in all of nature and seeking to manifest Godself there, then our life is diminished when we fail to interrelate with nature. As such, it is critical from a theological point of view to restore the human relationship with nature everywhere as a place God loves, as a place where God is at work, and as a place where God encounters us and we encounter God.

God in the Depths and All Around

Understanding God as in, with, and under all creation leads us to perceive incarnation not only as an incarnation of God *as Jesus* but also—precisely through this incarnate Word (John 1:1)—as an immanent presence of God in *all* things. "The whole earth is filled with God's glory!" (Isa 6:3). In taking this point of view, we shift the focus of our image of God from space to Earth, from *out there* to *in here*. We tend to think of God as "up in heaven," for example, when we look "up" to pray. When we do this, we associate God with what is airy rather than with what is earthy. We connect God with what is ethereal rather than with what is material, as if God's Spirit is transcendent alone and not also fully present in all things. We now need to take seriously that God is profoundly immanent, that God is not only "up" but also "down" and "around" and "within." If the whole Earth is filled with God's glory, then this is where we shall find

12. Cited by Bornkamm, *Luther's World of Thought*, 189. The passage comes from Luther's treatise, "That These Words of Christ, 'This is my Body,' etc., Still Stand Firm against the Fanatics," found at *LW* 37:59–60.

God—in the *depths* as well as the heights, among us *in* creation and all *around* us. This insight invites us to change the way we perceive things.

Sacramental Theology

These reflections are an affirmation of the Lutheran sacramental view of life. While environmentalists may talk about the re-enchantment of nature, Christians talk about the re-sacralizing of nature, seeing nature as a creation in which God is everywhere present. As we open our eyes and ears to the sacredness of life, we will love Earth for its own sake and we will cherish Earth because it blesses us in relationship with God. Life is experienced as *communion*—communion with one another, with nature around us, and with God.

Nowhere is this more true than in the Eucharist and in baptism. If we can be assured by the word of Christ that God is already in, with, and under such ordinary elements as grapes and grain and water, then God is indeed present in *every* ordinary thing in life. Luther believed that matter mattered, that the material world was good, that the finite could bear the infinite, that creation could be a vehicle of the divine. The sacraments confirm this ubiquity of God's sacramental presence everywhere.[13]

Reverence as the Basis for Right Use

The (in)sight that all of life is sacramental is critical for our ethical commitments. What we believe shapes how we act. How we see things affects how we relate to them. If we see all of life as sacramental, then a posture of reverence will be central to our Christian life. In the primary consumer model of our culture, we look at the rest of nature as resources to be tapped, materials to be used, places to be exploited, sites to be developed, and opportunities for financial gain. Nature is treated as if it were made up of lifeless things without mystery and devoid of God's glory—all there for *us* to use as we please.

By contrast, when we see nature as God's creation, then reverence will be the basis for our use of it. If we have deep respect and love for something, we will not abuse it or misuse it or neglect it. So, in an ecological re-formation, we begin with reverence for all things and then

13. On this topic see the essays in this volume by Benjamin M. Stewart and Lisa E. Dahill.

make use only of what we need without greed and exploitation; and we make sure that everyone has enough. We treat animals, plants, and land with respect, and then make sure they have the conditions to survive and thrive. When we see God's glory everywhere, then our appreciation for the sanctity of life leads us to live in ways that are sustainable and restorative.

THE CHANGING ROLE OF HUMANS IN CREATION: A NEW LUTHERAN ANTHROPOLOGY

To address the eco-crises we face, we also need to conceive anew what it means to be human. We have imagined ourselves living *on* the Earth rather than embedded in it and thoroughly dependent on it. We have focused on the well-being of humans to the neglect of the well-being of all living things. But humans cannot survive and thrive unless the whole planet is thriving. And, likely, it will not be enough to secure the life of human beings unless we are committed to restoring the Earth community of the planet *for its own sake*. Hence, we must rethink what it means to be human. What is our personal and collective role? What does it mean to be in solidarity and to have a sense of kinship with all else? And how can the insights from the sixteenth century Reformation provide a foundation for these transformations?

Justification by Grace Liberates Us for Love of Neighbors— All of Our Neighbors

Justification by grace is at the core of our identity as Lutherans. In the context of our twentieth-first century world, we find that justification becomes foundational for a Reformation in support of Earth.

Lutherans, like other Christians, have tended to think of redemption primarily in terms of the forgiveness of "my" personal sins and whether "I" will go to heaven when "I" die. We try to follow "the law" and then ask for forgiveness when we fall short. In order to insure our place in heaven, this approach can easily become a self-serving project of trying to justify ourselves by our good works. By contrast, justification offers a different model of redemption from that of forgiveness.[14] Justification

14. For example, see "Justification Rather than Forgiveness," in Stendahl, *Paul*, 23–39. See also Rhoads and Roberts, "Justification by Grace."

by *grace* means that we have been wholly set right by God and with God freely apart from the "laws" and any other standards by which we seek to justify ourselves, and apart from our efforts to earn our own redemption.

In other words, in justification, God accepts us apart from all the social, economic, and cultural mores by which societies seek to define people and by which people seek to justify themselves, including, for example, the standards of a market system of economic growth. Redemption is not just a matter of my own personal salvation. Freely-given grace also undercuts the power of the systems that bind us, systems that demand allegiance, systems that exclude, oppress, and marginalize, systems that lead the powerful to dominate and exploit other people and Earth.

Once we are justified unconditionally by God and freed from laws and standards, we are thrown into relationships in response to God's grace to create a new creation marked by love, in spite of the constraints of the current standards of society. Once we are justified freely by grace, we are freed to love our neighbor unconditionally, freed to be a citizen who works for justice and mercy, and, now, also, *freed to care gratefully, joyfully, and boldly for God's creation.*

Justification Liberates Us for Vocation

This new life of freedom in justification by grace comes to fruition in *vocation*—our human response to God's love for us. God became human so that we might have the vision and capacity to become the human beings we were created to be. The book of Genesis reveals our most basic human vocation. Humans are called to share dominion with God in caring for creation. In the first creation story, God creates humans last in order to share in the responsibility to care for the garden Earth and to see that God's creation thrives (Gen 1:26–31). Lest we think of this responsibility as dominating Earth, even in acts of stewardship, the second creation story calls humans "to serve and to keep." The word commonly translated "till" is a term of service used for those who "serve" priests and kings. So we are to exercise our responsibility to care for Earth from a position of service, a position from "below" (Gen 2:15). Centuries later, Jesus affirmed our vocation of service when he told his disciples not to lord over but to be "least of all and servant of all" (Mark 9:25). Imagine that! Our human vocation is to serve the rest of creation!

Imagining a New Creation

Once we are freed from the systems that bind us, we have an open future. There is "new creation" (Gal 1:4; 6:15). In the biblical understanding, new creation is apocalyptic, but not primarily in the sense of the end of the world. Rather, it is new creation in the sense of the end of one way of being in the world and the onset of another way. As Paul says, "the world has been crucified to me and I to the world" (Gal 6:13). And he adds that the only thing that matters is "new creation" (Gal 6:15). Entering this new creation, we are freed to address new circumstances, liberated to imagine love and justice, open to a world that treats people and nature with reverence, a world that does not exploit or dehumanize.

Furthermore, when we expand the Christian vocation to include serving creation, we expand the realms in which that vocational mission might take place. In traditional Lutheranism, our human vocation is played out in two arenas: the kingdom related to the church and the kingdom related to civil society, including political as well as economic structures and activities. Both of these are spheres of God's action and of human responsibility. Now we can multiply these kingdoms to encompass the animal kingdom and the plant kingdom as spheres of God's activity and arenas of human responsibility.

THE CHURCH'S VOCATION: EARTH-KEEPING

This human vocation as Earth-keepers is the communal mission of the church. As a collective community, our purpose and mission now include the natural world. Hence, it is time to re-form our church order to its possibilities for our day. This means we can integrate creation care into our congregational life: worship, evangelism, stewardship, education, responsibility for property, discipleship at home and work, social ministry, and advocacy. Other institutions of the church can do the same.[15] None of this means that care for creation is simply added onto our current vocation or our church's stated missions as one more task. Rather, creation is the encompassing orbit within which we carry out our responsibilities and

15. For an Eco-Reformation in the life and mission of congregations and other church institutions, explore the creation-care programs and resources at www.lutheransrestoringcreation.org. For a Rwandan example of integration of ministry and creation care, see the essay by Victor Thasiah in this volume.

relationships in *all* realms—regions of reality in our lives that interweave and overlap in one seamless web of creation.

Worshiping with Creation

In the sixteenth-century Reformation, the key to transformation in worship was to provide unmediated access to God—no venerated saints, no statues, and no indulgences, only the power of word and sacraments. In that day, however, people were still experiencing access to God in the natural world: living close to nature, growing food and raising animals, surrounded by unspoiled areas of forests, mountains, and meadows. Today, urban Christians have much less access to God through nature in their daily routines. Hence it is more important than ever to bring nature into relationship with our worship of God. For twenty centuries, many of our liturgical practices have focused on the God-human and the human-human relationships, and we have neglected the God-creation relationship and the human-creation relationship.

Yet worship can provide an opportunity for us to relate to the presence and revelation of God in and through nature, in ways that make our relationship with creation pervasive and unmistakable. This dimension of an Eco-Reformation is especially significant in that worship is the central event for which the community gathers, week after week. When we incorporate creation care thoroughly into weekly worship, we go a long way toward making creation-care integral to our congregational life and mission.[16]

This worship does not take place among humans alone. One of the most striking things about the biblical understanding of nature is that all creation is enjoined to worship God.[17] Scripture is downright exuberant about creation's praise of God. "May the heavens be glad and the Earth rejoice. Let the fields exalt and everything in them, let the trees of the forest sing for joy, let the oceans roar and all that is in them" (1 Chr 16:29–34). Indeed, "Let them [all creation] praise God!" (Ps 148:13); and

16. For "A Theology of Liturgy in a New Key: Worshiping *with* Creation," see *The Season of Creation*, 16–53. See also Stewart, *A Watered Garden*; and Santmire, *Ritualizing Nature*. On preaching, see Schade, *Creation-Crisis Preaching*. For resources on creation-centered worship throughout the lectionary years and the optional liturgical "Season of Creation," visit www.letallcreationpraise.org. For attention to moving worship location outdoors, see Dahill, "Indoors, Outdoors: Praying with the Earth."

17. On this point see the essay in this volume by Paul Santmire.

"Let everything that breathes praise the Lord!" (Ps 150:6). We humans are called not just to thank God *for* creation but to praise God *with* creation. Earth is the real sanctuary in which we worship, and we can transform our worship so that we are invoking and confessing and giving thanks and praising God and making prayer petitions and offering ourselves in solidarity with *all of life*. Praying and praising *with* creation changes our fundamental relationship with creation.

Eco-Justice Ethics

Care for creation requires a thorough rethinking of our ethical commitments and actions.[18] Most of the ways we configure our personal behavior focuses almost exclusively on our relationships with people. If we expand our personal commitments to encompass relationships with nature, our behavior will change. For example, we may become aware that personal decisions we make on a daily basis in our living spaces contribute to almost all of the ecological problems we face. Consider the electricity entering our homes from coal-fired power plants, carbon emissions pouring from our chimneys, water coming into and going out of our homes, and chemicals on our lawns that enter the watershed. Furthermore, the food we eat, the clothes we wear, and the products we purchase require energy to produce and transport in ways that contribute to pollution. Garbage from packaging and from discarded possessions goes to landfills and is frequently toxic. And on and on. The point is that, in the common actions of our daily lives, usually without being aware of it, we make personal decisions that contribute to our ecological problems—or, in positive ways, serve to allay them. Can we change our ethical actions so as to mitigate or eliminate these negative impacts and in turn take actions that restore nature? And can we make these actions integral and habitual to our personal discipleship?

Furthermore, an Earth ethic encompasses and expands systems of social justice. Many issues of social justice are rooted in and related to ecological conditions, from environmental illnesses, polluted air, unclean water, and lack of access to healthy food, to overcrowding or lack of access to green spaces. Much of these conditions are not accidental.

18. On ecological ethics, see especially Rasmussen, *Earth Community, Earth Ethics* and *Earth-Honoring Faith*. See also Jenkins, *Ecologies of Grace*; Moe-Lobeda, *Resisting Structural Evil*; Martin-Schramm, *Climate Justice*; and Martin-Schramm, et al., *Earth Ethics*.

Industrialists have regularly and intentionally put incinerators and factories that pollute in impoverished neighborhoods, often populated primarily by people of color. Such environmental racism is extensive. We need to take the blinders off our understanding of injustice to see how the underlying conditions are related to degraded ecological conditions. Unless we address the urgent issue of climate change, for example, we will see an exponential increase of injustices manifested in refugee populations, starvation, and mass suffering.[19] As we reassess churchwide efforts to minister to those who are suffering, we can explicitly name and explicate the interrelationship between ecological conditions and programs we sponsor: immigration and refugee services, disaster relief, hunger programs, among many others.

Lutheran ethics has always represented a commitment to the most vulnerable, for our ethics is grounded in the theology of the cross. In the cross, God expresses solidarity with the rejected, the weak, the oppressed, the poor, and the marginalized. The Lutheran church has a long tradition of creating and maintaining institutions and programs serving the vulnerable: the elderly, orphans, the sick and those who are mentally ill, the strangers and the marginalized, the poor and the oppressed, people of color and ethnic groups subject to racism, people with disabilities, people who are victims of disaster, those who suffer from diseases such as malaria, and the hungry. We have a remarkable legacy of care for the vulnerable people of the world.

Now we are also challenged to widen the circle of our neighbors to encompass our vulnerable kin in creation—including endangered species, distressed ecosystems, polluted air, land, and water. The crises we face are about humans, but they are also about other living animals and plants created by God as good and loved by God. This leads us to reconfigure our commitments as commitments to *all* the vulnerable of Earth community. Earth-care is not one more item or cause on a list of critical concerns. Rather, it is all interrelated. Earth is the matrix in which all of these realities of injustice are embedded and encompassed. This is why Pope Francis calls for an "integral ethic" whereby we see human and ecological conditions together as one dynamic complex to be addressed by "faith active in love."[20]

19. On this topic see the essays in this volume by Aana Marie Vigen and Cynthia Moe-Lobeda.

20. Francis, *Laudato Si'*, 85–99.

Life in the Spirit in an Eco-Reformation

The ecological crisis is a spiritual problem having to do with our fractured relationship with the rest of nature. Since, as the Nicene Creed confesses, the Holy Spirit is the sustainer of creation, we need to enter the flow of that Spirit in nature. To awaken to the world around us, we have to *see* it differently. We have to *be in* it differently. Many accounts of mystical experiences describe a vivid awareness of oneness with creation, the dissolving of the boundaries between the individual self and the cosmos. To the extent that the ecological problems we face have resulted from our human alienation and estrangement from the rest of nature, they will not be adequately addressed without a restoration of this relationship. We have failed to see our biological and spiritual kinship with all forms of life, our shared DNA, our exchange of oxygen and carbon dioxide with plants, and our shared emotional intelligence with other animal species. Our life is profoundly diminished by our failure to relate to and interact with nature on an intimate and continuous basis. And our relationship with God is greatly diminished in so far as we are estranged from oneness with all creation. The church community needs to find ways to enliven our communion with all other living relatives. We need a conversion to Earth.[21] We need to have a love affair with nature, because we will not save what we do not love.

How can we find the spiritual resources to care for creation? What will motivate us for this labor of love? What will sustain us for the duration? Will we be motivated by fear? We have reason to be afraid, but fear will not sustain us for long, and it certainly will not motivate others. Will we be motivated by guilt or shame? These emotions might lead us to realize our culpability and make some changes, but, again, these will not sustain us for the long haul. We certainly may be motivated by anger and outrage at how much wanton destruction is happening and how little is being done about it, especially at the corporate and governmental levels. But anger will exhaust us before long and throw us into bitterness and resentment. What about grief at the loss of life as we have known it? Again, this is an appropriate response but certainly not life-sustaining. We may see all these emotions as alarm systems—fear, guilt, shame, anger, grief—all as appropriate signals in a warning system that alerts

21. Frohlich, "Under the Sign of Jonah." Eco-conversion is also a key theme of Pope Francis's encyclical.

us that something is very wrong. But they are not adequate grounds for making wise decisions or for providing the nurture needed to sustain us.

In the end, we discover the answer with the very God of creation who impels our personal vocation and our communal mission. What can sustain us is the presence of the Spirit of God in, with, and under all of life, the very grace present in Jesus Christ now to be discerned everywhere. Gerard Manley Hopkins referred to this presence as the "dearest freshness deep down things."[22] Wendell Berry names it as "that fund of grace out by which alone we live."[23] This reservoir of God's presence and grace, God's love for all creation, does not quit. It only generates more love and more grace. This is the stream of life that empowers and sustains us for a new Reformation.

CONCLUSION: A NEW ECCLESIOLOGY

An Eco-Reformation will provide a much-needed infusion of new life into the church by deepening and widening our life together in relation to God's creation and by revivifying our mission to the world. In the first century, early Christians created communities that served as pockets of counter-cultural living—alternatives to the destructive and oppressive economic, social, political, and popular values and customary relationships of the Roman Empire. The church has an opportunity now to pioneer alternative communities[24] that are dedicated to restorative values addressing the impending ecological crises we face in our day. It is time for us to embrace this great work of our age. It is time to be renewed by the challenges and transformations of such a high calling. It is time for an Eco-Justice Reformation.

BIBLIOGRAPHY

Berry, Thomas. *The Great Work: Our Way into the Future*. New York: Bell Tower, 1999.
Berry, Wendell. "Original Sin." In *Given*, 35. Berkeley: Counterpoint, 2006.
Bornkamm, Heinrich. *Luther's World of Thought*. Translated by Robert H. Bertram. St. Louis: Concordia, 2001.

22. Hopkins, "God's Grandeur."

23. Berry, "Original Sin."

24. One way to express an alternative community publically is to reconfigure church grounds. See Rhoads, "From Church Property to Earth Community." A congregation that has embraced this approach is Advent Lutheran Church in Madison, Wisconsin.

Dahill, Lisa E. "Indoors, Outdoors: Praying with the Earth." In *Eco-Lutheranism: Lutheran Perspectives on Ecology,* edited by Karla Bohmbach and Shauna Hannan, 113–24. Minneapolis: Lutheran University Press, 2013.

ELCA. "Caring for Creation: Vision, Hope, and Justice." 1993. https://www.elca.org.

Francis, Pope. *Laudato Si,' mi' Signore (Praise to You, My Lord): On Caring for Our Common Home.* Brooklyn: Melville House, 2015.

Frohlich, Mary. "Under the Sign of Jonah: Studying Spirituality in a Time of Ecosystemic Crisis." *Spiritus: A Journal of Christian Spirituality* 9 (2009) 27–45.

Habel, Norman, ed. *Readings from the Perspective of Earth.* The Earth Bible Series 1. Cleveland: Pilgrim, 2000.

Habel, Norman, David Rhoads, and Paul Santmire. "A Theology of Liturgy in a New Key: Worshiping *with* Creation." In *The Season of Creation: A Preaching Commentary,* edited by Norman Habel, et al., 16–53. Minneapolis: Fortress, 2011.

Hopkins, Gerard Manley. "God's Grandeur." In *The Poems of Gerard Manley Hopkins,* 66. Oxford: Oxford University Press, 1967.

Jenkins, Willis. *Ecologies of Grace: Environmental Ethics and Christian Theology.* Oxford: Oxford University Press, 2008.

Luther, Martin. "That These Words of Christ, 'This is my Body,' etc., Still Stand Firm against the Fanatics." In *Word and Sacrament III,* edited by Robert H. Fischer, *LW* 37:3–150. Philadelphia: Muhlenberg, 1961.

Martin-Schramm, James. *Climate Justice: Ethics, Energy, and Public Policy.* Minneapolis: Fortress, 2010.

Martin-Schramm, James, et al. *Earth Ethics: A Case Method Approach.* Ecology and Justice Series. Maryknoll, NY: Orbis, 2015.

Moe-Lobeda, Cynthia. *Resisting Systemic Evil: Love as Ecological-Economic Vocation.* Minneapolis: Fortress, 2013.

Rasmussen, Larry. *Earth Community, Earth Ethics.* Ecology and Justice. Maryknoll, NY: Orbis, 1996.

———. *Earth-Honoring Faith: Religious Ethics in a New Key.* Oxford: Oxford University Press, 2013.

Rhoads, David. "From Church Property to Earth Community: Ethical Action for the Land." *Journal of Lutheran Ethics,* February 2015. http://www.elca.org.

———. "Reflections on a Lutheran Theology of Creation: Foundations for a New Reformation." *Seminary Ridge Review* 15 (Autumn 2012) 1–49.

Rhoads, David, and Barbara Rossing. "A Beloved Earth Community: Christian Mission in an Ecological Age." In *Mission after Christendom: Emergent Themes in Contemporary Mission,* edited by Ogbu Kalu and Peter Vethanayagamony, 128–43. Louisville: Westminster John Knox, 2010.

Rhoads, David, and Sandy Roberts. "Justification by Grace: Shame and Acceptance in a County Jail." In *The Shame Factor: How Shame Shapes Society,* edited by Robert Jewett, 86–102. Eugene, OR: Cascade Books, 2011.

Santmire, H. Paul. *Ritualizing Nature: Renewing Christian Liturgy in a Time of Crisis.* Minneapolis: Fortress, 2008.

Schade, Leah. *Creation-Crisis Preaching: Ecology, Theology, and the Pulpit.* St. Louis: Chalice, 2014.

Stendahl, Krister. "Justification Rather than Forgiveness." In *Paul among Jews and Gentiles,* 23–39. Philadelphia: Fortress, 1976.

Stewart, Benjamin. *A Watered Garden: Christian Worship and Earth's Ecology.* Minneapolis: Fortress, 2011.

Tucker, Mary Evelyn, and John Grim, eds. Religions of the World and Ecology Series. Cambridge: Harvard University Press, 2000–.

Watson, Philip. *Let God Be God: An Interpretation of the Theology of Martin Luther.* New York: AMS Press, 1947.

2

Creation—Not for Sale

—LARRY L. RASMUSSEN

Our whole point is that this is a sacred universe. Cosmology without ecology is empty. Our future is at stake. Is there anything more important?

MARY EVELYN TUCKER[1]

Everything is garbage and everything is sacred.

ROBIN NAGLE, ANTHROPOLOGIST AT THE NEW YORK CITY DEPARTMENT OF SANITATION[2]

The best thing we can do for the planet is reinvent the sacred.

N. SCOTT MOMADAY, KIOWA NATION[3]

---

1. Tucker, "Interview with Jamie Manson."
2. Goff, "The Landscape of Liturgy," para. 2.
3. See Kauffman, *Reinventing the Sacred*, 291, n1.

IN 2017 THE LUTHERAN World Federation (LWF) will commemorate the five-hundredth anniversary of the Reformation with three themes: Salvation—Not for Sale; Human Beings—Not for Sale; Creation—Not for Sale.

Salvation—Not for Sale earned Luther vilification as a heretic. The papal bull excommunicating him on June 15, 1520, begins: "*Exsurge Domine*—Arise, O Lord—and judge thy case. A wild boar has invaded thy vineyard."[4] That wild boar did serious damage to the churchly landscape, grew a dark beard, went into hiding with a price on his head as Junker Georg, was never caught, and "Salvation—Not for Sale" stands.

"Human Beings—Not for Sale" is true by degrees. It is the case for the law in most societies, if not for global sex trafficking, wages at the bottom end of global supply lines, and the legacies of slavery. Yet "Human Beings—Not for Sale" was hard-core heresy for millennia. What Aristotle calls "natural slaves" belong to the created order itself. Slavery was in place in the church, too, off and on for eighteen centuries.

Which brings us to Creation—Not for Sale.

Of course creation is for sale. What *is* the LWF thinking? Planetary creation mounts the auction block daily. Check Wall Street. To propose otherwise for colonized, industrialized, marketized, and monetized Earth is rank heresy, though never named as such. Nor will it be so named, since any good heresy is someone else's favorite orthodoxy.

For us that economic orthodoxy is global corporate capitalism. And for capitalist economies, even the parental elements of life are for sale: earth (soil), water, fire (energy), and, if you have the right zip code, air. (I know churches happily bailed from debt because they sold their air rights on Manhattan Island. I was a member of one that is still in debt because it couldn't.) Creation—Not for Sale is as heretical for us as slavery's unthinkable abolition was for the Greek philosophers, the Roman Empire, and centuries of Christian slaveholders. Nothing is more routinely operational than nature as a resource rather than a relative. When we talk of planetary creation, we are not talking family; we're talking utility. We're certainly not claiming with Tucker, Nagle, and Momaday that creation is sacred. Creation as Sacred would be heresy number two, right behind Creation—Not for Sale.

The Lutheran World Federation knows this. The text accompanying "Creation—Not for Sale," by Martin Kopp, may not be as bracing as the

---

4. Quoted in Bainton, *Here I Stand*, 147.

papal encyclical, *Laudato Si': On Care for our Common Home*, but it joins the Pope in essential ways.[5] Because Kopp's commentary also serves as a succinct state-of-the-planet summary I cite it in full.

> Does nature have a price? It is a fact that it is all there to buy: land, islands, minerals, water, fruits, vegetables, trees, fish, birds and animals of all species. There seems to be no limit to trade. Nature in its diversity has become a commodity. In fact, those wealthy enough are buying ever more. Accumulating. Longing for the newest. Discarding. Replacing. Since the beginning of the Industrial Revolution, ever more countries have entered a seemingly never-ending process of economic growth and turned into consumer societies where money and possessions are believed to make the good life.
>
> But nature is already presenting us with the bill. Grounds are drying and crops cannot grow without inputs. Water and air are polluted and our health is suffering. Biodiversity is declining and we are at the eve of the sixth great extinction of species. Climate is rapidly changing and is threatening our ecosystems and societies. In a word, we have entered the "Anthropocene," or the "era of the human being," our species having become the main driver of nature's state. And we know the wheel is pointing in the wrong direction.
>
> The time has come to rediscover the significance and implications of the first article of our Creed: our confession of God as the almighty Father, Creator of Heaven and Earth. We do not own the earth and all that is in it, but are creatures ourselves. We are not the masters of nature, but God's children entrusted with the wellbeing of God's creation. We cannot possess and exploit, but shall cultivate and guard.
>
> So let us get to work! There is a theology to spread, lifestyles to change, parishes and institutions to make green. There is a reform to be undertaken in our hearts, minds and deeds. For if nature has a price, creation is priceless—it is not for sale.[6]

To repeat: "So let us get to work! There is a theology to spread, lifestyles to change, parishes and institutions to make green. There is a reform to be undertaken in our hearts, minds and deeds." The "reform to be undertaken" is a comprehensive eco-Reformation. Let that be the next

---

5. As does the powerful *Islamic Declaration on Global Climate Change* issued in Istanbul by world Muslim leaders on August 20, 2015.

6. Kopp, "Creation—Not for Sale."

chapter of the Lutheran Reformation, this time joining the Pope and all persons of good will.

Because only a little can be done in the span of these pages, I choose the first item on the LWF list, "a theology to spread," and, within that, attention to "creation."

NATURE

Did you catch the sharp distinction in the last line of the LWF commentary? "For if nature has a price, creation is priceless—it is not for sale." That follows the topic sentence of the previous paragraph: "The time has come to rediscover the significance and implications of the first article of our Creed."

What *is* the LWF thinking, contrasting "nature" and "creation" and calling for a rediscovery of the first article? "Nature" and "creation" are synonyms, are they not?

Given what the text lays out before—commodified nature in all forms on sale everywhere—the juxtaposition might be this: "nature" in our daily practice is living and non-living goods and services that we seek to control in order to survive and thrive. Though we are nature, too, we are essentially abstracted from it. We are the active subject while the rest of nature is object. We are owners, nature is owned. The ruling relationship is subject-to-object, with nature's goal its usefulness for human ends. The relationship is a pragmatic utilitarian one.

A few fundamental assumptions control this working relationship. They have reigned since the onset of the Industrial Revolution. Their range and grip have increased with advancing technological and scientific powers, however, and now include ecosystems and biological systems. They underlie what for a long while was simply called "Progress." They essentially define "modern nature."

- Nature is a limitless storehouse of resources for human use. It possesses no intrinsic value of its own. It is malleable and can be reconfigured for human ends.

- Humans possess properties and abilities that render us categorically different from the rest of nature. There is no essential or ontological connection between humans and the rest of nature. We are unique.

- Humans have the right, even the calling, to use natural resources for an improvement in humankind's material standard of living.

- The most effective means to raise standards of living is ongoing economic growth directed to ever-expanding material abundance. The good life is one of productive labor and material well-being.

- There is freedom in material abundance. When people have more, their freedom of choice is expanded and they can and will *be* more.

- Modern science and technology, coupled with democracy, have helped achieve a superior civilization, first in the West, then for the rest. A combination of capitalist, democratic, and self-interested values and institutions is best.

- The things we create are under our control.[7]

The bottom-line theological-moral principle here is that modern nature's value is its value for *Homo sapiens* life. The end value of anything, dead or alive, rests with its benefit to humans.

The default relationship of this baseline principle is domination-based and nonreciprocal. There is no inherent demand for nature's regeneration on its own terms and timelines, nor are there ways to represent and institutionalize the needs of future generations of humankind and otherkind. Few laws protect the natural world's integrity for the long haul. The relationship is systemically impersonal, transient, and pragmatic.

This relationship is also severely anthropocentric. Modern nature is divested of subjectivity and any transcendent status and meaning. Communal feelings of intimacy do not well up within us. From a *relational* point of view, nature is effectively dead. Or, if you prefer, even living nature is machine-like, with our connection an instrumental one. God as Creator may not make an appearance at all; but if God does, it is the God who, through creation, meets *our* wants and needs, for *our* good. Even redemption plays out on the axis that runs solely between God and humankind.

It was a clergyman, William Derham, who preached this theological ethic most plainly. His book, *Physico-Theology: or, A Demonstration of the Being and Attributes of God, from His Works of Creation*, was published at the onset of the Industrial Revolution, in 1768. It includes this: "We can, if need be, ransack the whole globe, penetrate into the bowels of the

---

7. Birch and Rasmussen, *The Predicament of the Prosperous*, 44–45, considerably abbreviated and modified here.

earth, descend to the bottom of the deep, travel to the farthest reaches of this world, to acquire wealth."[8]

And we have.

Two hundred fifty years later, the same center of gravity holds. It was nicely captured in a recent ExxonMobil shareholder meeting as CEO Rex Tillerson answered those who asked the giant energy corporation to stop using the atmosphere for a sewer. He posed his own question in response. It was meant to quash any further conversation. "What good is it to save the planet if humanity suffers?"[9]

Nature and the planet here have the same standing as mountains have for Jason Bostic, Vice President of the West Virginia Coal Association. He asked the critics of strip-mining, "What good is a mountain just to have a mountain?"[10] Like Tillerson's, the plain sense of Bostic's question was meant to settle the issue. Both questions answered their interlocutors with the logic of modern conventional wisdom. In this moral world, the mountain's sole value is its value as natural capital, whether as a resource for human use or for recreation. This is how it is "good," to use Bostic's vocabulary. That is how nature is "good."

This, to remember the LWF commentary, is nature with "a price," nature "become a commodity," nature as "all there to buy: land, islands, minerals, water, fruits, vegetables, trees, fish, birds and animals of all species."

The Pope's summary is the following: "Modern anthropocentrism has paradoxically ended up prizing technical thought over reality, since 'the technological mind sees nature as an insensate order, as a cold body of facts, as a mere 'given', as a mere 'space' into which objects can be thrown with complete indifference.' The intrinsic dignity of the world is thus compromised."[11] Nature is not sacred.

What, then, is "Creation—Not for Sale," that is "creation" as "priceless"? What kind of world carries "intrinsic dignity" that is not "compromised" by utility or indifference?

Recall the epigraphs from Tucker, Nagle, and Momaday. Creation is what modern nature is not—sacred, personal, and invested with meaning.

---

8. Derham, *Physico-Theology*, 110; cited from Klein, *This Changes Everything*, 171.

9. Cited from Gore, "The Turning Point," 11.

10. Klein, *This Changes Everything*, 337.

11. Francis, *Laudato Si',* para. 115.

CREATION

The peoples who have treated creation as sacred, personal, and inherently meaningful are precisely the peoples most disdained by the powers of colonized, industrialized, and marketized Earth—the peoples displaced by the forces of modernity itself: namely, indigenous peoples around the globe. At the same time, they are the ones who have the best track record for living ecologically and sustainably when they have been able to exercise sovereignty over their own lands.

To explore creation in the register of the sacred, consider the Aboriginal Indigenous Peoples' Declaration at the United Nations. It was formally offered at the UN Climate Summit in New York City, September 22, 2014. In just over two pages the words "sacred," "sacredness," and "sanctity" appear twenty-five times, including the title itself: *Beyond Climate Change to Survival on Sacred Mother Earth*. Were "the sacred" or "sacredness" itself the main subject, it might have been even more prominent. But planetary creation as sacred is not the main point; getting beyond climate change to survival is. Much of the text is thus descriptive of changes to "Sacred Mother Earth," changes that follow upon "modern living and all that it encompasses," i.e., changes that follow upon the Industrial Revolution and its centuries of colonization and "Progress."

> The Air is not the same anymore. The Water is not the same anymore. The Earth is not the same anymore. The Clouds are not the same anymore. The Rain is not the same anymore. The Trees, the Plants, the Animals, Birds, Fish, Insects and all the others are not the same anymore. All that is Sacred in Life is vanishing because of our actions.[12]

That paragraph begins, "There is no more time for discussion on preventing 'Climate Change'. That opportunity has passed. 'Climate Change' is here."[13] "Not the same anymore" is the new normal. This is not the statement's first paragraph, however. There the theological framework and moral foundation for the full declaration is laid out. "All Creation has a right to live and survive on this Sacred Earth and raise their Families where the Creator placed them to be."

"Raise their Families," means the families of "all Creation." Insects, birds, fish, plants, et al., have families. Citizens of Sacred Earth, all of

12. Aboriginal Indigenous Peoples' Council, *Beyond Climate Change*, 1.
13. Ibid.

them, are personal in the manner of family members. We're talking family here.

The declaration goes on to list changes beyond the ones cited above. There is no need to add them, there is only need to say what the document says: The planetary changes all follow from the kind of economic orthodoxy that has ravaged Sacred Earth and its families, that has brought climate change and survival stakes in its wake, and that violates ways of life that are congruent with creation as sacred.

The problem of moving to survival under these circumstances is compounded, the document says, because we presently "lack leadership." "We have misplaced our trust in governmental leaders and the leaders of industry. They failed us by trying to maintain their profits, economies and their power over the people."[14]

No more need be said in order to show the conflicting moralities and theologies we have outlined: the contrast of personal and impersonal, creation as sacred and modern nature as profane. Suffice it to end with a sentence of such gravity that the declaration offers it in bolded uppercase:

> TO SURVIVE CLIMATE CHANGE AND SEE THE FUTURE WE MUST RESTORE THE SACRED IN OURSELVES AND INCLUDE THE SACREDNESS OF ALL LIFE IN OUR DISCUSSIONS, DECISIONS, AND ACTIONS.[15]

SACRAMENTAL IMAGINATION: UP CLOSE AND PERSONAL

As part of the necessary transition from this world to "Creation—Not for Sale," allow me a gloss on "personal" and "impersonal." This simple contrast highlights how Lutherans might rediscover the First Article of the Creed for eco-reformation work.

The sacred is always deeply personal. Orthodox theologian John Chryssavgis writes, "It has always been a source of great comfort to me that Orthodox spirituality retains a sacramental view of the world, proclaiming a world imbued by God and a God involved in the world—a sacrament of communion." He then goes on to say what the world as sacrament means: "We should respond to nature with the same delicacy,

14. Ibid.
15. Ibid., 2.

sensitivity, and tenderness with which we respond *to a person in a relationship*, and our failure to do so is the fundamental source of pollution."[16] "The time has come," he says elsewhere, "to stop treating even things like things."[17]

Differently said, in a profoundly personal relationship I experience a deep companion *feeling* for the other, whether the other is animate or inanimate, a fellow creature, a mountain or river, a helpless newborn or an emblazoned horizon at day's onset or end. Even things are not treated as "things."

The feeling accompanying the sacred is so deeply personal that any of our core moral emotions—empathy, sympathy, love, compassion, awe, reverence, righteous anger, or a heartfelt loyalty to place—might well up. "The more I wonder, the more I love," is Alice Walker's version.[18] Love, that most personal of all communal connections, is subject joined to subject in a common life. As such, love might pertain to anything and all things, a friend, a mountain, a plain, a forest, a village, city, county, or life itself and the starry night. "I love it here" professes true, simple belonging. Of that which really counts, love even surpasses faith and hope. St. Paul thinks so.[19]

The impersonal, by contrast, is instrumental and mechanistic. Its relationship is means-to-end, with no moral emotions or claims attached, other than all those pleasures of being waited upon and enjoying the life of the consumer. The impersonal is the world as my oyster, the world in which I am the "taker," but not the "giver" or "leaver." As impersonal, it has no claims upon me; I have claims upon it. As subject to object, I-to-it, no genuine reciprocity exists, either. The world is useful but it is a world without soul, a world manipulated but not revered, a world needed but not loved. The impersonal imitates the personal and sacred in only one way; that is, the impersonal, too, can pertain to anything and all things— that mountain, plain, forest, village, the next-door neighbor, or the stars.

At its historical extreme, impersonal logic is the logic of master-slave. And this is, according to Jennifer Harvey, precisely the "shared hinge" on which "European-Indigenous-African relations"[20] have swung.

---

16. Chryssavgis, "Panel Comments at the Living Cosmology Conference."

17. Chryssavgis, *Beyond the Shattered Image*, 15.

18. Walker, *The Color Purple*, 290.

19. 1 Cor 13:13.

20. Harvey, *Whiteness and Morality*, 14.

James Cone, in "Whose Earth Is It, Anyway?" lays out what for him is
that hinge. "The logic that led to slavery and segregation in the Americas,
colonization and apartheid in Africa, and the rule of white supremacy
throughout the world is the same one that leads to the exploitation of
animals and the ravaging of nature. It is a mechanistic and instrumental logic that defines everything and everybody in terms of their contribution to the development and defense of white world supremacy."[21]
Cone argues that this centuries-deep instrumentalist economic logic
still prevails, with other-than-human life the irreplaceable slave alongside exploited humans. Moreover, and like Pope Francis later in *Laudato
Si'*, Cone underscores the causal links, whether the parties acknowledge
them or not. Like justice, injustice, too, is indivisible. "People who fight
against white racism but fail to connect it to the degradation of the earth
are anti-ecological—whether they know it or not. People who struggle
against environmental degradation but do not incorporate in it a disciplined and sustained fight against white supremacy are racists—whether
thy acknowledge it or not. The fight for justice cannot be segregated but
must be integrated with the fight for life in all its forms."[22]

Carl Anthony's observation confirms and extends Cone's and Harvey's. "Historic moments of excessive abuse—slave trade, colonization,
genocide—developed in tandem with humanity's unsustainable relationship to the environment."[23] The instrumentalist and impersonal ethic of
consistent utility is a destructive master-slave ethic, destructive for nature
and other humans.

Anthony might have added "patriarchy." Early on in both the second wave of feminism and the modern environmental movement, the
entrenched pattern of treating women and the rest of nature as property
and the subject of patriarchal privilege and authority was exposed. This
too, was a rendition of master-slave morality. Furthermore, women's
equality and nature revered as kin was viewed as the contrasting ethic
of liberation. All this had been powerfully presented already in 1975
with the publication of Rosemary Radford Ruether's *New Woman, New
Earth*.[24]

21. Cone, "Whose Earth Is It, Anyway?," 23.

22. Ibid.

23. Anthony, "Interview with Jamie Manson."

24. Ruether, *New Woman, New Earth*. For more, including international forms of
eco-feminism, see the essay by Wanda Deifelt in this volume.

Yet this is to stray from the earlier point. While it may surprise most Euro-Americans, the *personal* can be, and in the cosmology and practices of Indigenous peoples and many ancient civilizations has been, a relationship embracing *both the animate and inanimate worlds.* We are soil people, or water people, or deer people, or mountain people, because we share a common origin, energy and spirit with other natural entities. We are companions to all that is, companions to all that participates in being. In many indigenous traditions, as well as some religions, the birds are a nation, too, as are insects, animals and plants. The *Qur'an's* version is: "All the creatures on earth, and all the birds that fly with wings, are communities like you" (6:38).

"Person" ethics does not erase difference—birds, plants, insects, animals, winds, waters, and mountains are distinguished from one another in wildly different ways. Like human persons, each knows uniqueness and each has a life, with this personal ethic granting citizenship to all. The universe is home to a communion of subjects, not a collection of objects.[25]

Again the papal encyclical, *Laudato Si'*, has the distinctions right. Francis quotes the German bishops: "We can speak of the priority of *being* over that of *being useful.*"[26] This is the priority of "creation" over "nature" in the LWF theme.

Put it this way. "Things change according to the stance we adopt toward them, the type of attention we pay to them, the disposition we hold in relation to them."[27] Values arise with the relationships they express. Different values belong to different kinds of relationships. If my relationship is instrumental and impersonal, values appropriate to a mechanistic and decontextualized world will rule. If nature and some humans are without use, they are essentially what strip-miners call "overburden." Their value is means-only.

By contrast, if I respond to the same world "out there" as sacred creation rather than modern nature, then some place, event, or natural phenomenon of that world appears in a different light. It is deeply personal and internal rather than extrinsic and at arms' length. There is no controlling design, no instrumental purpose in view such that I seek to possess it for some end other than its own. The experience is one of awe

25. Berry, *Evening Thoughts*, 17.

26. Francis, *Laudato Si'*, para. 69.

27. McGilchrist, *The Master and His Emissary*, 4.

and wonder, reverence and respect, rather than manipulation. Here I belong in a relationship of reciprocity rather than narrow self-reference. I am a member of a self-transcending community to which others and I belong, together.[28] For believers this is "a world imbued by God and a God involved in the world—a sacrament of communion" (Chrysavvgis). In this sacred and sacramental world, creation is not for sale.

THE DIFFERENCE IT MAKES

Of course we use the world. All creation does. It must, in order to live. Life even requires the taking of life for the sake of ongoing life. How, then, might the sacred and utilitarian be joined? Or, what difference would it make if "being" (sacred creation) had priority over "being useful" for a world that, in essential ways, *must* be used (nature)?

The sketch might go like this, a la Martin Luther and Thomas Berry. The Lutheran insistence that the finite bears the infinite and the transcendent is utterly immanent (*finitum capax infiniti*) means that God's abode is the material universe. Luther is boldly pan-en-theistic on this—all is in God, God is in all. In a thoroughly sacramental stance, he writes: "How can reason tolerate it that the Divine majesty is so small that it can be substantially present in a grain, on a grain, over a grain, through a grain, within and without, and that, although it is a single Majesty, it nevertheless is entirely in each grain separately, no matter how immeasurably numerous these grains may be?"[29] This is the ordinary (a grain) in a different and extraordinary light (God present in each grain). This is creation as sacred.

One difference a sacred universe like this might make would be the primacy and priority of creation for the policy principles that govern the human use of nature. Thomas Berry's maxim says it well: "Planetary health is primary and human well-being is derivative."[30] This in turn renders "the preservation of the Earth economy" the first law of economics.[31]

28. These paragraphs on relationship and different modes of attention are indebted to Iain McGilchrist's discussion of the left and right hemispheres of the brain in McGilchrist, *The Master and his Emissary*. I am drawing most directly from the subsection "Conclusion," 174–75.

29. Bornkamm, *Luther's World of Thought*, 189. The German original is from the *Weimarer Ausgabe* of Luther's writings, 32:134.34–136.36.

30. Berry, *Evening Thoughts*, 19.

31. Berry, "Conditions for Entering the Ecozoic Era," 10.

It also merges economics and ecology to become "eco-nomics," with all human economic activity embedded within the ecological limits of nature's economy, limits ignored in global capitalism's working notion of modern nature.

A parallel exists for energy policy. Almost all attention to energy is about energy resources and use. Do we have enough to do what we want to do, namely, continue to grow the economy to meet human needs? How do we secure energy independence? How will energy be distributed fairly? These discussions all go on without *first* asking what sources and uses are mandated by the planet's climate-energy system, the way the planet regulates the incoming solar heat that keeps Earth from being a barren rock and no more. Energy policy discussions assume that human energy use is primary; then we'll deal with the side effects. (These effects now include climate change.) But *human* primacy and priority—"being useful"—is exactly backwards. The first law of energy is preservation of the planet's climate-energy system as conducive to life. Human energy use is *derivative of the planet's*. This is the energy parallel to Berry's principle that the first law of the human economy is the preservation of the planet's economy. It is also a conviction that flows from creation, or "being," as sacred. The well-being of creation comprehensively is its due, and the starting point for human use of it.

The same holds for water policy and the hydrological system. What does water require of us for its life and work? What does our watershed require for human life and healthy community for other-than-human life? We would start with water's requirements for its own health and its roles in sustaining the community of life, then factor in our needs as they fit creation's life. "Being" has priority over "being useful" (to us).

We need not spell out the other principles that would follow—the primacy of the atmosphere's dynamics, or ecosystem requirements. All of them frame policy with nature's requirements for its own regeneration and renewal.

Yet getting policy principles right, vital though it be, is likely insufficient for a genuinely sacramental life. Without a virtue ethic that forms character and shapes conduct in keeping with first principles and the conviction that we inhabit a sacred universe, moral resolve will falter and moral emotions will fail. We will not escape the grip of the master-slave ethic of impersonal utility without a soul-deep, personal *feeling* for the families of creation, a gut connection that is profoundly personal, Earth-honoring, and Earth-healing. This subjective knowing of the other expresses a moral universe that nurtures certain ecological virtues, many of which have not been the coin even of Christian social justice traditions—wonder, awe, and reverence, for example, with all of "being" a companion and neighbor across time and space. These join virtues already at home in social justice—respect, empathy, and sympathy yoked to a passion for fairness and equality in lives that matter. In all events, the religious conviction that all creation is sacred backs the formation of character and conduct in such a way that creation justice includes social justice.

Is there more?

For religious devotees, especially those in theistic traditions, a sacred universe confesses God in all and all in God. But which God? To match what we now know about the universe, worthy "God-talk" would gather in all of Earth's voices to sing the hymn of creation: God-talk that encompasses all 13.8 billion years of the universe's pilgrimage to date and the immense wheeling of one hundred billion galaxies, each swimming with billions of stars and who knows how many planets; God-talk that gathers in all species come and gone, as well as those leaving as we speak; and God-talk that embraces the whole drama of life in all its misery and grandeur. In a sacred universe, worthy God-talk is about the mystery of matter and its drama—all of it, past, present, and future. It is an invitation to "sing with all the people of God and join in the hymn of all creation"[32] so as to give voice, however partially and inadequately, to the carnal presence of the "uncontained God."[33] The uncontained God is the God of creation. In the language of third century Christian texts, God is a sphere whose center is everywhere and circumference nowhere.[34]

An upgraded understanding of ourselves is another critical element, an improved anthropology, if you will. Our present segregated sense of ourselves as a master species is a miserably shrunken grasp of who we are in the grand scheme of things. From both a scientific and a religious point of view we are "fearfully and wonderfully made," to use the singer's words (Ps 139). We are the handsome fruit of two wombs, our mother's and Mother Earth's. So the psalmist sings of God:

---

32. From the ELCA Eucharistic liturgy, *Evangelical Lutheran Worship*, 101.

33. Levertov, "Annunciation," 85.

34. McGilchrist, *The Master and His Emissary*, 448–49. McGilchrist is drawing on the *Corpus Hermeticum*, a body of early Christian texts from Hellenic Egypt.

For it was you who formed my inward parts;
>   you knit me together in my mother's womb.
I praise you, for I am fearfully and wonderfully made.
>   Wonderful are your works;
>   that I know very well.
My frame was not hidden from you,
>   when I was being made in secret,
>   intricately woven in the depths of the earth.
Your eyes beheld my unformed substance.
In your book were written
>   all the days that were formed for me,
>   when none of them as yet existed. (Ps 139:13–16)

To be "fearfully and wonderfully made" across the stop-and-start eons of evolutionary life, to belong to life's drama and grandeur and have a perch of our own in the great Tree of Life, is our glory. To breathe the same air Jesus breathed and stand before the same waters Moses did, to share DNA with most of life and be comprised of atoms 14 billion years old, this is enough. "I just try to act my age," quips Joanna Macy. "My atoms are 14 billion years old."[35]

These elements, then, together with deep changes in policy that prioritize the requirements of life's generative elements and systems, explain what it would mean to merge the sacred and the utilitarian. Creation would be deemed sacred and given primacy and priority for baseline principles, character would be formed and conduct shaped by ecological virtues, God-talk worthy of the uncontained God would be the language of praise and lament, and a "fearfully and wonderfully made" understanding of ourselves would recognize that we are precious members of a sacred cosmos. Such might be one way Lutherans rediscover the First Article of the Creed for an Eco-Reformation.

BIBLIOGRAPHY

Aboriginal Indigenous Peoples Council. *Beyond Climate Change to Survival on Sacred Mother Earth.* Bozeman, MT: American Indian Institute Traditional Circle of Indian Elders and Youth, 2014.

Anthony, Carl. "Interview with Jamie Manson." *National Catholic Reporter*, November 21, 2014. http://ncronlineorg.

Bainton, Roland H. *Here I Stand: A Life of Martin Luther.* Nashville: Abingdon, 1950.

35. Macy, "The Greening of the Self," 155.

Berry, Thomas. "Conditions for Entering the Ecozoic Era." *Ecozoic Reader* 2 (Winter 2002) 10–11.

———. *Evening Thoughts: Reflecting on Earth as Sacred Community.* San Francisco: Sierra Club, 2006.

Birch, Bruce C., and Larry L. Rasmussen. *The Predicament of the Prosperous.* Biblical Perspectives on Current Issues. Philadelphia: Westminster, 1978.

Bornkamm, Heinrich. *Luther's World of Thought.* Translated by Martin H. Bertram. St. Louis: Concordia, 2001.

Chryssavgis, John. *Beyond the Shattered Image.* Minneapolis: Light & Life, 1999.

———. "Panel Comments at the Living Cosmology Conference," Yale Divinity School. *National Catholic Reporter,* November 21, 2014. http://ncronline.org.

Cone, James H. "Whose Earth Is It, Anyway?" In *Earth Habitat: Eco-Injustice and the Church's Response,* edited by Dieter Hessel and Larry Rasmussen, 23–32. Minneapolis: Fortress, 2001.

Derham, William. *Physico-Theology: or, A Demonstration of the Being and Attributes of God, from His Works of Creation.* London: Printed for Robinson and Roberts, 1768.

Evangelical Lutheran Worship. Minneapolis: Augsburg Fortress, 2006.

Francis. *Laudato Si': On Care for our Common Home.* Rome: Vatican Publishing House, 2015.

Goff, Ashley. "The Landscape of Liturgy: Garbage Can Turned Into Font." *God of the Sparrow: An Earth-Honoring Blog,* March 25, 2014. http://godofthesparrow.com.

Gore, Al. "The Turning Point: New Hope for the Climate." *Rolling Stone,* June 18, 2014. http://www.rollingstone.com.

Harvey, Jennifer. *Whiteness and Morality: Pursuing Racial Justice through Reparations and Sovereignty.* New York: Palgrave Macmillan, 2007.

Islamic Declaration on Climate Change. Istanbul, August 20, 2015. http://islamicclimatedeclaration.org/.

Kauffman, Stuart A. *Reinventing the Sacred: The New View of Science, Reason, and Religion.* New York: Basic Books, 2008.

Klein, Naomi. *This Changes Everything: Capitalism vs. The Climate.* New York: Simon & Schuster, 2014.

Kopp, Martin. "Creation—Not for Sale." *The Lutheran World Federation.* January 20, 2015. https://2017.lutheranworld.org.

Levertov, Denise. "Annunciation." In *The Door in the Hive,* 86–88. New York: New Directions, 1984.

Macy, Joanna. "The Greening of the Self." In *Spiritual Ecology: The Cry of the Earth,* edited by Llewellyn Vaughn-Lee, 145–56. Point Reyes, CA: Golden Sufi Center, 2013.

McGilchrist, Iain. *The Master and His Emissary: The Divided Brain and the Making of the Western World.* New Haven: Yale University Press, 2009.

Ruether, Rosemary Radford. *New Woman, New Earth: Sexist Ideologies and Human Liberation.* San Francisco: Harper & Row, 1975.

Tucker, Mary Evelyn. "Interview with Jamie Manson." *National Catholic Reporter,* November 21, 2014. http://ncronline.org.

Walker, Alice. *The Color Purple.* New York: Washington Square, 1982.

3

A Haunting Contradiction, Hope, and Moral-Spiritual Power

—CYNTHIA D. MOE-LOBEDA

GOD'S BELOVED HUMAN CREATURES— CALLED TO LOVE

IT IS AN ASTOUNDING moment in history to be people who serve the God revealed in Jesus, the Hebrew Scriptures, and Earth itself.[1] We who stake our lives on the promises of this God have been given truths that shake the foundations of the world.

- The first is God's love. Nothing is surer, no truth stronger than this breath-taking claim of Christian faith: that God—the creating, liberating, healing, sustaining Source—loves this world and each of us with a love that will neither cease nor diminish, a love more powerful than any other force in heaven or earth. That is the beginning point.

- And next, this God is at play in the world, breathing life into it. This Spirit is present within, among, and beyond us.

1. This essay is a revised and shortened version of two keynote addresses delivered at Trinity Lutheran Seminary for its conference titled "How Then Shall We Live? Manifesting Lives of Eco-Justice, Faith, and Love" (March 17–18, 2014). The essay was first published in *Currents in Theology and Mission* (August 1, 2014) and is reprinted here in a revised form with permission.

- But that is not all. We human creatures are created and called to recognize this gracious and indomitable love, receive it, relish it, revel in it, and—most important of all from a Lutheran perspective—to trust it.

- And finally, after receiving and trusting that love—being claimed by it—we are then to embody it in the world by loving as God loves. We are beckoned to join with God's Spirit of justice-making, Earth-relishing Love in its steadfast commitment to gain fullness of life for all. We are called to "love as God loves."

According to widespread understanding of the Christian story, this is the human vocation, our life's work. We are called and given this reason for being.

Two millennia of Christians and the Hebrew people before them have sought to heed this calling: "to love the Lord your God" (Deut 6:5), and "to love your neighbor as yourself" (Lev 19:18). "The whole thrust of biblical religion," writes Dan Maguire, "is toward the recovery of the broken human capacity to love."[2] "Our responsibility as Christians," Martin Luther King, Jr. declared, "is to discover the meaning of this command and seek passionately to live it out in our daily lives."[3] What love is and requires is the great moral question permeating Christian history. In each time and place Jesus' voice resounds: "You shall love your neighbor as yourself." The human response rings out: What does it mean to "love neighbor as self" or to "love neighbor as God loves" in our day and place?

What does this vocation mean for the world's high consumers if we are, through climate change, threatening Earth's God-given capacity to generate life? Never before in this three or four millennia old faith tradition have the stakes in heeding our calling been so high. What do I mean?

GOD'S BELOVED HUMAN CREATURES: UNCREATING AND KILLING

I am haunted by the contradiction between this reason for being—to love as God loves—and the hidden realities of our collective lives. Please note two things: We are talking about the *impact* of our lives, not our

2. Maguire, *The Moral Core of Judaism and Christianity*, 208.
3. King, "Strength to Love," 48. Here King is speaking specifically of the commandment to love enemies.

intentions, and we are talking about the impact—and therefore the moral weight—of our *collective* lives, not just our *individual* lives. Daring to heed these concerns draws us into the stark and seemingly godforsaken landscape of structural or systemic sin. It is a terrain from which we would far rather flee.

But please have the courage to go with me into this terrain of structural sin. I do promise that this is not where we will end. The great truth shaping all that I say is the truth of cross and resurrection. Despite death and destruction at their fullest, God's life-giving, life-saving love ultimately is the shape of the future. Even where God seems absent, God is present with us. So we step with courage to look briefly at the unprecedented two-fold moral crisis now facing the generations of people on Earth as a consequence of our collective lives.

The first dimension of the crisis is ecological. The intimate Mystery that we call God must have an insatiable hunger for life and, moreover, for life that creates ever-more abundant and complex life forms. This God uses even death and brokenness to further *life.* Indeed, the monotheistic traditions hold in common this claim: God created a fruitful, fecund Earth, a planet that spawns and supports life with a complexity and generosity beyond human ken. Fundamental to Christian and Jewish faith is the claim that it is "good" (Gen 1:31). According to Genesis's first creation story, "God saw that it was *ṭov.*" The Hebrew *ṭov,* while often translated as "good," also implies "life-furthering." And God said time and again that this creation was *ṭov*—a good that is life-furthering.

Here we arrive at a frightening theological problem. The primal act of God (creating) is not merely to create a magnificent world. This God creates a magnificently *life-furthering* world. Here lies the scandal. We are *undoing* that very *ṭov,* Earth's life-generating capacity. We are "uncreating." We—or rather, some of us—have become the "uncreators."[4] One young and dangerous species has become a threat to Earth's life-generating capacity. *Homo sapiens* are using and degrading the planet's natural goods at a rate that Earth's ecosystems cannot sustain. The credible

---

4. A good example is the "terminator seed" developed by Monsanto, one of a few companies that control a large part of the world's "seed business." The terminator seed is designed to be incapable of reseeding itself. It enables a company to make more profit from small subsistence level farmers around the globe. Each season, instead of using saved seed, the farmer who has been sold the terminator seed must rebuy seed. The terminator seed seems to me to be a quintessential illustration of "uncreating" the life-furthering capacity of life.

scientific community is of one accord about this basic reality, and hundreds of its widely respected voices have been for over two decades.

Less widely accepted, however, is a corollary point of soul-searing moral import. It is this: The horrific consequences of climate change, toxic waste, and other forms of ecological degradation are not suffered equally by Earth's people. Nor are the world's people equally responsible. Those least responsible for Earth's crisis are suffering and dying first and foremost from it.

Here we have moved into that ominous link between ecological degradation and social injustice and the second dimension of the moral crisis shaping our world today. It is the social justice impacts of ecological degradation. Eco-justice is the term used to designate this nexus of social and ecological concerns.

While working in India with the National Council of Churches of India and a number of theological seminaries, I realized more fully the extent to which race-based and class-based climate injustice permeates our lives. Climate change may be the most far-reaching manifestation of white privilege and class privilege yet to face humankind. Climate change is caused overwhelmingly by the world's high-consuming people who are disproportionately descendants of Europe. Yet climate change is wreaking death and destruction first and foremost on impoverished people who also are disproportionately people of color.[5] The millions of current climate refugees are primarily Asian and African. That number will increase dramatically in the years ahead, and will represent overwhelmingly people of Asia, Africa, and low-lying Pacific Islands.[6]

---

5. The environmental refugees whose lands will be lost to rising seas if Antarctica or Greenland melt significantly will be disproportionately people of color. So too the people who will go hungry if global warming diminishes crop yields of the world's food staples—corn, rice, and wheat. The forty percent of the world's population whose lives depend upon water from the seven rivers fed by rapidly diminishing Himalayan glaciers are largely not white people. See Tupouniua, "Statement of H. E. Mr. Mahe," 1, #4: climate change "represents the gravest of threats to the survival" of some island nations, some of which could cease to exist as countries as a result of rising sea levels. It goes without saying that these nations are composed of people who are predominantly not white.

6. According to former U.N. Deputy Higher Commissioner for Refugees Craig Johnstone, "Given the primary, secondary and tertiary effects I have described, it is unlikely we will get as much precision as we would like. Current estimates seem to range between 250 million and a billion people who will be forcibly displaced [by climate change] by 2050." See Johnstone, "The Climate Change Future is Now."

Rise in sea levels will not force economically privileged people like me from our homes and livelihoods. Not true for many of the world's more impoverished people in low-lying areas. The Maldives, a nation of islands no more than a mile wide at any point, is threatened with loss of its entire land mass. The entire nation may be forced to relocate. Martin Parry, chair of the Intergovernmental Panel on Climate Change (IPPC), Working Group II, declares: "The people most affected by climate change are and will be those living in developing countries . . . and within those regions it will be the poor that will be most affected . . ."[7] Even a slight degree of warming decreases the yield of the world's food staples—wheat, corn, barley, rice—in seasonally dry areas.[8] Subsistence farmers and people with little money will go hungry. The coastal peoples without resources to protect against and recover from the fury of climate-related weather disasters are not the people largely responsible for greenhouse gas emissions. Nor are they, for the most part, white. Many voices of the Global South recognize this injustice with the terminology of climate debt, climate colonialism, or climate imperialism.

The social justice implications of environmental issues are, of course, not limited to climate change. Environmental racism within the United States and globally is pervasive, devastating, and hidden from view for

7. Parry, "IIED Interviews: Martin Parry on Climate Change."

8. Parry, et al., *Contributions of Working Group II*.

people not oppressed by it.[9] In theological terms, these are manifestations of "structural sin."[10]

Enough! Danger lurks; facing realities such as these breeds despair and powerlessness. To acknowledge the widespread suffering that may be linked to my material abundance would be tormenting. How could I live with the knowledge if I truly took it in? And if I dare to see, then I view also the power and complexity of structural injustice and the relative insignificance of individual efforts at change. Where would I find the moral-spiritual power to transgress tidal waves of cultural, political, and economic forces pushing me to accept and maintain the way things are? A sense of inevitability sucks away at hope. Hope for a more just and

9. The term *environmental racism* was coined in 1987 by Benjamin F. Chavis Jr., a civil rights leader, in the groundbreaking study, *Toxic Wastes and Race*, published by the United Church of Christ Commission for Racial Justice. While initially referring to environmental discrimination based on race alone, environmental racism has come to denote the disproportionate distribution of environmental dangers not only in communities of color but also communities of economically marginalized people. Environmental racism within the United States is pervasive. The aforementioned study documented horrendous environmental and health effects, and found that the disproportionate numbers of racial and ethnic minorities living in communities with hazardous waste facilities was *not a random occurrence* but rather a *consistent pattern*. Environmental racism on an international level includes climate change but extends beyond, and much is easily hidden from the public eye, except for the people who suffer from it. The transfer of ecologically dangerous production plants to countries of the two-thirds world is one manifestation. Over two thousand *maquiladoras* (factories) line the Mexico side of the US–Mexico border. Many of them are relocated from the U.S. in order to profit from weaker environmental and labor protection regulations on the Mexico side. The maquiladoras are notorious for appalling degrees of dangerous—even deadly—environmental pollution. Even more explicit is the practice of "transboundary dumping" across national borders. Much of U.S. citizens' waste ends up in landfills in the Global South. Computers and other electronic goods that are discarded by consumers in the industrialized nations are often shipped to urban areas and rural villages across Asia, Latin America and Africa where residents disassemble them for re-sale or where they are simply dumped as waste. Because computer monitors contain highly toxic materials, this constitutes an enormous transfer of hazardous waste products from Global North to South, poisoning watersheds in Bangladesh, China, India, Philippines, and elsewhere. These are examples of environmental racism.

10. Structural sin refers to the harm caused by social structures that damage some people in order to benefit others, even though the people benefiting may not be doing anything wrong as individuals and may not even be aware of the harm caused by the systems from which they benefit. Racism and patriarchy are examples. With the rising ecological awareness in religious thought, the understanding of structural sin has expanded to include unnecessary harm to other-than-human parts of creation. On these questions, see also the essay by Larry Rasmussen in this volume.

sustainable world may fade before ever it sees full bloom, and with it moral vision and power.

WHY FACE STRUCTURAL SIN?

Why, then, spend time with the disheartening reality of our entanglement in structural sin? I believe that doing so—despite the pain involved—is crucial and deeply faithful. Consider three reasons.

The first is theological. Christians profess that the first step in freedom from sin is repentance. Where we do not repent, we remain in bondage to sin. The power of structural sin is so fierce, so mesmerizing, so seemingly impenetrable precisely because—failing to recognize it—we fail to confess it and repent of it. Christian traditions must bring to our perilous situations of climate debt and environmental racism the call to repent. It is a call to confess, repent, and then lament collectively for our collective sin. This may be a necessary step toward freedom from it.

The second reason is also theological. If sin is structural, not only individual, then so too is the force that counters sin: love. Love in our day takes structural form—more specifically ecological and economic form. In the face of eco-injustice, the church will meet God's call to seek justice in all the Earth to the extent that we rethink our calling to love—our principal guideline for life—as not only an interpersonal calling but also an ecological-economic calling. Luther insisted that love be the guide for every aspect of life, including the economic part of our lives. More on that shortly.

The third reason for facing our implication in the structural sin of climate change and other forms of environmental injustice is more practical. In seeking to understand how they work, we gain knowledge necessary to undo them. You cannot dismantle a complex structure and rebuild it differently without some sense of how it is put together in the first place.

If faith calls us to face the structural sin of environmental injustice, including climate change, how can we protect ourselves from the despair and hopelessness that may attack us when we do so?

THEOLOGICAL SEEDS OF HOPE AND MORAL POWER[11]

This—the testing point of human history—is the time for the world's great faith traditions to abandon preoccupation with privatized morality, conflict with each other, and conflict with science, and instead to embrace collaboratively the sacred calling of our day: forging a sustainable relationship between the human species and planet Earth, and doing so in ways that shrink—rather than grow—the vast gap between those who have too much and those who have not enough.

Religious traditions are called to plumb their depths for wisdom to meet this epic moral challenge. All religious traditions have particular gifts to bring. We are called to put these religious traditions and their wisdoms in dialogue with each other, and with other bodies of knowledge including the natural and social sciences.

Our focus in this volume is on Christian traditions. What do Christian traditions offer to the church and to the broader society in the quest for sustainable Earth-human relations marked by social justice? And what are the practical implications of these gifts? Let us sink our hearts and minds into four particular resources inherent in Lutheran traditions.

Resurrection

The first is the promise of resurrection: life in God is more powerful than all forms of death and destruction. I write now very personally. I am easily tempted toward despair when I acknowledge the insidious nature of structural injustice and the projected consequences of climate change. A subtle but deep voice within me whispers that things will continue as they are despite our best efforts. However, the cross and resurrection defy that voice and promise otherwise. This I believe with my whole being.

The power of God liberating all of creation from the bonds of oppression, destruction, and death is stronger than all forces of evil that would undermine God's promise that all shall have life and have it abundantly. God "will not allow our complicity in . . . evil to defeat God's being for us and for the good of all creation."[12] We have heard the end of the story, and it is resurrection. Soul-searing, life-shattering destruction and death is not the last word, in this moment or forever. In some way that

11. The following section is drawn from my book, *Resisting Structural Evil*, chap. 6.
12. Morse, *Not Every Spirit*, 249.

we do not grasp, the last word is life raised up out of brutal death. In the midst of suffering and death—be it individual, social, or ecological—the promise given to the Earth community is that life in God will reign. So speaks the resurrection.

In all honesty, I do not know what this promise means for us and for Earth's community of life. It does *not* lessen our call to devote our lives to building a more just, compassionate, and sustainable world; it does *not,* that is, allow us to sit back and let God do the work. That conclusion would be absurd, because God works through human beings as well as other creatures and the cosmos itself. Nor does the hope of cross and resurrection ensure our survival as a species in the face of climate change. It *does* ensure that the radiant Good beyond comprehension that is above, beyond, under, and within all, ultimately will bring all to the fullness of love and life in God's realm. We are to live trusting in that promise. In Martin Luther's imagery, if the world is to end tomorrow, one ought to plant an apple tree. The resurrection promise, then, is one profound source of hope and moral power.

The Cross

The cross offers a second source of life-sustaining hope for those of us who have glimpsed even momentarily the horror of being wealthy Christians in a world of hunger or the horror of what we are doing to Earth and what it will mean for our children.[13] We may run from this knowledge because it implies too much brokenness and evil present in our lives.

Jesus' execution by imperial power, however, demonstrates that even in the furthest reaches of human brokenness and in bondage to structural sin, the saving Christ is present, is healing, and is liberating. This truth enables seeing the structural brutality of which we are a part without being destroyed by that knowledge. Canadian theologian Douglas John Hall says it well: "The central message of the cross "is not to reveal that our condition is one of darkness and death; it is to reveal to

---

13. Jesus' execution by Roman officials has been understood differently throughout church history. As I have noted elsewhere, there is good reason to distrust many interpretations of the cross. It is a much abused and controversial symbol of Christian faith. See my essay, "A Theology of the Cross for the Un-Creators." Yet in many contexts, the image of the cross continues to unfold dimensions of God's infinite love and ubiquitous life-saving presence. It holds particular promise for this inquiry into seeing and resisting systemic evil.

us the One who meets us in our darkness and death. It is a theology of the cross not because it wants to put forth this ghastly spectacle as a final statement about life in this world but because it insists that God . . . meets, loves, and redeems us precisely where we are: in the valley of the shadow of death."[14]

God's presence in the depths of our brokenness means that God with grace is present even where I am the perpetrator of violence against others. God is present even if I have no awareness of God's presence and have no faith that God is present. A central message of what became known as Luther's theology of the cross is that where God seems *absent,* there God is. God's saving power is hidden in God's apparent absence.[15] Nothing, "neither death nor life, neither angels nor demons, neither the present nor the future, nor any powers . . . neither height nor depth, nor anything else in all creation will be able to separate us from the love of God in Jesus Christ" (Rom 8:38–39). This means that God's liberating love, working through this world, can move us from *perpetrating* ecological and economic violence to *dismantling* it, even if that seems impossible. Salvation is "both from the *affliction* of evil and from the *infliction* of evil."[16]

This saving claim makes possible seeing reality, rather than pretending that the economic systems that create our wealth are beneficial to all. Lutheran theologian Winston Persuad says it well: When reality seems "distorted and sinful, and seemingly God-forsaken . . . a theologian of the cross is not afraid to recognize reality for what it is."[17] In Luther's words, "A theologian of glory calls evil good and good evil. A theologian of the cross calls the thing what it actually is."[18] This too is a profound source of hope.

God Indwelling Creation

Consider a third wellspring of hope within Lutheran traditions. Let us call it the indwelling God. Multiple streams of Christianity, from its earliest centuries, have affirmed the *mysterium tremendum* (awesome mystery)

14. Hall, *Lighten Our Darkness*, 149.

15. The saving power of God is hidden in the form of its opposite (*sub contrario suo abscondita sunt*). See also the essay by Wanda Deifelt in this volume.

16. Morse, *Not Every Spirit*, 225.

17. Persaud, "Luther's Theologia Crucis," 265–66.

18. Luther, "Heidelberg Disputation," *LW* 31:39–58.

that God, the Source of life itself, the One who is saving and has saved, abides within human beings and within the entirety of creation.

This claim is particularly striking when uttered by theologians not commonly recognized for it. Luther is one. He insists in various sermons and treatises that God inhabits the things of Earth. Hear Luther: ". . . the power of God . . . must be essentially present in all places even in the tiniest leaf."[19] God "is in and through all creatures, in all their parts and places, so that the world is full of God and He [sic] fills all . . ."[20] "Christ . . . fills all things . . . Christ is around us and in us in all places . . . he is present in all creatures, and I might find him in stone, in fire, in water . . ."[21] In these claims Luther is by no means alone. The assertion of God indwelling all of creation has been present in Christian theology since its beginning.

Fascinating to me and relevant here are the implications for moral-spiritual power. According to Luther: "The Word of God, whenever it comes, comes to change and renew the world."[22] If God is present within the trees, waters, winds, and creatures—human creatures included—then God is at play within us and our earthy kin to change and renew the world. We are called to hear the healing, liberating, and transforming Word of God in the creatures and elements of Earth. Stop for a moment to take this in. Close your eyes simply to contemplate what it might mean to take seriously the Christian claim that God lives within the creatures and elements of this good Earth. What better place than Lutheran churches, seminaries, colleges, and universities to explore prayerfully, gratefully, humbly, and jubilantly this very Lutheran faith claim. How will we prepare leaders of the church to learn from the trees and gardens? How will we—who may never have sought Christ's saving presence in the growing things around us—cultivate that capacity in Christ's church?

For now let us say this: If Christ indwells the Earth, then our hope and power for the work of love will also be fed by God within the created world.

19. Luther, "That These Words of Christ, 'This is My Body,'" *LW* 37:57.
20. Ibid., 59.
21. Luther, "The Sacrament of the Body and Blood of Christ," 321.
22. Luther, "The Bondage of the Will," *LW* 33:52.

Paradoxical Moral Anthropology

Who we think we are matters. Who are we? The Bible teaches that we humans are—in the words of second century theologian Irenaeus of Lyons—"mud creatures," crafted from soil (*adam* from *adamah*). Incidentally, in the biblical texts, it is the same soil from which other animals are made.[23] We are children of stardust and the elements that spewed forth some fifteen billion years past in the birth of the cosmos. This is crucial; we will live as integral *parts of* Earth's great economy—rather than *apart from* it—or we will not live at all into the future. Moreover we are an integral and utterly dependent species in Earth's tapestry of life.

But who are we as *moral* beings? Christian theology throughout the ages teaches that we are paradoxically two opposing things at one time. We are sinners, in bondage to the human condition of sin, including structural sin. And simultaneously, we are the body of Christ on Earth, abode of the God whose passionate life-giving love is more powerful than any other force in Heaven or Earth; we are lovers of all that God has made. While we are implicated in cruel forms of oppression and exploitation, we also are an abode of the living Christ. The Spirit of God abides within and among us. We are empowered by the Spirit to receive God's love, trust it, and then to embody that justice-making mysterious and marvellous love into the world. We are here to let God work through us, in us, and among us to bring healing from all forms of sin that would thwart God's gift of abundant life for all. This is an ancient faith claim—that God's love in Christ lives in and among us as justice making, self-respecting, Earth-honoring love. Now hear this clearly: biblical faith insists that this face of our being is more truly who we are and ultimately will prevail over our bondage to sin.

This love is the counterpoint of structural evil. Although embedded in systemic evil, we humans are nevertheless charged with seeking the widespread good, abundant life for all, through ways of justice-making love. For fulfilling this calling, the Spirit brings divine and indomitable love to abide in us. This is a Word of hope for us given the irrefutable perils of climate change and our responsibility for it.

For us who are paradoxically both structural sinners and bearers of divine justice-making love, the way forward within this duo moral anthropology, I think, is this:

---

23. 'Adam and 'adamah are the Hebrew words in Genesis's second creation story meaning respectively "human being" and "soil."

1. Recall that we are first and foremost mud creatures—humans made from humus, an utterly dependent part of the great web of life.

2. Strive to see ever more clearly our entanglement in collective or structural sin so that we may repent of it and resist it.

3. Embody the promise that we are also bearers of a life force that is greater than all forces of death and destruction.

4. With all of our resources—spiritual and material, scientific and artistic—feed and water that side of our being while we repent of the other.

For this feeding and watering, I offer an image again from Irenaeus of Lyons (who was, incidentally, a leader of a community martyred by Rome for their allegiance to God over allegiance to Caesar). According to Irenaeus, our task as mud creatures is to remain moist with the dew of the Holy Spirit dispersed through all the Earth so that the two hands of God—Word and Wisdom, or Christ and Spirit—can mold us and through us all of creation into its destiny of union and communion with God.

In our congregations and communities, we will ask: What practices of liturgy, prayer, home-making, eating, transportation, organizing, advocacy, demonstrating, and more will keep us moist and feed our being as God's beloved who love with God's love? We will not remain moist alone or just as households, but rather as communities. I no longer think about what I can do, but rather about what I—as a part of a greater "we"—can do.

Christian traditions offer countless wellsprings of hope. We have noted four:

1. Life in God is more powerful than all forms of death and destruction.

2. God is present and healing even in the depths of our brokenness as complicity in ecological devastation and economic exploitation.

3. The life-saving and life-savoring power and presence of God is coursing through all of creation.

4. While we are indeed complicit in structural sin, we also are the abode of God's justice-making, Earth-honoring love.

In short, moral-spiritual power lies in a trust that the sacred forces of life, known in Jewish, Christian, and Muslim traditions as God, flows within this good creation, is bringing about healing and liberation despite all evidence to the contrary, and is forgiving all forms of human brokenness.

PRACTICAL IMPLICATIONS

What then are we to do? If we seek to repent of the structural sin in which we are embroiled, if we long to align our lives with the Spirit of God flowing and pouring through all things working and willing that all might have life and have it abundantly, what then are we to do?

The path from heartfelt longing for more just and Earth-honoring lives to change at the societal level seems to travel through a thick and swirling fog. The complexity and vastness of the possibilities are confounding. Needed is a framework for unraveling what that conversion entails. In my recent book I have proposed such a framework.[24] It is a framework for expressing neighbor-love as an ecological-economic vocation, not only an interpersonal vocation. And it translates neighbor-love into secular terms for public life.

Here I point to three elements of that framework. One key element is to recognize that we are not primarily "I's." I am part of a "we." Whatever I do is one part of an infinitely vaster movement—a cloud of witnesses spanning ages and continents, seeking more just and sustainable ways of living on Earth.

A second key element is to recognize the different arenas of social life in which change happens and to realize that when you work for change in one of these, you actually are opening doors to change in the others. They are:

1. Household or individual
2. Institutions of civil society such as congregations, churches, seminaries, universities, etc.
3. Business ranging from global corporations to small businesses
4. Public policy or government at all levels
5. Worldview or consciousness

Often my students will say that lifestyle change does not matter; my gardening or riding bikes instead of cars will not change the world. What

24. Moe-Lobeda, *Resisting Structural Evil,* chap. 9.

we need is change in public policy and other social structures. Other students argue the opposite; social structures will not change until people change how they live.

I love to help them realize that both dimensions work together, feeding each other, needing each other. Always see your efforts in one of the arenas as also impacting the other arenas. For example in Seattle, countless people's decision to bike or bus has had profound impact on city policy, which in turn makes it much safer for people to bike. And these changes in lifestyle and public policy make it more possible for institutions—such as universities—to consider divestment from companies that extract, refine, or distribute fossil fuel.

A third element in this framework for living love as ecological-economic vocation and resisting structural sin is recognizing the various forms of actions that need and nourish each other. I like to think of them as fingers on the hands of radical change. They include:

- Lifestyle changes
- Economic advocacy—boycotts, buying fair trade, socially responsible investing, etc.
- Legislative advocacy and electoral advocacy
- Community organizing campaigns
- Education and consciousness-raising
- Public witness—demonstrations, civil disobedience (some refer to this as "evangelical defiance")
- Charitable giving and service
- Economic alternatives such as small-scale local business and agriculture
- Worship, Bible study, and prayer

Let us dwell a moment on one of those "forms of action": worship. The church claims that Christian worship forms and empowers believers to heed God's call. Worship does this by enacting a vision of the world and an epic story in which we are players.

If indeed the moral life of worshipers is formed by liturgical enactment of a "vision of the world," then the "vision of the world" enacted *matters,* and it matters much. Perhaps worship will better form the people for love as an economic-ecological calling if worship enacts an alternative "vision of the world" in which humans are creatures with all the other creatures, dependent—for example—upon millions of microbes inhabiting our bodies enabling us to sing and to taste and digest the bread and wine. Or what if the alternative vision of the world embodied in worship portrayed water, trees, and bodies—rather than buildings—as sacred abodes of God?

If the moral life of worshipers is formed also by an epic story told through the process of worship, then what epic story is "told" matters. What if the story we told in the sermon, songs, sacraments, and sacred art highlighted the Christian heritage of resistance to structural sin? What if the practice of worship taught our children that they stand in a long line of courageous resisters who stood up against structural evil even at cost of life? There are many examples:

- Daring Hebrew midwives who rescued Moses from the Pharaoh's deadly hand.

- Jesus and the early martyrs who refused to comply with the imperial demands.

- Abolitionists who opposed slavery.

- "Righteous gentiles" who defied Hitler's death machine.

- Huguenots in the village of Le Chambon whose quiet resistance saved four thousand Jews even while they were occupied by fascist forces.

What if our children frequently heard sermons such as that preached by one of my pastors: "I could empathize with Paul in prison," she declared, "because last time I was in prison, I too was in solitary confinement." She had been jailed many times for protesting the Trident nuclear submarines stationed near Seattle. What if our congregations were morally formed to see themselves as walking in the footsteps of fiercely loving resisters? What if the story told, including us as characters, truly honored our rich heritage of resistance to dominant powers where they demanded people to transgress God's commandment to love God and to love neighbor as self? Telling this story would not be too strange, for that heritage is at the heart of Christian scriptures. Were this story told in worship, might we be more fertile ground for love that renounces structural sin? Would we not offer and embody hope for a planet in peril?

CLOSING

Humankind hovers on a climate change precipice. One side of the precipice does not look good. The other side however is the potential before us: the vision that we all hold—in varied forms—of a world in which all people have the necessities for life with dignity and Earth's eco-systems flourish. A great choice, a "great calling," is before us. It requires radical change on all levels of being. No humans before us have had to face and renounce the systemic sin of "uncreating" and the horrible damage it does to vulnerable sisters and brothers the world over whom we are called to love. However, the One who calls us also works within us enabling us to move from death to life, from inflicting ecological devastation to ecological healing.

Where something new is required of humankind, something new is required of religion. The task of religion in the early twenty-first century (the end of the petroleum era) is to plumb the depths of our religious traditions for the moral-spiritual wisdom to answer our calling, and bring this wisdom to the table of public discourse. The church is called to offer the resources of Christian traditions. If we let them go untapped, then the world is deprived of what the church has been entrusted to bring to the world.

Christian teachings at their best are in the service of hope and life. That word of hope comes in many forms. As professed by Hadewijch of Brabant, a fourteenth century poet and mystic, God's love "will never cease in all the endless age to come."[25] The God who called this world into being loves it with a love beyond human imagining that will never die. It is our blessed call to live that love into the world as individuals and as parts of social systems. As our Lutheran heritage insists, that love cannot be taken from us by any force in heaven or on Earth.

BIBLIOGRAPHY

Hadewijch of Brabant. *Hadewijch: The Complete Works*. Edited and translated by Mother Columba Hart. Classics of Western Spirituality. Mahwah, NJ: Paulist, 1981.

Hall, Douglas John. *Lighten Our Darkness: Toward an Indigenous Theology of the Cross*. Philadelphia: Westminster, 1976.

25. Hadewijch of Brabant, *Hadewijch*, 60.

Johnstone, Craig. "The Climate Change Future is Now." Address at the Institute of Public Policy Research Conference, Climate Change and Forced Migration, April 29, 2008. http://www.unhcr.org.

King, Martin Luther, Jr. "Strength to Love." In *A Testament of Hope: The Essential Writings and Speeches of M. L. King, Jr.*, edited by James M. Washington, 491–516. San Francisco: Harper & Row, 1986.

Luther, Martin. "The Bondage of the Will." In *Career of the Reformer III*, edited by Philip S. Watson and Helmut T. Lehmann. *LW* 33:15–295. Minneapolis: Fortress, 1972.

———. "Heidelberg Disputation." In *Career of the Reformer I*, edited by Harold J. Grimm and Helmut T. Lehmann. *LW* 31:39–58. Philadelphia: Fortress, 1957.

———. "The Sacrament of Body and Blood of Christ—Against the Fanatics." In *Martin Luther's Basic Theological Writings*, edited by Timothy F. Lull, 314–40. Minneapolis: Fortress, 1989.

———. "That These Words of Christ, 'This is My Body,' etc., Still Stand Firm against the Fanatics." In *Word and Sacrament III*, edited by Robert H. Fischer. *LW* 37:3–150. Philadelphia: Muhlenberg, 1961.

Maguire, Daniel. *The Moral Core of Judaism and Christianity: Reclaiming the Revolution.* Minneapolis: Fortress, 1993.

Moe-Lobeda, Cynthia. *Resisting Structural Evil: Love as Ecological-Economic Vocation.* Minneapolis: Fortress, 2013.

———. "A Theology of the Cross for the Un-Creators." In *Cross-Examination: Interrogating the Cross for its Meaning Today*, edited by Marit Trelstadt, 181–95. Minneapolis: Fortress, 2006.

Morse, Christopher. *Not Every Spirit: A Dogmatics of Christian Disbelief.* Valley Forge, PA: Trinity, 1994.

Parry, Martin. "IIED Interviews: Martin Parry on Climate Change." International Institute for Environment and Development. http://www.iied.org.

Parry, Martin et al. *Contributions of Working Group II.* New York: Cambridge University Press, 2007. https://www.ipcc.ch.

Persaud, Winston. "Luther's Theologia Crucis: A Theology of 'Radical Reversal': In Response to the Challenge of Marx's Weltanschauung." *Dialog* 29 (Fall 1990) 265–66.

Rasmussen, Larry. "Luther and a Gospel of Earth." *Union Seminary Quarterly Review* 51 (1997) 1–28.

Tupouniua, Mahe 'Uli'uli Sandhurst. "Statement of H. E. Mr. Mahe, U.S. Tupouniua, Permanent Representative of the Permanent Mission of the Kingdom of Tonga, Chair of the Pacific Small Island Developing States for the Intergovernmental Negotiations on the Post-2015 Development Agenda, Follow-up and Review." New York: United Nations, 2015. http://www.un.org.

United Church of Christ Commission for Racial Justice. *Toxic Wastes and Race in the United States: A National Report on the Racial and Socio-Economic Characteristics of Communities with Hazardous Waste Sites.* New York: United Christ of Christ, 1987.

United Nations Conference on Sustainable Development. "The Future We Want." Resolution adopted by the United Nations General Assembly, July 27, 2012. http://www.un.org.

4

Out of Brokenness, a New Creation

Theology of the Cross and the Tree of Life

—WANDA DEIFELT

CARE FOR CREATION IS a central theme in theological discourse and practice, even if Christians do not always agree on what this teaching should entail.[1] Some Christians interpret environmental degradation, climate change, and planetary doom as signs of the end time—not only to be disregarded but actually welcomed (even hastened) as a sign of the coming apocalypse.[2] Others, however, stemming primarily from mainline Protestant, Orthodox, and Roman Catholic churches, want to work together to resist social and ecological destruction in order to create viable alternatives to corporate globalization.[3] To understand the tension between these two approaches, it is necessary to recognize the connections between theology and justice, peace, and ecological sustainability.

The World Council of Churches (WCC) has been instrumental in articulating a vision of a common household, an *oikoumene*, celebrating the diverse unity of the whole inhabited planet. Already in the 1970s the

1. An earlier and abridged version of this chapter appears as "From Cross to Tree of Life" in Bohmbach and Hannan, *Eco-Lutheranism*, 169–77. It is reprinted here with permission.

2. Mooney, "New Study Reaffirms the Link between Conservative Religious Faith and Climate Change Doubt."

3. Forum on Religion and Ecology at Yale, "World Council of Churches (WCC) Justice, Peace, and Creation (JPC)."

WCC began to recognize the need for broad paradigms to address environmental degradation and socio-economic disparities. In 1983, at its sixth assembly in Vancouver, the WCC encouraged member churches to address environmental concerns as part of a common effort to promote Justice, Peace, and the Integrity of Creation (known as the JPIC process). Originally intended as a program priority, it was subsequently expanded to include churches that are not members of the WCC, regional and national ecumenical organizations, and other movements committed to these issues.

Vancouver intended these elements (justice, peace, and the integrity of creation) to be viewed as three aspects of one reality: as a single vision towards which we work and as three entry points into a common struggle in these areas. The addition of the term "integrity of creation" to help clarify "the biblical vision of peace with justice" was particularly useful. Besides alluding to the damage being done to the environment and the threat posed to the survival of life, the term also gave a new prominence to the doctrine of creation and the opportunity to re-affirm our Trinitarian faith, beginning with God as Creator and therefore also Liberator and Sustainer.[4]

From a Lutheran perspective, there are a number of potential theological approaches that can further the ongoing dialogue on the wellbeing of creation. Luther's theology offers sound principles for how a Christian ought to live in this world and give witness of the Word of God. In doing so, Christians live in the promise of God's love, who gives us concrete ways to ensure not only human wellbeing, but that of the entire creation. God promises "to govern with justice for the political sphere, *politia*, to care about the needs of God's creatures for the sphere of economics, *oeconomia*, and to communicate God's Word to our hearts and minds in the sphere of communal life, *ecclesia*."[5] These promises point to ways we too can be better citizens of the entirety of creation.

4. Niles, "Justice, Peace, and the Integrity of Creation."
5. Ulrich, "On the Grammar of Lutheran Ethics," 29.

THE ENVIRONMENTAL QUESTION
IS A THEOLOGICAL QUESTION

Ivone Gebara, along with many other ecofeminists, asserts that eco-justice is closely related to our perceptions of the divine.[6] She points out that the consequences of our theological views are not restricted to metaphysical queries or eschatological assumptions. Rather, our theology profoundly affects how humans act, interact, and see purpose in life. The question of God is ultimately the question of the perception of humanity and the consequences of its behavior and life direction. This has profound implications if we want to pursue justice for the whole creation, including—but not limited—to vulnerable humans. Ivone Gebara draws a connection between Western thought, Christianity, and environmental destruction. She argues that Earth-healing requires that humans become converted to a new relationship with the cosmos by recognizing God's sacred and immanent presence among creation.

The same idea has long been articulated by Rosemary Radford Ruether. The destructive relation between ruling and subjugated human groups is profoundly related to the destruction of the entire biotic community.[7] The dominating and destructive relations to the planet are inter-related with gender, class, and racial domination, as well as colonialism and imperialism. The healing of creation cannot be realized simply through technological solutions but demands a social critique and reordering to bring about just and loving relations. It also requires a reorientation of humanity itself—not apart from nature but as an interdependent part of it. Humans cannot speak of eco-justice without addressing the disparities of access to basic resources between women and men, races and nations. The creation of systems of subjugation and stratification not only prevents flourishing but has proven to be deadly.

Thus, we are called to conversion: our attitudes and behaviors must change radically on both personal and socio-political levels. As in the time of the Reformation, a *metanoia*—a deep change of mind, heart, and attitudes—is needed. As human beings, we must hear what we need, and not necessarily what we want. This was a key realization for Martin Luther as he described the life of the Christian as a theologian of the cross, as opposed to a theologian of glory. As Douglas Hall points out, what Luther intended with his critique of *theologia gloriae* (theology of glory)

6. Gebara, *Longing for Running Water*.
7. Ruether, *Gaia & God*.

is triumphalism, a fundamentally human phenomenon of excessive ex-ultation over one's privilege, success, or achievements.[8] A theology of glory leaves little or no room for debate, doubt, difference of opinion, and openness to dialogue—let alone repentance or change.

CREATION AS THE "OTHER"—
THE NEIGHBOR IN NEED

Nature is often understood as separate from the human sphere, yet, due to a dualistic framework, certain social groups have been deemed as clos-er to nature—and therefore deemed as inferior or expendable. Women, for instance, have been identified with nature through their reproduc-tive function. Proximity to nature was not seen as an advantage. To the contrary, in the list of dualities, female is to nature as male is to culture. The same ideology applied to other groups, such as Indigenous popula-tions and African nations. In the expansion of European colonial powers, all those outside the realm of the European "civilization" were subject to exploitation. As pointed out by James Axtell: "To Europeans, 'others' might appear in an infinite variety of shapes, hues, and habits, but they were always and distinctively unlike Europeans, and for the most part, therefore, regarded as inferior."[9]

In the colonial enterprise, the creation of "others" is another ex-ample of how the command for dominion in Genesis 1 could be mis-construed. This dominion was amplified to include male-European rule over the entire world, including another's land, resources, and people. In post-colonialism, the rhetoric might have changed. Nevertheless, in the name of economic advantage, development, or civilization, the cre-ation of "others" continued. Difference in ethnic or religious beliefs was a ground for othering, i.e., what is different is either inferior or should be feared. In Christianity, this is implied in preaching domination over the Earth along with loathing the body and contempt for the material world. Creation itself becomes the other. Only a redefinition of the role of humanity vis-à-vis creation, in its construction of otherness, will make explicit what being its curators or caretakers might entail.

Two theorists, Emmanuel Levinas and Enrique Dussel, have ad-dressed "otherness" (alterity) in ethics. Levinas engages in a creative

---

8. Hall, *The Cross in Our Context*, 17.

9. Axtell, *Beyond 1492*, 31–32.

interpretation of Judaism (particularly the asymmetrical relation between God and humans) and applies this principle also to the relationship between human beings.[10] The other is absolutely other, not the same, not the self. The other is an infinitely transcendent reality that cannot be fully grasped by knowledge. For Levinas, dialogue begins with the ethical interruption of the other: there is no self outside the response to otherness, to the claims posed by the other. The encounter with the other, the "face of the other," the other who is "infinitely foreign," needs to be acknowledged before using reason or forming judgments. To recognize difference and to validate the experiences of others are key elements in the ethics developed by Levinas.

Enrique Dussel takes a similar approach but articulates his thought from a Christian perspective. The other, in Dussel's liberationist ethics, is embodied by the concrete disenfranchised of society: women, poor, indigenous people, former slaves, etc. He proposes mutuality as a form to encounter the divine and to experience "the reign of God as the absolute face-to-face," through symmetric participation and transformative praxis.[11] For Dussel, there is no ethics unless the cultural, social, and economic "others" are taken into consideration. Ethics is the concern for and concrete actions carried out to ensure the dignity and freedom of all the members of the community, particularly those who are not representative of normative discourse or beneficiaries of structures of political and economic power.

In light of the current environmental crisis and the urgency of addressing climate change, the ethical categorizations that Levinas and Dussel articulate gain a new impetus and pose fresh questions for the role of humanity vis-à-vis the "non-human" natural world. While there is a clear connection between humanity and the totality of creation (after all, we are all creatures) we need to further reflect on the theological parameters and ethical discernment that this position entails. What would a care for creation based on the values of "otherness," as established by Levinas and Dussel, look like? Can humanity and creation sustain a distinction between "self" and "other" in a manner that realizes agency as well as relationality? How can Martin Luther's theology help in the conversation?

Luther's ethics could be summarized with his statement that Christians live not in themselves but in Christ and in their neighbor. They live

---

10. Levinas, *Totality and Infinity*.

11. Dussel, *Ethics and Community*.

in Christ through faith and in their neighbor through love.[12] This is where Luther's theology of the cross leads to concrete acts for the benefit of the disempowered and disenfranchised. "While *theologia gloriae* [theology of glory] keeps people in a state of contemplation, *theologia crucis* [theology of the cross] thrusts them into the decision of faith."[13] Martin Luther's theological insights—ranging from the centrality of justification by faith through grace, the use of the Scriptures, his two kingdom theory, the notion of vocation and the priesthood of all baptized believers, among other key themes—are developed to answer the question of the human condition in our relationship to God and to one another.

Creation is an intrinsic part of this and some of the most important theological thinking today is working to redefine and clarify how human beings perceive themselves, their relationship to God as creator, and the entire created world. It is appropriate, therefore, to talk about creation as the neighbor. It is an opening to the other. This way of looking at the world expands us beyond our selfish interests (upheld by greed and consumerism) to become concerned for the wellbeing of the entire creation. Christians live in Christ through faith and in their neighbor through love. By faith Christians are caught up beyond themselves into God. By love they reach out to their neighbor. While Christians are citizens of heaven, they are also citizens on Earth, and in this capacity they advocate for their neighbor and strive to promote the common good. Care for the neighbor includes creation care.

To care for the neighbor is to assure dignity and life in abundance, act for justice and peace, and enable that another may flourish. It is to look out for the other, to welcome diversity, difference, and divergence.[14] For those who have been privileged by the world's colonial history and neo-colonial economy, this care requires abnegation and a commitment to rectify wrongs. The desire for justice needs to be instilled because it is not a given reality. A genuine concern for the neighbor's need—the groaning in pain of the entire creation (Rom 8:22)—requires the willingness to change our own lifestyles and to promote sustainability. It takes vision, political courage, and discernment for societies of all socio-economic levels to meet the needs of the present with equity and justice without compromising the ability of future generations to meet their own needs.

12. Luther, "The Freedom of a Christian," 79.

13. Dreher, "Luther's Theology of the Cross in the Context of Liberation Theology," 105.

14. A more comprehensive reflection is found in Deifelt, "Heterotopic Citizenship."

Lutheran orientation to the needs of the neighbor nourishes this commitment to action, service, and advocacy. This then obliges us to attend to the unequivocal scientific findings on climate change, for instance, and spurs our transformative efforts to embody the gospel in its fullness in this endangered world. The neighbor—creation—is not a mere receiver of one's favor or charity. The neighbor is the other with whom I engage as an equal, the one who brings me closer to Christ, and the one for whom I am Christ.

CREATION AS GOD'S MASK

It is easy to identify the goodness of God in relationship to creation. As proclaimed by Martin Luther, we look at creation and can only fall on our knees in sheer awe and admiration for all God has made and so generously bestowed. There is no other attitude but gratefulness that can meet God's generosity. In creation itself we have a manifestation of divine grace. Some authors emphasize that, for Luther, the physical world is not only a vehicle of spiritual life but is itself permeated by God.[15] Luther writes:

> How angry can God really be if He [*sic*] lets His sun rise for us every day, if He gives us good weather, if He lets all kinds of plants, fruits, and nourishment grow for us, if He favors us with healthy bodies and members? If we could look at these things properly, we would have to say: "He surely has given us great treasures—above all, peace and joy toward Him and, in addition, all kinds of physical benefactions on earth, visible and palpable evidence of His mercy and His willingness to help us." Therefore, we should learn not to be afraid or fainthearted before Him.[16]

It is less simple to talk about a theology of eco-justice that also takes into account the destructive, chaotic, and devastating aspects of creation that come in the form of tsunamis, earthquakes, hurricanes, wildfires,

---

15. See Strier, "Martin Luther and the Real Presence in Nature," 289. "Luther develops his conception of the presence and activity of God in the unique and concrete facticity of each created thing. In these passages in the Eucharistic tracts, Luther presents physical things not only as the essential vehicles of the spiritual life but as themselves permeated by God."

16. Luther, *Sermons on the Gospel of St. John: Chapters 14–16*, LW 24:180.

floods, or droughts.[17] We would be remiss if we were not to reflect theologically also on these aspects of creation. Luther's notion of the hiddenness of God can be helpful in this endeavor. If we speak of creation
as God's mask, creation both reveals God's presence and conceals it. It
contains both the pleasurable and hurtful. While creation allows us to affirm God's generosity and benevolence, it is equally a reminder that God
is more than that. God is also manifested in wrath and fury—in ways that
are not always comprehensible to our reasoning. Because God escapes
our understanding, we are prevented from domesticating God and limiting the divine to the aspects of creation that please and appease us.

Luther develops the notion that God is ever present and ever concealed within the intricate mask of creation. It is when our own masks become distorted by evil that the traps Satan has set for us become our way
of life, as Luther attests in his interpretation of the bondage of the will.
Our actions are not only a matter of personal choices but also of systemic
entrapments.[18] Vitor Westhelle summarizes this with the statement:
"Humans, as God's creatures, are God's masks through which we observe,
experience, and interact with God's masks on creation in general."[19] If
we are God's masks and are part of creation, then creation as a whole
is equally God's mask. This both implicates us and compels to think of
God employing different categories, such as relatedness and interdependence.[20] For Luther, this can be done only through a grateful and prayer-
ful heart, as taught in the fourth petition of The Lord's Prayer—Give us
today our daily bread:

> But especially is this petition directed against our chief enemy,
> the devil, whose whole purpose and desire it is to take away or
> interfere with all we have received from God. He [sic] is not
> satisfied to obstruct and overthrow spiritual order, so that he
> may deceive men [sic] with his lies and bring them under his
> power, but he also prevents and hinders the establishment of
> any kind of government or honorable and peaceful relations on
> earth. This is why he causes so much contention, murder, sedi-
> tion, and war, why he sends tempest and hail to destroy crops
> and cattle, why he poisons the air, etc.[21]

17. On this topic see the essay in this volume by Terence E. Fretheim.
18. Altmann, *Luther and Liberation*.
19. Westhelle, *The Scandalous God*, 97.
20. See Gebara, *Longing for Running Water*, 101–35.
21. Luther, "The Large Catechism," 451.

To think of creation as God's mask allows us to deal with the paradoxical language of Luther's theology: a God who is at the same time revealed and hidden. This notion of a concealed God confronts us with the question whether God is revealed in evil as well as good. In our times, it is easier to talk about glory, forgiveness, and joy. It is more difficult to talk about God's wrath and vengeance—unless it is used towards others (those we consider our enemies). An angry God who passes judgment does not fit our culture or our society. This is also why it is so difficult for us to talk about evil. So, is God revealed in evil? If so, how are human beings supposed to address it?

Westhelle believes that God is concealed in evil and wrath just as God is concealed in the goodness of creation.[22] We cannot just select creation as God's mask because of its beauty, but also because it contains aspects of divine relation that we cannot fully grasp. When confronted with natural disasters, for instance, we might be tempted to embrace two of these stances: either ascribing full responsibility to God (asking, for instance, how God allows bad things to happen) or claim human ownership (stating that we reap the consequences of our own actions). For Luther, the solution is to stress the paradox of the God preached (the Word of God) and the God hidden (God's own self).[23] In the opposite of what is good, in evil, we realize that the visible is not able to fully reveal God. It would be a mistake to name as God what is the mask, confusing the creature for the creator, even if the mask conveys in part what it hides. The existence of evil cannot be used to demonstrate the existence of a God who permits evil to happen. Although we can know God from what is visible and revealed (in what is good and bad), there is an inscrutable part to God as well. Thus, with creation as God's mask, God is not to be seen behind the mask (for this belongs to the hiddenness of God) but in and through it, for creation also reveals the absence of God, the concealment, and our own blindness to God's revelation. The question, therefore, is not only where God is in the midst of pain and suffering, but also where we, as creatures and God's masks, place ourselves.

22. Westhelle, *The Scandalous God*, 98.

23. Luther, "The Bondage of the Will," 191. "God does many things which He [*sic*] does not show us in His Word, and He wills many things which He does not in His Word show us that He wills. Thus, He does not will the death of a sinner—that is, in His Word; but He wills it by His inscrutable will. At present, however, we must keep in view His Word and leave alone His inscrutable will; for it is by His Word, and not by His inscrutable will, that we must be guided."

A THEOLOGY OF THE CROSS

Because the environmental question is a theological question, it cannot rely solely on ethical imperatives—extending the values instilled by Jesus' teachings about the Reign of God—in order to give witness to the Good News of life in abundance to all. It also requires a theological reassessment, placing emphasis on what faith the church professes and how it empowers Christians for their role in the world. This calls for a deeper and urgent conversation about faith.

The hidden God, *Deus Absconditus*, is revealed in the cross, in the suffering of Christ. For Luther, the Word of God does not bring us to philosophical principles, speculations, or assertions. Rather, the Word brings us back to the core of the Christian message: the cross. Revelation is seen in the suffering of Christ rather than in striving for moral perfection or good works. In his *Heidelberg Disputation*, Luther talked about the "theologian of the cross" in contrast with a "theologian of glory." Whereas a theologian of glory "calls the bad good and the good bad," the theologian of the cross "says what a thing is."[24] Luther himself seldom talked about a theology of the cross *per se*. More than a theological subject, the cross is a way of doing theology that requires continuous transformation. The cross is a "crossing over" that brings us closer to love and truth not because of our merits, but because of God's mercy and grace. In other words, Christians do not carry out good works for the purpose of salvation but for the wellbeing of the neighbor in need. Today, the neighbor in need is creation itself.

Luther's understanding of the centrality of the cross comes hand-in-hand with the understanding of God. In the *Heidelberg Disputation* he clarified that only faith can understand and appreciate that God's revelation comes in unexpected ways, defying logic and reason (paraphrasing Paul in 1 Cor 1:23). The truth of the Gospel is different from philosophical truth. God's revelation is indirect and concealed, as explained in the notion of the hidden God. In Theses 19 and 20 Luther states:

19 The one who beholds what is invisible of God, through the perception of what is made [cf. Rom 1:20], is not rightly called a theologian.

20 But rather the one who perceives what is visible of God, God's "backside" [Exod 33:23], by beholding the sufferings and the cross.[25]

24. Luther, "Theses for the Heidelberg Disputation," 503.
25. Ibid., 502.

Because of humanity's fallen condition, one can neither understand the redemptive Word nor can one see God face to face. Here Luther's allusion to Exodus 33, where Moses seeks to see the glory of God but instead sees only the backside, refers not only to the indirect exposure to God but also to God's presence *sub contrario* (under God's opposite). No one can see God face to face and live, so God reveals Godself on the backside, that is to say, where it seems that God should not be: in the indecent exposure, the scandal of the cross, in the "rearward parts" of God (*posteriori Dei*). God is concealed in the vilified and broken body, in the human nature of Christ, in weakness and suffering. All of this presents a stumbling block to belief and appears as foolishness to human logic.

Larry Rasmussen interprets God's weakness and wretchedness in connection to the wellbeing of creation, particularly Jesus entering into the predicament of others who are suffering. He draws from Luther's affirmation that only the cross is our theology (*crux sola nostra theologia est*) to establish a connection between the cross and the suffering of the entire creation. He, too, draws on the notion of creation as God's mask and goes further to draw from it the ethical implications that responsible stewardship entails, concluding that human actions are God's mask as well:

> There is a major moral and a major theological assumption here, but they merge so as to be indistinguishable in practice. The moral assumption is that the farther one is removed from the suffering present in creation, the farther one is from the central moral reality of the situation; and the closer one is to the suffering, the more difficult it is to refuse participation in that life, human or extrahuman. Compassion (suffering with) is the passion of life itself, even as joy is. Both are a corollary of the fact that the only way we can be human is to be human together.[26]

Luther stresses that what is revealed is the crucified God. In other words, the God who is revealed in Jesus Christ is revealed in hiddenness. The theologian of the cross names this reality of brokenness. For Rasmussen, Luther's thesis has concrete consequences in naming as "theology of glory" what has commonly been idealized and called "good" (as in, "the good life") while imposing suffering and abusing power, leading to the exhaustion of the environment and the degradation of the planet.[27] Co-

26. Rasmussen, "Returning to Our Senses," 49.

27. Ibid., 52–53.

lonial enterprise, imperial expansion, and unlimited economic growth are intertwined in this reflection about the common good. If Luther was correct in identifying not only creation but also human actions as God's masks, then a theology of the cross also has ethical implications for the entire wellbeing of creation. The neighbor for whom good is done is creation itself.

The suffering of creation, which moans in pain, is described by Paul in Romans 8:22: "the whole creation has been groaning in travail together until now." The suffering of creation, of the world, is formally identical with the suffering of Christ at the cross, and it too finds redemption in it. In creation, then, we find both a manifestation of divine presence, as God's mask, but also an opportunity for engagement, as human beings (ourselves part of this creation) become God's mask and stand with the suffering world. God's creative power is paradoxically present—revealed and hidden—in the suffering of creation and the solidarity (compassion) of the creatures. God's continuous work of creation is manifested also at the cross: "through the theology of the cross the suffering in and of the world is recognized as the locus of God's creative work."[28] Our image and likeness in God empowers us not to move away from creation, but rather to become the active citizens that we are gifted to be.

FROM CROSS TO TREE OF LIFE

To say that creation is God's mask, and that creation is in pain (Romans 8), is to say also that God is in pain. The centrality of the cross and the awareness of divine suffering, however, are not an affirmation of divine displeasure with creation. Neither is it an idealization of pain or violence. To the contrary: it is a categorical "no" to meaningless death and imposed suffering. The pain of creation invites solidarity. Similar to the experience of the cross, where death is overcome through resurrection, there is anticipation that creation too is renewed and that it finds its rebirth in divine resurrection. The pain of creation is embraced by God and is in God. And so is the promise of resurrection.

The solidarity of those moved by this pain and committed to the wellbeing of the entire creation finds in the tree of life, as described in Revelation 22:2, a powerful symbol.[29] It is the tree in the garden whose

28. Westhelle, *The Scandalous God*, 104.
29. On this point see the essay in this volume by Barbara R. Rossing.

leaves are for the healing of the world. The hopeful solidarity of Jesus' friends at the foot of the cross empowers and gives transformative hope. The tree carries within it the seed of resurrection and insurrection, of transformation and renewal. That which is a symbol of suffering and violence, a scandal, carries within it the seed of transformation that announces hope and new life. The cross becomes the tree of life![30]

Ecofeminist theologians—particularly Rosemary Radford Ruether, Sallie McFague, and Ivone Gebara—point out that Christian theology's emphasis on a new creation typically comes with some sort of condemnation of the current world. This is done more often not to transform the current order and restore creation, but to completely abandon it and overemphasize the otherwordly. But the emphasis on a new creation has implications for the here and now. In metaphorically describing the universe as the body of God, for instance, McFague aims to express both divine transcendence and immanence, radicalizing both the mystery and the nearness, inviting us to see the creator in the creation.[31] Creation, then, enables us to identify not only the suffering of the world but also the signs of resurrection that the tree of life symbolizes.

It might seem surprising that the tree of life can spring forth from the cross, especially in light of the abuses the cross itself has endured. In many parts of the world, the cross has led to the idealization of suffering—not in the sense that Christians will eagerly undergo pain, but that Christians do not question the violence that leads to suffering. Eschatological explanations are used to make sense of suffering, offering a heavenly compensation for the pain endured in the present. This idealization of the cross does not question the reality that leads to the cross because it so quickly and easily remits to its salvific dimension. In pointing out this problem, I do not mean to imply that the cross is not salvific. I am pointing out a concern, however, that we too easily move from the suffering in this world—including the suffering of creation—into an eschatological dimension that diminishes the actual suffering and the causes that lead to it, and that our fixation with the reality after this world supersedes and surpasses our involvement in the present reality.

As the theology of the cross is a disruption of human expectations and projections, the tree of life is a disruption of passivity toward suffering and an annunciation of healing. As Paul says, the cross is foolishness

---

30. Deifelt, "Da Cruz à Árvore da Vida," 13–30.

31. McFague, *The Body of God*, 133.

because it presents us with God's vulnerability and pain. But through the cross there is also reconciliation, transformation, and hope. The repentance and renewal that the cross engenders finds in the tree of life, whose leaves are for the healing of the world, a way to announce the wellbeing of the entire creation. As the wounds of God on the cross offer healing, and the wounds of the world invite our solidarity and advocacy, so God's promise to ensure the wellbeing of the entire creation finds in the tree of life the affirmation of resurrection.

When Luther affirms, "Christ's body is everywhere because the right hand of God is everywhere,"[32] he confesses that everything is full of Christ through and through. So, also, is the redemptive Word that is spoken in Christ: "Christ is around us and in us in all places . . . Although he is present in all creatures, and I might find him in stone, in fire, in water, or even in a rope, for he certainly is there, yet he does not wish that I seek him there apart from the Word . . ."[33]

That which is redemptive, transformative, and salvific in the cross finds its fulfillment in the tree of life. It announces the resurrection that could only happen because of and through the cross. It propagates life in abundance, for the tree exists for the healing of the world. This life in abundance is not only for human beings, but for the entirety of creation. God's being and action is revealed with the cross, and in it is a proclamation of grace, a transformative power that can be expressed through the vitality of the tree that offers healing. God's saving action involves wholeness—restoring all of creation back to its dignity and beauty.

CONCLUSION

Although Martin Luther did not elaborate a theology or ethics of eco-justice, his reflections offer a framework that allow us to do so today. Three theological insights in particular can aid us in spelling out the complexity of the relationship between God and creation: Luther's paradoxical language about God as being both hidden and revealed, a theology of the cross that thrusts us into care for the well-being of the neighbor, and the eschatological hope of moving from the cross to the tree of life. These categories offer a nuanced way to overcome the dichotomy between

32. Luther, "Confession Concerning Christ's Supper," 376.

33. Luther, "The Sacrament of Body and Blood of Christ—Against the Fanatics," 321.

humanity and nature, the notion of creation as separate from the divine, and to insist on the mutual interdependency of humanity and the larger natural world. The environmental question is a theological question. If, for so long, religious discourse justified apathy and even abuse toward creation, it also has the potential to analyze, critique, and envision alternatives that foster justice, peace, and the integrity of creation.

BIBLIOGRAPHY

Altmann, Walter. *Luther and Liberation: A Latin American Perspective.* 2nd ed. Translated by Thia Cooper. Minneapolis: Fortress, 2015.

Axtell, James. *Beyond 1492: Encounters in Colonial North America.* New York: Oxford University Press, 1992.

Deifelt, Wanda. "Da Cruz à Árvore da Vida: Epistemologia, Violência e Sexualidade." In *Epistemologia, Violência e Sexualidade,* edited by Elaine Neuenfeldt et al., 3–30. São Leopoldo: Sinodal, 2008.

———. "From Cross to Tree of Life: Creation as God's Mask." In *Eco-Lutheranism: Lutheran Perspectives on Ecology,* edited by Karla G. Bohmbach and Shauna K. Hannan, 169–77. Minneapolis: Lutheran University Press, 2013.

———. "Heterotopic Citizenship." In *Kirche—befreit zu Widerstand und Transformation/Church—Liberated for Resistance and Transformation,* edited by Karen Bloomquist and Ulrich Duchrow, 161–78. Berlin: Lit Verlag, 2015.

Dreher, Martin. "Luther's Theology of the Cross in the Context of Liberation Theology." In *Kirche—befreit zu Widerstand und Transformation/Church—Liberated for Resistance and Transformation,* edited by Karen Bloomquist and Ulrich Duchrow, 95–111. Berlin: Lit Verlag, 2015.

Dussel, Enrique. *Ethics and Community.* Translated by Robert R. Barr. Theology and Liberation Series. Maryknoll, NY: Orbis, 1988.

Forum on Religion and Ecology at Yale. "World Council of Churches (WCC) Justice, Peace, and Creation (JPC)." http://fore.yale.edu.

Gebara, Ivone. *Longing for Running Water: Ecofeminism and Liberation.* Translated by David Molineaux. Minneapolis: Fortress, 1999.

Hall, Douglas John. *The Cross in Our Context: Jesus and the Suffering World.* Minneapolis: Fortress, 2003.

Levinas, Emmanuel. *Totality and Infinity: An Essay on Exteriority.* Translated by Alphonso Lingis. Pittsburgh: Duquesne University Press, 1969.

Luther, Martin. "The Bondage of the Will." In *Martin Luther: Selections from His Writings,* edited by John Dillenberger, 166–205. New York: Anchor, 1962.

———. "Confession Concerning Christ's Supper." In *Martin Luther's Basic Theological Writings,* edited by Timothy F. Lull, 375–403. Minneapolis: Fortress, 1989.

———. "The Freedom of a Christian." In *Martin Luther: Selections from His Writings,* edited by John Dillenberger, 42–85. New York: Random House, 1962.

———. "The Large Catechism." In *The Book of Concord: The Confessions of the Evangelical Lutheran Church,* edited by Timothy J. Wengert and Robert Kolb, 377–480. Minneapolis: Fortress, 2000.

————. "The Sacrament of the Body and Blood of Christ—Against the Fanatics." In *Martin Luther's Basic Theological Writings,* edited by Timothy F. Lull, 314–40. Minneapolis: Fortress, 1989.

————. *Sermons on the Gospel of St. John. Chapters 14–16,* edited by Jaroslav Pelikan. *LW* 24. Saint Louis: Concordia, 1961.

————. "Theses for the Heidelberg Disputation." In *Martin Luther: Selections from His Writings,* edited by John Dillenberger, 500–503. New York: Anchor, 1962.

McFague, Sallie. *The Body of God: An Ecological Theology.* Minneapolis: Fortress, 1993.

Mooney, Chris. "New Study Reaffirms the Link between Conservative Religious Faith and Climate Change Doubt." *Washington Post,* May 29, 2015. https://www.washingtonpost.com.

Niles, D. Preman. "Justice, Peace, and the Integrity of Creation." *World Council of Churches Ecumenical Dictionary,* November 2003. http://www.wcc-coe.org.

Rasmussen, Larry. "Returning to Our Senses: The Theology of the Cross as a Theology for Eco-Justice." In *After Nature's Revolt: Eco-Justice and Theology,* edited by Dieter T. Hessel, 40–56. Minneapolis: Fortress, 1992.

Ruether, Rosemary Radford. *Gaia & God: An Ecofeminist Theology of Earth Healing.* New York: Harper Collins, 1992.

Strier, Richard. "Martin Luther and the Real Presence in Nature." *Journal of Medieval and Early Modern Studies* 37 (2007) 271–303.

Ulrich, Hans G. "On the Grammar of Lutheran Ethics." In *Lutheran Ethics at the Intersection of God's One World,* edited by Karen L. Bloomquist, 27–48. Geneva: Lutheran World Federation, 2005.

Westhelle, Vítor. *The Scandalous God: The Use and Abuse of the Cross.* Minneapolis: Fortress, 2006.

5

The Two Voices of Nature

Further Encounters with the Integrity of Nature

— H. PAUL SANTMIRE

As kingfishers catch fire, dragonflies draw flame:
As tumbled over rim in roundy wells
Stones ring; like each tucked string tells, each hung bell's
Bow swung finds tongue to fling out broad its name;
Each mortal thing does one thing and the same.
Deals out that being indoors each one dwells;
Selves—and goes itself, *myself* it speaks and spells:
Crying *What I do is me: for that I came* . . .

GERARD MANLEY HOPKINS, "AS KINGFISHERS CATCH FIRE"

THEOLOGIANS, ETHICISTS, SPIRITUAL WRITERS, philosophers, professional ecologists, and many other authors and activists have, in recent decades, taken to railing against anthropocentric readings of nature.[1]

---

1. The term "nature" is notoriously difficult to define. I will take it to mean "the natural world," as used in ordinary speech. I will also presuppose *a theological definition*. For this definition, see my study *The Travail of Nature*, 11–12. There, drawing on the language of Genesis 1, about God creating "the heavens and the earth" (Gen 1:1), I identify "nature" with "the earth" in biblical parlance. Drawing on the language of

71

Frequently, this prophetic denunciation has taken the form of a passionate rejection of a spectrum of inherited approaches to biblical interpretation, especially the idea of human dominion over nature.

Call this the critical ecological wisdom of our era. And claim this
wisdom we must, on theological, ethical, spiritual, and biblical grounds.
Pope Francis has told us precisely that in his celebrated encyclical, *Laudato Si'*: "We [humans] have come to see ourselves as [Earth's] lords and
masters, entitled to plunder her [*sic*] at will."[2] And: "Clearly, the Bible
has no place for a tyrannical anthropocentrism unconcerned for other
creatures."[3]

Yet, as prophecy sometimes tends to be, this kind of critique has
often been clearer about what is to be rejected than about what is to be
affirmed. Anthropocentrism is bad. But what is good? At this point, a
number of prophetic voices sometimes seem to have faltered.

Fortunately, a variety of theologians have taken up the anti-
anthropocentrism cause in a thoughtful manner in recent decades, beginning publicly already in the middle of the last century. One group,
whom I have called theological *reconstructionists*, has tended to assume
that the classical Christian tradition is ecologically bankrupt, precisely
because of its evident anthropocentric tendencies and, more particularly,
due to its deeply seated androcentrism.[4] Ecofeminists such as Rosemary
Ruether and Sallie McFague, for example, have projected non-anthro-
pocentric theologies of Earth or Gaia.[5] In doing so, they have radically
reinterpreted traditional Christian symbols and, more particularly, have
envisioned the world itself, humans and nature together, as the Body of
God. This is a dramatic way to affirm the Divine standing of nature as
well as humanity, thus avoiding anthropocentrism.

---

the Nicene Creed, likewise, I identify "nature" with what that Creed calls "all things
visible." In this sense, I suggest that "nature" is the material-vital dimension of God's
creation. I want to thank Clifford Green, Paul Jersild, and Panu Pihkala for reading
earlier versions of this paper and for offering valuable comments. I particularly want
to thank Dr. Pihkala for drawing my attention to the Hopkins sonnet. I, of course, take
full responsibility for this final version of the paper.

2. Francis, *Laudato Si'*, para. 2.

3. Ibid., para. 68. Pope Francis discusses "The Crisis and Effects of Modern Anthropocentrism" at length in paras. 115–21.

4. For this typology of the reconstructionists and the revisionists—along with
the apologists—see my discussion in *Nature Reborn*, 6–10. I am not dealing with the
apologists here, since their approach has often been, if not always, anthropocentric.

5. Ruether, *Gaia and God*; McFague, *The Body of God*.

A second group of theologians, with whom I myself have identi-fied, I have called the theological *revisionists*.[6] These thinkers have also responded to today's critical ecological wisdom, but in a way that hon-ors classical Christian reflections about God as transcendent as well as immanent, about God as Trinity, about Christ as the center of creation-history, from alpha to omega, and about the special calling of the church to witness to all these things. Perhaps the most significant recent contri-butions by revisionist theologians have been made by Jürgen Moltmann and Elizabeth Johnson.[7] Both have developed theocentric theologies of God and the whole creation in terms of classical theological symbols and have adopted ecological categories as their own, thus rejecting anthro-pocentrism and also, with thinkers like Ruether and McFague, rejecting androcentrism.

A number of Lutheran theologians, particularly in the U.S., laid strong foundations for continuing developments in this revisionist dis-course, roughly from 1962 to 2012.[8] These contributions were wide-ranging: Christology (Joseph Sittler), anthropology (Philip Hefner), eschatology (Ted Peters), ethics (James Childs), biblical studies (Terence Fretheim), liturgical studies (Gordon Lathrop), and historical studies (myself).[9] Early on, I sought to identify the importance of this kind of revisionist thinking, particularly by accenting the integrity of nature, in my programmatic 1970 study, *Brother Earth: Nature, God, and Ecology in a Time of Crisis*.[10]

On the other hand, Lutheran thought and practice has sometimes strongly resisted this kind of discourse, by default, if not self-conscious-ly.[11] The thought of Luther himself, though rich with sensibilities for

6. See n. 4.

7. Moltmann, *God in Creation*; Johnson, *Ask the Beasts*.

8. For an overview of this theological trajectory, see Santmire, "American Lu-therans Engage Ecological Theology." For a much more comprehensive study of such trends, see the detailed analysis of Pihkala, *Joseph Sittler and Early Ecotheology*.

9. Fretheim, *God and World in the Old Testament*; Childs, *Ethics in the Com-munity of Promise*; Hefner, *The Human Factor*; Lathrop, *Holy Ground*; Peters, *God—the World's Future*; Sittler, *Evocations of Grace*.

10. Santmire, *Brother Earth*.

11. Thus in 1984, fourteen years after the first Earth Day, at the time when Jür-gen Moltmann was giving his Gifford Lectures, *God and Creation* (1985), a major, two-volume summary and synthesis of Lutheran teachings, *Christian Dogmatics*, ap-peared, with chapters written by a number of leading U.S. Lutheran theologians at that time. That massive 1190 page work did not have an index entry for "ecology." Not

nature, had a certain anthropocentric character, particularly given his accent on justification of the sinner by faith.[12] Lutheran revisionists have, as a matter of course, celebrated that accent on justification, but they have also given equal voice, in various ways, to Luther's rich theology of creation and of nature, in particular.[13] My purpose in this essay is to continue and, where necessary, to deepen that kind of Lutheran accent on nature. Thankfully, in this respect, all revisionist Lutheran ecotheologians can now work in a new ecumenical partnership with the Church of Rome, in a way that would have probably shocked Luther himself.

In my view, Pope Francis can be considered to be a revisionist eco-theologian, insofar as we have, to this point, been made aware of his still unfolding thought. In *Laudato Si'*, the Holy Father is very much aware, as we have already seen, of the dangers of anthropocentrism. In response, he has developed what he calls an "integral ecology,"[14] based on teachings from the classical Christian tradition. This papal construct, however, is more comprehensive than the concept of *the integrity of nature* that I want to highlight in this essay. Integral ecology addresses social and political issues as well as themes from the theology of nature. Simply expressed, as I am employing the construct theologically, the integrity of nature means that God values nature for itself and blesses nature with its own goodness, in a way that is distinct from God's valuing and blessing of humans.[15]

---

too much should be made of this fact, to be sure. But it was symptomatic of a certain kind of Lutheran mind-set at that time (not shared by one of its authors, Philip Hefner [see n. 9]). Most of these authors had other axes to grind. The underlying issue in this respect appears to be this: how do Lutherans read Luther, tending toward the anthropocentric or more comprehensively? For this, see my discussion in "American Lutherans Engage Ecological Theology," 41–44.

12. For Luther and the Lutheran tradition, see Santmire, *The Travail of Nature*, 121–44.

13. In my judgment, a new generation of Lutheran revisionist theologians and practitioners is now espousing an ecological theology most impressively. See the essays in Bohmbach and Hannan, eds., *Eco-Lutheranism*, and the extensive historical research done by Pihkala in his study of Joseph Sittler's theology (see n. 8).

14. *Laudato Si'*, para. 10. Pope Francis discusses his view of integral ecology in detail in paras. 137–42.

15. Pope Francis affirms the integrity of nature in his encyclical, under the rubric of his "integral ecology." Thus he specifically talks about the integrity of the Earth (para. 8), of the creation (para. 130), of the environment (para. 136), and of ecosystems (para. 227). Francis also explicates that theme in various contexts. For him, all creatures are valuable in themselves (paras. 33, 69, 76, 78). This is a typical comment, para.

This theme merits the continuing attention of revisionist theologians, precisely as an alternative to the dominance of anthropocentrism in our culture and in some theological traditions.[16] *If members of our church communities do not hear their pastoral leaders constantly affirming that nature has its own integrity, that it has a Divine standing of its own, then nature will tend to be understood in those communities, by default, in terms of God's relationship with humanity, reinforcing the anthropocentric theology our churches must self-consciously move beyond in this, our ecological era.*[17] In these times, Christians must understand that nature has intrinsic value for God (*coram Deo*) and that, therefore, "Each mortal thing does one thing . . . Crying *What I do is me: for that I came*" (Hopkins).

Informed by the rich biblically rooted theological discussions of nature that have flourished in recent years[18] and encouraged by Pope

---

77: "Every creature is thus the object of the Father's tenderness, who gives it its place in the world. Even the fleeting life of the least of beings is the object of his love, and in its few seconds of existence, God enfolds it with his affections." God, for Francis, is also "intimately present to each being" (para. 80) and, eschatologically, God will redeem all things (para. 83). So Francis states, with particular reference to the theme of anthropocentric dominion (para. 83): "Here we can add yet another argument for rejecting every tyrannical and irresponsible domination of human beings over other creatures. The ultimate purpose of other creatures is not to be found in us. Rather, all creatures are moving forward with us and through us towards a common point of arrival, which is God, in that transcendent fullness where the risen Christ embraces and illumines all things. Human beings, endowed with intelligence and love, and drawn by the fullness of Christ are called to lead all creatures back to their Creator." All this points to a certain consistent affirmation of the integrity of nature in *Laudato Si'*.

16. For anthropocentrism in Christian theology, see my study of historic Christian attitudes toward nature, *The Travail of Nature*. There I identify two classical Christian approaches to nature; the one ecological, the other spiritual. The latter tends to be anthropocentric in many respects.

17. Absent such teaching by both theologians and pastoral leaders, the default theology in many church communities will at best be "responsible stewardship." For all the positive meanings this construct has had in American churches, responsible stewardship is fundamentally an anthropocentric idea: the notion that God has given humans the responsibility to act toward and on nature. The construct of responsible stewardship says nothing about God's affirmation of and purposes with nature in itself; that is, nothing about the integrity of nature. See my discussion, "On the Ambiguities of 'Stewardship,'" in *Ritualizing Nature*, 231–38. Of interest in this respect is this fact. In his book-length encyclical, Pope Francis mentions "responsible stewardship" only once and the human calling to be "stewards" only once, in both cases without discussion. Francis is much more at home with the notion of humans caring for nature as a world in its own right, than in humans exercising stewardship over nature.

18. For a comprehensive overview, see Horrell, et al., eds., *Ecological Hermeneutics*.

Francis' proposal for an overarching integral ecology, in particular, I want to show that *the particular theme of the integrity of nature, in addition to everything else it means, also points, more evocatively, to a certain kind of complex expressiveness on the part of nature* coram Deo (in the presence of God). To that end, I will develop a metaphor I have used before, the two voices of nature: the groaning of nature and the praising by nature.[19] I will also call these the two choruses of nature, in order to underline the rich diversity of each of nature's two voices. My premise is that when God hears all the complex expressivity of nature, its virtually infinite numbers of sounds, God hears the creatures of nature both groaning and praising.

THE VOICES OF NATURE AND THE GOD WHO HEARS

But wait: Nature has voices!? And God hears them!? Biblical interpretation of the last century largely discounted this idea on the grounds that it is merely poetic license or that it is an expression of some "primitive" sensibility. In a more nuanced manner, a number of prominent scholars today hold that when, in the Bible, nature is called upon to praise God, what is really being affirmed is that the creatures of nature are being called upon "just *to be* themselves."[20] According to this view, when the biblical writers call on nature to praise God, they are really just asking those creatures to affirm their own existence and value before God. But if the creatures of nature do not have a voice in some identifiable sense, how can they affirm themselves? When they are called upon to praise

---

Worthy of special mention is the Earth Bible Project launched by Norman C. Habel et al. See especially the discussion by the Earth Bible Team, "The Voice of the Earth: More than Metaphor?," and, in particular, that team's conclusion, 28: "The metaphor of voice is more than metaphor: it opens for us a domain of reality about Earth as subject and leads us to explore dimensions of that reality which Indigenous people know first-hand and some biblical writers reflect in poetic modes. The metaphor of voice is more than a rhetorical device; exploring this metaphor becomes another hermeneutical tool to enable us to move beyond the dualisms that we as a team have inherited as Western thinkers, and to begin relating to Earth as kin rather than commodity, as partner and co-creator rather than property." On the other hand, valuable as the work of the Earth Bible Project is, it must be approached critically, too. For an entry into this discussion, see Conradie, "What on Earth is an Ecological Hermeneutics?"

19. See *Brother Earth*, 137–39, and, more fully, *Before Nature*, 194–202, 207–11.

20. See, e.g., Fretheim, "Nature's Praise of God in the Psalms," 29–30; Bauckham, *Living with Other Creatures*, 147–84; Hardy and Ford, *Praising and Knowing God*, 82; and Coad, *Creation's Praise of God*.

God, what are they being asked to do that they are not already doing simply by being?

The character of this view of creation's praise is perhaps revealed most clearly in Dominic John Coad's work. His approach sounds plausible, theologically speaking. For Coad, "praise is the essential aspect of created existence."[21] And the "theme of creation's praise encourages us to realize that the rest of creation exists, in a particular relationship to God, with or without interference from us."[22] Coad quotes Daniel Hardy and David Ford, *Praising and Knowing God*, in agreement: "Since God's blessing is given by letting each creature, animals or not, be itself, and by enabling it, with infinite respect for its nature, to participate in the drama of the universe, then *creation's response is primarily its very existence.*"[23] Nature's voice is here reduced to its being: "Creation praises God by being itself, creation's being itself consists in its orientation towards God; in its orientation toward God creation participates in God's goodness; in participating in God's goodness in all its diversity creation praises God."[24]

The question as I see it is this. In order to affirm the meaning of nature praising or groaning before God, is it helpful to *reduce* nature's voice/s to almost nothing, to allow it to be swallowed up, as it were, by the sheer being of the creatures? Or is it better, as I propose, to understand the voices of groaning and praise heard by God—*metaphorically in all cases*—for all creatures, not only humans? Can we imagine God hearing the voices of humans and baboons and nightingales and elephants and volcanoes, let us say, without having to reduce the meaning of "voice" to something belonging solely to humans?

A revealing biblical case in point is that classic psalm of praise, Psalm 148.[25] The psalmist stands in the midst of the vibrant, even ecstatic—human—praises of the temple, or is clearly imagining him- or herself standing there. And that could be, and often was, a world of *very loud music*, clashing cymbals and all the rest, as Psalm 150 attests. Without so much as missing a beat, then, the poet of Psalm 148 *calls on all the creatures of nature to do the same thing.* Likewise the poet of Psalm 150, after celebrating all the holy noise of the temple liturgy, says: "Let every-

---

21. Coad, "Creation's Praise of God," 15; see 144 for a lengthier statement.

22. Ibid., 80.

23. Ibid., 80–81, emphasis added.

24. Ibid., 144.

25. I discuss this psalm more fully below.

thing that breathes praise the Lord!" (Ps 150:6). My reading of Psalms 148 and 150 suggests that *all* the creatures of nature have a voice in ways that are like human voices—and musical instruments.[26] This, I believe, is nature's complex expressivity, as attested by the psalmists: *every creature has a voice, not just humans*—with these voices being understood by us metaphorically in all cases.

Such an assertion not only challenges implicit anthropocentrism (the assumption that God hears only *human* voices). It also obliges us to recognize that God's hearing—that great biblical metaphor of attentive presence—is not just restricted to sounds that we humans *might* hear if *we* had the right technologies or the right kind of cultural formation. In the history of evolution on Earth, God listened when the morning stars sang together, when primeval beasts roared for their prey, when the great sea monsters communicated with one another in the depths of the seas, when the birds and the insects of aboriginal jungles sang forth, each in its own way, their cacophony of sounds. Even today, far from human hearing—although now, thanks to exquisite technologies, sometimes recorded by humans—the hare groans as it feels the teeth of the cougar in its neck, *and God hears*; elephants mumble what seem to be sounds of contentment among themselves, as all gather in their own communal space, free, for a time, from predators and the pressures of foraging for food, *and God hears*; the nightingale sings its hauntingly beautiful crescendos in the darkness, *and God hears*; the gibbons of Indonesia, bonded in pairs, lift up songs at the sunrise, as Bernie Krause explains, with "elaborately developed vocal exchanges unique to each couple . . . ,"[27] *and God hears*.

And, of course, God's hearing is not just terrestrial. God heard when the Big Bang happened, something very distantly akin, I imagine, to a human hearing of Beethoven's Ninth Symphony. God hears when a planet is sucked into oblivion in its host star, as planet Earth will be in five billion years, something very distantly akin, I imagine, to a human hearing of the "Dies Irae" from Mozart's *Requiem*. God hears when infinitesimal, subatomic particles collide or pass through each other in every corner

26. True, the poet of Psalm 19 (here, as throughout, using the best available translation), in talking about the heavens telling the glory of God and the firmament proclaiming God's handiwork (v. 1), does say: "There is no speech, nor are there words; their voice is not heard" (v. 3). But then the poet immediately says: "yet their voice goes out through all the earth, and their words to the end of the world" (v. 4). I read this as a more nuanced witness to the voices of nature, not as in any way contradicting the witness of Psalms 148 and 150.

27. Regarding the gibbons, see Krause, *The Great American Orchestra*, 92.

of the universe, in all of its billions of galaxies, something very distantly akin, I imagine, to a human hearing of a Bach fugue.

THE SOUNDS OF NATURE AND DIVINE HEARING

If we are to think of the Divine hearing metaphorically, as we must, it is critically important to have concrete images of the richness of human hearing of the sounds of nature in mind and heart. For self-conscious metaphorical discourse, in other words, it is best to have a phenomenological threshold, which will allow us to say of the Divine hearing that it is in some measure akin to human hearing, but "all the more so" in itself: infinitely richer and infinitely more complex than human hearing and therefore profoundly challenging to the theological imagination. I have already given examples along the way of human hearing of the sounds of nature, but I want to fill in the picture more completely here, with a brief phenomenological description of human hearing of nature and its riches and complexities. I will begin with Bernie Krause's scientific discussions.

Krause's accounts of the sounds of Earth-creatures border on the astounding, many of them dependent on the use of sophisticated technical listening devices. Every organism and every site on Earth has its own acoustic signature.[28] So for the marine environment: "Some of the fish create acoustic signals with their swim bladders. Others signify their presence by gnashing their teeth . . . From animals as small as protozoa, copepods, and phytoplankton to large whales, each species creates an acoustic sound-mark. The world's waters are saturated with living chatter, sighs, drumming, glissandos, cries, groans, grunts, and clicks."[29] Shorelines, too, have distinct sounds: "The water sounds at each beach have their own acoustic signatures as a result of the beaches' rakes, offshore and shoreline depths, currents, composite materials, weather patterns, salinity, water temperature, climate, season, surrounding terrestrial environment, geological features, and a range of other dynamic components."[30] Even "the mass of a constantly moving glacier is a geophysical sound

---

28. Krause, *The Great Animal Orchestra*, 27. See also Rothenberg, *Bug Music,* and Rothenberg and Ulvaeus, eds., *The Book of Music and Nature.*

29. Krause, *The Great Animal Orchestra*, 6.

30. Ibid., 42.

source—a category that also includes avalanches, earthquakes, and thermal mud pots."[31]

Planet Earth is full to overflowing with sounds from many sources, the non-biological (geophony), the general biological sources (biophony), as well as particularly generated human sounds (anthrophony).[32] The biophony, in particular, seems to have a kind of orchestral structure.[33]

Then there are the immensities of the whole universe, which is replete with unimaginable sounds that scientists have now—remarkably—begun to hear, if only in the most miniscule of ways, but hear nevertheless. In February 2016, according to press reports, a team of scientists "heard and recorded the sound of two black holes colliding a billion light years away, a fleeting chirp . . . , which rose to the note of middle C . . ." Said one of the scientists: "Finally, astronomy grew ears. We never had ears before."[34]

Humans have heard the sounds of nature throughout the ages, in an even greater variety of ways, not just with the ears of a scientist such as Bernie Krause or of the scientific team that recorded that echo of black holes colliding a billion light years away. Consider the listening to the sounds of nature that is common in the lives of many indigenous peoples in our time and has apparently been commonplace in indigenous communities throughout the human ages. The listening to the sounds of nature that such peoples have taken for granted far exceeds in scope and complexity the hearing practices of most modern Westerners. As Krause explains: "it turns out that many human groups have likely understood how wild sound is layered since our ancestors first began to hunt and forage for food. The ability to correctly interpret the cues inherent in the biophony was as central to our survival as the cues we received from our other senses."[35]

---

31. Ibid., 50.

32. Ibid., 80.

33. Ibid., 97: "In biomes rich with density and diversity of creature voices, organisms evolve to acoustically structure their signals in special relationships to one another—cooperative or competitive—much like an orchestral ensemble . . . The combined biological sounds in many habitats do not happen arbitrarily: each resident species acquires its own preferred sonic bandwidth—to blend or contrast—much in the way that violins, woodwinds, trumpets, and percussion instruments stake out acoustic territory in an orchestral arrangement."

34. Overbye, "With Faint Chirp, Scientists Prove Einstein Correct," A 1, A 12.

35. Ibid., 89.

Even some modern Western sensibilities appear to be revealing, more intuitive than the ears of scientists, more akin to the ears of indigenous peoples. Was John Muir merely the victim of some pathetic fallacy, for example, when he observed that "Music is one of the attributes of matter, into whatever forms it may be organized"?[36] And:

> Drops and sprays of air are specialized, and made to splash and crunch in the bosom of a lark, as infinitesimal portions of air splash and wing about the angles and hollows of the sand-grains, as perfectly composed and predestined as the rejoicing anthems of the world; but our senses are not fine enough to catch the tones. Fancy the waving, pulsing melody of the vast flower-congregations of the Hollow flowing from the myriad voices of tuned petal and pistil, and heaps of sculptured pollen. Scarce one note is for us; nevertheless, God be thanked for this blessed instrument hid beneath the feathers of a lark.[37]

Had Muir developed or been gifted by sensitivities to nature that many other citizens of his world had not? Could he have crossed some kind of a threshold, from the quotidian to the liminal? As when he observed, "Nature is ever at work building and pulling down, creating and destroying, keeping everything whirling and flowing, allowing no rest but in rhythmical motion, chasing everything in endless song out of one beautiful form into another."[38]

Rich and complex as the human hearing of the sounds of nature has been over the centuries, surely the Divine hearing of the voices of nature is infinitely richer and infinitely more complex. The scope and depth of God's hearing of the voices of nature infinitely surpasses ours, even in its most sophisticated forms. Yet such human hearings of nature's expressiveness offer us a rich metaphorical threshold that makes it possible for us to think about what that Divine hearing of nature beyond that threshold may be like and, more particularly, to grasp some of the nuances suggested by the two biblical images before us in this essay: nature's groaning and nature's praising. I will first consider the groaning.[39]

36. Muir, *The Story of My Boyhood and Youth & A Thousand Mile Walk to the Gulf*, 406.

37. Ibid.

38. Muir, *Our National Parks*, 106–7.

39. I discuss these themes throughout *Before Nature*; see especially 194–98, 203–11. There I refer to the groaning as nature's second voice and the praising as nature's first voice. Here I reverse the order, a minor change, for which I hope readers will give

THE INTEGRITY OF NATURE
AND THE FIRST VOICE OF NATURE: GROANING

The groaning of nature appears to be a self-authenticating theme.[40] It has sometimes been said that original sin is the only empirically demonstrable Christian truth.[41] Perhaps we could broaden this dictum to include the groaning of the whole creation. Be that as it may, if we step back and survey not just human history, but cosmic history and particularly the whole history of life on Earth, we soon grasp that ours is a cosmos of dramatic destructivity.[42] No galaxy, as Brian Swimme and Thomas Berry explain, "escapes the reality of ongoing destruction. In the center of our own Milky Way galaxy a black hole churns, sucking suns into its destruction as a spider at the center of a net transforms brilliant insects into black tombs."[43]

At the very end, according to many cosmological physicists, the whole universe is destined for a vast collapse of some kind, perhaps some universal slow-down to a dead frigidity. After countless billions of years, during which many billions of galaxies have come into being and died, together with all their stars and planets and other astral bodies and particles, infinitely large and infinitely small, everything in the universe will have come to an end (*finis*), a kind of universal, grinding cosmic halt. Not "Love Supreme" (John Coltrane) but Death Supreme will reign at the very end of our cosmos, according to current scientific projections.

Then consider the history of life on Earth. Darwin's picture of the unfolding of terrestrial evolution is full of blood and gore.[44] We humans

---

me the benefit of the doubt.

40. I am employing the terminology of groaning here because of its particular use in Romans 8. Further explorations of this theme will benefit from studies of the closely related biblical theme, lament. My thanks to Lisa Dahill (private communication), for raising this question.

41. This quip is said to have appeared first in the *Times Literary Supplement* and was then given currency by Reinhold Niebuhr, according to a number of his interpreters.

42. I employ the seldom used word "destructivity" here because it appears to me to be less abstract than "destructiveness." In ordinary speech it brings with it more of the nuance of a negative form of "activity."

43. Swimme and Berry, *The Universe Story*, 50.

44. Wesley Wildman has helped to fill in this picture with his explorations of nature at the *microbial* level. Evolutionary destructivity is perhaps most striking in that context. See Wildman's essay, "Distributed Identity."

understandably highlight the story of *human* suffering on Earth, focusing particularly on events such as the Holocaust. But such colossal tragedies in human history are only a minuscule part of a vast story of destruction and death over the course of many billions of years, spanning the whole history of the cosmos.

Destructivity, therefore, is indeed a key construct we can invoke to describe the "Great Story" (Thomas Berry) of our universe, since its first moments. This is not to say that the Great Story is not also a story of creativity (Gordon Kaufman), as the biblical creation narratives also attest. There appears to be a universal dialectic of destructivity and creativity unfolding throughout the universe.[45] Thus, on Earth, as old forms of life are destroyed, new forms of life emerge. Emergent life, in this sense, presupposes death.[46]

The biblical narratives of this first voice of nature appear to be closely related to those experienced realities of destructivity, pain (at least on the part of some creatures), and death. My fiducial premise here, predicated on a certain reading of biblical narratives, is that *God hears the phenomenologically discernible destructivity of nature as the groaning of nature.* Later, I will also suggest that *God hears the phenomenologically discernible creativity of nature as nature's praise.*

This is not the place to undertake a comprehensive survey of the biblical theme of the groaning of the whole creation.[47] I will consider here,

45. Cf. Swimme and Berry, *The Universe Story,* 51: "Is the universe ultimately destructive or creative? Violent or cooperative? The more closely we look at any place in the fifteen billion years of the universe's story, the more we realize that the universe is both violent and creative, both destructive and cooperative. The mystery is that both extremes are found together. We even find it difficult to determine when violence is simply destructive or when violence is linked to creativity."

46. Cf. the hermeneutics of nature taken for granted by Muir, as he contemplates the mountains of Yosemite, *Our National Parks,* 106: "If among the agents that nature has employed in making these mountains there be one that above all other deserves the name of Destroyer, it is the glacier. But we quickly learn that destruction is creation. During the dreary centuries through which the Sierra lay in darkness, crushed beneath the ice folds of the glacial winter, there was a steady invincible advance toward the warm life and beauty of today; and it is just where the glaciers crushed most destructively that the greatest amount of beauty is made manifest. But as these landscapes have succeeded the preglacial landscapes, so they in turn are giving place to others already planned and foreseen. The granite domes and pavements, apparently imperishable, we take as symbols of permanence, while these crumbling peaks, down whose frosty gullies avalanches are ever falling, are symbols of change and decay. Yet all alike, fast or slow, are surely vanishing away."

47. For reflections about creation's groaning in biblical perspective, with specific

in short compass, the *textus classicus* of that theme, Romans 8:18–23, particularly as it allows us to understand what for faith is the groaning of nature.[48] I begin with some comments about the context of this text. Although Paul is preoccupied in his Letter to the Romans with a number of particular issues in the church of his time, above all with the relationship between Jews and Gentiles, he also presupposes two grand narratives. The first is the story of the rise and the power of Rome and its claims for ultimacy. The second is the story of the world's creation, human sin, the redemption of all humans, and the consummation of the whole world, the narrative of the biblical God's ultimacy.

The first story was celebrated by the poet Virgil. He announced the dawning of a golden age in the reign of Caesar Augustus. But as Paul and the Roman Christians to whom he wrote would have known well, the facts on the ground radically belied such imperial propaganda. Rome was a ruthless, militaristic culture predicated on slave labor and vast exploitations of nature. In particular, both Paul and his audience "could well have thought about how imperial ambitions, military conflicts, and economic exploitations had led to the erosion of the natural environment throughout the Mediterranean world, leaving ruined cities, depleted fields, deforested mountains, and polluted streams."[49]

Roman culture was also undergirded by the violent cult of animal sacrifice in every major city of the Empire. We know that early Christian writers, surrounded by this pervasive culture of bloody sacrifice, as Gordon Lathrop has explained, engaged in a vigorous polemic against ritual killing and its violence.[50] Still, such animal sacrifice "was the central ritual act of late antique society, bearing and sustaining a conception of world, including the gods, into the heart of daily experience."[51] Violence made the Roman world go round. This was no golden age.

Hence the expression "the groaning of the whole creation" is in all likelihood implicitly linked, for Paul, with the thought of the desecration of Earth by the powerful and a culture of violence more generally, violence against animals and slaves and subjugated peoples as well as against

---

reference to nature, see Fretheim, *Creation Untamed*. For an instructive theological discussion of these issues, see Southgate, *The Groaning of Creation*.

48. Here I am following my exposition of this text in *Before Nature*, 205–11. See that discussion for references to the extensive scholarly literature.

49. Jewett, "The Corruption and Redemption of Creation," 37.

50. Lathrop, *Holy Things*, 144.

51. Ibid.

forests and fields and rivers. There is also ample precedent in biblical traditions that would have inclined Paul and other first-century Christians
to believe that this situation presupposed what for us could be called a
divinely mandated feedback loop: that God judges human sinfulness, in
part at least, by "cursing the ground" (Gen 3:14–19) because of sinful
humans and their violence. In response to human sin, in other words,
God reshapes the human experience in nature so that it is no longer a
blessing as God had intended it to be, but a curse, especially under the
hegemony of Roman power. This is why, at least in part, according to this
way of thinking, creation groans.

It appears, furthermore, that the motif of the groaning of creation
brings with it some reference to a kind of suffering that is endemic to
nature, apart from the interventions by the powers of Rome and apart
from human sin more generally. Consider, in this respect, the eschatological expectations of many first-century Christians. Those hopes were
shaped, in some measure at least, by the prophecies of Isaiah, which envisioned the messianic age as a time of cosmic peace, a time when "the
wolf shall live with the lamb, the leopard shall lie down with the kid,
the calf and the lion and the fatling together, and a little child shall lead
them" (Isa 11:6).[52] First-century Christians must have had some sense,
then, that animal suffering, in particular, was not only real, but that it was
ultimately to be overcome. Was that one of the reasons why in the early
church animal sacrifice was opposed so strongly?

It seems clear, furthermore, that the expression "the groaning of
the whole creation" presupposes that *God hears* that groaning. Such an
observation is strengthened when we examine the word Paul uses for
groaning. It calls to mind traditional mourning practices of Paul's Jewish
heritage, which were often replete with loud cries of grieving. Paul, as a
matter of course, attributes the same kind of emotional intensity to the
groaning of *all* the creatures. All the creatures cry out loud because of
their misery! Paul seems to have a real, public expression of universal
grief in mind, predicated on the firmly held conviction that God hears all
those cries of grief. Thus the destructivity that is omnipresent in nature,
driven by many creatures, including the human creature, is not merely
destructivity, theologically speaking. It can also be understood as *groaning*, because *God* hears that destructivity as groaning.

---

52. See also Isa 11:7–9; 65:26.

THE INTEGRITY OF NATURE
AND THE SECOND VOICE OF NATURE: PRAISING

We can speak theologically of the integrity of nature, I have been suggesting, for a number of reasons, among them this: nature has its own
complex expressiveness. God hears the destructivity and the creativity
of nature as its groaning and its praising. And God reveals that hearing,
in some small measure, to those who have ears to hear in the household of faith and its worship. It is no accident that most of the biblical
calls to nature to praise God are found in the Psalms and rooted in the
practices of worship, as similarly in the Book of Revelation.[53] Here I will
again focus on a *textus classicus*, in this case Psalm 148, to which I have
already referred.[54] This Psalm was used daily for centuries in monasteries throughout the West. It undoubtedly helped shape a major ecological
strain in Western Christian theology and spirituality.[55] St. Francis, for
one, sang this Psalm every day at *Lauds*; and it was in all likelihood much
in his mind and heart when he composed his *Canticle of All the Creatures*.

In Psalm 148 the creation moves into worship, as it were. Here
the voices of praise become the primary theme, as the mind of the poet
ranges over the very world of many creatures that the composers of Genesis 1 and Psalm 104 envisioned. Psalm 148 is an itinerary of the whole
creation, immersed in the creation traditions of ancient Israel, spoken
from the context of the temple liturgy. Heavenly creatures are called upon
to praise God, then sun and moon and stars, and "the waters above the
heavens" (vv. 1–4). Thereafter the primal realities of Earth, reminiscent
of Psalm 104, are invited to join in: "sea monsters and all deeps, fire and
hail, snow and frost, stormy wind fulfilling [God's] command" (vv. 7–8).
Every creature of nature, is to have its part: "Mountains and all hills, fruit
trees and all cedars! Wild animals and all cattle, creeping things and fly-
ing birds!" (vv. 9–10) Humans of every rank and age are also asked to join
in the song of the whole creation (vv. 11–12). Finally, the Psalm comes to
a kind of frenzied rest with the cultic affirmation of "the name of [Yah-
weh]" in the midst of the people called to praise that name. As they lift up
their voices with the whole creation, they stand in awe before God, "the
horn" of their salvation (vv. 13–14).

53. See Bauckham, "Creation's Praise of God in the Book of Revelation."

54. Cf. the commentary of Weiser, *The Psalms*, 836–38.

55. Centuries of ritual use of Psalm 148 surely gave impetus to the ecological
trajectory of Christian theology that I identified in *The Travail of Nature*.

The plot thickens when we turn to the Orthodox interpretation of worship. According to the Orthodox view, *the human celebrant* offers the praise of the whole creation to God as a priestly mediator of Christ.[56] Of interest here, too, is the fact that Dominic John Coad, in his earlier-cited study, espouses a similar position. For him, "[I]t is the non-human creation's privilege to have its praise offered to God by humans, the priests of creation."[57] He views humans as "the priests of creation" who have "the privilege of leading creation into the everlasting glory of God."[58] Without this human mediation, he says, creation's praise "is left disparate and un-united."[59] Jeremy Begbie, in *Voicing Creation's Praise: Towards a Theology of the Arts,* notwithstanding the suggestiveness of his title, adopts the same position: "Our calling . . . is to articulate and extend [creation's] praise in ever fresh ways, to be 'priests of creation.' In humankind, creation finds a voice . . . Through the human creature, the inarticulate (though never silent) creation becomes articulate."[60] These perspectives seem to suggest that apart from human mediation, non-human praise of God means next to nothing. The creatures of nature do not have a voice of their own *coram Deo.* To be heard by God, that voice must always be mediated by a human figure.[61]

Richard Bauckham suggestively takes issue with this view in his book, *Living with Other Creatures*:

> Through [the Eucharistic] offering to God of what belongs to him [*sic*], according to John Zizioulas, "creation is brought into relation to God and not only is it treated with the reverence that belongs to God, but it is also liberated from its natural limitations and is transformed into a bearer of life." . . . This Eucharistic relationship to creation is then treated as a kind of model for all of human relationships with creation. Humanity's priesthood is exercised in human creativity that brings creation to a fulfilment it could not have otherwise . . . Of this arrogant assertion

56. For an oft-cited—apparently normative—statement of the Orthodox position, see Zizioulas, "Preserving God's Creation" (1989), 1–5, 41–45; and (1990), 1–5.

57. Coad, *Creation's Praise of God*, 248.

58. Ibid., 275; see also 279.

59. Ibid., 262.

60. Begbie, *Voicing Creation's Praise*, 177.

61. Soberingly, Pope Francis *appears* to adopt this kind of teaching, *Laudato Si'*, para. 83. But his is a singular and undeveloped reference to the idea, and does not seem to express his consistent affirmation of the integrity of nature; for the latter, see n. 15 above.

that only through human mediation can the rest of creation be itself in relation to God there is not a trace in the Scriptures.[62]

I agree. In themselves, the voices of the many creatures of nature beyond humans are not "disparate and un-united" (Coad) or "inarticulate" (Begbie). Long before humans emerge in the picture, "the heavens are telling the glory of God; and the firmament proclaims his handiwork" and "their voice goes out through all the earth" (Ps 19:1, 4). Again, humans had yet to appear in the world when "the morning stars sang together" (Job 38:7). The creatures of nature do not need human mediation, thank you. They can sing before God—and be heard by God—all by themselves.

In fact, divine hearing is the *sine qua non* (essential condition) of the voices themselves. God hears the destructivity of nature as nature's groaning. God hears the creativity of nature as nature's song of praise. And we who participate by faith in the worship of the household of faith then can join in the hymn of the whole creation, our baptismal birthright along with all other creatures.

CELEBRATING A STRONG THEOLOGY OF THE INTEGRITY OF NATURE

As it stands, this essay could leave a mistaken impression. In order further to develop the theme the integrity of nature, I have been preoccupied here with the construct of God's hearing the two voices of nature. But the image of a hearing God is by no means the whole story. The God whose universal history with the creation is disclosed to us in the Scriptures of the household of faith is no *Deus otiosus*, as Luther and Calvin often reminded us, some idle Deity who sits in heaven, as James Joyce once observed, "paring his fingernails," just listening. The God attested by the Church's scriptures is the God who is incessantly active and immediately present to every creature. This God, as I have elsewhere narrated, is the omnipresent cosmic Christ and the omni-active cosmic Spirit.[63] The theme of the two voices of nature, in a word, if it is to be rightly understood, must be construed in terms of the fullness of the Church's Trinitarian traditions.[64]

62. Bauckham, *Living with Other Creatures,* 150–53; the quote is from 152.

63. See Santmire, *Before Nature,* 129–80.

64. Had space permitted, I would wish to explore a Christological theme in this context. Can we identify "signs" of Christ's presence (*vestigia Christi*) in nature, once

But it must also be construed for itself. We must be able to hear all the creatures of nature "Crying *What I do is me: for that I came*" and then tell the story of that integrity. This is the judgment on which this whole essay is predicated. If nature has no integrity or if that integrity is only weakly affirmed, theological discourse will end up being defined by a kind of default anthropocentrism, if not a self-consciously developed anthropocentrism. In particular, the kind of "integral ecology" that Pope Francis has begun to set forth, were it not to incorporate, as it continues to unfold, a strong theology of the integrity of nature at each step along the way, could be weakened, even to the point of requiring life support.

Finally, this plea. The theme, the integrity of nature, if I may say so, needs all the help it can get. Anthropocentrism is still rampant in our culture and also, sadly, in the preaching and practices and theologies of more than a few of our churches. While, therefore, it is critically important for us to show what a strong theology of the integrity of nature can mean, as I have tried to do in this essay, it is all the more important for us to celebrate that theology, constantly and enthusiastically, in the identity-forming matrix of the church's liturgical and spiritual practices.[65]

And more. In this era of NDD, "nature deficit disorder" (Richard Louv), it may well be necessary for Christians to worship outdoors as often as they can, if they are to be existentially attuned to the two voices of nature.[66] Likewise, in this era of pervasive and destructive climate change, much of it induced by humans, it may well be necessary for those

we have affirmed its integrity *coram Deo*? Could we think of nature's groaning and praising in light of the Cross and Resurrection? Could we invoke a widely attested traditional theological saying about nature *breathing* Christ's Resurrection (think of a field of blossoming lilies, on the one hand, and Easter, on the other), also in terms of nature breathing Christ's Cross (think of an animal slaughter-house, on the one hand, and Good Friday, on the other)? Could we say: *Natura spirat Crucem et Resurrectionem* (Nature "breathes" the Cross and the Resurrection)?

65. For this, see my study *Ritualizing Nature*. More particularly, see Stewart, "Baptismal Water in Lutheran Worship and on the Earth"; Schade, "Preaching and Ecofeminist Theology at the Crossroads"; and Dahill, "Indoors and Outdoors." Such attention to the renewal of the Church's liturgical practices necessarily requires, as well, a fresh approach to the Church's spiritual practices. For the latter, see my book *Before Nature*; also see Chase, *Nature as Spiritual Practice* and *A Field Guide to Nature as a Spiritual Practice*. Of importance in this context, too, are the many works of Belden C. Lane, such as *Backpacking with the Saints*.

66. See especially Dahill, "Bio-Theoacoustics." In her Presidential Address to the Society for the Study of Christian Spirituality, "Into Local Waters," Dahill argues persuasively that in today's world the goal should be that *all* Christian baptisms will be outdoors. See her essay derived from this address in the present volume.

of us who are members of the household of faith, insofar as we have the stamina and the opportunity and the vision, to get out into the streets and to join with other citizens of our global community to demand that the powers that be, at all levels, zealously keep addressing the issues of climate justice, thus affirming not only the integrity of humanity, but also the integrity of the nature. Today the whole Earth community is profoundly at risk, the creatures of nature no less than human creatures. For sure, then, talking the talk about the integrity of nature, critically important as that is, is not enough.[67] We need an Eco-Reformation.

BIBLIOGRAPHY

Bauckham, Richard. "Creation's Praise of God in the Book of Revelation." In *Living with Other Creatures: Green Exegesis and Theology*, 163–84. Waco, TX: Baylor University Press, 2011.

———. *Living with Other Creatures: Green Exegesis and Theology*. Waco, TX: Baylor University Press, 2011.

Begbie, Jeremy. *Voicing Creation's Praise: Towards a Theology of the Arts*. Edinburgh: T. & T. Clark, 1991.

Braaten, Carl E., and Robert W. Jenson, eds. *Christian Dogmatics*. Philadelphia: Fortress, 1984.

Brown, William P. *The Seven Pillars of Creation: The Bible, Science, and the Ecology of Wonder*. New York: Oxford University Press, 2010.

Chase, Steven. *A Field Guide to Nature as a Spiritual Practice*. Grand Rapids: Eerdmans, 2011.

———. *Nature as Spiritual Practice*. Grand Rapids: Eerdmans, 2011.

Childs, James M., Jr. *Ethics in the Community of Promise*. Minneapolis: Fortress, 2006.

Coad, Dominic John. "Creation's Praise of God: An Ecological Theology of Non-Human and Human Being." PhD diss., University of Exeter, 2010.

Conradie, Ernst. "What on Earth Is an Ecological Hermeneutics? Some Broad Parameters." In *Ecological Hermeneutics: Biblical, Historical and Theological Perspectives*, edited by David Horrell, et al., 295–314. London: T. & T. Clark, 2010.

Dahill, Lisa E. "Bio-Theoacoustics: Prayer Outdoors and the Reality of the Natural World." *Dialog* 52:4 (Winter 2013) 292–302.

67. The identity-forming liturgical and spiritual practices referred to in the preceding two notes are, of course, not sufficient in themselves either. The integrity of nature must also be affirmed by theological ethicists, by the church's public policy advocates, and by grassroots church activists. For a baseline for the ethical reflection, see the classic study by James Nash, *Loving Nature*. To explore practical issues, see James Martin-Schramm, Laura Stivers, and Daniel Spencer, *Earth-Ethics*. For one entry into the Church public policy and grassroots activism arena, see the website of Lutherans Restoring Creation: www.lutheransrestoringcreation.org.

————. "Indoors and Outdoors: Praying with the Earth." In *Eco-Lutheranism: Lutheran Perspectives on Ecology*, edited by Karla G. Bohmbach and Shauna K. Hannan, 112–123. Minneapolis: Lutheran University Press, 2013.

————. "Into Local Waters: Rewilding the Study of Christian Spirituality." *Spiritus: A Journal of Christian Spirituality* 16 (2016) 141–65.

Francis. *Laudato Si': On Care for Our Common Home*. Rome: Libreria Editrice Vaticana, 2015.

Fretheim, Terence E. *Creation Untamed: The Bible, God, and Natural Disasters*. Grand Rapids: Baker Academic, 2010.

————. *God and the World in the Old Testament: A Relational Theology of Creation*. Nashville: Abingdon, 2005.

————. "Nature's Praise of God in the Psalms." *Ex Auditu* 3 (1987) 29–30.

Habel, Norman C., and Earth Bible Team. "The Voice of the Earth: More than Metaphor?" In *The Earth Story in the Psalms and the Prophets*, ed. Norman C. Habel, 23–28. Cleveland: Pilgrim Press, 2001.

Hardy, Daniel W., and David F. Ford. *Praising and Knowing God*. Philadelphia: Westminster, 1985.

Hefner, Philip. *The Human Factor: Evolution, Culture, Religion*. Minneapolis: Fortress, 1993.

Horrell, David G. et al., eds. *Ecological Hermeneutics: Biblical, Historical and Theological Perspectives*. London: T. & T. Clark, 2010.

Jewett, Robert. "The Corruption and Redemption of Creation: Reading Romans 8:18–23 within the Imperial Context." In *Paul and the Roman Imperial Order*, edited by Richard A. Horsley, 25–46. Harrisburg, PA: Trinity, 2004.

Johnson, Elizabeth A. *Ask the Beasts: Darwin and the God of Love*. New York: Bloomsbury, 2014.

Krause, Bernie. *The Great American Orchestra: Finding the Origins of Music in the World's Wild Places*. New York: Little, Brown, 2012.

Lane, Belden C. *Backpacking with the Saints: Wilderness Hiking as Spiritual Practice*. New York: Oxford University Press, 2015.

Lathrop, Gordon. *Holy Ground: A Liturgical Cosmology*. Minneapolis: Fortress, 2003.

————. *Holy Things: A Liturgical Theology*. Minneapolis: Fortress, 1993.

Martin-Schramm, James B., et al. *Earth-Ethics: A Case-Method Approach*. Ecology and Justice. Maryknoll, NY: Orbis, 2015.

McFague, Sallie. *The Body of God: An Ecological Theology*. Minneapolis: Fortress, 1993.

Moltmann, Jürgen. *God in Creation: A New Theology of Creation and the Spirit of God*. Translated by Margaret Kohl. San Francisco: Harper & Row, 1985.

Muir, John. *Our National Parks. The Works of John Muir*. Manuscript Edition, VI. Boston: Houghton Mifflin, 1916.

————. *The Story of My Boyhood and Youth & A Thousand Mile Walk to the Gulf. The Works of John Muir*. Manuscript Editions I. Boston: Houghton Mifflin, 1916.

Nash, James. *Loving Nature: Ecological Integrity and Christian Responsibility*. Nashville: Abingdon, in cooperation with the Churches Center for Theology and Public Policy, Washington, DC, 1991.

Overbye, Dennis. "With Faint Chirp, Scientists Prove Einstein Correct." *New York Times* (February 12, 2016) A 1, A 12.

Peters, Ted. *God—The World's Future: Systematic Theology for a Postmodern Era*. Minneapolis: Fortress, 1992.

Pihkala, Panu. "Joseph Sittler and Early Ecotheology." PhD diss., University of Helsinki, 2014.

Rasmussen, Larry. "The Integrity of Creation: What Can It Mean for Christian Ethics?" In *The Annals of the Society of Christian Ethics* 15 (1995) 161–75.

Rothenberg, David. *Bug Music: How Insects Gave Us Rhythm and Noise.* New York: St. Martin's, 2013.

Rothenberg, David, and Marta Ulvaeus, eds. *The Book of Music and Nature: An Anthology of Sounds, Word, Thoughts.* Middletown, CT: Wesleyan University Press, 2001.

Ruether, Rosemary Radford. *Gaia and God: An Ecofeminist Theology of Earth Healing.* San Francisco: Harper, 1992.

Santmire, H. Paul. "American Lutherans Engage Ecological Theology: The First Chapter, 1962–2012, and Its Legacy." In *Eco-Lutheranism: Lutheran Perspectives on Ecology*, edited by Karla G. Bohmbach and Shauna K. Hannan, 17–54. Minneapolis: Lutheran University Press, 2013.

———. *Before Nature: A Christian Spirituality.* Minneapolis: Fortress, 2014.

———. *Brother Earth: Nature, God, and Ecology in a Time of Crisis.* New York: Thomas Nelson, 1970.

———. "Creation and Nature: A Study of the Doctrine of Nature with Special Attention to Karl Barth's Doctrine of Creation." PhD diss., Harvard University, 1966.

———. "Ecology, Liturgy, Justice." In *Theologians in Their Own Words*, edited by Derek R. Nelson, et al., 217–32. Minneapolis: Fortress, 2013.

———. "I-Thou, I-It, and I-Ens." *Journal of Religion* 47 (1968) 260–73.

———. *Nature Reborn: The Ecological and Cosmic Promise of Christian Theology.* Minneapolis: Fortress, 2000.

———. *Ritualizing Nature: Renewing Christian Liturgy in a Time of Crisis.* Minneapolis: Fortress, 2008.

———. *The Travail of Nature: The Ambiguous Ecological Promise of Christian Theology.* Minneapolis: Fortress, 1985.

Schade, Leah D. "Preaching and Ecofeminist Theology at the Crossroads: Homiletic Theory and Praxis in Dialogue with a Lutheran Ecofeminist Christology." In *Eco-Lutheranism: Lutheran Perspectives on Ecology*, edited by Karla G. Bohmbach and Shauna K. Hannan, 100–111. Minneapolis: Lutheran University Press, 2013.

Sittler, Joseph. *Evocations of Grace: The Writings of Joseph Sittler on Ecology*, edited by Steven Bouma-Prediger and Peter Bakken. Grand Rapids: Eerdmans, 2000.

Southgate, Christopher. *The Groaning of Creation: God, Evolution, and the Problem of Evil.* Louisville: Westminster John Knox, 2008.

Stewart, Benjamin M. "Baptismal Water in Lutheran Worship and on the Earth: A Living, Sacramental Landscape." In *Eco-Lutheranism: Lutheran Perspectives on Ecology*, edited by Karla G. Bohmbach and Shauna K. Hannan, 87–99. Minneapolis: Lutheran University Press, 2013.

Swimme, Brian, and Thomas Berry. *The Universe Story: From the Primordial Flaring Forth to the Ecozoic Era: A Celebration of the Unfolding of the Cosmos.* San Francisco: HarperSanFrancisco, 1992.

Tillich, Paul. "Nature and Sacrament." In *The Protestant Era*, 94–111. Translated by James Luther Adams. Chicago: University of Chicago Press, 1948.

Weiser, Artur. *The Psalms.* Translated by Herbert Hartwell. Old Testament Library. Philadelphia: Westminster, 1962.

Wildman, Wesley. "Distributed Identity: Human Beings as Walking, Thinking Ecologies in the Microbial World." In *Human Identity at the Intersection of Science, Technology, and Religion,* edited by Nancey Murphy and Christopher Knight, 165–78. Burlington, VT: Ashgate, 2010.

Zizioulas, John D. "Preserving God's Creation: Three Lectures on Theology and Ecology." *King's Theological Review* 12 (1989) 1–5, 41–45; and 13 (1990) 1–5.

6

Joseph Sittler and the Ecological Role of Cultural Critique

A Resource for Eco-Reformation

—ROBERT C. SALER

INTRODUCTION: STABILITY AND DISPLACEMENT

To ASSESS THE PROSPECTS of Lutheran contributions to the larger project of ecological justice requires decisions as to the relative fluidity of key Lutheran concepts.[1] Ecologists and eco-philosophers alike have spent decades attempting to move public discourse about nature past the stage of simple romanticism wherein nature could be relied upon as a stable, "given" category rather than a contested field of concepts imposed onto uninterpreted and constantly changing material realities. This means that any responsible talk about "nature" must recognize it to be the fluid, shifting category of scientific and cultural analysis that it is.[2]

Similarly, a tension within Lutheran theology—one that is sometimes generative, sometimes debilitating—has to do with the fluidity or plasticity of historic Lutheran understandings of such core theological concepts as "justification," "old/new Adam," "salvation," "revelation,"

---

1. Earlier portions of this chapter appeared as Robert C. Saler, "Joseph Sittler as Theologian of the 21st Century," *Let's Talk* (Feb. 4, 2014). http://mcsletstalk.org/joseph-sittler/joseph-sittler-theologian-21st-century/. Reprinted by permission.

2. Cf. Morton, *Ecology without Nature.*

etc. While most theologians within the Evangelical Lutheran Church in America may not spend much time worrying about older Lutheran debates of *quia* ("because") vs. *quatenus* ("insofar as"), affirmations of subscription to the Lutheran Confessions, the animating concern behind that debate remains vital: are sixteenth century Lutheran theological categories true and universal reflections of contemporary reality (including "nature" in its shifting physical and conceptual terrain), or should the changing circumstances of our societies and our planet prompt ongoing testing and (if necessary) revision of these categories, sometimes in thoroughgoing fashion?

When one puts the question that way, of course, then it becomes clear that the choice is not a strict either-or. In changed circumstances, even the assertion of a theological formulation from the past becomes a "fresh" event (including in situations where the result is more retrograde than helpful). Most theologians and pastors would argue that it is not a zero-sum game between repristinating past formulations and creative innovation, but rather that all theology is necessarily an interweaving of historical and contemporary sources. What the Roman Catholic theologian Hans Urs von Balthasar said about Catholic theology in relation to patristic and medieval theological authorities applies, I would suggest, to Lutherans assessing their heritage as well:

> Being faithful to tradition most definitely does not consist . . . of a literal repetition and transmission of the philosophical and theological theses that one imagines lie hidden in time and in the contingencies of history. Rather, being faithful to tradition consists much more of imitating our Fathers in the faith with respect to their attitude of intimate reflection and their effort of audacious creation, with are the necessary preludes to true spiritual fidelity. If we study the past, it is not in the hope of drawing from it formulas doomed in advance to sterility or with the intention of readapting out-of-date solutions. We are asking history to teach us the acts and deeds of the Church, who presents her treasure of divine revelation, ever new and ever unexpected, to every generation, and who knows how, in the face of every new problem, to turn the fecundity of the problem to good account with a rigor that never grows weary and a spiritual agility that has never dulled.[3]

---

3. Von Balthasar, *Presence and Thought*, 12. Quoted in Martin, *Hans Urs von Balthasar*, 14–15.

In this essay, I want to suggest that the legacy of a self-consciously constructive and daring Lutheran eco-theologian, Joseph Sittler (1904–1987), can provide insights into how the blending of past and present Lutheran theological formulations can engage the subtleties of "nature" as a material and cultural reality that is in constant flux. I will be arguing that what is needed (and what Sittler models) is not simply a mix of past and present Lutheran theological themes, but an integration of eco-theological analysis with an analysis of "creation" as a modality within culture.

SITTLER'S LEGACY

To a large extent, Joseph Sittler was a theologian of his time and place. While he would often remark that his reputation as an academic theologian is not sufficient to place him among the giants of twentieth century theology, his life and work do serve to reflect many of the issues that defined the twentieth century North American church scene. His first book, *The Doctrine of the Word*, was published in 1948 as inherited notions of biblical inerrancy prevalent in North American circles were beginning to strain under the pressures of historical biblical criticism, emerging scientific consensus, and the awareness that adherence to doctrines of inerrancy were producing a kind of spiritual aridity in theology and church practice. His assertion that the "word" of God cannot be reduced to the text of scripture, and that scripture is spiritually rich despite its not being completely factual, was disturbing to large sectors of the Lutheran world even as it corresponded well with emerging trends in liberal and neo-orthodox theology. Later, his extensive work with the World Council of Churches (which he often referred to as his "graduate school" in theology, having never finished a doctorate himself) coincided with the heyday of ecumenical optimism in the later twentieth century. Meanwhile, his early insistence upon the need to rethink issues of nature and grace in light of a growing consciousness of our responsibility to the environment, while predating public consciousness of ecological issues by nearly a decade, would become informative for a whole generation of "ecological" theologians by the century's end.

In other respects, though, Sittler was an odd enough fit in the twentieth century that we might risk cliché and describe him as a thinker ahead of his time. While most of the aforementioned work took place amidst the heyday of liberal Protestant Christendom in the United States, Sittler very much saw ahead to a time when the "mainline" would wane, at least in terms of prestige and cultural influence. Indeed, he was vexed by what he saw as the banality that resulted when the church traded the historic thickness of its liturgical and spiritual heritage for fleeting "relevance" within popular culture. That said, he was also strikingly willing to rethink aspects of that heritage in light of insights from contemporary science, literature, film, and philosophy. And his tools for such work were sporadic borrowings from a host of theological currents without any consequent indebtedness to any of them; for instance, even though he taught in the heart of "Chicago-school" process and empirical theology, he casually appropriated what he liked from those methods without ever feeling the need to fully commit himself to their limitations. In articulating a given theological theme, he was as likely to cite Melville, Whitman, or Joseph Conrad as he was to appeal to Barth or Schleiermacher. Such eclecticism might be a given in our own day, but it was a bit of a novelty in most of the settings in which he taught.

To borrow an old term, Sittler was a "churchman" through and through—but he was a churchman who wanted the church to always shape its proclamation in ways that would speak in nimble and mutable fashion to the large trajectories of human endeavor on display in his time. And the trajectories that began in Sittler's time have continued in ours, but with even more profound twists and turns than what Sittler himself might have anticipated. His work against biblical literalism—which he saw as a fight to keep "good poetry from turning into bad science"[4]—has become even more significant as Lutheranism continues to grapple with the growth of evangelical/fundamentalist strands of Christianity in the United States. His assertions that, at any given point in human history, the fine arts (literature, film, poetry, etc.) and *not* theology or sermons might be speaking more effectively to the pathos of the human condition take on deep resonance now, when growing numbers of North Americans turn away from churches and towards movie theaters and the Internet in order to find meaningful discourse on the ambiguities of life in a postmodern age. And, perhaps most significantly, his "ecological" insistence that Christians needed to rethink such fundamental theological themes as "nature" and "grace," *not only* to address the gathering ecological crisis but also to proclaim the gospel to human beings now capable of shaping

4. Cf. Sittler's audio lecture, "His God Story."

their environment in unprecedented ways, becomes more prophetic with each passing day.

NATURE AND CULTURE

The two groups of topics upon which the still relatively small field of Sittler studies has focused most of its scholarly attention have been his theological readings of culture, on the one hand, and on the other his "pioneering" insistence upon the need for Christian theology to take ecology and environmentalism seriously, particularly the various ecological crises that were just beginning to arrive at the forefront of public consciousness in Sittler's day. Sittler was far ahead of the curve. He was writing about theology and ecology in the early 1950s, whereas Rachel Carson's *Silent Spring* was not published until 1962.

When scholars have dealt with these two areas—Sittler's theological reading of culture and his ecological theology—they've tended to treat them more or less in isolation from one another. Numerous ecological theologians have claimed Sittler as a forebear without saying much about his work as a theological critic of cultural expression; meanwhile, many fine presentations about Sittler's work on culture have not had occasion to connect that work to ecology in the environmental sense. It should be said from the outset that this is quite understandable, since Sittler himself—who always insisted that he was not a "systematic" theologian—almost never made any explicit connection between the two either, at least not in any programmatic way.

That being said, I would argue that Sittler's theological writings on environmentalism and his work on theology of culture both proceed from an integrated view of theology and aesthetics; truth and beauty were not fully separable in his work. Moreover, that integrated vision is foundational to Sittler's thought. This suggests that we can gain more insights into Sittler's ecological writings when we read them in conjunction with his theological probing into human culture—the arts, architecture, music, and especially literature—and also vice versa. It would be an argument for viewing him, if not as a systematic theologian, at least as one with an integrated set of concerns. And these concerns that animate Sittler's work largely center on the connections between what he saw as humanity's God-given mandate to care for God's creation on the one hand and, on the other hand, our God-given abilities to shape that creation by being creative, that is, by using the products of our own creative imagination (art, literature, politics, technology, and so on). In short, care for the environment and the ethics of cultural production were linked in Sittler's mind.[5]

Another way of putting it would be to say that what's in play here are two senses of creation: creation as the theological name for nature, and creation as the human ability to bring about new things within that ecological matrix. Sittler helps us to see that, because nature as God's creation is fundamental to Earth's identity, and creativity in interacting with nature (that is, producing novelty, initiating movement within nature, and indeed shaping such previously unalterable structures as mountains and atoms) has become, for better or for worse, an inescapable part of contemporary humanity's self-image, proper human care for our natural environment must be reflected in proper human exercise of our own creative capacities. And this is true whether we're talking about humanity's ability to design buildings and remove mountaintops, or our impulses to, say, produce film, write poetry, philosophize, and so on. Just as nature has, in many ways, become shapeable (or "plastic," as some environmental philosophers have put it) to human intervention, so also the realms of the arts and the humanities are deeply and necessarily caught up in our ability to live as responsible citizens of God's creation.

The theological document for which Sittler is best remembered is his 1961 speech to the third assembly of the World Council of Churches (WCC) in New Delhi, India. Sittler, who had already begun thinking about what the Christian gospel might have to do with the natural world and its ecological crises as early as 1954, used the forum of the WCC as a stage to articulate a theological vision that posited the unity of the churches, not as a catholicity derived from agreement about inner-theological resources, but as a consequence of the churches responding to a call issuing from outside their walls—the call to articulate the gospel in such a way that it names all of creation, not just the churches and not even just all of humanity, as the site of God's redemption. As Sittler puts it in the speech, "Unless the reference and power of the redemptive act [of Christ] includes the whole of man's [sic] experience and environment, straight out to its farthest horizon, then the redemption is incomplete."[6] In other words, those expecting yet another call for ecumenical table talks

5. Cf. Saler, "Creativity in Earthkeeping," 126–35.
6. Sittler, "Called to Unity," 40.

between churches found themselves listening to a theologically nuanced call for what Sittler later called "a theology of grace as applied to nature" (as distinct from a theology of nature itself, which Sittler repudiated).[7]

In contrast to such an ecologically disastrous understanding of redemption, Sittler offers a vision—which he derives mainly from Eastern Christianity, Irenaeus in particular—in which all of nature becomes an intimate part of the redemption of humanity. As he puts it, "We are being driven to claim the world of nature for God's Christ just as, in the time of Augustine, the church was driven to claim the world of history as the city of God."[8] If speaking of the redemption of history was the task of previous generations, then speaking of—indeed preaching about—our inability to responsibly conceive of history's redemption apart from the salvation of the natural realm is our task.

Indeed, in his ecological writings, particularly the sermon "The Care of the Earth," Sittler added theological and philosophical substance to this claim by making a point that has now become familiar to those of us working in the area of eco-philosophy. Sittler argued that human identity is, in a quite literal and rigidly material sense, porous to nature in such a way that it makes increasingly little sense to speak of an individual's identity apart from its matrix of interactions with its surrounding environment. As Sittler puts the matter in his essay "The Scope of Christological Reflection": "I am what I am not only as one with, among, and in self-forming transactions with men (sic); I am who and what I am in relation to the web, structure, process, and placenta of nature . . . If the self is to be redeemed by Christ, and if that self is unspecifiable apart from its embeddedness in the world as nature, then 'the whole creation' of the book of Genesis and of Romans 8 is seen as the logically necessary scope of christological speech."[9]

In other words, for Sittler—and here his debts to process theology, which he acknowledged but never systematized, become more clear[10]— to talk of a given individual as some kind of bounded set that can be ab-

---

7. Sittler, *Gravity and Grace*, 67. Sittler for the most part did not think that nature *per se* provides specific material for theology; rather, his interest was in reconceiving the relationship between nature and grace in such a way that preaching and theology could understand nature as a site of grace and redemption. For further engagement with questions of nature and grace, see the essay by Terra S. Rowe in this volume.

8. Sittler, "Called to Unity," 45.

9. Sittler, "The Scope of Christological Reflection," 196.

10. Cf. Pikhala, "Joseph Sittler and Early Ecotheology."

stracted from the hundreds of thousands of environmental interactions that make up a typical day in my life is misleading on strictly material, not to mention theological, grounds. One of the upshots is that a common view of salvation, which talks of the salvation of individuals or even human communities as a removal of these humans to some otherworldly plane abstracted from nature, is not only ecologically problematic but is actually a misconstrual of our own human identities. Sittler puts the matter nicely, and in Trinitarian terms, in his book *The Anguish of Preaching*:

> The Christian doctrine of creation acknowledges that the earth is the Lord's; the Christian doctrine of redemption by its affirmation of the incarnation declares that God who created man [*sic*] in the garden of history and nature does not will to redeem him [*sic*] in any other garden—or some angelic removal from all gardens. And the doctrine of the Holy Spirit declares that God, as sanctifier, sticks by his earthly decision as creator and redeemer. When the presence and gift of the Holy Spirit "filled the house where they were sitting" [Acts 2:2], the same spirit made clear that God does not empower a holy balloon-ascension out of nature and history, but rather that God empowers a new heaven and new earth to be constituted for humanity for whom "all things have been made new."[11]

Sittler sounded this note firmly throughout his career: only a "cosmic Christology," that is, a Christology that views the whole cosmos as the site not only of God's creation but of Christ's redemption, is a Christology adequate to speak to contemporary humanity's relationship with nature.

While he was insistent throughout his life that such a Christology was to be desired primarily for its fidelity to the biblical witness and not just because it has the advantages of speaking to the various environmental crises, he was certainly aware that these crises—e.g. pollution, loss of species diversity, and (preeminent in his mind) the ability of humanity to virtually destroy Earth's ecosystems through the use of nuclear weapons—did require a more Earth-friendly theology if Christians were to be anything other than bystanders or complicit in nature's destruction. With what I take to be an utter lack of hyperbole on his part, and in a manner evoking Luther's own rhetoric of the cosmic drama in which every human finds herself, he was in the habit of describing such a state of destruction as "damnation." This term is central to his integration of theology and culture in that the force of the term rests largely on aesthetic grounds.

11. Sittler, *The Anguish of Preaching*, 55.

This usage makes sense to the extent that we remember that for Sittler, humanity's capacity to experience beauty and its capacity to experience life as meaningful are intimately related. In an essay in his book *Gravity and Grace*, Sittler writes: "Now to know what in one's time one ought to make an effort to redeem depends on what one finds damnation to be. Redemption is a meaningful possibility only in the presence of damnation. I'm not sure that there is an absolutely clear, moral way to respond to many of the issues of our time. But I am absolutely clear that there is such a massive damnation existing in our time that if the church does not think and act on it, we will call down rightful judgment on ourselves."[12]

In the "Called to Unity" speech to the WCC, Sittler similarly appeals to damnation as the impetus behind the need to expand Christology to include the nature that is so vulnerable to human mismanagement:

> When millions of the world's people, inside the church and outside of it, know that damnation now threatens nature as absolutely as it has always threatened men [*sic*] and societies in history, it is not likely that witness to a light that does not enfold and illumine the world-as-nature will be even comprehensible. For the root-pathos of our time is the struggle by peoples of the world in many and various ways to find some principle, order, or power which shall be strong enough to contain the raging "thrones, dominions, principalities" which restrict and ravage human life. If, to this longing of all men [*sic*] everywhere we are to propose "Him of whom, and through whom, and in whom are all things," then that proposal must be made in redemptive terms that are forged in the furnace of man's [*sic*] crucial engagement with nature as both potential to blessedness and potential to hell.[13]

And finally, Sittler gives what I take to be his most comprehensive statement on what we might call the actual content of the threatened damnation in his sermon, "The Care of the Earth":

> If the creation, including our fellow creatures, is impiously used apart from a gracious primeval joy in it, the very richness of creation becomes a judgment. This has a cleansing and orderly meaning for everything in the world of nature, from the sewage we dump into our streams to the cosmic sewage we dump into the fallout.

12. Sittler, *Gravity and Grace*, 107.
13. Sittler, "Called to Unity," 45.

Abuse is use without grace; it is always a failure in the counterpoint of use and enjoyment. When things are not used in
ways determined by joy in the things themselves, this violated
potentiality of joy (timid as all things holy, but relentless and
blunt in its reprisals) withdraws and leaves us, not perhaps
with immediate positive damnations but with something much
worse—the wan, ghastly, negative damnations of use without
joy, stuff without grace, a busy, fabricating world with the shine
gone off, personal relations for the nature of which we have in-
vented the eloquent term "contacts," staring without beholding,
even fornication without finding.[14]

In Sittler's view, a proper theological appreciation for creation paves
the way for a proper ethic for the use of creation. Sittler was not a Luddite
or a "minimalist," in the sense of contemporary ecologists who advocate
for the least possible human intervention in the natural world. Com-
mendably, he was already anticipating the argument, common now in
our day since the work of Bill McKibben, that pure "nature" no longer
exists—all of the Earth's space, be it city or so-called wilderness, is now
"managed" space that bears the imprint of human shaping.[15] What Sittler is interested in doing is articulating the need for a theological appreciation for the natural world that can serve as some sort of check upon
humanity's empirically demonstrable appetite for consuming natural
resources at an unsustainable rate—for creating the conditions of its own
damnation. Amidst the shifts and contestations concerning the status of
"nature," its capacity to be a site of blessing or damnation remains central
for Sittler.

However, as we've seen, Sittler's articulation of the impact of environmental damnation draws heavily upon terms not just native to religion, or to the natural sciences. Rather, the vocabulary is also that of
the humanities—philosophy, literature, rhetoric, and so on. "Damnation"
as the failure of our human commerce with God's good creation is not
simply a description of a physically impoverished state in which our lives
and livelihood are cut short by ecological catastrophe; it also names what
we might term the existential emptiness of what it means to live in the
world alienated from what Sittler calls the "web, structure, process, and
placenta"—the life-source—of nature. Indeed, one of the earliest audio

14. Sittler, "The Care for the Earth," 97.
15. McKibben, *The End of Nature.*

recordings of Sittler in the Sittler archives is a lecture on twentieth century literature entitled, "Contemporary Witnesses to Damnation."

That Sittler would draw upon these humanistic disciplines, particularly literature, to give existential weight to the human dimensions
of unfaithful interactions with creation is not surprising. Sittler himself
made many references to the fact that he could not think about theological themes in abstraction from literature—*Moby Dick*, the works of
Joseph Conrad, Gerard Manley Hopkins, and T.S. Eliot, to name just a
few of his favorites. Indeed, he occasionally referred to himself as a "failed
literary critic." As I mentioned before, cultural critique is the other major
area of Sittler's work that has received attention from scholars; however,
based on what we have seen in his descriptions of the human dimensions of "damnation" (these "wan, ghastly, negative damnations of use
without joy, stuff without grace, a busy, fabricating world with the shine
gone off"), we can already begin to see how the two might come together
for Sittler. Just as one humanistic discipline—namely theology—had, for
Sittler, the potential to give focus to humanity's efforts to see the natural world as an inextricable part of its own identity, other humanistic,
creative, and aesthetic disciplines—literature, the arts, film, and so on—
could name and describe the vicissitudes of the human condition so as
to focus humanity's creative powers toward fostering saner dealings with
the natural world.

The arts have this power for Sittler because (in his view) at any given
point in human history the most penetrating, insightful, and evocative
descriptions of the human condition do not, perhaps unfortunately, oc-
cur in the discourse of the church through sermons, social statements,
and so on. This was not simply because Sittler was a famously cranky
assessor of the state of modern preaching, although he was that! Rather,
in any given age, Sittler observes, those artists and writers outside of the
church's walls might be the ones with the creative tools to give voice to
what Sittler constantly calls the "pathos" of an age, and to do it with more
creative verve and evocative power than that exercised by the church. In
a rather infamous quote, Sittler once said: "My whole career has been an
effort, not wholly successful, to drag my students out of the church—out
of the church!—into what's happening in the world, what is the reality of
the world, in order that their theological speech might intersect the kind
of world their listeners would take for granted."[16]

---

16. Sittler, *Gravity and Grace*, 67.

For Sittler, being responsible citizens of God's creation does not require that we hold off on the exercise of our own creative capacities—our
ability to shape, draw sustenance from, and in some respect manage the
natural world. Indeed, he saw quite clearly that we have no choice but
to be engaged in shaping the world. What faithfulness to creation does
require, though, is that we do so with a regard for creation that sees its
healthy functioning—and indeed, its beautiful functioning—as integral
to our own identities as beings created by God and redeemed by Christ,
and that we construct our ecological ethics accordingly. Moreover, the
building blocks of such an ethic do not only reside with what we might
call the "harder" ecological sciences alone, indispensable as they are.
Rather, the imaginative spirit of humanity in exercising its creation vis-
à-vis God's creation is also funded by its culture, its art—humanity's own
self-representation to itself about what is worthwhile in life. Thus, ecological ethics and close attention to culture are joined.

Here a concrete example is helpful. In a fascinating 1969 lecture entitled, "Time, Space, and the American Experience,"[17] Sittler drew upon
the work of the historian Frederick Jackson Turner (on the role of the
frontier in American life) in order to describe the non-eschatological
character of the American experience. By "non-eschatological," Sittler
meant that American culture, both in its literature and in its fascination
with technology, displays a sense that, while time is limited, space—the
new frontier—is limitless. There is always more land to claim; there
are always more boundaries to be pushed. In the lecture, Sittler draws
heavily upon American literature—Whitman, Melville, Twain, Tom
Wolfe, etc.—to describe the ways this literature reflects, in his words, the
"language-shaping vastness of this illimitable land."[18] Using example after
example from American cultural production, he shows how the idea—an
idea that's fictional, but compelling nonetheless—that available space is
unlimited has worked its way into the North American psyche.

Sittler contrasts this uniquely North American mentality to that of
the European countries that most of the settlers who came to America
left behind by choice; he acknowledges that his analysis here bypasses
the reality of Africans forcibly brought to North America, and he does
not mention those who had been native to this continent prior to European arrival. In these European countries, posits Sittler, the geographical

17. Sittler, "Time, Space, and the American Experience."
18. Ibid.

boundedness of their space meant that they had to be far more attentive to the persistence of time, the ability to invest meaning in the maintenance and care of the limited spaces they had. Absent a sense of limited space, an "eschatological" sense, Americans have not recognized the need to develop these procedures for enduring for generations in a given, bounded space.

After extensive exegesis on this point, however, Sittler moves on to consider American use of technology. Once the western shore of California has been reached and manifest destiny has reached its apparent limits, does this confronting of a geographical boundary represent a crisis in America's self-understanding? Not really, says Sittler, because what we see now in America is that the impulse to engage in ever-greater technological innovation has replaced the geographical frontier as the boundary which contemporary humanity aspires to breach at a rapid and constant clip. Technology, then, becomes a means of further eschatological evasion, the denial of boundaries and of the need to invest time—time in the sense of care for a given space across generations—with meaning.

Sittler then brings his point home: as North Americans confront the boundaries imposed upon their limitless "development" of technology by the environmental crises that have attended the rapacious development of natural spaces, we need to confront—at both practical *and cultural* levels—this deep-seated but ultimately erroneous notion in our American experience that space is unlimited, and that time will take care of itself. We need to embrace the experience of boundedness, not in order to cease development entirely (again, Sittler was aware that that is impossible), but to develop with an eye towards investing spaces with meaning and to preserve them for generations to come. And, as we have already seen, Sittler's christological vision was designed to aid in precisely that kind of revision of our consciousness: what Sittler, following St. Paul, liked to refer to as the "change in the *spirit* of our minds." This was his hope concerning the role played by theology in the ecological crisis.

I've highlighted this speech by Sittler because it represents one of the most interesting occasions in his writings where ecological concern and cultural analysis—and underneath both, a distinctive theological conception of our proper relationship to creation—come together to form an integrated analysis of how our cultural conceptions inform our ecological behavior, and vice versa. It is precisely this sort of integration and the insights it yields that make clear that Sittler was a theologian for whom discourses around art and aesthetics were necessarily and salu-tarily burdened with a powerful theological, and ethical, force.

CONCLUSION: SYSTEMATICS AND STYLE

The above examples also serve to exemplify Sittler's theological style. He is arguing that foundational theological themes—nature, grace, cre-ation, redemption—need to be rethought in light of both the ecological crisis and the growing plasticity of the natural environment to human technological interventions. However, such rethinking proceeds on the basis, not of wholesale theological innovation, but rather of recapturing heretofore submerged themes of the Christian tradition. Such themes are particularly useful to the extent that they outflank those aspects of the Western medieval, Reformation, and Enlightenment legacies that have proven to be incapable of remaining compelling in our own day (for in-stance, any facile belief in the inevitable progress of humanity towards more humane social arrangements, or any strong distinction between nature and humanity as sites of God's redemptive grace). What emerges from this sort of thinking is a kind of fragmentary, ever-provisional post-Enlightenment theology that is conversant across time and disciplines, particularly in relation to science and aesthetics. A theology that has *ta panta* (all things) as its scope will not be parochial or afraid of insights from other disciplines; rather, it will assume that any discipline that can speak authentically about what God creates and Christ redeems has its own contribution to make to our knowledge of the Christian drama of salvation, even if those contributions cannot be systematized in compre-hensive fashion.

Indeed, it may be precisely the fragmentary and provisional char-acter of Sittler's theological provocations that endear him to our century, even as these same characteristics kept his writings from finding a proper hearing among those swept up in previous eras' mania for multivolume systematic theologies. Sittler, like many of his contemporaries, recog-nized that he was living in a time when humanity at the global level was undergoing epochal sea changes in its understanding of itself and its environment. In a manner more prescient than many of his contempo-raries, however, he intuited that these transitions required a theological style that was less assertive and more probing, less "systematic" and more dialogical, less didactic and more evocative. In one of his most suggestive passages, he offers the following program for how such a theology might consider its own task:

> Knowledge gained by [humanity's] probing into the structure and process of the physical world, the accumulation of evolutionary, genetic, psychological and social facts, is so astounding as to shatter the sufficiency of older ways of specifying and relating grace and nature and, on the positive side, suggests a quite fresh and more comprehensive anthropology. While it may not be possible for our generation to fashion for its day and necessity a systematic theology and an ethics that shall have the coherent authority of the older systems, it may be possible by working obediently to wait creatively.[19]

Even as humanity suffers the uncertainty of a future in which previous givens have proven fallible, and venerable theological axioms have found themselves under increasing interrogation, the role of the ecclesial theologian proves even more valuable. It is theologians who, at their best, possess an understanding of God's redemptive activity in the world that is capacious yet fluid enough to follow our era through unprecedented twists and turns in its orientation towards the divine and the creation that the divine loves. Theology as a "creative waiting" holds, if not an exclusive claim, at least a unique potential in articulating both the pathos of our times and the address of grace to our ambiguities. To the extent that Sittler captures this potential in the writings he bequeaths to us, he remains well worth reading as we consider what needs to be retained and what needs to be reshaped in an age crying out for renewed Lutheran participation in the struggle for the soul of an Earth—and a culture—in peril.

BIBLIOGRAPHY

Martin, Jennifer Newsome. *Hans Urs von Balthasar and the Critical Appropriation of Russian Religious Thought*. Notre Dame: Notre Dame University Press, 2015.
McKibben, Bill. *The End of Nature*. New York: Random House, 2006.
Morton, Timothy. *Ecology without Nature: Rethinking Environmental Aesthetics*. Cambridge, MA: Harvard University Press, 2009.
Pikhala, Panu. "Joseph Sittler and Early Ecotheology." PhD diss., University of Helsinki, 2014.
Saler, Robert C. "Creativity in Earthkeeping: The Contribution of Joseph Sittler's *The Structure of Christian Ethics* to Ecological Theology." *Currents in Theology and Mission* 37 (April 2010) 126–35.

19. Sittler, *Essays on Nature and Grace*, 18.

———. "Joseph Sittler as Theologian of the 21st Century." *Let's Talk* 18.1, Lent 2013. http://mcsletstalk.org.

Sittler, Joseph. *The Anguish of Preaching*. Philadelphia: Fortress, 1966.

———. *The Care of the Earth and Other University Sermons*. Philadelphia: Fortress, 1964.

———. *Essays on Nature and Grace*. Philadelphia: Fortress, 1972.

———. *Evocations of Grace: Writings on Ecology, Theology and Ethics,* edited by Peter Bakken and Steven Bouma-Prediger. Grand Rapids: Eerdmans, 2000.

———. *Gravity and Grace: Reflections and Provocations*, edited by Linda-Marie Delloff. Minneapolis: Augsburg Fortress, 1986.

———. "Time, Space, and the American Experience." University of Chicago Divinity School, August 13, 1969. http://www.josephsittler.org.

von Balthasar, Hans Urs. *Presence and Thought: Essay on the Religious Philosophy of Gregory of Nyssa*. San Francisco: Ignatius, 1995.

7

Bonhoeffer, the Church, and the Climate Question

—JAMES B. MARTIN-SCHRAMM

THE LUTHERAN TRADITION CONTAINS a host of theological perspectives that can and should form the foundation of a robust Earth ethic.[1]

For example, Lutheran perspectives on the doctrine of creation emphasize God as the Creator of all. This theocentric perspective is a much-needed antidote to the rampant anthropocentrism that plagues many of us in the global north. While human beings are created in the image of God (*imago dei*), Luther emphasized that we are like God not because we substantially possess consciousness or reason, but rather because we have the capacity to relate to all of creation with the care and affection of God.[2] The Lutheran theocentric perspective emphasizes that human

---

1. This essay is an updated version of "Lutheran Theology and The Environment," which was published in Bohmbach and Hannan, *Eco-Lutheranism*, 55–63. I am grateful to Lutheran University Press for their permission to reprint a revised version in this volume. I focus on the foundations for an *Earth ethic* because I think the conventional distinction between social and environmental ethics perpetuates a dualistic way of thinking that separates nature from culture and denies the integrated nature of all reality. I prefer to talk about an ethic of ecological justice that seeks to integrate the fields of social and environmental ethics. See Martin-Schramm, *Climate Justice*, 23–44.

2. Luther writes: "If these powers [consciousness or reason] are the image of God, it will also follow that Satan was created according to the image of God, since he surely has these natural endowments, such as memory and a very superior intellect

beings are not set above other creatures but rather are set apart to serve the flourishing of all whom God has made. The *dominus* (Jesus) is the model of *dominion*. Our call is to care for our kin.

The doctrine of the incarnation similarly challenges the rampant dualism of our era. It insists on the unity of body and soul and cherishes the presence of God in all of earthly reality. Here, laid in a manger, and surrounded by animals, the finite bears the infinite. Bodies are affirmed, protected, and valued. All bodies. All that God has made has value. We are not fundamentally individuals but rather social and ecological creatures who share in common the goodness of bodily life. We cannot live without each other. We are Earth creatures. We were formed from the dust, and to the dust we will return. "[T]he Word became *flesh* and lived among us . . . full of grace and truth" (John 1:14).

One of the hallmarks of the Lutheran tradition, however, is also a robust doctrine of sin. Despite being created in the image of God and being saved through Christ's death on the cross, Luther believed all human beings remained in bondage to the powers of sin, death, and the devil. This notion that human beings are both saints and sinners (*simul iustus et pecator*) yields a realistic view of human nature that forges a middle way between naive idealism and cynical pessimism. Even in Luther's day this awareness of sinful behavior extended well beyond the individual into the systems, powers, and structures that shape human behavior and thus influence all of life. This Lutheran emphasis on the structural pervasiveness of sin enables and requires us to look carefully at the laws and policies that wreak havoc on ecological systems and jeopardize the welfare of all who are poor and vulnerable.

While the notion of being both a saint and sinner has the potential to yield a paralyzed ethic, the Lutheran doctrine of justification by grace through faith empowers Christians to live out their vocation. We are not justified by our works to "save the planet." Instead, our justification by grace through faith enables us to make our faith active in love through the care and redemption of all that God has made. As David Rhoads explains so well in his essay in this volume, this empowerment is rooted positively in God's grace and mercy rather than in human fear or despair.

My goal with this brief overview is to demonstrate that the Lutheran theological tradition provides a solid foundation for an ethic of ecojustice. As an ethicist, however, the question is whether this tradition shapes

---

and a most determined will, to a far higher degree that we have them." *LW* 1:61. Cited in Hall, *Imaging God*, 101.

what we do and who we are. We have inherited these Lutheran insights from those who have gone before us, but what have we done with this inheritance? Are these Lutheran theological traditions reflected in our communities and are we applying them to the most pressing issues of our time? What might it mean to do so?

The rest of this essay focuses on a Lutheran theologian who took his theological heritage seriously and applied it to his day. I have chosen intentionally in the title to mirror Dietrich Bonhoeffer's provocative essay on "The Church and the Jewish Question," which was published in June 1933.[3] The essay grew out of a controversial talk Bonhoeffer delivered in April 1933 to a group of pastors as the Nazi regime dictated a series of new laws that dispossessed many of their rights, especially those deemed to be Jews.[4] Bonhoeffer drew on Luther's doctrine of the two kingdoms as he addressed what he and others called "the Jewish question." I want to draw upon the same two kingdoms tradition to reflect on the climate question, which I believe is the most pressing issue we face today.

Before I begin, however, I need to say a bit more about the doctrine of the two kingdoms. Luther was not a modern person. While he was a key hinge between the medieval and modern eras, Luther had an apocalyptic worldview that tends to be off-putting to those of us schooled by the Enlightenment. When Luther looked out his window he saw God at war with Satan. Luther believed that God fought Satan in two ways—as the Creator and as the Redeemer of the world.[5] Luther believed God as Creator established the institution of government in God's "Kingdom of Temporal Authority" to enforce laws that would preserve a modicum of peace with justice in the world. It was precisely because human beings remain subject to the forces of sin, death, and the devil that their sinfulness needed to be restrained by the coercive power of the sword. At the

---

3. Bonhoeffer, "The Church and the Jewish Question," 361–70.

4. One reason this essay has been controversial is because it begins with two anti-Jewish quotes from Luther. It also contains a section which assumes Jews "must endure the curse" for rejecting Christ and asserts "[t]he conversion of Israel is to be the end of its people's sufferings." These sentiments and Luther's views are deeply offensive to Jews. Recent scholarship has revealed, however, that none of this material was contained in any of Bonhoeffer's three drafts of this essay. Larry Rasmussen was the editor for this volume in the English edition of the *Dietrich Bonhoeffer Works*. He suggests the editor of the journal, *Der Vormasch*, which published Bonhoeffer's essay in June 1933, may have added these materials. See footnotes 1 and 15 in Bonhoeffer, "The Church and the Jewish Question."

5. Luther, "On Temporal Authority," 81–129.

same time, Luther believed God as the Redeemer of the world established the institution of the church in the "Kingdom of Spiritual Authority" to use the Word of God to preach the gospel of love and mercy. In a world subject to the powers of Satan, Luther believed God protected human beings through both the work of government and the church; God was at work in *both* but it was vital to distinguish between the two and not collapse the one into the other. The church should not subsume the state, and the state should not meddle in the affairs of the church.

Dietrich Bonhoeffer brought Luther's two kingdoms tradition to bear on the rapidly rising anti-Semitism in Germany after Adolf Hitler became Chancellor on January 30, 1933. When the German parliament building, the Reichstag, was destroyed by fire on February 27, Hitler issued an emergency decree "For the Protection of People and State" that abolished virtually all constitutional rights. On March 22, the first concentration camp was opened in Dachau to incarcerate those who protested the loss of their civil rights and others who were viewed as threats to the Nazi regime. On April 7, Hitler announced the "Law for the Reconstitution of the Civil Service," which precluded any non-Aryans from functioning as civil servants. Because university professors and Protestant pastors were regarded as civil servants, this law had a direct impact on Bonhoeffer's brother-in-law, a professor of constitutional law, and Bonhoeffer's best friend, who wanted to become an ordained Protestant pastor. Both were baptized Christians with one or more Jewish parents or grandparents, which rendered them non-Aryans under this new Nazi law.

BONHOEFFER ON "THE CHURCH AND THE JEWISH QUESTION"

Bonhoeffer's talk and subsequent essay, "The Church and the Jewish Question," was divided into two parts. The first focused on how and whether the church can judge the actions of the state. The second focused on how the church should regard the status of baptized Jews in the church. This essay focuses on the first part of Bonhoeffer's comments regarding the relation of the church to the state. Bonhoeffer identified two concerns regarding the state's responsibility for promoting law and order, and he identified three possible responses to these concerns.

Bonhoeffer began by emphasizing that the church "has to affirm the state as God's order of *preservation*."[6] Bonhoeffer chose his words carefully here. He refused to refer to government as one of God's "orders of *creation*" because many conservative Lutheran theologians had used such rhetoric to promote uncritical obedience to the current governing authorities that had presumably been "instituted by God" (Rom 13:1). Bonhoeffer emphasized that governments exist to preserve what God has made from the evil forces of Satan that still abound, and that they are accountable to God for that task. This doesn't mean, however, that the church is indifferent about the actions of the state. Bonhoeffer writes: "Instead, [the church] can and must, precisely because it does not moralize about individual cases, keep asking the government whether its actions can be justified as *legitimate state* actions, that is, actions that create law and order, not lack of rights and disorder . . . In doing so the church will, of course, see the state limited in two ways. Either *too little* law and order or *too much* law and order compels the church to speak."[7]

Bonhoeffer was very clear about what constituted "too little law and order." It occurs "wherever a group of people is deprived of its rights."[8] Any state that deprives people of their legal rights is acting in a lawless manner and thus loses its legitimacy and divinely appointed authority. Bonhoeffer was referring here to all whose constitutional rights had been vitiated by Hitler's emergency decree, not only the Jews.

Bonhoeffer was also clear about what constituted "too much law and order." This occurs when the state interferes in the affairs of the Church and uses its force "to rob the Christian faith of its right to proclaim its message."[9] Here Bonhoeffer was referring to baptized Jews who had been singled out for discrimination in the "Law for the Reconstitution of the Civil Service," and to rising cries among German Christian Nazi sympathizers that demanded Jewish Christians be excluded from Protestant congregations. As noted earlier, the law prevented baptized Jews from serving as Protestant pastors since pastors were civil servants. The German Christians wanted to extend this racial discrimination further to affect all lay people who were baptized Jews or had Jewish heritage. Bonhoeffer drew a bold line in the sand and emphasized that such unlawful

6. Bonhoeffer, "The Church and the Jewish Question," 362.

7. Ibid., 363–64; emphasis original.

8. Ibid., 364.

9. Ibid.

and unchristian acts of discrimination not only violated the integrity of the Christian gospel but also violated the obligations of the state to preserve legitimate law and order.

Bonhoeffer argued that the church had three actions it could take in situations like these in which the state was preserving too little law and order in society, or was wielding too much law and order by interfering in the affairs of the church. Each action was radical in its own way for Bonhoeffer's principally Lutheran audience and community of accountability.

The first action was for the church to question the state "as to the legitimate state character of its actions; that is making the state responsible for what it does."[10] This confrontation of the state by the church was largely inconceivable among Lutherans in Bonhoeffer's day because most had radically and incorrectly separated Luther's doctrine of the two kingdoms and thus were honoring Hitler with naive, uncritical obedience.

Regardless whether the state responded to the church's questions and changed its actions, Bonhoeffer argued the second action the church should take was to engage in "service to the victims of the state's actions" because "[t]he church has an unconditional obligation toward the victims of any societal order, *even if they do not belong to the Christian community*."[11] Here Bonhoeffer was making it clear that Christians needed to come to the aid of Jews and all others who had become the victims of the Nazi state. He was not confining his concern to Jewish Christian victims of Nazi discrimination, and thus he was not allowing Christian communities to be concerned only about themselves. Bonhoeffer argued that the followers of Jesus have an obligation to all who suffer whether they confess Christ's name or not.

Bonhoeffer saved his most radical contention for last. "The *third* possibility is not just to bind up the wounds of the victims beneath the wheel but to seize the wheel itself. Such an action would be direct political action on the part of the church."[12] At this point some of the pastors left the room.[13] What Bonhoeffer was proposing was scandalous to their

---

10. Ibid., 365.

11. Ibid.; emphasis added.

12. Ibid., 365–67.

13. Eberhard Bethge reports "Leonhard Fendt, one of the most influential members of the [pastors] group and a man whose sermons Bonhoeffer admired, decided to leave as a result of the discussion." Bethge, *Dietrich Bonhoeffer*, 272. Elizabeth Raum writes, "some pastors got so upset that they left the room." Raum, *Dietrich Bonhoeffer*, 65.

ears. Not only did it violate their false understanding about the separation of church and state, what Bonhoeffer was proposing was treason-
ous—the penalty for which was death. His remarks were not idle, fuzzy,
or insignificant. To take them seriously would be to risk one's life, which
is precisely what Bonhoeffer did.

THE CHURCH AND THE CLIMATE QUESTION

I think Bonhoeffer's views on "The Church and the Jewish Question" offer a template with which to think about the church's response to global
warming and climate change. Almost ten years before the "Final Solution" was adopted at the Wannsee Conference in January 1942, I doubt
most of the pastors who attended Bonhoeffer's talk in April 1933 thought
"the Jewish question" was the most important issue facing their nation.
They probably were more concerned about Germany's poor economy,
high unemployment, and diminished stature in global politics. A parallel
is certainly true in the United States today. According to a recent poll conducted by the Pew Research Center, 75 percent of the U.S. public thinks
the economy and terrorism should be the top priorities for Congress and
the Obama administration. Only 38 percent think climate change should
be a top priority; it ranked third to last in a list of eighteen policy issues.[14]

Reality does not match public perception.

Recently the United Nations Intergovernmental Panel on Climate
Change (IPCC) issued its Fifth Assessment Report in four volumes.[15]
The following are two of their key findings:

- Human influence on the climate system is clear, and recent anthropogenic emissions of greenhouse gases are the highest in history.
  Recent climate changes have had widespread impacts on human
  and natural systems.

- Continued emission of greenhouse gases will cause further warming
  and long-lasting changes in all components of the climate system,
  increasing the likelihood of *severe, pervasive, and irreversible impacts
  for people and ecosystems.* Limiting climate change would require

---

14. Pew Research Center, "Budget Deficit Slips as Public Priority."
15. Intergovernmental Panel on Climate Change, Fifth Assessment Report.

substantial and sustained reductions in greenhouse gas emissions, which, together with adaptation, can limit climate change risks.[16]

The IPCC report emphasizes Earth's atmosphere has warmed about 1.5° Fahrenheit (0.85° Celsius) since 1880. If carbon dioxide and other greenhouse gases continue to be emitted at the current rate, temperatures will rise 3.6° F by 2050. By 2100, temperatures could be 6.7° F warmer. *This rate of warming is unprecedented in human history* and throughout most of the planet's history as well. The IPCC emphasizes failure to reduce greenhouse gas emissions will lead to food shortages due to disrupted and reduced agricultural production, refugee crises spurred by the flooding of major cities and low-lying areas, rapid extinction of many plant and animal species, and an increase in heat waves that will make it dangerous for people to be outside during the hottest times of the year. In order to limit warming to 3.6°F (2°C), the report states global greenhouse gas emissions must be reduced 40–70 percent *below pre-industrial levels* by 2050, and by the end of the twenty-first century the nations of the world would have to remove more carbon dioxide from the atmosphere than they are emitting.

It is for these reasons that I think the "climate question" is the most important issue facing us today. A recent report by the United Nations Development Program (UNDP) summarizes the situation this way:

> Climate change demands urgent action now to address a threat to two constituencies with little or no political voice: the world's poor and future generations. It raises profoundly important questions about social justice, equity and human rights across countries and generations . . . Dangerous climate change is the avoidable catastrophe of the 21st Century and beyond. Future generations will pass a harsh judgment on a generation that looked at the evidence on climate change, understood the consequences, and then continued on a path that consigned millions of the world's most vulnerable people to poverty and exposed future generations to the risk of ecological disaster.[17]

I am convinced Dietrich Bonhoeffer would share UNDP's grave concerns about the welfare of the poor and future generations. Climate change

16. IPCC Secretariat, "Headline Statements from the Summary for Policymakers." Emphasis added.

17. United Nations Development Program, *Human Development Report 2007/2008,* Summary/Overview, 2.

poses great threats to social justice and human rights for present and future generations. Bonhoeffer thought the church should confront the state when its actions resulted in too little or too much law and order. The facts are that the U.S. Senate refused to ratify the Kyoto Protocol, it has not passed any laws to reduce greenhouse gas emissions, and U.S. greenhouse gas emissions per person remain higher than almost every other nation in the world.[18] All of these facts reflect a situation of too little law and order.[19]

So has the church confronted the state? In fact, the ELCA and many of its ecumenical partners have been quite assertive through their public policy advocacy ministries with respect to global warming and climate change. By supporting regulations developed by the Environmental Protection Agency (EPA) and cap-and-trade legislation in Congress, the ELCA has joined others in pointing the way to a world with more law and order regarding global warming and climate change. The question is whether that is enough. It is easy to talk the talk, but it is harder to walk the talk. To what extent are the various expressions of the ELCA attempting to reduce their own greenhouse gas emissions? While there is no substitute for the force of law and the need for structural and systemic change, there is a place for moral witness, social responsibility, and even strategic direct political action.

I am pleased some of the twenty-four ELCA colleges and universities are concerned about global warming and climate change. I coordinate a page on the Lutherans Restoring Creation website that provides links to things ELCA colleges and universities are doing all over the nation.[20] I am proud my own institution, Luther College, is one of seven ELCA schools that have joined the American College and University Presidents Climate Commitment.[21] Luther's Board of Regents approved a Climate

18. World Resources Institute, "6 Graphs Explain the World's Top Ten Emitters."

19. National Energy Policy Institute, Energy Forum, "World Greenhouse Gas Emissions Per Capita By Country." The only mitigating factor is the decision by the EPA to regulate greenhouse gas emissions under the Clean Air Act. Predictably, however, the fossil fuel industry and its defenders have decried the EPA's proposed Clean Power Plan. Ironically, they are claiming EPA regulation of greenhouse gas emissions would constitute too much governmental intervention in economic life; that is, *too much law and order.* When this book went to press the legal status of the EPA's Clean Power Plan was pending before the U.S. Supreme Court.

20. Lutherans Restoring Creation, "Colleges and Universities."

21. The seven ELCA schools that are signatories of the American College and University Presidents Climate Commitment are: Augsburg College, California Lutheran

Action Plan in 2012 that challenges the college to reduce its campus carbon footprint 50 percent by the end of 2015, 70 percent by 2020, and to become carbon neutral by the year 2030.[22] Luther College has met its first goal through major investments in energy efficiency as well as wind and solar power.

It is also encouraging that, as of May 2016, twenty of the ELCA's sixty-five synods have passed forty different resolutions since 1999 about climate change and related issues like hydraulic fracturing, fossil fuel divestment, energy stewardship, and care for creation. Five synods thus far have urged the ELCA to include a focus on eco-reformation as the ELCA commemorates the five hundredth anniversary of the Protestant Reformation.[23] Perhaps most importantly, the 2016 ELCA Churchwide Assembly voted to work towards discontinuing any investment by the church in fossil fuel companies, and to reinvest in corporations that are taking positive steps toward a sustainable environment.[24] It is harder to know what is happening locally within nearly ten thousand ELCA congregations. I know of some congregations that have made major investments in energy efficiency and others that have hosted workshops to help members reduce emissions produced by their households and daily activities.

In my opinion lay and ordained leadership regarding climate change is critical within our synods and congregations. In some places it is strong, but in other places it is weak. For example, a few years ago I invited all three ELCA bishops in Iowa to sign on to a statement by faith leaders about climate change that was drafted by Iowa Interfaith Power & Light. Two of the bishops quickly agreed to sign, but the third declined saying he would not do anything that might cause more congregations to leave his synod. I reminded the bishop that the ELCA's "Vision and Expectations" policy expects ordained leaders "to speak on behalf of this earth, its environment and natural resources, and its inhabitants." This made no impact on the bishop. We would certainly have a different church if our Presiding Bishop disciplined pastors and bishops for failing

University, Gettysburg College, Gustavus Adolphus College, Luther College, Pacific Lutheran University, and Wittenberg University.

22. Luther College Public Information, "Luther College Sets Goals for Achieving Carbon Neutrality by 2030."

23. LRC, "ELCA Resolutions."

24. LRC, "Churchwide Votes Toward a Fossil-Free Future."

to live up to the ELCA's vision and expectations regarding peacemaking, justice, and stewardship of Earth.[25]

I think there is no question Bonhoeffer would urge the church in the United States to compel the state to live up to its obligations to protect present and future generations from the perils of climate change. He would condemn this lack of law and order in the face of climate change. I find myself thinking, however, that Bonhoeffer might supplement his counsel by asking the church whether it is living up to its obligations. If the work of the state is to preserve law and order, the work of the church is to preach the gospel of love and mercy. Drawing upon his critique of cheap grace, Bonhoeffer might claim that the church's reluctance to grapple with global warming and climate change is due to the church too often peddling a gospel of cheap grace that expects too little in terms of Christian discipleship in an era of rapid global climate change.

Regardless, Bonhoeffer insists Christian communities have an obligation to tend the victims of injustice whose wounds are inflicted by a state's actions or inactions. A quick check of the ELCA's website for disaster response reveals a long list of places within the United States and around the world where the ELCA is reaching out via its congregations, social ministry organizations, Lutheran World Relief, and ecumenical partners to bind up the wounds of those harmed by natural disasters.[26] The majority of these locations are places where people have been the victims of severe droughts, huge floods, and devastating tornadoes. Meteorologists and climate scientists emphasize that extreme weather events are becoming more frequent and more violent as global warming increases. Are we ready as a church to provide the increasingly large financial resources that will be needed as the consequences of climate change become more severe? Will we be tempted to focus our aid on our Lutheran brothers and sisters, or will we maintain our "unconditional obligation toward the victims of any societal order, even if they do not belong to the Christian community"?[27]

This brings me to the third and most radical action Bonhoeffer said the church could take in relation to the state. If the church's questions fall on deaf ears, and if the victims of the state's actions or inactions continue to increase, then Bonhoeffer said the church should seize the wheel of

25. ELCA, "Vision and Expectations."

26. ELCA, "ELCA Disaster Response: Our Work."

27. Bonhoeffer, "The Church and the Jewish Question," 365.

the state to prevent further injustice. It is no wonder some of those present left the room at this point. Such an action would be extreme in any age. Perhaps we should just dismiss Bonhoeffer on this point because his context was so different from our own. After all, in a few short months he had witnessed the loss of constitutional rights and the rise of the Hitler dictatorship. Our context is different. We live in a democratic society. Our constitutional rights are still intact. The state is not muzzling the churches. All of us have the franchise and can vote in the next election. The ELCA's public advocacy officers are still able to do their work in Congress and in several state capitals.

That said, the U.S. Congress has still not passed any legislation designed to reduce the nation's greenhouse gas emissions. In the meantime, horizontal drilling technology and hydraulic fracturing have produced a boom in U.S. oil and natural gas production. When combined with the ocean of oil trapped in Canadian tar sands, these new fossil fuel resources are leading some to dream of the day when the United States can once again be energy independent. The problem, of course, is that the combustion of these fossil fuels releases even more greenhouse gases into the atmosphere. Scientists around the world are telling us we cannot continue business as usual. There is near universal consensus that we need to reduce greenhouse gas emissions 80 percent by 2050 in order to avoid catastrophic climate change.

On the basis of these scientific findings and claims, some have resorted to civil disobedience to stop further emissions. Bill McKibben and his grassroots organization, 350.org, recently conducted sit-ins at the White House.[28] They were protesting the Keystone XL pipeline that would ferry oil derived from Alberta tar sands through the United States to the Gulf Coast where it can be refined and exported to the world. They claim tar sands oil is twice as carbon intensive as conventional oil because so much fossil fuel has to be used to mine the sand and heat the oil to remove it from the sand. In addition, vast swaths of boreal forest are being cut down to gain access to the oil that lies sequestered in the tar sands beneath.

The last time many Lutherans in the United States participated in organized civil disobedience was during the Civil Rights era. Have we

28. Tracy, "Dozens Arrested at Protest of Oil Pipeline." More recently Bill McKibben has encouraged college students to urge their institutions to divest their endowment investments in the fossil fuel industry. See "Global Warming's Terrifying New Math."

arrived at a similar time when civil disobedience should be practiced to protest the state's inaction regarding the impact of climate change on the poor and vulnerable in both present and future generations? Might it be better to try as hard as we can to get our own house in order by reducing greenhouse gas emissions within the ELCA? Yes, we should do this. Might it be better to focus on less controversial and more constructive approaches to changing public policy? Probably, but isn't that what we have been doing? Are things changing for the better? To borrow a phrase from Martin Luther King, Jr., the climate scientists are urging us to face "the fierce urgency of now"[29] In earlier years I tended to view civil disobedience with regard to climate change as self-righteous, but I find myself thinking increasingly that it is justified. At what point does one draw the line and say that things must stop? At what point does one look up and say, "I can go this far but no farther?"

Bonhoeffer asked himself these questions from 1933 through his death in 1945. At first he focused on the imposition of the Aryan Clause upon the life of the church. Along with other leaders of the confessing church movement who issued the Barmen Declaration in 1934, Bonhoeffer believed anti-Semitism within the church violated the integrity of the gospel and thus required a stand of confession. Later, he joined a conspiracy that worked to depose Hitler and ultimately tried to assassinate Hitler three times. His goal was to restore the rule of law, to secure human rights, and to bring peace to a war-torn world. He gave his life for present and future generations who were the victims of some of the worst injustice our world has ever seen. The Nazi era is a stark blight on the past, but the virulence of the climate change we face in the near future may well match or exceed it in terms of horror and destructiveness. How will we respond as Christian disciples to the most pressing issue of our day? How will the church respond to "the climate question"?

CONCLUSION

There were two questions that drove Bonhoeffer's theological and ethical reflection: "Who is Jesus Christ for us today?" and "What is the responsibility of Christians in the modern world?" I find it very interesting that Bonhoeffer told his eldest brother in a letter in January 1934: "I am becoming more convinced every day that in the West Christianity is approaching

29. King, "I Have a Dream."

its end—at least in its present form, and its present interpretation."[30] This is one reason why he was attracted to Mohandas Gandhi. Bonhoeffer thought this Hindu took Jesus more seriously than most Christians. He wanted to visit Gandhi and learn more about his nonviolent resistance movement because, in my view, he thought Gandhi and his movement for non-violent social change may be the form Christ was taking in the world in his day. Later, in *Ethics,* he asserts that values like "reason, justice, culture, and humanity" all spring forth from Christ who is their origin and the center of all reality.[31] As the confessing church gradually receded in significance, Bonhoeffer found himself working with many people who had not darkened the door of a church in a very long while, if ever. What united them was their common desire for a state that preserved justice through the rule of law and the protection of human rights. Bonhoeffer believed Christ blessed those who suffered for these values because they suffered for a just cause.[32]

I find these views of Bonhoeffer to be inspiring and hopeful because they remind me that *God is at work in the world outside the church.* God is at work in the world among all who strive on a daily basis to reduce greenhouse gas emissions and seek to help those who are harmed by climate change. God is at work among all those people and organizations who are concerned about the welfare of present and future generations imperiled by climate change. God is at work in the world among who are calling for climate justice. I think Christ is taking form in the world today in all of these ways and in many others.

BIBLIOGRAPHY

Bethge, Eberhard. *Dietrich Bonhoeffer: A Biography.* Minneapolis: Fortress, 2000.

Bonhoeffer, Dietrich. "The Church and the Jewish Question." In *Berlin: 1932–1933,* edited by Larry L. Rasmussen, 361–70. Translated by Isabel Best and David Higgins. *DBWE* 12. Minneapolis: Fortress, 2009.

———. "Church and World I." In *Ethics,* edited by Clifford J. Green, 339–51. Translated by Reinhard Krauss, Charles C. West, and Douglas W. Stott. *DBWE* 6. Minneapolis: Fortress, 2005.

———. "Letter to Karl-Friedrich Bonhoeffer." In *London: 1933–1935,* edited by Keith Clements and translated by Isabel Best. *DBWE* 13, 81–82. Minneapolis: Fortress, 2007.

30. Bonhoeffer, "Letter to Karl-Friedrich Bonhoeffer," 81.

31. Bonhoeffer, "Church and World I," 341.

32. Ibid., 346.

ELCA. "Vision and Expectations." http://www.elca.org.

Ge, Mengpin, et al. "6 Graphs Explain the World's Top Ten Emitters." *World Resources Institute*, November 25, 2014. http://www.wri.org.

Hall, Douglas John. *Imaging God: Dominion as Stewardship*. Grand Rapids: Eerdmans, 1986.

IPCC. *Fifth Assessment Report (AR5)*. http://www.ipcc.ch/report/ar5.

IPCC Secretariat. "Headline Statements from the Summary for Policymakers." *Climate Change 2014: Synthesis Report*. http://www.ipcc.ch.

King, Martin Luther, Jr. "I Have a Dream," August 28, 1963. http://www.americanrhetoric.com/speeches/mlkihaveadream.htm.

Luther, Martin. *Genesis Chapters 1–5*, edited by Jaroslav Pelikan and translated by George V. Schlink. *LW* 1. Saint Louis, Missouri: Concordia, 1958.

———. "On Temporal Authority: To What Extent It Should Be Obeyed." In *Christian in Society* II, edited by Walther I. Brandt. *LW* 45:81–129. Philadelphia: Muhlenberg, 1962.

Luther College Public Information. "Luther College Sets Goals for Achieving Carbon Neutrality by 2030." http://www.luther.edu.

Lutherans Restoring Creation. "Churchwide Votes Toward a Fossil-Free Future." http://www.lutheransrestoringcreation.org.

———. "Colleges and Universities." http://www.lutheransrestoringcreation.org.

———. "ELCA Resolutions." http://www.lutheransrestoringcreation.org.

Martin-Schramm, James B. *Climate Justice: Ethics, Energy, and Public Policy*. Minneapolis: Fortress, 2010.

———. "Lutheran Theology and the Environment: Bonhoeffer, the Church, and Climate Question." In *Eco-Lutheranism: Lutheran Perspectives on Ecology*, edited by Karla G. Bohmbach and Shauna K. Hannan, 55–63. Minneapolis: Lutheran University Press, 2013.

McKibben, Bill "Global Warming's Terrifying New Math." *Rolling Stone*, July 19, 2012. http://www.rollingstone.com.

National Energy Policy Institute. "World Greenhouse Gas Emissions Per Capita By Country," February 24, 2012. http://energyforumonline.com

Pew Research Center. "Budget Deficit Slips as Public Priority." January 21, 2016. http://www.people-press.org/.

Raum, Elizabeth. *Dietrich Bonhoeffer: Called by God*. New York: Continuum, 2002.

Tracy, Tennille. "Dozens Arrested at Protest of Oil Pipeline." *Wall Street Journal*, August 20, 2011. http://online.wsj.com.

United Nations Development Program. "Fighting Climate Change: Human Solidarity in a Divided World." *Human Development Report 07/08*. New York: United Nations, 2008. http://hdr.undp.org.

8

Issues of Interdependence in Matters of Creation

An Old Testament Perspective

—TERENCE E. FRETHEIM

THE CONCERN OF THIS volume for matters of Eco-Reformation right-fully includes reflections on related Scriptural perspectives. This essay focuses on Old Testament texts that contain remarkably mature insights with respect to environmental issues. Greater attention to these texts will enhance our ecological reflections and practices.

The biblical accounts of creation make clear that God is not the only subject of the creative process.[1] God chooses to catch up all creatures in creative activity, not only human beings. Perhaps we could even speak of divine "dependence" upon that which is not God in the ongoing task of bringing the creation into being.[2] At the least, God's engagement in the creative process is more dependent upon the creature's involvement in creation than is commonly suggested. "Interdependence" at the divine

1. Most scholars think that two major sources are used in the Genesis creation accounts, commonly named the Priestly writer (1:1—2:4a) and the Yahwist (2:4b—3:24). At the same time, what we have explicitly available to our reading is only a *combination* of sources, which may be the Priestly writer's work, using various resources, including the Yahwist, and inviting readers to read the text as a unit.

2. Fretheim, "Divine Dependence upon the Human," 25–39. See the bibliography at the conclusion of this article for helpful resources regarding related issues.

initiative may be the best language.[3] God did not (and does not) create the world alone.

A careful look at images of God in Genesis 1–2 demonstrates that creatures are engaged by God in a creative role in these chapters; they are given a more enhanced standing by God than is commonly claimed. Indeed, creaturely activity is represented in the text as indispensable in the becoming of creation. These texts suggest a relational model of creation; God and all of God's creatures have key roles in the creative process. This understanding suggests certain levels of interdependence, in which God gives power and responsibility to the creatures in the becoming of creation. This move on God's part seems to be more than an entrusting of human beings with responsibilities in the world, though it includes that. The creation is given a degree of openness and unpredictability wherein God leaves room for genuine creaturely decisions and actions that shape the future of creation.

I am particularly interested in the image of divine self-limitation for God's activity in creation.[4] Fundamental to such an understanding of the God of the Old Testament is this claim: God is in a genuine relationship with the world and, by definition, such a relationship entails self-limitation, making room for the other in relation to oneself. God gives humans and all other species power and responsibility in a way that commits God to a certain constraint and restraint in the exercise of power in the creation. This is a risky move for God, for creatures may misuse the power they have been given and thus reclamation of creation will be needed.[5] Such an understanding fits well with Eco-Reformation emphases.

3. The 2015 encyclical by Pope Francis, *Praise Be to You (Laudato Si')*, has thoughtful references to biblical texts, including Genesis 1–2. At the same time, the encyclical does not engage issues of the interpretation of Genesis 1–2 as one might have hoped, especially regarding images of God. Traditional images of God are especially prominent and shape the document in ways that, to my mind, are not true to the text. One example has to do with divine power and control. In addition, creation seems to be understood as originally harmonious and only human sin has messed things up. See my *Creation Untamed*.

4. For more detailed reflections on divine power, see Fretheim, *The Suffering of God*, 71–78; "The Self-Limiting God of the Old Testament and Issues of Violence," 159–71.

5. It is common to say that God created the world alone, with overwhelming power and absolute control, working independently and unilaterally. But, if this understanding of God in creation is correct, then those created in God's image could *properly* understand their role regarding the rest of creation in comparable terms. Such

A GENESIS OPENING

In the first chapter of Genesis, God exhibits a certain style in the work of creation. For example, creation is not a sudden one-day or one-minute affair. God does not flick the divine wrist and immediately bring the creation into being. Creation is more drawn out. God takes time in creating: there was evening and morning, one day, two days . . . The fact that the creation is brought into being over time—whether seven actual days or the days as emblematic of any stretch of time—signals that creation is to be understood as a dynamic process and not a finished product. Indeed, God does not hand over the creation to human beings and other creatures in a bright red box, commanding: "Keep it exactly like it was at the end of the sixth day." Creation is ongoing.

Moreover, this Creator God chooses not to take an "I'll do it by myself, thank you very much" kind of approach to creation. God deliberately catches up the creatures along the way to participate with God in ever new creations. On days three, five, and six, God invites all creatures to be involved in further creative acts. Already in Genesis 1:11–13, God says: "Let the earth bring forth . . . and the *earth* brought forth." The earth is the subject of the creative activity. God authorizes and the earth acts.

Or, later in Genesis 1: "Let the *waters* bring forth"; "Let the *earth* bring forth" (Gen 1:20, 24); "Let *us* create humankind" (Gen 1:26). In these cases, God is the subject of the creating verb that follows (1:20–21, 24–25, 26–27). Yet, given the pattern established by 1:11–13, this formulation does not take away from the co-participation of the waters and the earth in these acts of creation. God chooses not to do the creating alone; God invites the earth and the mountains and the microorganisms—the list seems endless—into the creative activity. And God invites humankind, each of us, into that process (1:28): Be fruitful and multiply, and fill the earth and subdue it; and have dominion. Each human being, myriads of other creatures, and even geological forces such as glaciers and earthquakes and volcanoes, have a part to play in the becoming of creation!

And that divine command echoes down through the millennia in various forms. One expression of that divine vision would be: Take care of the environment. Importantly, however, the issue for human beings is not simply a matter of the *care* of the environment, as important as care is. Sometimes we make that language sound as if our task was to

---

a perspective is all too common. That said, this perspective does not deny or set aside divine omnipotence.

keep everything the same! Rather, our task is that of being an imaginative co-creator with God, energetically and constructively working *with* the creation through continuing changes as it makes its way into the future. What we do with respect to the environment will shape the future of the world in which we live. What we do counts! It counts for the world and it counts with God.

As we have noted, these texts make clear that it is not only human beings who are blessed and invited to be fruitful, multiply, and fill the earth. God shares creative powers with all that God has made (Gen 1:22). Human beings created in the image of God are kin with all other forms of life. Such creative capacities are thus not a uniquely human prerogative. All creatures are given a vocation with respect to the future of the creation. God gives power over to all species to propagate their own kind. God has made a world in which creatures could make themselves.

This interpretation of the kind of God portrayed in Genesis 1–2 has implications for how one understands human beings as created in the image of such a God.[6] To affirm that God shares power with creatures says something very important about what it means for human beings, created in the image of God, to use power. "The democratization of the image . . . suggests an egalitarian conception of the exercise of power."[7] I believe that the "image of God" language is amonarchial, even anti-monarchical. Kings in that era would not have appreciated the social leveling that "image of God" language represents![8] Given the creation of human beings in the image of God, human behaviors are to be patterned after God's actions. One important dimension of this discussion, with significant implications for contemporary understandings of creation, is that Genesis 1–2 portrays creation in non-violent terms.[9] Such a patterning could shape how one understands human "dominion" in 1:28: namely, to embody God's concern for the flourishing of life.

6. See the extensive discussion of "image of God" in Middleton, *The Liberating Image*.

7. Ibid., 205. Middleton's understanding of "image of God" is very helpful, but may retain too many links to royal images for God.

8. See Fretheim, *God and World in the Old Testament*, 47–55.

9. See the extensive discussion of the issue of Genesis 1–2 as a combat myth, and the rejection thereof, especially in Middleton, *Liberating Image*, 250–69.

GOD CREATES A GOOD BUT NOT PERFECT WORLD

At the end of each day of creation, God looks out over the developing landscape and makes an evaluation of what the divine eyes have observed: It is good. It is very good. But, pray tell, why would God ever need to *evaluate* what *God* has done? Would not God's creative work inevitably be perfect? Well, apparently not—because God chose not to do the creative work alone. You will recall that God's first word to the newly created human beings (Gen 1:28) included this command: subdue the earth. Subdue? What would such a word mean in a time when there was not yet sin? Apparently, the earth continued to need action with respect to that which was disorderly. So, God's evaluation of the earth as "good" must not mean perfect, or there would be nothing left for human beings to subdue.

In the wake of God's creative work, there is continuing *disorder* in God's *good* world that needs to be subdued; even with all of that disorder, the creational result is still evaluated as "good." As Genesis commentator W. Sibley Towner explains: "If there were no freedom in this creation, no touches of disorder, no open ends, then moral choice, creativity, and excellence could not arise. The world would be a monotonous cycle of inevitability, a dull-as-dishwater world of puppets and automatons."[10] So, this ongoing *disorder* in the world is a *good* thing, contributing to the continuing creativity of the world. *Disorder* is an integral part of the ongoing creative process. That suggests that disorder should be subdued, but not eliminated.

I have suggested that the best sense for the verb "subdue" is "to bring order out of continuing or ongoing disorder."[11] The command to "subdue" (which has the same grammatical standing as the commands "be fruitful, multiply," and "fill the earth") assumes that the earth is not fully developed; there is no once-for-all givenness to the creation at the end of the seventh day. The command is given in the service of developing God's creation *toward* its fullest possible potential. God's creation is a dynamic reality; it is a long-term project, ever in the process of becoming—as the history of nature shows, with the Earth-changing activities of such creatures as glaciers, earthquakes, volcanoes, and tsunamis.

All of God's creatures must adapt to these changing forces and can even contribute to them. God builds this potential of creaturely becoming

10. Towner, *Genesis*, 21.

11. See Fretheim, *God and World in the Old Testament*, 52–53.

into the very structures of the world. For human beings to "subdue the earth," together with the continuing creative activity of other creatures, means that over time the creation would look quite different than it did on the seventh day. Somewhat ironically, God gives to the human being this "natural law" in order that the created order would *not* remain the same. At the same time, even this natural law must be on the move in view of the changing world. "Fill the earth"? Sorry, it's already full!

In summary, God's first move with respect to the newly created human being is a power-sharing move for the sake of a relationship of integrity (Gen 1:28).[12] God gives to the human being a key role in the ongoing development of creation, of bringing the world along to its fullest possible creative potential. A highly dynamic state of affairs is created in which the future remains open to a number of creative possibilities, among which human activity will prove crucial in the development of the world. To reiterate, taking care of the environment is not a matter of attempting to keep it unchanged.

A DIVINE RISK

Such a creative move on God's part entails risk. Human creatures in their finitude may fall short in the use of their creative potential. Or, more negatively, in their sin they may misuse the creation so that it is damaged, with more levels of disorder than creativity calls for. So, whether in view of human finitude or in view of human sin, giving the human such a high level of participation in ongoing creation is risky on God's part. God's creative work entails risks.

Eugene Peterson speaks of "the mess of creativity": "I can never be involved in creativity except by entering the mess. Mess is the precondition of creativity."[13] He adds that risks abound in every creative enterprise; indeed, risk is essential to the meaning of creativity. False starts, failures, frustrations, embarrassments—all seem to be integral to the creative process. Watch children at play! Nevertheless, out of the mess, love, beauty, and peace often slowly emerge. Creative activity is itself finally unmanageable. When the Spirit of God is at work, you cannot apply time management techniques or hire efficiency experts. To be a creator entails an almost infinite tolerance of messiness, of inefficiency. The moment

12. Ibid., 13–22.
13. Peterson, *Under the Unpredictable Plant*, 63.

that tidiness and strict orderliness become the rule of the day, creativity is inhibited and the appearance of the genuinely new slows way down. For some disorder to persist beyond God's originating creative activity is necessary for the creative development of the creation. On the other hand, too much disorder can create havoc. The biblical account seems to thread a dynamic, evolving way *between* these poles, allowing humans tremendous latitude in shaping the continuing face of the planet and its life, within God's larger creative activity. So, subdue the earth! For example: control forest fires!

This theme of God's creating in and through existing messy matter continues in Genesis 2, where God assumes human form (and later in Gen 3:8, God will go walking in the evening breeze). God comes incredibly close in the creative process by molding the first human being out of the dirt. That is a wonderful image of God. God gets down on the ground to gather and shape the dust into a human being. Getting dirt under the divine fingernails! The ground (*adamah*, a play on *adam*) proves to be a crucial ingredient for the creation of the human. Human beings are not created "out of nothing," but out of the ground, an already existent creature, a creature that has creative capacities (already voiced in Gen 1:11–13, 20, 24). The common notion that the Creator is (completely) external to the creation in the creative process is not present here. God is imaged as a potter who molds a human being (and animals, Gen 2:19) out of the dust of the earth; God here works from *within* the world, not on the world from without.[14]

Moreover, God is further imaged in this text as a surgeon; God puts Adam to sleep, removes a part of his body (probably his side, not just a rib) and creates a woman. We often forget that, short of some kind of magic, this would have been a bloody process indeed! Creation is messy! The testimony of Genesis 1 to the *goodness* of all forms of material reality is undergirded in Genesis 2 with respect to God's *tactile* engagement with the Earth's creatures.

Again, God is creating from *within* creation, not from without. God is bringing new creatures into being with the help of already existing creatures. Creation is an *interdependent* act. Presumably, God could have simply spoken a word and "poof," a new creature would have been brought into existence—a not uncommon way of thinking about creation, unfortunately. But that is not God's way in the testimony of this

14. Most scholars these days do not take an "out of nothing" approach to Genesis 1–2. For initial reflections on this question, see Fretheim, *God and World*, 34–40.

text. From the first moment and on, God works with what is already there in creating something new. From the beginning, God chooses to create interdependently.

The environmental implications of God's creating in this earthy and breathy way are considerable. Briefly, God deeply values the messy stuff of earthy life; it is creative material out of which new creatures can (continue to) be brought into being. The text makes clear that this earthy stuff is indispensable for developing new creatures, for developing creation as we know it, including human life. And, if this earthy stuff is of value to God, certainly it is of value to human beings and all creatures who are engaged in creative activity.[15]

In summary, in these Genesis 1–2 texts God speaks *with* already existing creatures and involves them in creative activity. This is not immediate creation; it is mediated creation. This is creation from within rather than creation from without. God's creating here is not presented as a unilateral act; it is multilateral. God's creating is not done alone; God involves already existing creatures in ongoing creative activity. God chooses interdependence rather than independence in continuing to bring the creation into being. Given the common "in control" understanding of God, these types of creative moves are remarkable *for God* (!) and they need more attention than they have been given in the discussion regarding creation.

All of God's creatures have a genuine *vocational role* in enabling the creation to become ever new.[16] That story has certainly been repeated again and again over the millennia as ever new creatures come into existence, mediated by the activity of existing creatures, from volcanoes to earthquakes to typhoons. How creative the creatures are! Messy, but creative! Much of the beauty that we see in the natural world around us is due to the ongoing activity of such diverse creatures. Indeed, many of the most spectacular vistas of nature are due to the creative activity of such creatures (e.g., mountains and valleys carved out by glacial movement over the millennia), which in turn is due in significant part to

---

15. This theme stands against any notion that continuing creation beyond Genesis 1–2 is really only "preservation." Moreover, newness is a reality in the *ongoing* life of the world, and creation—from the beginning—entails working with already existing creatures. See Fretheim, *God and World,* 1–21.

16. See Fretheim, *God and World,* 273–84, regarding the word "vocation" for the activity of God's creatures. The language of vocation should be used more often for all of God's creatures and not only for humans.

God's decision to work interdependently rather than alone. So, issues of environmental protection and care have implications for the continuing creativity potential of the world.

Activity on behalf of the environment is not simply a human task; all creatures are caught up by God in the continuing work of creation. Now, this will certainly be a messy process, so one ought not look at the creational results and expect to use the word "orderly" or "neat" (the dominant use of "orderly" language for describing the rhythm of Genesis 1–2 can be misleading[17]). Indeed, as we have stated, messiness enhances the creative potential of the environmental activity.

In this connection, it might be noted that the phrase "natural disasters" may be a misnomer.[18] Natural "disasters" certainly result in much damage to one or another aspect of the created order, but these events also have the potential of enhancing the beauty of creation. They harbor deep creative potential. It appears God purposely created a world filled with what humans call natural disasters, precisely in the interests of creativity and beauty.

CREATION AND SUFFERING

For earth and waters to so participate in creation means that the process will be disorderly. Indeed, much *suffering* (for all creatures) will follow in the wake of the world's becoming. And inevitably so! Earth and waters are not machines that work in precise and predictable and orderly ways. God has created such a dynamic world; not only earthquakes and tsunamis, but storms, bacteria, and viruses have their role to play in the becoming of the world—in both a pre-sin world and a post-sin world. Because humans are a part of such an interconnected world, we may get in the way of the workings of these creatures and get hurt by them. The potential for "natural evil"[19] was present from the beginning of God's *good* creation.

These creatures of God function in an orderly process in many ways, but randomness also plays a role; in the words of Eccl 9:11, "time and

17. For some detail, see Middleton, *The Liberating Image*, 278–89.

18. For a lengthy discussion, see Fretheim, *Creation Untamed*. Given anthropogenic climate change, moral evil and natural evil may no longer be distinguishable, in certain situations.

19. This may not be the best language to use, but it is common in theological reflection and makes an important distinction between natural evil and moral evil.

chance happen to them all." Randomness is a God-given part of the created order, even with all the accompanying risks, at least in part because
it enhances Earth's creative potential. Do you have room in your understanding of God for risk and chance? God created a world filled with
dangers. Think about water; it is necessary for life, but it is also dangerous—and not just because of sin, but also because of finitude. Or, think
of the law of gravity; it is also indispensable for life, but it works on either
side of a cliff! Let me repeat: God created a dangerous world, and at least
one reason for God's creation of that kind of world is the increase in the
potential for creativity and beauty. However costly it might be.

In summary, what are the environmental implications of the fact that
God in Genesis 1–2 calls upon existing creatures to bring about still other
creatures, indeed entirely new creatures? Once again, the text demonstrates the immense value of all creatures *for God*, not least a remarkable
value for the process of continuing creation. This move is so important
because *God* determines to involve these creatures in the creation of still
further creatures. Without the help of all beings, God's creation would
not live up to its potential of becoming; it would not be nearly the creative
place it is and continues to be. Indeed, without the help of all of God's
creatures, this world would be a much less beautiful and less creative
place. God has decided to take an *interdependent, relational* route in the
continuing development of the creation by involving such creatures in
addition to human beings. And God has decided not to micromanage or
control their work. One effect of such a creational dynamic in the world's
becoming may be not only messiness, but horrendous suffering. As the
book of Job teaches us, especially as seen in the creation chapters (Job
38–41), suffering has no necessary relationship to sin. Even without sin,
suffering is an integral part of life and its becoming.[20]

GOD'S CREATION MAY NOT BE "GOOD"

Moving back into Genesis 2, God's own observations of the creation lead
to God's preliminary conclusion that something is not good. God says
(Gen 2:18): "It is not good that the man should be alone." *God* has created
something that is not good! And so God has to make further creative
moves before creation could be called good. In this case, God chooses to

20. For a study of Job's understanding of creation, see Fretheim, *God and World*,
219–47.

involve the human being in moving the creation from not good to good. Whereas God does all the evaluating of creatures in Genesis 1, God now gives to the human being a key evaluative role in the next stages of creation. God brings all the animals before the newly created human being and asks for an evaluation as to whether any of them would help meet the God-identified problem of human aloneness. The *human* makes an evaluative move that shapes the next stages of creation. The animals: No, they won't do. The woman: Yes! This, again, is a power-sharing, creative move on God's part.

God had determined that something was not good and decided that additional creative work was needed; a partner was needed for the first human. But God chose not to make all the creative decisions relative to this development. God drew the human into the evaluative process and, in the language of Genesis 2:19, "whatever the man called every living creature, that was its name." God determined that the human being was to be a key decision-maker with respect to the future shape of the creation.

This evaluative role given to the human by God is not a one-time event. That responsibility continues through the ages. God continues to draw in the human creatures to participate in the *ongoing* evaluation of creation. This role is already revealed in God's first word to the newly created human being in Genesis 1:28, wherein God makes a remarkable, power-sharing move. God says, in effect: "I am not going to retain all power to myself; I am giving you something to do and the power with which to do it." God chooses to share power with the creature. What might it mean that the first thing, the *first* thing that God says to the newly created human beings is a sharing of power with that which is not God? God's first move with humankind is *an explicit act of self-limitation.*[21] What human beings do and say counts in the shaping of the future of the creation. Human words and actions make a difference with respect to the future of all creatures, not just other human beings.

In sum, God so *values* every human being that God will entrust them with tasks and responsibilities beyond their present knowing. That evaluation of God may run something like this: what you do and say about the environment is good, but *the way in which you say it and do it* may make the "what" even better. Style counts with God and it makes a difference with respect to the shape of the future of creation.

---

21. This divine self-limiting move continues with the divine rest in Genesis 2:1–3.

CREATIONAL RESPONSIBILITIES AND THE SHAPE OF THE FUTURE

How we think about the care of creation is closely associated with how we think about the future, the future of the world. In fact, how we think about the future is probably the most decisive factor with respect to our perspective on the human role in the care of the environment.

A friend of mine had a close call in a car accident and his reply was: "It wasn't my time." As if there were some specific time determined for everyone when they would die! Smoke three packs of cigarettes a day; my time is all set. Take as many risks as you like; the time is all set. That's not faith, that's fate.

Through the powers that human beings have been given by God, they are capable of giving shape to their future and to the future of others. A text such as Jeremiah 22:1–5 illustrates this perspective:

> Thus says the Lord: Go down to the house of the king of Judah and speak there this word, and say: Hear the word of the Lord, O King of Judah sitting on the throne of David—you, and your servants, and your people who enter these gates. Thus says the Lord: Act with justice and righteousness, and deliver from the hand of the oppressor anyone who has been robbed. And do no wrong or violence to the alien, the orphan, and the widow, or shed innocent blood in this place. For if you will indeed obey this word, then through the gates of this house shall enter kings who sit on the throne of David, riding in chariots and on horses, they, and their servants, and their people. But if you will not heed these words, I swear by myself, says the Lord, that this house shall become a desolation.

According to this neglected text, two specific future possibilities are open to king and people, depending upon their exercise of justice. What people do and say and pray regarding matters of justice and the environment can have a genuine effect on the shape of their future. If they do obey this word, they will experience one kind of future; if they do not, they will experience another kind of future. At the same time, as I have noted elsewhere, "the actions of the people will not only affect their own future, they will affect God's future as well. What God will do in the future is said to depend at least in part on what the people do. Even more, for both of these options to have integrity, they must be genuine possibilities, for both God and people."[22]

We could say that the future is both settled and unsettled, even for God. There will be a new heaven and a new earth; God will raise you and me from the dead. But between now and then, various courses of action regarding, say, peace, justice, and the integrity of creation will help shape the character of that future. The creating of the new heaven and earth could be said to be a "quilt-making" enterprise.[23] Your "patch" will be included—what will it be like? How lovely or sophisticated will it be? What people do makes a difference; it makes a difference to God and to the *nature of the future* of their world. Our words and deeds with respect to matters of creation will make a difference with respect to the shape the future takes, indeed what the shape of the new heaven and new earth will be.

Sometimes it is thought that God is in total control (an ambiguous word that is much-misused; think of, say, absolute control, crowd control, ultimate control, and controlling) of the future and that, for example, on the way into that future, "God will not give you any more than you can handle." Well, God may not give you more than you can handle, but the tyrants of this world like Hitler might do so!

Sometimes an unqualified language creeps into our talk about God and the future: The future is in God's hands; the future is settled. I think that that kind of statement about God may lead to incoherence in the minds of those who hear it. What difference then do our words and deeds make? Perhaps if we regularly qualified such a statement—the future is *ultimately* in God's hands—we would be clearer. But, if we just say that the future is in God's hands, people can easily conclude that it makes little, if any difference what they do about matters of, say, justice or the environment. God has got the future all mapped out and what humans do is finally irrelevant.

There are those who think that Earth is in its last minutes of existence. God is about to wrap up the history of the world in our lifetime, and some people have been "clued in" regarding its final stages. So, care for the environment is largely irrelevant. Such a perspective could be called a "theology of demolition." We don't need to take any care for the environment; it's going to be destroyed soon anyway. We don't need to take any

22. Fretheim, "Divine Dependence upon the Human," 33–34.

23. Quilt-making is a complex metaphor. It should be made clear that the patches of such quilts have different shapes, sizes, and qualities.

special care of the less fortunate; heaven will be theirs soon, in any case. This perspective is disempowering. Nevertheless, we will continue to be subjected to speculation about the end of the world, as we have been for centuries. We need to remember that how we think and speak and act about God and the future, including the future of the environment, can have a deep effect on the shape of the present/future of the creation.

Such a perspective could also lead to a certain level of passivity relative to, say, one's own life and health. A member of my family died of colon cancer because for many months he ignored the symptoms and refused to see a doctor, claiming that God would take care of him. His future was in God's hands. Remember when the Devil tempted Jesus (Luke 4:9–13): "Jump off the pinnacle of the temple and God will save you from the rocks below. Jump, Jesus, jump; do you trust God to take care of you or not!?" Jesus responded: "You shall not tempt the Lord your God." Prepare your own list: I will not prepare for my retirement; I will not care for the environment; I will not worry about injustice. I submit that all such behaviors are a violation of Jesus' word: you shall not tempt the Lord your God. *Ultimately*, yes, we put ourselves in the hands of God, but in the meantime we must consider how people might hear such language. What we do and say makes a difference, not only for our own life and that of the Earth; it makes a difference to God. In addition, God continues to decide not to do everything all by Godself. God catches us up in this work—what we do counts with respect to the environment and the shape of the future of this world. And, it counts with God.

I conclude with a homiletical note. *You* are God's garden of imagination. God the creator *values* you and every other creature for the creation you are, for the gifts you have, for the imaginative possibilities you bring to moments of life. God has chosen to work interdependently with you and other creatures; may that work among you proceed with energy and creativity.

BIBLIOGRAPHY

Bauckham, Richard. *The Bible and Ecology: Rediscovering the Community of Creation*. Waco, TX: Baylor University Press, 2010.
Brown, William P. *The Seven Pillars of Creation: The Bible, Science, and the Ecology of Wonder*. New York: Oxford University Press, 2010.
Brueggemann, Walter. *Genesis*. Interpretation. Atlanta: John Knox, 1982.
Davis, Ellen. *Scripture, Culture, and Agriculture: An Agrarian Reading of the Bible*. New York: Cambridge University Press, 2009.

Edwards, Denis. *Ecology at the Heart of Faith*. Maryknoll, NY: Orbis, 2006.

Francis. *Praise Be to You (Laudato Si'): On Care for Our Common Home*. San Francisco: Ignatius, 2015.

Fretheim, Terence E. *Creation Untamed: The Bible, God, and Natural Disasters*. Grand Rapids: Baker Academic, 2010.

———. "Divine Dependence upon the Human: An Old Testament Perspective." In *What Kind of God? Collected Essays of Terence E. Fretheim*, edited by Michael J. Chan and Brent A. Strawn, 25–39. Siphrut: Literature and Theology of the Hebrew Scriptures. Winona Lake, IN: Eisenbrauns, 2015.

———. "Genesis and Ecology." In *The Book of Genesis: Composition, Reception, and Interpretation*, edited by Craig A. Evans et al., 638–708. Vetus Testamentum Supplements 152. Leiden: Brill, 2012.

———. *God and World in the Old Testament: A Relational Theology of Creation*. Nashville: Abingdon, 2005.

———. "The Self-Limiting God of the Old Testament and Issues of Violence." In *What Kind of God? Collected Essays of Terence E. Fretheim*, edited by Michael J. Chan and Brent A. Strawn, 159–71. Siphrut: Literature and Theology of the Hebrew Scriptures. Winona Lake, IN: Eisenbrauns, 2015.

———. *The Suffering of God: An Old Testament Perspective*. Overtures to Biblical Theology. Minneapolis: Fortress, 1984.

Habel, Norman C. *An Inconvenient Text: Is a Green Theology of the Bible Possible?* Adelaide, SA: ATL Press, 2009.

Habel, Norman C., and Peter Trudinger, eds. *Exploring Ecological Hermeneutics*. SBL Symposium Series 46. Atlanta: Society of Biblical Literature, 2008.

Habel, Norman C., and Shirley Wurst, eds. *The Earth Story in Genesis*. Earth Bible 2. Sheffield: Sheffield Academic, 2000.

Hiebert, Theodore. *The Yahwist's Landscape: Nature and Religion in Early Israel*. New York: Oxford University Press, 1996.

Middleton, Richard J. *The Liberating Image: The Imago Dei in Genesis 1*. Grand Rapids: Brazos, 2005.

Peterson, Eugene H. *Under the Unpredictable Plant: An Exploration in Vocational Holiness*. Grand Rapids: Eerdmans, 1994.

Santmire, H. Paul. *The Travail of Nature: The Ambiguous Ecological Promise of Christian Theology*. Philadelphia: Fortress, 1985.

Simkins, Ronald A. *Creator and Creation: Nature in the Worldview of Ancient Israel*. Peabody, MA: Hendrickson, 1994.

Towner, W. Sibley. *Genesis*. Westminster Bible Companion. Louisville: Westminster John Knox, 2001.

Westermann, Claus. *Genesis 1–11: A Commentary*. Translated by John J. Scullion. Continental Commentaries. Minneapolis: Augsburg, 1984.

9

The World Is about to Turn

Preaching Apocalyptic Texts for a Planet in Peril

—BARBARA R. ROSSING

My heart shall sing of the day you bring.
Let the fires of your justice burn.
Wipe away all tears, for the dawn draws near,
And the world is about to turn!

"CANTICLE OF THE TURNING," RORY COONEY[1]

THE JOYFUL "CANTICLE OF the Turning," a musical setting of Mary's Magnificat to an Irish tune, proclaims the message of hope at the heart of apocalyptic biblical texts: The world is not about to *end*. Rather: the world is about to *turn*.[2]

---

1. Cooney, "Canticle of the Turning."

2. This essay is dedicated to the memory of Richard R. Caemmerer Jr., artist, founder of the Grunewald Guild, visiting professor at the Lutheran School of Theology at Chicago from 1991–2010, with whom I co-taught "Visualizing Revelation" on art and apocalypse. Notre Dame University's "Human Distinctiveness" Project, with support from the John Templeton Foundation, provided funding for a research leave during which this essay was written.

A "revolution of the imagination" is how John Collins describes the apocalyptic worldview.[3] Apocalypses are essential to our preaching. They empower radical witness. They give us a sacramental imagination, taking us on a journey into the heart of God's vision for our world. Apocalypses pull back a curtain so people can see the world more deeply—both the beauty of creation and also the pathologies of empire, experienced as plagues against creation. Apocalypses show us the throne of God, the Alpha and Omega. Then they take us back to our lives with our vision transformed, to join with victims of injustice who cry out, "How long O Lord?" (Rev 6:10), and to live according to an alternative community vision.

We need such a radical transformation of our imaginations for Eco-Reformation today. In a time of climate injustice, greed, food insecurity, environmental racism, species extinctions, ocean acidification, and ecological trauma, the visionary world of apocalypses can renew our hope. They can help us see both the perils we face and the urgency of God's promised future, turning the world for justice and healing, "on Earth as in heaven." The preacher cultivates an apocalyptic imagination by helping people recognize God's future breaking into the present, even in times of despair.

My goal is to encourage preaching on apocalyptic scripture so people hear the urgent good news: God's kingdom is drawing near. New birth is dawning on Earth. Scripture is coming to life. Healing is springing forth. The world is about to turn. And God's people participate in that apocalyptic turning, as living witnesses to the hope and healing Eco-Reformation can bring.

PREACH HOPE IN A CULTURE OF FEAR

We preach in a culture "full of fear."[4] The world itself looks increasingly fearful and apocalyptic to many people. As Karoline Lewis notes, hearers of sermons bring a sense that "there *are* signs in the sun, the moon, and the stars, and on the earth distress among nations . . . people *are* fainting from fear and foreboding of what is coming upon the world."[5] Preaching on texts such as Jesus' apocalyptic discourse in Luke 21:25–36 "has

3. Collins, *The Apocalyptic Imagination*, 283.

4. Robinson, "Fear."

5. Lewis, "Why Advent?"

to start with naming what appears to be all too true." But it cannot stop there. The preacher must empower people to move beyond fear to hope.

Fear is not the only apocalyptic pitfall. When preaching on biblical apocalyptic texts we also run up against dualism, determinism, moralism, judgmentalism, otherworldliness, end-times violence, escapism, heavenism, doom and gloom: if we are not careful, these are the messages our hearers will take home from the scripture readings, especially if we frame them as primarily about the end of the world. For the ecological preacher, additional perils include the premillenialist interpretation of environmental calamities as biblical "signs" predicting the end-times, or worse, an environmental fatalism, despairing that "it's too late, there's nothing we can do."

Polling data documents the problem: people do not hear apocalypses as a message of hope for Earth. If our goal is to give people hope for this world's future—for God's healing and liberation in their lives and in our world—then our sermons need to do a better job. Pope Francis' visit to the United States in September 2015 increased acceptance of the science of global warming among all Americans, with biggest gains among Evangelical Christians.[6] Yet several recent polls confirm a strong American tendency to correlate apocalyptic end-times interpretations of the Bible with denial of global warming. According to a poll conducted in 2014 by the Public Religion Research Institute and the American Academy of Religion, "the number of Americans who believe that natural disasters are evidence of the apocalypse has increased" over the past couple years. More white evangelical Protestants attributed the severity of recent natural disasters to the biblical "end times" (77%) than to climate change (49%). Black Protestants agreed that natural disasters are a sign of the apocalypse (74%), while they also say they are evidence of climate change (73%).[7] These results echo a 2013 study by sociologists David C. Barker and David H. Bearce, "End-Times Theology, the Shadow of the Future, and Public Resistance to Addressing Global Climate Change," which was widely reported in *The Huffington Post*, *Raw Story* and other publications, correlating climate change denial with Christian end-times belief.[8]

While I would quibble with the specific phrasing of some of the polls' questions, the correlation between many American Christians'

6. See *The Francis Effect*.

7. "Believers, Sympathizers and Skeptics," 23.

8. Barker and Bearce, "End-Times Theology," 267–79; see Dolan, "Belief in Biblical End-Times."

end-times beliefs and climate change denial is irrefutable. One of the most extreme climate change deniers in the U.S. Congress, Missouri Synod Lutheran Rep. John Shimkus from Illinois, brought his Bible to a March 2009 hearing of the U.S. House Subcommittee on Energy and Environment. Shimkus cited God's promise to Noah in Genesis 8:23, as well as Jesus' apocalyptic discourse in Matthew 24:31, to argue against the existence of human-caused global warming. Such entrenched denial raises the question of how religious communities can hope to address climate change if large percentages of people, including elected officials, attribute natural disasters to biblical end-times rather than to climate change.

Exacerbating the problem is the whole "Left Behind" pre-millennial dispensationalist story, which claims that Christians have an escape from Earth prepared for them in heaven.[9] Another part of the problem is our culture's fascination with secular apocalyptic narratives. People hear apocalyptic end-times elaborations not only in religious communities but also in the broader culture, through movies, television shows, political speeches, and Internet sites. Dystopic apocalypses—*The Hunger Games*, zombie apocalypses, and more—shape people's apocalyptic imaginations.

Part of the problem is also the choice of scripture texts in the lectionary, the concentrated way the church assigns apocalyptic readings for November and December, ending the church year and leading into Advent. We saturate parishioners with Day of the Lord imagery, divine vengeance, and weeping and gnashing of teeth (one of the Gospel of Matthew's favorite phrases). The most difficult sequence of readings leads directly from Matthew's apocalyptic discourse into the first and second Sundays of Advent, with the exhortation to hasten the day "when the earth will burn," from 2 Peter 3—truly the most dangerous text, ecologically, in our entire lectionary.[10] A pastor candidly said, "I hate November," which means I hate preaching on the fear-filled texts the lectionary serves up in November.

PREACH APOCALYPSES AS NARRATIVE: IMAGINING OURSELVES IN THE STORYLINE

"How do they see the end of the world?" This is the question the butterfly scientist asks protagonist Dellarobia Turnbow in Barbara Kingsolver's

9. Rossing, *The Rapture Exposed*.
10. See Rossing, "Hastening the Day When the Earth Will Burn?"

novel about climate change, *Flight Behavior*. Faced with the rainiest winter in memory, floods, and a disruption in monarch butterflies' migration, residents in Dellarobia's rural Appalachian community doubt the scientist who tries to tell them it's climate change. It does not fit with their reading of the Bible or their understanding of God. Dellarobia tells the scientist, "People can only see things they already recognize."[11]

Biblical apocalypses persuade not by logical proofs or arguments, but by creating a "world of vision."[12] They use highly pictorial and visionary language. They give people new eyes to recognize deep truths about the world, empowered with a sense of urgency and hope. They draw on stories from the prophets, the Exodus, and Israel's past to help people "see things they already recognize," to use Kingsolver's words. Apocalypses were written at crucial times in Israel's life, to offer what liberation theologian Pablo Richard calls a "spirituality of resistance" in a time of political crisis. They were written to rebuild people's imaginations, when all seemed hopeless.[13] Apocalypses take the form of a narrative, "once upon a time," drawing us into a dramatic story of conflict between God and evil. So it is important for preachers to know how to tell the big story we are in: how to rebuild people's scriptural imaginations for recognition, for hope, and for radical turning. Where are we located in the apocalyptic narrative?

Let's begin with Revelation 12, one of Martin Luther's favorite apocalyptic scenes, a story that can help us locate ourselves in God's big story, both spatially (*topos*, "place," Rev 12:6, 8, 14) and chronologically (*kairos*, "time," Rev 11:18; 12:12).[14] This apocalyptic story can furnish a framework for preaching other apocalyptic texts, whether from the gospels or Pauline epistles, or Revelation. This story of the heavenly woman of Revelation 12 comes at the center of the book of Revelation. It is one of the most deeply symbolic and mythic of all apocalyptic texts in the Bible. Few Protestants preach on Revelation 12, since this chapter does not appear in the Revised Common Lectionary. (Roman Catholic churches assign her story for the Day of the Virgin of Guadalupe, December 12, and

---

11. Kingsolver, *Flight Behavior*, 282.

12. Schüssler Fiorenza, *Revelation*, 22.

13. Richard, *Apocalypse*, 3–4.

14. On *topos* and spatial eschatology, see Westhelle, "The Way the World Ends," and *Eschatology and Space*.

for the Assumption of Mary, August 15.) It was a favorite of mystics such as Hildegard of Bingen, William Blake, and many poets and artists.[15]

The story opens with a pregnant heavenly woman in the throes of labor. She gives birth to a son, the Messiah, Jesus. When a dragon chases the woman, she is given two wings of a great eagle to escape to a safe place. Both the woman and the dragon are called "signs" (*sēmeia*, 12:1, 3), underscoring the symbolic character of these stories and their imagery. Into this story of the woman's childbirth and rescue in the wilderness, Revelation sandwiches an even more fantastic story, the epic heavenly battle story of the "dragon-slayer."[16] The archangel Michael, a figure familiar from the biblical book of Daniel, defeats the dragon and his angels, throwing them down from heaven to Earth. (This story is appointed for the Feast of St. Michael and All Angels, September 29.)

Time is not linear in apocalypses. Although these scenes come in the middle of the book of Revelation, they are most likely flashbacks. Most scholars think the victory scenes in Revelation 12 portray Jesus' already-accomplished victory through the cross and resurrection—when God defeated the dragon and evil once for all. Heaven rejoices over the defeat of the dragon (Rev 12:10–12). God's people rejoice because their accuser no longer has a place in the heavenly courtroom from which to bring accusations (Rev 12:10). But Earth is not yet able to rejoice. "Alas for you, earth and sea," a voice from heaven laments (Rev 12:12).[17]

Who is the dragon? In Revelation's time, the dragon represented all the powers behind the reality of evil, namely the deception embodied in the Roman imperial system with its predatory economic and military regime. John of Patmos regarded Rome as idolatrous, violent, and deceptive, enslaving peoples and lands. He modeled the dragon on Hebrew Bible references to foreign nations as dragons (Egypt as dragon, Ezek 32:2).

Who is the heavenly woman? In the biblical palette of imagery, she probably represents the people of God, depicted in cosmic terms. For Luther, she represents the church. Countering Roman Catholic interpreters in the sixteenth century who viewed her as the Virgin Mary, Luther wants us to see ourselves as the heavenly woman—engaged in a great struggle,

15. See Huber, *Thinking and Seeing With Women in Revelation*.

16. Sanchez, *From Patmos to the Barrio*.

17. I translate the Greek word *ouai* as "Alas" rather than the standard "Woe," in order to emphasize that this is a lament, not a curse against Earth. See Barbara Rossing, "Alas for the Earth."

yet protected and nourished by God. Luther even wrote a hymn about this woman, "To Me She's Dear, the Worthy Maid."[18]

John's story of the heavenly woman in Revelation 12 can give preachers guidance for how to preach apocalyptic hope for eco-reformation today. First, Revelation persuades by using images and narrative. It evokes people's visual imagination. We too live in a culture of stories and images; our culture, like the ancient cultures of the Bible, is saturated with story. The Romans told an eschatological story of eternal Rome as "empire without end." Biblical apocalypses challenged that core imperial narrative. Today, hearers of our sermons have multiple competing narratives in which to see themselves. One core story is what climate activist Naomi Klein calls "winner-take-all capitalism." The crisis of climate change represents not just an environmental and economic crisis, but a "profound narrative crisis for Western civilization," raising questions of worldview, spirituality, and how we understand our relationship to nature.[19] In order to challenge the narrative of extractive capitalism, as Klein underscores, we need a different narrative, a different social imaginary.

Over and against the Roman imperial narrative—proclaimed in sculptures, monuments, and propaganda for all to see—New Testament authors boldly positioned their counter-world perspective, declaring an imminent "end." John of Patmos re-told the Exodus story in his own time by scripting Rome as Egypt, and Jesus as a new Moses. He called on people to exit that unjust imperial system that was coming to an end. For us today, the Bible can declare an "end" to our own cultures' multiple negatives—whether to the narrative of unfettered economic growth, unlimited fossil fuel consumption, the endless war on terrorism, or to other eschatological narratives. Apocalyptic imagination creates a counter-world, because "hope's greatest power is to negate the negatives of present experience," as Richard Bauckham notes.[20]

PREACH NEW BIRTH

The second point to note in the story of Revelation 12 is that the pregnant woman is in the throes of giving birth. This is good news. Birthing and

18. *LW* 53 ("Liturgy and Hymns").

19. Mowe, interview of Naomi Klein, "Spiritual Questions and Climate Change." See also Klein, *This Changes Everything*.

20. Bauckham, "Conclusion," 681.

labor pains (*ōdinō*, Rev 12:2) figure prominently in Hebrew Bible and New Testament apocalyptic texts, as images of vulnerability and hope. The world is about to turn. We and the whole creation participate in this birth together. Creation "co-groans and co-labors with us," the apostle Paul says—using the same birth-pain word, prefixed with *syn*, "together with" (Rom 8:22). Jesus likewise uses birthing imagery to portray the urgent end of the unjust system and the turning of the world (Mark 13:8, Matt 24:8).

Preaching on apocalyptic texts today can mean helping people frame painful experiences of change as birth, and asking: What new birth is happening in our lives today? How is our experience of the "end" of the current system also an experience of new life? Regime change brings agonies. But these agonies are birth pains—the travail of new birth, laboring for God's new reign of justice. Ecologically, the promise of new birth can help us find hope today.

The third element to underscore from the story is that the woman is nourished by God. Twice John emphasizes that a safe place (*topos*) has been prepared for the woman, where she is "to be nourished" (*trephetai*, 12:6, 14) for an interim time. In this strange pictorial way, Revelation locates readers as living in a brief "in-between" reality, symbolically portrayed as the time and space after Satan's expulsion from heaven, and before God locks Satan down in the abyss (20:3, 10). Things will get worse on Earth before they get better, but this is finite, a short time, symbolically identified as 1,260 days (Rev 11:3, 12:6). For Revelation's audience, this is the short time before God's final judgment against the Roman Empire.

When we preach, we and our hearers are now located in this brief in-between—a safe place where we are nourished by God. We must preach not doom and gloom but a narrative of hope. Evil has already been defeated through Christ's victory. The in-between place and time in which we live may seem chaotic or hopeless, but *it is the turning of the ages. It is a safe place.* It is new birth, when we and the world are liberated. "The kingdom of this world has become the kingdom of our Lord and of his Christ" (Rev 11:15), an event that has already happened! Only temporarily does evil imperil God's creation. It may feel like things are getting worse. But John assures us that where we are in the story is a time and place of protection and nourishment by God. It is a very hope-filled time and place. In fact, God's people themselves play a crucial role in the struggle.

PREACH COMMUNITY SOLIDARITY: WE DEFEAT EVIL BY WITNESSING TO HOPE

This leads to the fourth eco-reformation truth to preach in this story: God's people are not passive spectators in the battle against injustice. We participate, as agents of hope. We actually defeat Satan by our witness and testimony. According to the victory song in Revelation 12:11, the community itself participates in the defeat of the dragon—not by joining in violence but by the blood of the Lamb Jesus, and by giving testimony. This verse gives God's people a starring role in the key theme of "conquering" that has been so important to the whole book of Revelation. The way God's people conquer evil is twofold: by their communion in Jesus, and by the power of witness or "testimony" (the Greek word *martyria*). The term comes from a courtroom context. We conquer by putting the unjust empire on trial and telling the truth about it. As Pablo Richard names his own experience during the Pinochet regime in Chile in the 1970s, "testimony always has a power to change history."[21]

Rescue from dragons and heavenly women with wings may seem more like science-fiction or fairy-tale imagery than theology. But what if we engage our imaginations pictorially, in ways similar to how Revelation engaged its first-century audience's imagination? What if we explore our role as participants in a great transformative drama, called to give our witness and testimony to how the world and its structures of power are on the edge, about to turn?

Public witness makes a difference, John of Patmos says.[22] Communities of faith today can draw on this truth in organizing public actions against climate change. Skits, dramatic liturgical actions, climate marches, and blockades can put fossil fuel companies "on trial." We make visible what corporate interests try to hide. The root meaning of the term "apocalypse" is to expose, to reveal, to make visible. Using apocalyptic imagination from the Hebrew prophets, John himself performed a funeral liturgy in advance for the unjust Roman Empire and its economic system (Rev 18). He brilliantly invoked Isaiah's taunt over the death of the king of Babylon (Isa 14:4–21) to taunt the unjust Roman economy of his own day. By means of satirical laments for Rome's merchants, kings, and mariners—"Alas, alas, alas" (Rev 18:10, 16, 19)—he helped his hearers envision the end of the imperial economic system. Today, imagina-

21. Richard, *Apocalypse*, 33.
22. See Blount, *Can I Get A Witness?*

tive apocalyptic witness and lament can serve a public, even liturgical, function. Our action has the performative power to expose and conquer climate injustice, and to embody hope.

The purpose of the apocalyptic story is to empower an alternative community as followers of the Lamb Jesus (Rev 14:4) and to strengthen people's witness to God's reign of love and hope in the face of evil. By our testimony we have already defeated evil. The preacher's job—whether preaching on Jesus' apocalyptic discourses, on Paul's epistles, or on Revelation—is to inspire that testimony.

PREACH EARTH'S RESCUE, NOT ESCAPE INTO HEAVEN

Heavenly women with wings can also sound like "heavenism," leaving Earth behind.[23] But as N. T. Wright notes, such a narrow focus on an individual's soul leaving Earth for heaven after death may be more neo-Platonist than Christian.[24] For eco-reformation today, escapism and otherworldliness are two of the most challenging misconceptions about apocalyptic literature we still need to refute.

Until recently, Krister Stendahl's 1971 pessimistic description of apocalyptic literature's worldview as a "stance of despair, as to the possibility of mending the world,"[25] typified scholars' views. Many claimed the apocalyptic perspective reflected a flight from reality, unlike prophets' hope for transformation. Apocalypses were said to leave Earth behind. Rosemary Radford Ruether, for example, critiqued the dualism of apocalyptic writings as ecologically problematic, "based on the fantasy of escape from mortality . . . The very nature of the life of the biosphere . . . is denied."[26]

But recent scholarship has convincingly shown that apocalyptic hope "does not leave the world behind." Rather, apocalypticists give us "hope

---

23. The term "heavenist" was coined by Norman Habel: "'Heavenism' is the belief that heaven, as God's home, is also the true home of Christians . . . Earth, by contrast, is only a temporary 'stopping place' for Christians en route to heaven." See "Ecojustice Hermeneutics," 3–4.

24. See Wright, *Surprised by Hope*, 18–19; see also Wright, "Jesus Is Coming—Plant a Tree!"; and Conradie, *Hope for the Earth*.

25. Stendahl, "On Earth as It Is in Heaven," 59.

26. Ruether, *Gaia and God*, 82–83.

for the radical reformation of life on earth."[27] Early Jewish apocalypses
such as Daniel and 1 Enoch functioned as resistance literature, engaging historical crises of oppressive empires. Apocalypses are not escapist.
They look for the renewal of Earth.[28] When apocalypses employ imagery
sometimes labeled as "cosmic catastrophe" (earthquakes, plagues, the sun
darkening and moon turning to blood) they do so for political critique,
portraying empires' brutality as so severe that the very ordering of the
world is "de-created."[29] Like prophets, apocalyptic authors fully engage
the world. In the three-tiered cosmology of apocalypses, heaven functions
to reveal the transcendent dimension to all reality. John of Patmos travels
to heaven in Revelation 4:1 not to escape Earth but in order to receive a
visionary message for communities on Earth. Especially in times of social
and cultural collapse, apocalypses can play a vibrant role. As John Collins
underscores: "[T]here is no doubt that the social and cultural worlds we
inhabit are constantly crumbling. Christianity inherited from the Jewish apocalypses a way of affirming transcendent values, those things we
should affirm even when the world around us collapses."[30] As we face the
collapse of fossil-fuel based economy and transition to a different way of
life, apocalypses can help us today.

In the storyline of Revelation 12, the dragon once more tries to sweep
the woman away, with a flood. Out of its mouth the evil dragon spews a
toxic river to drown the woman. But Earth itself comes to her rescue,
opening its mouth to swallow up the flood (Rev 12:16).[31] This active role
for Earth is typical of apocalypses, where animals and waters and other
elements of the cosmos speak and participate in God's story. Personifying
Earth with a mouth to "swallow up" evil recalls the Exodus story, when
Earth opened its mouth to swallow the Egyptians (Exod 15:12). Medieval
illuminated manuscripts of Revelation portray this scene with Earth (Gē)
as a fully personified feminine figure, with a literal mouth. The imagery
is deeply metaphorical, inviting us to play with images at a more visually
symbolic level.

27. Keller, "Eschatology, Ecology, and a Green Ecumenacy," 338.

28. Horsley, *Revolt of the Scribes*. For a critique of the entire construct of "apocalypticism" re-visiting the legacy of Albert Schweitzer and others, see Horsley, *The
Prophet Jesus and the Renewal of Israel*.

29. Portier-Young, *Apocalypse against Empire*, xxiii.

30. Collins, *The Apocalyptic Imagination*, 282.

31. See Kahl, "Gaia, Polis and *Ekklēsia* at the Miletus Market Gate."

How can we envision Earth coming to our help today? Ecologically, the message of hope is particularly important as a counter to despair. Courageous preaching can help us recognize and imagine hope unfolding in our world. It is easy to despair, claiming it is too late to find healing for our Earth. Well-known climate skeptic and economist *Washington Post* columnist, Robert Samuelson, seems to have taken this position on climate change, after years of climate denial.[32] I think we will see more and more cynical people claiming it is too late to do anything, which is a convenient way to avoid action and responsibility.

Scriptural imagination can help people imagine what hope can look like, aided by Earth itself. Whatever dangerous river Satan spews out at us—whether a flood of carbon pollution, or denial, or hopelessness—is not the last word. The church must open up the space between denial and despair. Scientists tell us that Earth still has the power to sequester huge amounts of carbon in its soils and forests, through biochar and other low-tech participatory means. We have the technology to bring fossil fuel use to zero. Decisions we make in this next decade will be critical for the next ten thousand years, climate scientists tell us.[33] It is not too late. We are truly living in what the Greek Orthodox Patriarch Archbishop Bartholomew calls a "*kairos* moment." The church must lead. It is easier for people to imagine fear than hope. Apocalyptic images and stories help foster imagination that is not just dystopic.

PREACH ESCHATOLOGY AS HEALING, NOT HELLFIRE AND JUDGMENT

Michelangelo's Sistine Chapel's huge last judgment scene, like many medieval cathedrals' entrances, used hell as a way to foster fear, visually reminding people of their own end and judgment. Dante Alighieri's fourteenth-century allegorical journey through hell leads the reader on tours of layers of the underworld to make a terrifying case for individual repentance. In a *Science* magazine column entitled "The Beyond-Two-Degree Inferno" National Academy of Sciences president, geophysicist

32. See Samuelson, "On Climate Change, We Have No Solution."

33. See Clark, et al., "Consequences of Twenty-First-Century Policy: "Policy decisions made in the next few years to decades will have profound impacts on global climate, ecosystems and human societies—not just for this century, but for the next ten millenia and beyond."

Marcia McNutt, draws on Dante to warn of the peril of continuing on the current trajectory of fossil-fuel burning:

> In Dante's *Inferno*, he describes the nine circles of Hell, each dedicated to different sorts of sinners, with the outermost being occupied by those who didn't know any better, and the innermost reserved for the most treacherous offenders. I wonder where in the nine circles Dante would place all of us who are borrowing against this Earth in the name of economic growth, accumulating an environmental debt by burning fossil fuels, the consequences of which will be left for our children and grandchildren to bear?[34]

Such use of apocalyptic imagery by scientists may help to raise public awareness of the urgency of avoiding a climate inferno. But such use of apocalyptic imagery can also backfire, especially if it sounds moralistic. "Sinners in the hands of an angry earth" is how New Yorker author Jonathan Franzen caricatures environmentalists.[35]

Moreover, a moralistic focus on individual judgment was never the primary focus of Revelation or other biblical apocalypses. The purpose of the visionary rhetoric of Revelation, and of the apocalyptic teachings of Jesus and Paul, was to strengthen the community's identity and solidarity in the face of empire.[36] Only later, in the second and third centuries, did the church come to read apocalypses as primarily threats about individual judgment after death, influenced by texts such as the popular second-century Apocalypse of Peter. Later texts focused on graphic punishments of the individual sinner, rather than on transformation of the community and the world. Unfortunately we have tended to read biblical apocalypses through later moralistic lenses, fueling fear.

Instead of sin and judgment, I am starting to frame Revelation more in terms of sickness and healing.[37] I picture John as a doctor, who

---

34. McNutt, "The Beyond-Two-Degree Inferno," 7.

35. See Franzen, "Carbon Capture," 56: "Climate change has given us an eschatology for reckoning with our guilt: coming soon, some hellishly overheated tomorrow, is Judgment Day. Unless we repent and mend our ways, we'll all be sinners in the hands of an angry earth."

36. As Schüssler Fiorenza demonstrates, apocalyptic language can function in two ways, either to control the behavior of individuals or to provide an alternative vision and encouragement of new community structures in the face of oppression (as with Revelation). See "The Phenomena of Early Christian Apocalyptic," 313.

37. In liturgical theology, Benjamin Stewart suggests a similar shift to framing climate change in terms of sickness and healing (rather than primarily sin and

gives us a diagnosis of what ails us and the world. Like a radiologist, John is able to diagnose the evil of the Roman system, by putting up on the screen slides of previous empires (Assyrians, Babylonians, Seleucids). Or perhaps he is an epidemiologist, who can see the public health consequences of something others cannot yet see—like the colorless methane escaping from a massive leak in the Porter Ranch community near Los Angeles, or the lead poisoning drinking water in Flint, Michigan.

Healing is crucial. How we diagnose our current situation, how we frame the trajectory of the illness of climate change today, shapes how people respond. For some, the fever of climate change can feel like a terminal illness. That's how the scientist in Barbara Kingsolver's novel *Flight Behavior* diagnoses the dystopic situation when sheep-farmer Dellarobia's wooded hill in Kentucky has unexpectedly become the winter hibernation grounds for the entire species of monarch butterflies. Scientist Ovid Byron sets up a lab in Dellarobia's barn to study the butterflies on the hill, to see whether they can perhaps be saved. His reading of the butterfly species' future in the face of climate change is dire: "'I am a doctor of natural systems. And this looks terminal to me.' In the branches over their heads, small bursts of butterflies exploded into the sun like soundless fireworks. The beauty was irresistible. 'I just can't see it being all that bad,' she said. 'I'd say most people wouldn't.'"[38] But by the end of the novel, Dellarobia also comes to realize the terminal consequences of what she is seeing. The monarch butterflies' presence on her hill means we are now living on a different planet.

In one way, the book of Revelation is similar to the scientist's project: to help people see that it is "all that bad." John of Patmos, like Ovid Byron, is a "doctor of natural systems." John diagnoses the entire Roman imperial system as terminal, toxic, even satanic. For twenty chapters, he shows pictures of Rome's sickness, leading to its doom. The trajectory the Empire is on will lead to its own destruction, he says. Its death will be the logical result of the way Rome poisons the whole world with its idolatrous worship, its violent militarism, and its predatory economy.

Yet unlike the scientist, John is also a healer. Dr. John has a two-fold project: He not only diagnoses the situation as terminal but also prescribes the medicine, a different vision of hope for healing. That hope comes in Revelation 21–22, the New Jerusalem vision of renewed community on a

judgment). See Stewart, "What's the Right Rite?", and the essay by Aana Marie Vigen in this volume.

38. *Flight Behavior*, 282.

renewed Earth. That hope comes in the vision of the tree of life growing in the middle of the city, on either side of the river of life, with fruit for everyone and leaves for healing. That hope comes in the invitation, "Let everyone who is thirsty come" (Rev 22:17).

John leads readers through twenty chapters of dire diagnosis. His mission is to help Jesus' followers see the inevitable "end" that lies ahead, and then to give them the courage to "come out" of the sick system before it is too late (Rev 18:4). The empire's illness is terminal, he says. But that does not mean it is the sickness unto death. There is healing beyond empire, echoing God's promises of healing for ancient Israel beyond the "diseases of Egypt" (Exod 15:26). John leads his communities on an exodus journey out of the sick system of Rome into Jesus' vision of healing. By washing the toxic sickness from its life the community receives a wondrous blessing, "so that they will have the right to the tree of life and may enter the city by the gates" (Rev 22:14).

No vision is more urgently needed for our climate sickness than Revelation's image of the healing tree of life. Doctor John of Patmos helped people find that medicine two thousand years ago. Christ, our healing tree of life, is laying healing leaves on our bodies, our souls, and on our whole wounded world. Preachers and artists can help people visualize that healing today. The importance of healing in Revelation and other apocalyptic texts taps into a sometimes-overlooked tradition dear to Patristic theology and also to the Reformers, the tradition of *christus medicus* (Christ the Healer).[39] The biblical Greek word *sōzō*, often translated "save," also means "heal."[40] The image of healing can give a vision for future life on Earth, in contexts where climate change and drought are already causing suffering.[41] In Revelation, healing comes not directly from God but from the leaves of a tree, from a specific part of God's creation.

39. The identification of Christ as Physician begins with Ignatius of Antioch ("For there is one physician . . . Jesus Christ, our Lord," *Ign. Eph.* 7:2) and comes to the fore with Augustine. See Arbesmann, "The Concept of 'Christus Medicus.'" Luther also loved the *Christus Medicus* metaphor. See Steiger, *Medizinische Theologie*.

40. John 3:17, for example, could be translated "God did not send the Son into the world to condemn the world, but in order that the world might be *healed* through him."

41. See Maathai, *Replenishing the Earth*.

VISUALIZING REVELATION'S HEALING TREE OF LIFE

Artists throughout Christian history draw on scriptural imagination to connect Revelation's tree of life to people's own lives and landscapes. Early Christian visual imagery focused on paradise, helping people visualize paradise already in their daily lives.[42] The rivers of paradise were envisioned in this world. The twelfth-century apse mosaic of the Church of San Clemente in Rome, for example, gave viewers a social imaginary that included nature as well as the cross. It invites Christians to imagine themselves in the paradisiacal tree of life—bringing "the cosmos into the cathedral," as Susan Power Bratton describes the Jesse Tree window in Chartres Cathedral.[43] At San Clemente, Christ's cross becomes the vine, growing out of a fountain of water where deer drink. Miniature scenes up in the branches of the tree show village life, embraced in God's cosmic tree: a woman feeding chickens, a shepherd tending sheep, birds nesting, deer and lambs grazing, food overflowing from baskets, and dolphins leaping.

Reformation art, similarly, brought the Bible to life in people's lives. Today, art can help us visualize healing and Eco-Reformation, inviting us to God's river of life and tree of life in the center of our lives.[44] Lucas Cranach, Luther's collaborator, resettled "popular biblical figures into present-day Saxony as if they had always lived there."[45] Various rivers in Saxony became the location for Christ's baptism. "Baptism of Christ by John the Baptist in the River Elbe" pictured Jesus in Wittenberg. The woodcut "Baptism of Jesus in the River Pegnitz before Nurnberg," similarly imaged the River Jordan flowing through the rivers of people's lives. Creating a woodcut for each chapter of Revelation, Cranach notably depicted the New Jerusalem vision of Revelation 21 as a radiant Saxon city. The picture invites viewers to be part of that scene.

In Revelation, the tree of life is located in the center of the renewed city, the radiant New Jerusalem. Earth is the location of salvation, since the city descends from heaven to Earth. Everyone is invited to enter and receive its gifts of life—even those with no money. Ezekiel's many trees

42. See Brock and Parker, *Saving Paradise*.

43. Bratton, *Environmental Values in Christian Art*, 118.

44. For a reading of Revelation through the woodcuts of Albrecht Dürer, see Smith, *Apocalypse*. See also Rossing, "Revelation."

45. Ozment, *The Serpent and the Lamb*, 149. See also Koerner, *The Reformation of the Image*.

on either side of the river become the single "tree of life," echoing the paradise of Genesis. The tree's leaves bring healing for all the "nations," for the whole world. Today, this expansive eschatological image of healing can speak to individuals, to relationships, to communities struggling against injustice, and to the many illnesses of our world.

The biblical tree of life can serve as a corrective to overly individualistic and non-relational readings of eschatology. The tree of life as an image of healing is not only metaphorical. It coheres with biological understandings of the healing power of trees. Ethnobotanists and pharmaceutical investigators recognize the healing properties of the leaves of some trees. Environmental engineers now recognize trees' capacity to create beneficial micro-climates, to prevent soil erosion, to filter toxins from water and air, and to sequester carbon from the atmosphere. The tree of life, understood biologically, stands at the interface of soil, air, and water. In its boughs and bark many species find their habitat, and through its roots and leaves the face of the Earth is renewed.

Christian eschatology must speak of a new creation that is "both transcendently new and yet in continuity with this creation, since it is the renewal of this world."[46] Visionaries and dreamers need images that point beyond literal meanings. The Rev. Dr. Martin Luther King Jr., for example, drew on Revelation's vision of the New Jerusalem to inspire hope among poor people in American cities in the 1960s.

The tree of life in art history also becomes Christ the vine, from John 15, declaring, "I am the vine, you are the branches." People's desire to see themselves as part of God's great tree, as branches of the vine, can foster ecological desire for renewal of this Earth. A Greek Orthodox icon of Christ as the vine, showing the twelve disciples up in the branches, elicits the response, "I want to be in the tree of life." The importance of seeing points to a crucial role for preachers. We can help people "recognize" things—our dire climate illness, but even more the way of healing. We can help people recognize Christ the tree of life who is also Christ the healer (St. Bonaventure).[47]

In the gospels, eschatology and healing are deeply connected in ways we have not always seen. "My daughter is at the *eschatos*," the synagogue leader Jairus tells Jesus (Mark 5:23). Come heal her! *Eschatos* means the

46. Bauckham, "Conclusion," 681.

47. On the ecological significance of St. Bonaventure's *Tree of Life*, see Deane-Drummond and Rossing, "The Eco-Significance of John 10:10."

edge, the edge of life and death. We are at the *eschatos* and we need healing! Come heal us.

Revelation concludes with a liturgical dialogue. The entire book has brought hearers on a transformative journey, through hearing the book read aloud in the worship service. This final scene is the homecoming. The antiphonal "Come" (Rev. 22:17—the spirit and the bride say come, let the one who is thirsty say come) may be part of a eucharistic liturgy in which the Spirit and the bridal new Jerusalem call the community to participate. The invitation to "take the water of life" (Rev 22:17) draws the apocalyptic vision to a sacramental close, gathering people around the tree of life on a renewed Earth.

The hope John proclaims is that unjust empires and systems will soon come to an end—in fact, they have already been defeated. The message of hope assures communities thirsting for justice that God hears their cries and that God dwells with them on Earth. The world is about to turn. The hope of Revelation centers on a slain Lamb and a radiant city with gates open to all, with a river of life and a tree that gives healing for the whole world, and healing for each one of us. It is to this hope that an Eco-Reformation and apocalyptic preaching can bear witness, as voiced in the final, summative words, "Amen. Come Lord Jesus."

BIBLIOGRAPHY

Arbesmann, Rudolph. "The Concept of 'Christus Medicus' in St. Augustine." *Traditio* 10 (1954) 1–28.

Barker, David C., and David H. Bearce. "End-Times Theology, the Shadow of the Future, and Public Resistance to Addressing Global Climate Change." *Political Research Quarterly* 66 (2013) 267–79.

Bauckham, Richard. "Conclusion: Emerging Issues in Eschatology in the Twenty-First Century." In *The Oxford Handbook of Eschatology*, edited by Jerry L. Walls, 671–89. Oxford: Oxford University Press, 2008.

Blount, Brian. *Can I Get A Witness? Reading Revelation Through African American Culture*. Louisville: Westminster John Knox, 2005.

Bratton, Susan Power. *Environmental Values in Christian Art*. SUNY Series on Religion and the Environment. Albany: SUNY Press, 2007.

Brock, Rita Nakashima, and Rebecca Ann Parker. *Saving Paradise: How Christianity Traded Love of This World for Crucifixion and Empire*. Boston: Beacon, 2008.

Clark, Peter U., et al. "Consequences of Twenty-First-Century Policy for Multi-Millennial Climate and Sea-Level Change." *Nature Climate Change* 6 (April 2016) 360–69.

Conradie, Ernst. *Hope for the Earth: Vistas on a New Century*. 2000. Reprinted, Eugene, OR: Wipf & Stock, 2005.

Collins, John J. *The Apocalyptic Imagination: An Introduction to Jewish Apocalyptic Literature*. 2nd ed. Grand Rapids: Eerdmans, 1998.

Cooney, Rory. "Canticle of the Turning." In *Evangelical Lutheran Worship*, #723. Minneapolis: Augsburg Fortress, 2006.

Deane-Drummond, Celia, and Barbara Rossing. "The Eco-Significance of John 10:10: Abundant Life through the Sabbath, Trinitarian Vestiges, and the Tree of Life." *Ecumenical Review* 65 (March 2013) 83–97.

Dolan, Eric. "Belief in Biblical End-Times Stifling Climate Change Action in U.S.: Study." May 1, 2013. http://www.rawstory.com.

Franzen, Jonathan. "Carbon Capture." *The New Yorker* 91 (April 6, 2015). http://www.newyorker.com.

Habel, Norman C., and the Earth Bible Team. "Ecojustice Hermeneutics: Reflections and Challenges." In *The Earth Story in the New Testament*, edited by Norman C. Habel and Vicky Balabanski, 1–14. The Earth Bible 5. Sheffield: Sheffield Academic Press, 2002.

Horsley, Richard A. *The Prophet Jesus and the Renewal of Israel: Moving Beyond a Diversionary Debate*. Minneapolis: Fortress, 2012.

———. *Revolt of the Scribes: Resistance and Apocalyptic Origins*. Minneapolis: Fortress, 2010.

Huber, Lynn R. *Thinking and Seeing with Women in Revelation*. London: T. & T. Clark, 2013.

Jones, Robert P., et al. "Believers, Sympathizers and Skeptics: Why Americans Are Conflicted about Climate Change, Environmental Policy, and Science." Public Religion Research Institute, November 22, 2014. http://publicreligion.org.

Kahl, Brigitte. "Gaia, Polis, and *Ekklēsia* at the Miletus Market Gate: An Eco-Critical Reimagination of Revelation 12:16." In *The First Urban Churches 1: Methodological Foundations*, edited by James R. Harrison and L. L. Welborn, 111–50. Writings from the Greco-Roman World Supplement Series 7. Atlanta: Society of Biblical Literature, 2015.

Keller, Catherine. "Eschatology, Ecology, and a Green Ecumenacy." In *Reconstructing Christian Theology*, edited by Rebecca Chopp and Mark Lewis Taylor, 326–45. Minneapolis: Fortress, 1994.

Kingsolver, Barbara. *Flight Behavior*. New York: HarperCollins, 2012.

Klein, Naomi. *This Changes Everything: Capitalism vs. The Climate*. New York: Simon & Schuster, 2014.

Koerner, Joseph Leo. *The Reformation of the Image*. Chicago: University of Chicago Press, 2008.

Lewis, Karoline. "Why Advent?" November 22, 2015. https://www.workingpreacher.org.

Luther, Martin. "To Me She's Dear, the Worthy Maid." In *Liturgy and Hymns*, edited by Ulrich Leupold. LW 53: 292–94. Philadelphia: Fortress, 1965.

Maathai, Wangari. *Replenishing the Earth: Spiritual Values for Healing Ourselves and the World*. New York: Doubleday, 2010.

Malbach, Edward, et al. *The Francis Effect: How Pope Francis Changed the Conversation about Global Warming*. Yale Program on Climate Change Communication, November 5, 2015. http://environment.yale.edu.

McNutt, Marcia. "The Beyond-Two-Degree Inferno." *Science* 349 (July 3, 2015) 7.

Mowe, Sam. "Spiritual Questions and Climate Change." *Tricycle* 25 (Fall 2015). http://www.tricycle.com/interview/capitalism-vs-climate.

Ozment, Steven. *The Serpent and the Lamb: Cranach, Luther and the Making of the Reformation.* New Haven: Yale University Press, 2012.

Portier-Young, Anathea E. *Apocalypse Against Empire: Theologies of Resistance in Early Judaism.* Grand Rapids: Eerdmans, 2011.

Richard, Pablo. *Apocalypse: A People's Commentary on the Book of Revelation.* The Bible & Liberation Series. Maryknoll, NY: Orbis, 1995.

Robinson, Marilynne. "Fear." *New York Review of Books* 62, September 24, 2015. http://www.nybooks.com

Rossing, Barbara. "Alas for the Earth: Lament and Resistance in Revelation 12." In *The Earth Story in the New Testament,* edited by Norman C. Habel and Shirley Wurst, 180–92. Earth Bible 5. Sheffield: Sheffield Academic, 2002.

———. "Hastening the Day When the Earth Will Burn? Global Warming, Revelation and 2 Peter 3 (Advent 2, Year B)." *Currents in Theology and Mission* 35 (2008) 361–71.

———. *The Rapture Exposed: The Message of Hope in the Book of Revelation.* Boulder, CO: Westview Press, 2004.

———. "Revelation." In *The New Testament: Fortress Commentary on the Bible,* edited by Margaret Aymer et al., 715–71. Minneapolis: Fortress, 2014.

Ruether, Rosemary Radford. *Gaia and God: An Ecofeminist Theology of Earth Healing.* San Francisco: HarperSanFrancisco, 1992.

Samuelson, Robert. "On Climate Change, We Have No Solution." *Washington Post,* May 11, 2014. https://www.washingtonpost.com.

Sanchez, David. *From Patmos to the Barrio: Subverting Imperial Myths.* Minneapolis: Fortress, 2008.

Schüssler Fiorenza, Elisabeth. "The Phenomena of Early Christian Apocalyptic: Some Reflections on Method." In *Apocalypticism in the Mediterranean World and the Near East: Proceedings of the International Colloquium on Apocalypticism, Uppsala, 1979,* edited by David Hellholm, 295–316. 2nd ed. Tübingen: Mohr/Siebeck, 1989.

———. *Revelation: Vision of a Just World.* Proclamation Commentaries. Minneapolis: Fortress, 1991.

Smith, Robert H. *Apocalypse: A Commentary on Revelation in Words and Images.* Collegeville: Liturgical, 2000.

Steiger, Johann Anselm. *Medizinische Theologie: Christus medicus und theologia medicinalis bei Martin Luther und im Luthertum der Barockzeit.* Studies in the History of Christian Traditions 121. Leiden: Brill, 2005.

Stendahl, Krister. "On Earth as It Is in Heaven—Dynamics in Christian Eschatology." In *The Eschaton: A Community of Love,* edited by Joseph Papin, 57–68. Villanova: Villanova University Press, 1971.

Stewart, Benjamin M. "What's the Right Rite? Treating Environmental Degradation as Sickness or Sin." *Currents in Theology and Mission* 43 (2016) 3–8.

Westhelle, Vitor. *Eschatology and Space: The Lost Dimension in Theology Past and Present.* New York: Palgrave Macmillan, 2012.

———. "The Way the World Ends: An Essay on Cross and Eschatology." *Currents in Theology and Mission* 27 (2000) 85–97.

Wright, N. T. *Surprised by Hope: Rethinking Heaven, the Resurrection, and the Mission of the Church.* San Francisco: HarperOne, 2008.

10

The Stream, the Flood, the Spring

The Liturgical Role of Flowing Waters in Eco-Reformation

—BENJAMIN M. STEWART

CLEAN, FLOWING WATER IS one marker of environmental health.[1] Such water is often an oasis of biodiversity. It is an *ecological* sign. Flowing water has also served as a *theological* sign of God's renewal of the church and the world. In fact, especially among Lutherans, we can say that the flowing waters of Earth have helped inspire reformation. This chapter proposes that as the church today seeks eco-reformation, flowing waters may again be a source of eco-theological renewal and wisdom, particularly as they flow through the landscape of the church's liturgical life. This chapter focuses on three patterns of flowing water: the stream, the flood, and the spring.

---

1. Parts of this chapter are adapted with gracious permission of the publishers from journal articles that appeared elsewhere as Stewart, "Flooding the Landscape" and "Water in Worship." A simplified version of this chapter appeared as "Stream, Flood, and Spring."

THE STREAM

Have you ever paused beside a stream to listen as the water rippled or cascaded by you? If you were in the wilderness, you might have knelt down to drink or to wash your face. You have at least seen photos: a flourishing creek flowing down over rocks and logs, in and out of sunlight, nourishing the landscape. The water reshapes the land even as it brings the ecosystem to life.

Water Flows

Water seems to want to flow. We speak of a water *cycle*, constantly in motion: rain, cascades, rivers, seeps, waves, tides, clouds. Our own bodies, mostly water, live only by remaining a part of this flowing watershed: drinking, pulsing, excreting, bathing, exhaling, birthing.

To understand water on Earth we cannot only consider a static substance comprised of elements on the periodic table, H_2O. There are indeed mysteries of water we can probe by isolating it and peering at it microscopically. But imagine what would be hidden from us if we did not step back to see water in motion. A map that traced water's path would reveal that it touches, flows through, and connects every living creature in Earth's history. At least on our home planet, the flowing nature of water is key to its significance.

The Contrasting Symbol of Light

First, however, in order to appreciate more fully the character of flowing water, briefly consider a different ecological motif in Christian liturgical tradition: the sun. Early Christianity regarded the rising sun as a partner in prayer.[2] Facing the sunrise to pray, Christians sang the *Benedictus*, proclaiming, "the dawn from on high shall break upon us, to shine on those who dwell in darkness and the shadow of death, and to guide our feet into the way of peace."[3] Church buildings were oriented to face the sunrise, as were graves. Christian worship was phototropic, like a field of sunflowers facing the rising sun. This sun-oriented tradition was at

2. From the third century on, evidence of sunrise facing prayer is "commonplace" throughout the Christian world. Taft, *The Liturgy of the Hours*, 15.

3. Luke 1:78–79.

times strongly Earth-embracing. For example, Origen, in advocating for sunrise-facing prayer, taught that the sunrise was to be preferred as a guide for prayer even over compelling human-built architecture, since "the natural is to be set before the artificial."[4] In many early Christian baptismal and funeral rites, the sunrise was portrayed as a symbolic compass point for guiding Christians in seeking a flourishing Eden, as Genesis described it, "in the east,"[5] still green and, in Christ, by grace, accessible to humans again.

The Gothic Vision

The image of the sun's light, however, could at times inspire some Earth-rejecting versions of Christianity. Rather than accenting how the sun gives abundant life to Earth's plants and animals, the sun's beams became something like ladders to follow away from Earth into the heavens. The goal of this spiritual pilgrimage could be portrayed as returning to the source of light in the sun, shedding the material body to become pure light. While there are healthy mystical uses of such imagery, it has also played a role in racist, biophobic, and escapist distortions of Christian faith.

Paul Santmire analyzes this imagery of ascent toward the sun's light in his *Nature Reborn: The Ecological and Cosmic Promise of Christian Theology*. In what he describes as "the ambiguity of the Gothic spirit," Santmire notes that while the symbolism of the sun's light can be portrayed as bidirectional (both bestowing life to Earth and leading away from it back to the source), the medieval Gothic spirit strongly accented ascent.[6] It was embodied in the soaring architecture of the age that drew the attention of worshipers upward toward the heights. Santmire focuses on liturgy as the critical point at which the question of ascent or descent

4. Origen, *On Prayer*, XX.

5. In Genesis, Eden is located "in the east" (Gen 2:8). For a fine overview of eastward oriented Edenic imagery in early Christianity, see "Baptism as the Beginning of the New Creation," in Jensen, *Baptismal Imagery in Early Christianity*.

6. Santmire, *Nature Reborn*, Kindle loc. 1145. Santmire notes that even the resurgent natural imagery of the era can be understood as part of an earth-transcending worldview: "The two trends [highlighting both ascent and earthly imagery] actually appear to have been one: the spiritual rising above and the mundane quest for mastery. The more the faithful aspired to transcend matter in order to be with God above the heavens, the more they also, in this era, engaged themselves with the earth below as mere matter, as a world at their disposal." Ibid., Kindle loc. 1204–1206.

is embodied. In the era preceding the Reformation, given the theological and architectural contexts, "the meaning of worship could move only in one direction finally, to accent the ascent of the soul to God, and the abandonment of the material world."[7]

The Reforming Trajectory: Descent

Santmire portrays Luther as leading reform in precisely the opposite direction. He describes Luther as having "canceled" the ascending half of the bidirectional schema of light.[8] Santmire writes that for Luther, "in particular with regard to worship, descent, not ascent, is the image that shapes every theological affirmation."[9] The trajectory that Luther emphasizes is God and God's goodness "continually overflowing into the created world."[10] To know the divine is to know "a Creator who is creatively and powerfully 'pouring' himself [*sic*] in, with, and under all things."[11] Notice that the descending imagery is expressed by metaphors of flowing water: flowing through, pouring out, and overflowing. The Lutheran emphasis on the action of God has special affinity with imagery of flowing water.

Such accent on divine initiative with an earthward flowing trajectory does not necessarily portray humanity as strictly passive. To the contrary, Cynthia Moe-Lobeda finds the image of God's life-giving power flowing through creation to be profoundly helpful in resisting the destructive and degrading dimensions of dominant economic systems. "It may be here that the role of religion is most crucial. It provides a sense of hope that the powers of greed, exploitation, and brokenness are not the final word, and that the sacred Source of all is flowing through creation, is healing and liberating, and ultimately will reign. We are not alone in our quest for just and Earth-honoring ways of living."[12]

Light can be portrayed as bidirectional—giving life and energy to Earth and also inviting a spiritual transcendence away from Earth to the source of light. As suggested above, the tendency in Christianity

---

7. Santmire, *Nature Reborn*, Kindle loc. 1190.

8. Ibid., Kindle loc. 1221.

9. Ibid., Kindle loc. 1276.

10. Ibid., Kindle loc. 1222.

11. Santmire, *Nature Reborn*, Kindle loc. 2719.

12. Moe-Lobeda, *Resisting Structural Evil*, 136. See her essay in this volume.

has sometimes been for such imagery to tend toward ascension and the ethereal. However, the imagery of flowing water in its liquid state (its most tangible form), like Luther's reformation emphasis, is strongly unidirectional and downward flowing. Edward Slingerland, in a cognitive-scientific analysis of religious imagery, notes the persuasive power of the imagery of flowing water "to introduce teleological and normatively charged features: the natural, 'internal' tendency of water is to flow downhill, and to go against this tendency requires the application of external force. Although it is possible under certain circumstances to make water flow uphill, this requires a huge expenditure of force and is ultimately unsustainable—going 'against the flow' of Nature-Heaven is bound to lead to failure."[13] It is this persuasive and powerful imagery that the prophet Amos invokes to describe a quest for justice that would mirror God's own faithfulness to Earth: "let justice roll down like waters, and righteousness like an everflowing stream."[14] Matthew's Jesus portrays the downward-falling rain as a sign of God's free generosity to all, especially to those who might be considered undeserving: God "sends rain on the righteous and on the unrighteous."[15] This universal divine benevolence is highlighted in Matthew as a countercultural model for emulation in human relationships. Thus, in both Amos and Matthew, humans are urged to reshape social structures according to qualities exemplified by downward-flowing water: charity should fall like rain and justice should flow down like water. In fact, today, the struggle for access to clean, free-flowing water for humans and other creatures may be helpfully considered through the conceptual-metaphorical structures of that very same endangered water: a pure, clean, flowing source for all creatures, not to be privately owned or hoarded. Lutherans especially may champion a theological ethic of metaphorical and literal downward-flowing water. A theological ethic of naturally flowing water may inspire activism and guide decision-making in questions related to irrigation, dam removal, riparian ecosystem

13. Slingerland, "Conceptual Blending, Somatic Marking, and Normativity," 578–79. I have elsewhere shown how conceptual metaphors based on free-flowing water tend to support arguments for "just sharing of resources, critique of hierarchy, sharing of knowledge, [and] freedom from strict governance" while metaphors based on channelized or dammed water "are associated with centralized control over other domains, including money, power, knowledge, communication, human nature and human behavior." Stewart, "The Role of Baptismal Water at the Vigil of Easter," 126–28.

14. Amos 5:24.

15. Matthew 5:45.

integrity, stream restoration, storm water capture, aquifer protection, and equitable access to clean drinking water.

Baptismal imagery may accent the flowing and pouring nature of God. *Evangelical Lutheran Worship* encourages ministers to pour water out into the font before or during the prayer over the water.[16] Prayers may image God as overflowing with goodness, such as this baptismal prayer, drawing on imagery of Psalm 104, "You water the mountains and send springs into the valleys to refresh and satisfy all living things."[17] Baptisms themselves may be generous in their use of pouring water, embodying the way our lives are caught up in the flow of God's blessing.[18] Paul Santmire writes that "[t]his theology encourages us to envision God cascading down, like a mountain river, into all things, binding them together and calling forth growth. It points us to God, working the divine purposes in, with, and under the whole creation."[19]

Against an overemphasis on the Earth-abandoning quest for God in the heavens, a Lutheran reforming accent instead points down toward Earth, like water flowing on the earth. This is the way God's goodness overflows. It calls us to contemplate—spiritually, liturgically, scientifically—the ways God's goodness is constantly flowing and pouring into and through the world. Rather than following a beam of light away from Earth into the heavens, Lutherans especially have emphasized the downward flowing trajectory of water as an image of the overflowing goodness of God coming down to Earth, flowing even to the dust. The trajectory of salvation history is the trajectory of flowing water. David Rhoads expresses the ongoing reforming nature of his own teaching regarding this trajectory: "In Scripture and in our Lutheran tradition, the movement of salvation has not been away from Earth but *toward* it. I sometimes tell my students that if you think of salvation only as dying and going to heaven, you may pass Jesus coming the other way! That is what incarnation is about: God becoming human, God coming to dwell with humans, Jesus returning to be with us."[20]

---

16. *ELW Leaders Desk Edition*, 586.

17. Ibid., Baptismal Prayer II, 587.

18. Water "is used generously in Holy Baptism to symbolize God's power . . ." (ELCA, *The Use of the Means of Grace*, Principle 26).

19. Santmire, *Ritualizing Nature*, 132–33.

20. Rhoads, "Reflections on a Lutheran Theology of Creation."

THE FLOOD

Have you stood at the edge of a flooding river? It may seem to be newly and fearsomely alive. It grows, roils, and rises. Beneath the surface, currents uproot trees, dislodge boulders, and move earthen banks. Kayakers and canoeists know the "funny water" of a flooded river—dangerously unpredictable currents formed when water surges through channels formed for smaller flows. Floods rise up and occupy land, encroaching on what we sometimes designate as "our" habitat.

Floods are natural reformers. They powerfully rearrange landscapes and disrupt boundaries that may have been considered more-or-less settled. Floods can irrigate land and deposit rich topsoil, giving life. They can strip away entire landscapes and destroy safe habitat, bringing death.

In the Reformation, the image of flood disrupted and reconfigured theology and cosmology. The centrality of the image of flood is one of Martin Luther's most distinctive contributions to the reform of baptismal theology and practice. This is especially evident in the prayer he composed to be prayed over the water at baptism. When Luther composed a version of the prayer over the water at baptism, he broke with tradition to make flood the central image of the prayer. Composed in 1523, the accent on the flood was so striking that Luther's prayer become known as the *Sintflutgebet*, or "Flood Prayer."[21] The prayer influenced other reforming traditions. It was used in Ulrich Zwingli's 1525 baptismal rite and Thomas Cranmer's 1549 *Book of Common Prayer*. Contemporary worship resources of Lutherans and others have continued to include versions of flood prayer and other baptismal prayers clearly marked by its influence.

Covering, Transforming Everything

Luther's prayer uses the flood of Noah as its orienting metaphor. The role of humans, the significance of other species, and the survival of life on the planet are all central themes in the Genesis narrative. In the biblical narrative, the flood covers *everything*.[22] The narrative repeats emphatically:

---

21. For a contemporary translation of the prayer see Senn, *Christian Liturgy*, 289.

22. "The waters swelled so mightily on the earth that all the high mountains under the whole heaven were covered; the waters swelled above the mountains, covering them fifteen cubits deep. And all flesh died that moved on the earth, birds, domestic animals, wild animals, all swarming creatures that swarm on the earth, and all human

every living creature outside of the ark was drowned. Even the highest mountains were deeply covered. After the flood, just as radically and completely, the new covenant extends out over the whole Earth, for all humans and all other living creatures, even toward all future creatures: "I am establishing my covenant with . . . every animal of the earth . . . never again shall there be a flood to destroy the earth."[23]

In the original biblical narrative out of which the metaphor of flood comes, the radical, world-encompassing extent of the flood's power is emphasized. Because Luther describes baptism in terms of the biblical flood, baptism is portrayed as touching, engulfing *everything*, leaving nothing the same. The extent of the meaning of baptism, says the flood prayer, is literally global; nothing on Earth or in the future stands outside of its reach.

Flood of Grace

Floods are often associated with destruction. But twice in his prayer Luther names the flood of baptism as a "*saving* flood." He writes in his 1519 sermon on baptism:

> Now baptism is by far a greater flood than was that of Noah. For that flood drowned [humans] during no more than one year, but baptism drowns all sorts of [humans] throughout the world, from the birth of Christ even till the day of judgment. Moreover *while that was a flood of wrath, this is a flood of grace*, as is declared in Psalm 29[:10], "God will make a continual new flood." For without a doubt many more people have been baptized than were drowned in the flood.[24]

The water of the flood that covers the Earth, that can kill and bring life to the entire creation, is transfigured, in baptism, to be a "saving flood," and,

---

beings; everything on dry land in whose nostrils was the breath of life died. [God] blotted out every living thing that was on the face of the ground, human beings and animals and creeping things and birds of the air; they were blotted out from the earth," Gen 7:19–23.

23. "I am establishing my covenant with you and your descendants after you, and with every living creature that is with you, the birds, the domestic animals, and every animal of the earth with you, as many as came out of the ark. I establish my covenant with you, that never again shall all flesh be cut off by the waters of a flood, and never again shall there be a flood to destroy the earth," Gen 9:9–11.

24. Luther, "The Holy and Blessed Sacrament of Baptism," *LW* 35:32 (my emphasis).

in Luther's preaching, not "a flood of wrath" but "a flood of grace." Thus, in baptism Luther would have us imagine grace extending even above the highest of the mountains, into the depths of the sea, and embracing all of the creation even into the future.

The Flood Prayer invites the baptizing assembly to imagine how grace can "drown" creation in order to bring everything to life. This is opposed to the "flood of wrath" which kills some in order to save the lives of others. We might say that the grace of God in Jesus Christ, according to Luther, "kills" sin metaphorically in baptism, while the flood of wrath "kills" sinful people literally and is the very flood in which Jesus himself is ultimately swept up. However, in Christ's death and resurrection, God announces an end to the flood of wrath once and for all, with some biblical imagery stretching to picture Christ preaching the good news of God's flood of grace even to those "spirits in prison" since "the days of Noah."[25]

While floods have long played an important role in a healthy global ecology, with anthropogenic climate change the image of flood today is recovering its ecologically apocalyptic resonance. Stronger storms, heavier rainfalls, thawing coastal permafrost, and rising sea levels combine to make flooding one of the more wrathful impacts of climate change. Remarkably, today's (ostensibly secular) cultural discourses sometimes frame this increased flooding as a form of divine wrath—a natural consequence of sinful social structures.[26] This conceptual framework is not wholly antithetical to Lutheran theology of Law and Gospel, and it is likely to be a helpful entry point into ecotheology. However, those who are likely to suffer the most wrathful consequences of climate change are often the least culpable for causing those changes. The carbon footprint of the rich presses on the back of the poor. The wages of carbon sin are often paid by someone other than the sinner. Even beyond these significant difficulties with understanding climate-accelerated flooding as divine punishment for sin, the Lutheran approach can never reach its *telos* in identifying a flood of wrath. As wrathful as the Genesis flood (or the rising waters of a hotter climate) may be, so the flood of baptism is even more full of grace and life giving. The flood of grace is the great desire of the God of the Gospel. Thus, for Lutherans, the very real image of the wrathful flood is always held in tension with its antitype. In the end, the gospel promise is an all-encompassing, world-changing, saving flood of

25. 1 Peter 3:18–20.

26. For reflection on the wider cultural use of "sin" as metaphor for environmental injustice, see my essay "What's the Right Rite."

grace. In the waters of baptism, the world, at last, is flooded not with wrath but with grace. At the heart of the ritual entry into Christian faith is a conversion from the ways of the flood of wrath into a life immersed and given to the flood of mercy for all.

All Water Is Holy Water

The Flood Prayer remembers that what God has done to water has been to "sanctify" it and "set [it] apart." This is the language of consecration usually used in blessings of the baptismal font. However, in the consecrations of Luther's day, the water was only sanctified when the Spirit was invoked and then descended into the local water, in a movement sometimes imaged in brutally mechanistic ways: the waters of the font became sanctified during the prayer and only the waters of the font received this sanctification. These consecrations were often interspersed with exorcisms of the "creature of water," so that evil spirits ("naturally" dwelling in water) were cast out.[27] In the Flood Prayer, not only are the consecratory and exorcistic elements eliminated, but the prayer also specifically identifies the baptism of Christ as having consecrated all water as saving flood. In other words, in Luther's prayer all water is known as consecrated, holy, flowing from God as part of the saving flood of baptism. Luther did not discard the category of holy water. He radically expanded it. Luther wrote, "Christ by the touch of his most innocent flesh has hallowed all waters, yes even all creation, through baptism."[28]

Luther's approach is consistent with an earlier theological tradition that understood the incarnation—and Christ's baptism in particular—to be a hallowing of all water and all creation. Maximus of Turin preached in the fifth century "Christ is baptized, not to be made holy by the water, but to make the water holy . . . For when the Savior is washed all water

27. See, for example, the blessing of the water at the Easter Vigil in the *Gelasian Sacramentary*, in Johnson, *Sacraments and Worship*, 143. There may be reason for such consecratory/exorcistic imagery in times and places in which people, unaware of the insights of contemporary microbiology, nevertheless correctly understand water to be teeming with powerful and threatening beings. Such life-threatening pollution may be even more widespread in waterways today. Among practitioners of exorcisms of such water, there is much more in the water than meets the eye. In most North American contexts today, however, the problem is the reverse: many people find in water "much less than meets the eye." i.e. there is little concern about the existence of powerful living creatures, natural or supernatural, that might inhabit the water.

28. Luther, "Fourteen Consolations" (1520), in *LW* 42:142.

for our baptism is made clean, purified at its source."[29] This approach
has been more widely recovered in the West especially since the mid-
twentieth century, when liturgical theologian Alexander Schmemann
introduced to wide audiences a cosmic and epiphanic approach to sacraments by way of his Orthodox tradition.[30] Catholic theologian Karl
Rahner expresses this sacramental nature of the cosmos, of which "the
sacraments" are focused expressions: "The sacraments . . . are not really to
be understood as successive individual incursions of God into a secular
world, but as 'outbursts' (if we can express it this way) of the innermost,
ever-present gracious endowment of the world with God himself [sic]
into history."[31]

A Flood of Grace Today

When those two words of the Flood Prayer, "all water," are spoken today,
they may call to mind profound and pressing questions of global ecological health. Luther's use of the metaphor of global flood in the baptismal
prayer—and his vision of all the waters of Earth participating in that saving flood of grace—has renewed significance for us who, like those in the
story of Noah, face the threat of global cataclysm. This image of flood,
which may serve as a key motif in a Christian map of the meaning of the
cosmos,[32] may contribute to the global project of re-mapping our industrial, social, and ecological world in the face of scientific discoveries of
both the wondrous interdependence of life through hydrological systems
as well as the profound degradation of those systems due to extensive and
intensive human manipulation of water.

In sum, Luther's Flood Prayer originally appears as part of a recovery of the central water-imagery of baptism and the institutionalization
of the theological concerns of the Lutheran Reformation. The metaphor
of flood hallows the entire planet (not just church or monastery) as the
arena of God's activity—the extent of this flood's reach is global and its

29. Maximus of Turin, Sermo 100 ("de Sancta Epiphania"), 1.3.

30. See especially his *Of Water and the Spirit* and *For the Life of the World.*

31. Rahner, "On the Theology of Worship," 143. I am grateful to Kristine Suna-
Koro of Xavier University for bringing this quote to my attention in a presentation of
her article at the 2016 Lutheran Caucus of the North American Academy of Liturgy:
Suna-Koro, "The Sign of Unity and the Bond of Charity," 140.

32. "The most powerful of Christian cosmological maps is the one set out in the
baptismal process." Lathrop, *Holy Ground,* 104.

intensity is radical. The reversal of the imagery of the flood-of-wrath is a powerful vehicle for Luther's theology of radical justification by grace. In our age, we do well to accent the interspecies salvation of the flood narrative. (While Luther mostly neglected this imagery to focus on the salvation of humans, contemporary theologian Cal DeWitt memorably called Noah's flood "the world's first endangered species act."[33]) The water metaphors of the flood prayer, referring both to the most local of water (that in the font) and to all the waters of Earth, urge us to know all water as holy water, a saving flood. Thus those who are baptized may be swept up in the flood of grace, to participate in the care and healing of Earth, in an age when the question of such participation has again begun to approach the global stakes of the biblical flood itself.

THE SPRING

Have you ever drunk from a spring in the wilderness? Perhaps on a summer hike you discovered the cool water bubbling up from the sandy bottom of a clear pool, or flowing out from among the rocks. Maybe after days of treating your drinking water drawn from less pristine streams, you marveled at the simplicity and sweetness of drinking directly from a spring.

Springs have long been signs of the goodness that mysteriously wells up in our world to sustain and refresh us. They are known for the purity of their water and for the cool temperatures with which they emerge from the earth. On the one hand, the location of a spring is precise and knowable. Since they rise at a particular location, they are plotted on a map not as a meandering stream but as an exact, locatable point. On the other hand, springs seem hidden and mysterious to us. Their overflowing source—all that makes them pure and refreshing (or, sometimes, hot and sulfuric)—is outside our field of vision, mostly inaccessible to us. So throughout human history, we have marked and remembered springs in order to find our way back to them. At the same time we have sought to guard springs against too much or too aggressive human contact. We especially protect them from human manipulation and misuse that fails to treat the spring as set apart, even sacred.

33. DeWitt, *Living on Earth.*

Rediscovering the Spring

Lutherans have tended to view the work of reformation as less like repairing a malfunctioning water treatment system and more like rediscovering a spring.[34] The Reformation of the sixteenth century called attention to the places where God had promised a gushing spring of abundant life and grace. Among these flowing springs of life are: the incarnate, crucified, and risen Christ with us in the world; the Sunday gathering around word and sacrament; the forgiveness of sins and justification by grace through faith; the vocations of the royal priesthood of the baptized; the importance and goodness of the arts, especially music; and the gift of mutually supportive and just human relationships, with special care and dignity for the least of these and those who especially share the sufferings of Christ. These are sources of renewal, promised by God to be constantly flowing with new life. The confessional documents of the Reformation of the sixteenth century can be seen in part as maps written to guide the church back to these forgotten or neglected springs.

Clearing Out the Spring

Sometimes, however, the work of reformation is not so much like rediscovery. It may be more like clearing out a spring that has become too familiar and taken for granted. Gordon Lathrop remembers John Vannorsdall, at his installation as president of the Lutheran Theological Seminary at Philadelphia, urging the seminary to its reforming task of "clearing out the spring," recalling "the old spring-house that used to stand on many American farms, and the relatively frequent task of clearing out the weeds and junk—even the broken-down house itself—so that the water could again flow, clear and accessible. The farmer did not make the water. But the farmer needed to clear out the spring. Our congregations always need to be clearing out the spring . . . We do not make the living water, but we can clear out the spring."[35] Vannorsdall and Lathrop suggest that the work of reformation is not only about recalling the forgotten gushing springs of God's abundant life. Sometimes the springs are familiar but obstructed or polluted. The church may be called to the work

---

34. On spring as an image for ongoing reformation, see Lathrop, *Holy Things*, 7, 122, 125.

35. Lathrop and Wengert, *Christian Assembly*, 137.

of dismantling systems or structures that pollute or impede access to the flowing springs of God's mercy.

Creation Itself Is a Spring

Today, the most pressing reform may be appreciating the creation as a life-giving spring itself, constantly flowing from its source in God. If Lutherans have identified clearly the flowing springs of word and sacrament, grace and vocation, we may today need at least equal vigor and clarity in proclaiming that Earth itself is a continually flowing spring-like fount of God's grace. Luther draws out the concept of the ongoing, overflowing act of creation in his explanation of the first article of the creed in his *Large Catechism*. At every moment, Luther writes, God the creator "constantly sustains" and "makes all creation help provide the benefits and necessities of life—sun, moon, and stars in the heavens; day and night; air, fire, water, the earth and all that it yields and brings forth; birds, fish, animals, grain, and all sorts of produce."[36]

I once heard an elementary-school-age Lutheran struggle to remember the name for what is typically known as the "The Big Bang." He furrowed his brow and asked, "what do you call it . . . 'The Great Overflowing?'" That may well be a better scientific conceptual frame for the origin of our universe. It certainly is an apt theological image for the ongoing divine act of creation, overflowing constantly, sustaining all things. This affirmation, sometimes known as *creatio continua*, predates Lutheran reforms, but it is given emphatic and ethical emphasis in the Reformation. Luther continues in the *Large Catechism*, "if we believed it [that the entire cosmos continually overflows with God's life-giving gifts] with our whole heart, we would also act accordingly, and not swagger about and boast and brag as if we had life, riches, power, honor, and such things of ourselves . . . This is the way the wretched, perverse world acts, drowned in its blindness, misusing all the blessings and gifts of God solely for its own pride, greed, pleasure, and enjoyment . . ."[37] While the ethical injunction is strong here, Luther understands the entire question in terms of grace. The continual overflowing goodness of the cosmos is

---

36. Luther's *Large Catechism*, from Luther's explanation to the first article of the creed, in Kolb, Wengert, and Arand, eds., *The Book of Concord*, 433.

37. Ibid.

an expression of God's grace: "All this [God] does out of pure love and goodness, without our merit."[38]

What would allow us to drink more frequently, directly, and mindfully from the spring of creation? In worship, we may ground every gathering in thanksgiving for the original gift of creation along with our own creaturehood shared with an unfathomably diverse choir of others. Some fonts with flowing water may flow upward into a bowl and overflow, suggesting the mystery of a spring. We may join with other human communities, especially indigenous communities, who seek to preserve and rehabilitate the fecund goodness of Earth from which we may drink directly: dark skies filled with stars; green spaces for beauty, recreation, and wild habitat for native species; enough quiet for the voices of fellow creatures to sing and be heard; clean air and water; rich land for human gardens and fresh local produce; buildings that feature natural light and surrounding landscape rather than hide it; structures and systems that work in harmony with Earth rather than against it.

FLOWING, REFORMING WATERS

These three forms of flowing water—the stream, the flood, and the spring—are metaphors from our textual traditions, they flow through our liturgical rites, and they are living ecological bodies of water on Earth. The work of eco-reformation renews our relationship with these waters in all three domains: textual/theological, liturgical, and ecological. Through water, a fellow creature with us, we encounter a witness to God, our common creator.

Even in yet another era in which humans have newly constructed religious and technological fantasies of fleeing Earth for the heavens, God comes to Earth as surely as water cascading from the mountain heights, flowing relentlessly, giving life to all of us creatures of dust. Against every scheme to save the world through destruction and violence, God desires to flood the world with mercy, saving every species on Earth, leaving nothing outside of this deluge of grace. This flood of baptismal mercy invites us to reform a too-stingy sacramentality so that we might see all water as holy water, a sign of God's desire to renew the cosmos. And the task of reformation calls us again to remember and clear out the life giving springs where God's mercy and goodness have been promised to

38. Ibid.

us. In this age of Eco-Reformation, we turn again to the first spring given to us earthly creatures: the fruitful Earth itself, overflowing with God's goodness. The call to Eco-Reformation is to help one another rediscover this spring, to drink from it deeply, and to clear out the pollution and obstacles that keep it from flowing freely for all creatures for generations to come.

BIBLIOGRAPHY

DeWitt, Calvin. "Living on Earth: The Good Book's Green Message." Interview by Steve Curwood, January 2, 2009. http://www.loe.org.

ELCA. *Evangelical Lutheran Worship: Leaders Desk Edition*. Minneapolis: Augsburg Fortress, 2006.

———. *The Use of the Means of Grace: A Statement on the Practice of Word and Sacrament*. Minneapolis: Augsburg Fortress, 1997.

Jensen, Robin Margaret. *Baptismal Imagery in Early Christianity*. Grand Rapids: Baker Academic, 2012.

Johnson, Maxwell E. *Sacraments and Worship: The Sources of Christian Theology*. Louisville: Westminster John Knox, 2011.

Kolb, Robert, Timothy J. Wengert, and Charles P. Arand, eds. *The Book of Concord: The Confessions of the Evangelical Lutheran Church*. Minneapolis: Fortress, 2000.

Lathrop, Gordon W. *Holy Ground: A Liturgical Cosmology*. Minneapolis: Fortress, 2003.

———. *Holy Things: A Liturgical Theology*. Minneapolis: Fortress, 1998.

Lathrop, Gordon W., and Timothy J. Wengert. *Christian Assembly: Marks of the Church in a Pluralistic Age*. Minneapolis: Augsburg Fortress, 2004.

Luther, Martin. "Fourteen Consolations" (1520). In *Devotional Writings* I, edited by Helmut T. Lehmann and Martin O. Dietrich. *LW* 42:169–182. Philadelphia: Fortress Press, 1969.

———. "The Holy and Blessed Sacrament of Baptism" (1519). In *Word and Sacrament* I, edited by E. Theodore Bachmann and Helmut T. Lehmann. *LW* 35:23–43. Philadelphia: Muhlenberg, 1960.

Moe-Lobeda, Cynthia D. *Resisting Structural Evil: Love as Ecological-Economic Vocation*. Minneapolis: Fortress, 2013.

Origen. *On Prayer*. Translated by William A. Curtis. N.d. http://www.ccel.org.

Rahner, Karl. "On the Theology of Worship." *Theological Investigations* 19, Faith and Ministry, translated by Edward Quinn, 141–49. New York: Crossroad, 1983.

Rhoads, David M. "Reflections on a Lutheran Theology of Creation: Foundations for a New Reformation." *Seminary Ridge Review* 15 (2012) 1–49.

Santmire, H. Paul. *Nature Reborn: The Ecological and Cosmic Promise of Christian Theology*. Minneapolis: Fortress, 2000.

———. *Ritualizing Nature: Renewing Christian Liturgy in a Time of Crisis*. Minneapolis: Fortress, 2008.

———. *The Travail of Nature: The Ambiguous Ecological Promise of Christian Theology*. Philadelphia: Fortress, 1985.

Schmemann, Alexander. *Of Water and the Spirit: A Liturgical Study of Baptism*. Crestwood, NY: St. Vladimir's Seminary Press, 1974.

————. *For the Life of the World: Sacraments and Orthodoxy*. Crestwood, NY: St. Vladimir's Seminary Press, 1977.

Senn, Frank C. *Christian Liturgy: Catholic and Evangelical*. Minneapolis: Fortress, 1997.

Slingerland, Edward G. "Conceptual Blending, Somatic Marking, and Normativity." *Cognitive Linguistics* 16 (2005) 557–84.

Stewart, Benjamin M. "Flooding the Landscape: Luther's Flood Prayer and Baptismal Theology." *CrossAccent: Journal of the Association of Lutheran Church Musicians* 13 (2005) 4–14.

————. "The Role of Baptismal Water at the Vigil of Easter in the Liturgical Generation of Eco-Theology." PhD Dissertation, Emory University, 2010. http://pid.emory. edu/ark:/25593/7mckz.

————. "Spring, Flood, and Spring: Water Renewing the Earth and the Church." *Living Lutheran* 1 (April 2016) 14–19.

————. "Water in Worship: The Ecology of Baptism." *Christian Century* 128 (Fall 2011) 22–25.

————. "What's the Right Rite: Treating Environmental Degradation as Sickness or Sin." *Currents in Theology and Mission* 43 (March 22, 2016). http://currentsjournal. org.

Suna-Koro, Kristine. "The Sign of Unity and the Bond of Charity: On the Eucharist as a 'Taskmaster' in the Context of Global Migration." *Dialog* 53 (2014) 138–48.

Taft, Robert F. *The Liturgy of the Hours in East and West: The Origins of the Divine Office and Its Meaning for Today*. Collegeville, MN: Liturgical, 1986.

11

Rewilding Christian Spirituality

Outdoor Sacraments and the Life of the World

—LISA E. DAHILL

In May 2012, a friend and I took an eight-day bicycle trip from Pittsburgh to Washington, DC. Our trek . . . began through the valley of the Youghiogheny River in western Pennsylvania. Tall trees shaded the trail; the shale hillsides were alive with water . . . All this water brought ladyslippers, trillium, buttercups, thick stands of laurel and rhododendron. The creeks were full of turtles and choruses of frogs and toads, air alive with dragonflies, butterflies, and songbirds. [In all directions,] in sound and sight and the sparkling (or rain-spattered) waters of the great river itself—life was teeming.

[Later in] the first day . . . the path moved under a high overpass. Far above us, motorists on I-70 were rocketing along at 65 mph, most presumably hardly noticing that a river snaked below. Passengers would have had to peer over the rail intently . . . as they zoomed past to have seen our bike path at all, let alone the two of us on it; and from that distance and speed all the wet complexity in which we were immersed and the creatures so vivid for us would have been a green blur disappearing as quickly as it had appeared.

I-70 is the interstate whose steady hum [was] audible from my backyard in Columbus, Ohio, and it gives travelers easy access to the seminary where I [taught]. I travel[ed] it regularly. So the experience of seeing that highway from far beneath . . .

was striking. From . . . the beautiful living thickness of the world itself in all its created reality, the oblivious world of the interstate seemed impossibly remote, even alien. We were perpendicular—cross-wise—to it in direction, and hundreds of yards beneath it in plane. That day on the Youghiogheny River gave form to a perception I am coming to call *perpendicularity*: the experience of the disconnection between much of contemporary human life from the living reality of the natural world.[1]

CONTEXT

We know the staggering dimensions of this alienation: the extent to which our current economic system and worldviews fail to take account of our planet's limits and our own place in the larger biological world on which our lives depend. We recognize—most of us, now and then, maybe in a rueful way—the extent to which our fossil-fueled lives charge along in more or less complete experiential detachment from the rest of the biosphere. We try to take in the scientific data tracking the effects of our global economic engines, culminating in the most recent IPCC report of the searing future we face if current greenhouse-gas emissions continue: "the likelihood of severe, pervasive and irreversible impacts for people and ecosystems."[2] What's going on down there, way below our interstates, off the edges of our screens, beyond our earbuds? The cascading patterns of disruption of our planet's core life-support systems, whole species and ecosystems wiped out and gone forever—exacerbating human trauma, dislocation, war, famine, and economic exploitation—*and* the astonishing beauty of the natural world itself, in its still-sustaining wildness and diversity and abundance: all this complexity and mystery of the biosphere is out there, both transcending us and withering under our attack.

To face this reality of climate chaos is the challenge Laurie Zoloth outlined in her 2014 presidential address to the American Academy of

---

1. Dahill, "The View from *Way* Below," 250–51. I first used the term "perpendicularity" in a companion piece published a year earlier. See "Bio-Theoacoustics." The present essay is revised from my 2015 presidential address to the Society for the Study of Christian Spirituality, titled "Into Local Waters: Rewilding the Study of Christian Spirituality." The original address is published in *Spiritus: A Journal of Christian Spirituality* (adapted here with permission).

2. IPCC, *Climate Change 2014 Synthesis Report*, 8.

Religion: to recognize this emergency for what it is, the shattering "inter-ruption" of our ordinary priorities and projects, the shock of our lives jolting all humans into new thinking and leadership and requiring us in whatever roles we serve in church or society to step up into leadership and activism. Each person needs to discern and give their own signal contributions toward turning this gigantic ship that is our shared Western economic system.[3] In this past summer's watershed encyclical, *Laudato Si': On Care for Our Common Home,* Pope Francis calls on all people of Earth to "acknowledge the appeal, immensity, and urgency of the chal-lenge we face" and to join in "a new dialogue about how we are shaping the future of our planet . . . a conversation that includes everyone, since the environmental challenge we are undergoing, and its human roots, concern and affect us all." Indeed, we need what Pope Francis calls "eco-logical conversion": a whole new way of being Christian and human.[4]

This essay is my response to these appeals from Zoloth and Pope Francis, along with the cries from all over Earth of those already suffering the effects of climate change and global economic injustice, and the great call echoing from the planetary systems necessary for the flourishing of life as we know it. How does Christian spirituality creatively cherish and respond to the new "Eaarth" we inhabit, the new geologic age we have entered?[5] Here I outline a Christian spirituality of biocentric sacramen-tal reimmersion into reality: "rewilding" Christian spiritual practice for the Anthropocene.[6] To summarize at the outset: I believe that Christian ecological conversion requires new and re-prioritized physical, spiritual, and intellectual immersion in the natural world. Thus I will argue for res-toration of the early church's practice of baptizing in local waters, for new

---

3. Zoloth, "2014 AAR Presidential Address," 3–24.

4. Pope Francis, *Laudato Si',* paras.14–15, 216–21. In this call to ecological con-version Francis echoes Thomas Berry's appeal to contribute to the Great Work of our time: "Our hope for the future is for a new dawn, an Ecozoic Era, when humans will be present to the Earth in a mutually enhancing manner." Berry, *The Great Work,* 55.

5 McKibben, *Eaarth.* On the data supporting scientists' coining and usage of the term "Anthropocene" to describe the new geological epoch into which human green-house emissions have already brought our planet, see Hamilton, et al., eds., *The An-thropocene and the Global Environmental Crisis.*

6. I use the language of "rewilding" in this essay in debt to George Monbiot, whose work *Feral* brought the movement of literal rewilding to a large readership. I am also influenced by Gary Snyder, *The Practice of the Wild,* and David Abram, whose books *The Spell of the Sensuous* and *Becoming Animal* model an immersive presence to the life and lives of the biosphere that I experience as authentically, i.e., *wildly,* baptismal.

forms of outdoor Eucharistic life, and for reclaiming primary attention to the Book of Nature alongside our attention to the Book of Scripture.

We hear the cries of Earth's most vulnerable precisely as *Christians*—bearing the distinctively Christian burden of responsibility for the present crisis. Lynn White famously articulated this responsibility in 1967 in his article, "The Historical Roots of Our Ecologic Crisis," asserting that Christianity is uniquely and dangerously anthropocentric, in a biocentric world marked by mutuality, not domination and dominion.[7] Despite decades of Christian contesting or nuancing of White's claims, they still accuse us. As a civilization based on historically Christian principles, in at least nominally Euro-American Christian societies, and sustained by continuing Christian legitimation, we are "losing track of nature" in ways now that White never imagined, via the ever-thickening layers of technology, video screens, virtuality, robotics, etc.[8] Thus, responding adequately to Lynn White's critiques—and to the appeals from Laurie Zoloth and Pope Francis—requires Christians perhaps above all to forge truly new forms of thinking and practice for our time: the Eco-Reformation to which this volume calls us.

For indeed Christian spirituality too is complicit in heedlessness to the natural world. Despite the incarnational and sacramental heart of the Christian vision, theologians and mystics through the ages have contributed to the formation of dualistic, otherworldly forms of piety that have had profoundly damaging effects. These are not the whole story of Christian spirituality, by any means; our traditions, including Lutheranism, are also full of Earth-loving spiritualities, the sacramental imagination, beauty and grace in every leaf. How can we then help explore and generate old or new forms of Christian practice that can creatively reconnect us to the larger life of the Earth? I ponder this question first within my own experience.

7. White, "The Historical Roots of Our Ecological Crisis."

8. The language of "losing track of nature" comes from Jennifer Price, *Flight Maps*, 164. Many scholars have documented the alienating effects of technology in human experience of the natural world. The psychic cost of this alienation is traced in work by, among many others, Paul Shepard: see, e.g., "The Domesticators." The popular examination of the human cost of alienation from nature received a boost from the work of Richard Louv, especially *Last Child in the Woods*.

BIOCENTRIC BAPTISMAL SPIRITUALITY

Since a sabbatical five years ago, I have felt increasingly uncomfortable in human religious worlds and discourse, all religious rooms, even the intimacy of prayer that was my home for so long. From within a long and intimate relationship with Jesus filling prayer, community, vocation, and sacramental worship, something began to shift. It was as if one day the chancel walls gave way and I stepped through and realized it's *all* chancel, this sacramental *world*, the real world. And so I've been living increasingly outdoors for years now—out in the creek, in the Ohio woods, now inside the California wind, its stunning oceanic expanse. What's harder is that I have no idea what is going on. It's disorienting: Jesus is dissolved, all that's left is the wind . . . the *literal* wind, the outdoor wind breathed from trees and cold fronts that fills my lungs and pushes against me on my bike and lifts pollen and petals and termites and spores up and out and this is all I seem to need, ever—but is this Christian? Is it really prayer? It's strange prayer, as it opens, this utter outdoor-ness. All I want is to live in the water—the literal water, the creek near my home in Ohio, actual rocks, with literal salamanders and mayflies, and those who fish here. Now the ocean, the elusive drenching California rain.

This was not my own idea; this sending simply *happened*, shoving me out into a vast world where religion doesn't matter to the salamanders on their own terms. I can't seem to come back inside; the creation itself is all I want, its wild particularity and beauty, its complexity. And having pondered this for years, slowly I began to realize that perhaps this urge out into the wildness of the world was an invitation not *out of* faith but further into some stranger face of God: being invited to learn from the creation about a Creator who speaks in wild languages I don't understand: bird languages, drought languages, smells and winds, predation, illness, death, life . . . the natural world my holy book.

This is hard. The surprise has been to realize with Job that being shoved out of human religious God-worlds into the scale and strangeness of the real world is itself divine address, the un-reading of Scripture, itself held within Scripture. The whirled interruption blows apart the closed-loop discourse Job and his friends have been exchanging. That airless airspace where human concerns are all that matter, the boring global static of endless human voices and debating: it all ends. The divine presence—the Name that cannot be spoken—breaks in with a radically *non*-anthropocentric vision, offensively, redemptively theo-centric, bio-centric.[9] And if even Job on his ash heap needs opening to the dazzling complexity and beauty of the layers of life cascading and interdependent on this gorgeous radiant miracle of a planet, out here on the far thin edge of the universe—to see the Creator's beauty and wisdom and logic filamented through every cell and star and membrane and muscle, every stem and fruit and feather—then how much more do we so-called privileged ones need this vision?

And so I began to see how the sacramental Word I had loved indoors, in so many gorgeous Eucharists and transforming contemplative monastic retreats—how this *Logos* lives *outdoors*. Jesus dissolved into the natural world. I experienced an ecstatic immersive baptism into the literal life of the world; with David Abram I discovered

> our carnal inherence in a more-than-human matrix of sensations and sensibilities. Our bodies have formed themselves in delicate reciprocity with the manifold textures, sounds, and shapes of an animate earth—our eyes have evolved in subtle interaction with *other* eyes, as our ears are attuned by their very structure to the howling of wolves and the honking of geese. To shut ourselves off from these other voices, to continue by our lifestyles to condemn these other sensibilities to the oblivion of extinction, is to rob our own senses of their integrity, and to rob our minds of their coherence. We are human only in contact, and conviviality, with what is not human.[10]

Out in that contact and conviviality I found an astonishing fullness of life that I slowly began to name *as* the baptismal life, a much wilder immersion than I had ever imagined. I have come to recognize that the ecological conversion to which we are summoned requires not only brilliant scholarship, new theologies, even papal encyclicals. Restoring 2.2 billion Christians to the passionate and intimate love of Earth requires Christians' literal re-immersion, through baptism the primal sacrament, back into the wild life of Earth's hydrologic system. And so my first and primary proposal is to restore the normative practice of Christian baptism into local waters.

---

9. See Schifferdecker, "Of Stars and Sea Monsters"; and McKibben, *The Comforting Whirlwind*. See too H. Paul Santmire's work in developing a "theo-cosmocentric" Christian spirituality in *Before Nature*.

10 Abram, *The Spell of the Sensuous*, 22.

The early church, like John the Baptist, practiced baptism in the rivers available; that was what "living water" meant—flowing water, a connection to a larger fullness of life considered intrinsic to the sacrament itself. In time this river-water was re-routed into indoor baptisteries and eventually separated from its river-source into ever tinier fonts, until what had been a fully immersive outdoor sacrament has become, in most communities around the world, an indoor rite using the minimum necessary amount of water. In his 1977 study, *Baptism,* historian Martin Marty notes how far Christian practice has moved from "the early understanding which involved relishing, drowning in, and enjoying the water of life. The baptismal river became a pool; the pool became a well or cistern; the cistern became a barrel; the barrel became a font; the font became a birdbath; the birdbath became a bowl; the bowl became a fingerbowl."[11] Even laudable efforts in liturgical communities more recently to learn what Baptists and others have been modeling all along—the transforming symbolic power of full immersion in baptism, and construction of fonts with the sounds of running water and immersive capacity—still result in baptisms taking place in indoor rituals more or less fully cut off from the actual biological life of the larger watersheds in which such communities are located.

I want to move back out: to step away from chlorinated tapwater in bowls or pools in climate-controlled rooms, and to restore the practice of Christian baptism into the uncontrolled, dangerous, transforming waters of a community's watershed.[12] We know that forms of practice powerfully shape belief, *habitus,* worldview; liturgical scholar Benjamin Stewart has demonstrated how powerfully the *form* of baptismal experience—full immersion or sprinkling—shapes in formative ways participants' spontaneous, untutored articulation of what their baptism *means.*[13] Thus the practice of indoor baptism, however powerfully enacted, does not necessarily translate, in people's imagination, into the sort of radical spiritual/

---

11. Marty, *Baptism,* 18. The earliest church practice of baptizing in rivers appears in the *Didache,* chapter 7: "baptize . . . in living water. If you do not have living water, baptize in other water; if you cannot in cold, then in warm; if you do not have either, pour water on the head three times . . ." (cited in Bradshaw, *Early Christian Worship,* 8).

12. Here I acknowledge my gratitude to the work and vision of Ched Myers, a pioneer in "watershed discipleship," or learning to practice Christian life in relationship with the creatures, forces, and features of one's actual local watershed. See "From 'Creation Care' to 'Watershed Discipleship.'"

13. Stewart, *The Role of Baptismal Water at the Vigil of Easter in the Liturgical Generation of Eco-Theology.*

ecological immersion into the actual local watershed and the largest life of Earth that we need today.

But what if baptism moves outdoors again? Some communities have never left: rural African-American communities in particular still baptize joyfully in rivers as they have done for centuries. And Russian Orthodox Christians' rites of blessing the waters at the Feast of the Baptism of Jesus in early January bring worshipers out to the local creek or lake in joyful—even immersive—connection to the larger baptismal blessing of these waters in Christ.[14] But for many of us, such immersion is new and strange. If baptism moves outdoors, can we baptize at Easter Vigils, in Northern Hemisphere cold? What about pollution? Is it safe? Will we die?

This is not an idle question. In many places in the world, local water sources are so polluted that immersion in them represents an immediate danger. Theologian Lynn Hofstad has traced the ecological and theological dimensions of the problem of pollution in river-based Hindu and Christian water rites in an essay titled, "Murky Symbols: How Contamination Affects the Symbolic Meaning of Water in Religious Rituals."[15] There she writes, "The result of [the] toxic mix of human, agricultural, and industrial waste [in rivers throughout India and Southeast Asia] is water that is not fit for human consumption or even use."[16] Needless to say, such poisonous water is also unfit for ritual, symbolic use: rather than bringing new *life,* it quite literally brings *death.*[17] As Hofstad's work and other analyses make clear, the safety and purity of local water for adequate symbolic use in Christian baptism is an urgent pastoral question in many places, regardless whether the rite takes place indoors or out.[18] But enough water to fill a font can be purchased by those with adequate means, whereas the watershed itself is all that's available for the poorest

14. See Denysenko, *The Blessing of the Waters and Epiphany.*

15. Hofstad, "Murky Symbols."

16. Hofstad, "Murky Symbols," 29. Footnote 70 (p. 23) describes the pollution in the Yamuna River in India: "The water from over 50,000 industries and over eight million people flows largely untreated into the river. The Yamuna water that leaves Delhi contains dangerous amounts of arsenic, cyanide, lead, mercury, and other industrial pollutants, as well as considerable amounts of human excrement. People get chemical burns and skin diseases from bathing in the water, and the government has declared all crops grown on the banks of the Yumana unfit for human consumption." See Haberman, "River of Love in an Age of Pollution," 348.

17. Hofstad, "Murky Symbols," 31.

18 Ibid., 30. See also McGann, "A Theopolitics of Water."

participants. If the practice of *all* Christian baptism moves normatively outdoors, this forces even the rich in a given area to have "skin in the game." If they can't just purchase water for indoor rites but must baptize their children in the local river with everyone else, might that not oblige the rich to use their political muscles differently?

Even in the U.S., where natural water sources are comparatively clean, the radical vulnerability such baptismal practice entails is part of its sacramental power: drawing us close to the incarnation, crucifixion, and resurrection of the *Logos* permeating all things, the effects of our own economy's devastation, the raw edges of many creatures' survival needs. We might run across people without permanent homes, camping among those trees; we might need to know how to distinguish poison oak from live oak. If we baptize in local waters we will need to know the local scientists who monitor pollution levels, to learn what is safe and what isn't, and to join the activists fighting to defend and restore this creek, this river, this lake or ocean. We will need to know the watershed more intimately than we ever imagined if we are to baptize out here. Restoring the practice of baptism outdoors thus dramatically broadens the meaning of being Christian: not excluding human-communal levels of spiritual meaning but extending those to include now also one's spiritual incorporation into experienced immersive kinship with the larger biological community in which one lives and into the hydrological cycle of the Earth itself, its jeopardy and beauty. Thus being Christian comes to mean, also, baptized into the full wildness of the world and its flourishing, and into this particular watershed. It is utterly *immersive*.[19]

I first sensed the power of this movement once home from that Youghiogheny trip, when I realized I wanted to go all the way in. I bought an inflatable kayak and set out for my first voyage late one June afternoon, deciding to explore Alum Creek near my home. I was astonished to realize that at kayak level in the water, the surrounding trees blocked all urban view except for the occasional bridge overhead, and these trees were filled with warblers, crows, vultures, hawks, the creek itself populated with ducks and herons, as well as the occasional kingfisher. Around the roots of the trees that first magical dusk voyage I saw a skunk, a mink, a family of raccoons climbing one of the sycamores overarching the river. But it was in the water—which from street view above I

19. Video games are also described with this adjective, of course. Thus my proposal for full-body immersion in local waters describes an alternative as well to the seductive and dis-placing grip of "virtual reality."

had assumed was basically dead—that the miracle happened. The golden light of the late afternoon somehow hit at just the right angle that the stream's depth lit up, and I was stunned to see masses of tiny fish darting in union, shadowy carp, many mollusk shells, riparian plants, some bass, even a water-snake. The water was clear as light, rich with nymphs and organisms, each milliliter of this urban stream full of life, and I knew for the first time that the water supporting life is *itself alive*. Living water is wild water. And I sensed how urgently Christianity and Christians and I needed to be baptized fully *into these actual waters,* these living waters. Over the years I kept kayaking, and began wading and swimming as well, getting to know this creek. I began designing seminary rites of baptismal remembrance along its banks, and I learned how the herons and riparian creatures and homeless folks at the edges of our circle pull ritual language out into all sorts of new connections.[20]

A student in this period, Robin Lutjohann, added his own testimony to my expanding baptismal vision.[21] Robin was a master's student at Harvard when he came to faith through his connection with the ministry of University Lutheran Church in Cambridge, Massachusetts. Desiring baptism, he asked if this rite could take place not in the sanctuary's font but in the Charles River; the pastor, Joanne Engquist, was happy to plan this with him. Robin describes his experience as a joyously public processional event, open to and engaging of bystanders and boaters struck by this community, following a cross, with streamers and violin and drum, toward a baptism into this river Charles with all its history and beauty and industry and legend. Robin emerged from those waters a Christian with a huge dripping joyful connection to *all* of this life.

His experience reminds me that we are baptized not only into the human Body of Christ, but into bodies of real water with their own public political and ecological life, and into the Body of God in Sallie McFague's sense: the biosphere, spoken into abundance of life by the Word itself.[22] Practicing baptism in this way—like Robin's—is harder than baptism in a room. It's more dangerous, more public, more political, more euphoric; it binds participants to the literal water of a given place at the heart of their experience of Christ, and it binds community members to one another and to all other forms of life in that place in an unforgettable intimacy.

20. See Dahill, "Life in All Its Fullness."
21. Personal communication, 2015.
22. McFague, *The Body of God.*

Such practice takes seriously the *biological and literal* dimensions of the Word becoming flesh, becoming matter, taking on and permeating and filling all created life.[23]

How might the Christian imagination and vocation—Christian spirituality itself—expand if all or most baptisms, as well as baptismal affirmations, took place out *in local waters*? How urgently might we and all the Christians of a given watershed take action, in that case, against degradation of these waters, endangering the vulnerable humans we long to baptize here, or against policies that dump toxic waste in certain zip codes, poisoning children and leaching into drinking water? How might the Spirit who fills all Earth's baptismal waters, oxygenated and alive, animate our protest of water's privatization, pollution, and waste? Could baptism into real waters break the catastrophic spell of otherworldliness for good—could it enact viscerally at last what being Christian means, today: our shared physical and spiritual participation in the threats and the aliveness of God in the life of the world itself?

REWILDING CHRISTIAN SPIRITUALITY: BAPTISM, EUCHARIST, WORD

Thus my first proposal for a re-wilding Christian spirituality is to move baptism outdoors to the fullest extent locally possible.[24] My proposal thickens and makes explicit what baptismal life means: the closest possible union with the biologically and ecologically incarnate, crucified, risen Christ, the *wild Logos* inhabiting all Earth's watery life, through whom indeed all things were made.[25] Baptism into this divine life filling all that is creates new kin in this wild *Logos*, a new Body of Christ: every species made of stardust, threaded with DNA, cycling life through its membranes, a whole new relationality in this Word and Wisdom to

23. Sacramentally oriented traditions have always insisted on the primacy of the literally embodied dimension of Word and sacraments, inseparable from their symbolic function; see, e.g., Lathrop, *Holy Ground*; and Gibler, *From the Beginning to Baptism*. My proposal draws this physicality explicitly into the larger biotic relationality essential today.

24. With this proposal I am in no way intending to deny the goodness also of indoor baptism, the womblike character of deeply enclosed watery ritual. But to effect and proclaim the ecological conversion our planet needs, the *primary or normative* site of Christian baptism needs to return outdoors, our fundamental physical and spiritual re-immersion into Earth's hydrological cycle and the life of a particular watershed.

25. John 1:1–5. On Logos theology, see Johnson, "Deep Christology."

which we're joined in the water. And an expanded vision of Christian life then calls for a fuller Eucharistic life as well, one adequate to this multiplicity of human, divine, and interspecies relations, stretchy enough to encompass and nourish this deep geo-/hydro-/biological immersion.

In 2012, I wrote about the power of such outdoor movement in Eucharistic experience, through a liturgy a seminary colleague and I had designed and led. The essay engages five dimensions of such outdoor experience: a) the question of the outdoors as "holy ground," b) the practice of sharing peace with other creatures, c) Eucharistic implications of the edibility of our own flesh to other animals, d) the practice of non-verbal rites connecting participants in direct sensory ways with the larger world, and e) the rethinking of questions of sending, thresholds, and liminality when worship takes place outside of a "sanctuary."[26] I continue to be intrigued with all of these questions, perhaps most of all with the one listed third here: the Eucharistic implications of that unsettling mystery of our bodies' edibility to other creatures.

> Lutherans cherish the physicality of the sacraments, the edibility of divine life as Jesus' body and blood permeate and incorporate ours. This physical theology experienced in one's own body in every Eucharistic celebration provides a crucial link to the physicality of all food, of all life, and to questions of poverty and abundance, hunger and delight, as these take flesh in billions of human bodies and the living land and water that feed us, all over our earth. Much Christian thinking over the centuries has pressed the ethical implications of our Eucharistic sharing in the "one bread" of the hungry in the one Body of Christ. We do not as often ponder further how our bodies' edibility by other creatures (from wolves to mosquitoes) provides a similarly Eucharistic ethic of our species' participation in the rest of creation. As privileged North Americans we may speak of "stewardship" of creation—from a position of dominance and inviolability—but too often shun uncomfortable questions of how Jesus' *kenosis* [self-emptying] models a similarly radical availability of our human flesh and life for the thriving of other species or ecosystems, and of marginalized human beings on Earth. Might movement outdoors . . . open us to the sacramental implications of our permeability to the rest of creation?[27]

26. Dahill, "Indoors, Outdoors."

27. Ibid., 115–16. For more on the holy and unsettling mystery of our bodies' edibility to other creatures, see the incisive work of Jewish environmental philosopher James Hatley: "The Uncanny Goodness of Being Edible to Bears"; and "Blood

In both of the primary Christian sacraments, joined in the flesh of the central sacrament that is Jesus Christ incarnate in all that is, therefore, we are invited *out*. More starkly than any previous generation of Christians, we face the choice to participate in the noticing and speaking and loving now of this living Word, in all its beauty and power, or to be increasingly complicit in the ongoing silencing of this Word, the very *Logos* of God in all that is. For it is precisely this living Word, the *Logos* permeating the creation in unique and marvelous forms all over this Earth, that our present economic systems are extinguishing, day after day after day.

Thus, in addition to moving the practice of Christian baptism and Eucharistic life outdoors, my final proposal is to learn again to hear and love this living Word not only in the Book of Scripture but also in what earlier centuries of Christians called the Book of Nature.[28] In proposing attention to the Book of Nature as a distinctive focus I am not asserting that nature on the one hand, and its religious apperception through Scripture and tradition on the other, really are fundamentally separate; in fact, it is precisely because the natural world itself participates in divine revelation that I am asserting the indispensability of attending to it. What that means, however, is complex. We are good at reading texts, but the text that is the natural world speaks in mysterious languages that are both increasingly remote from much of our daily experience and rapidly being destroyed in their intact wild life. How can we speak of attention to the Book of Nature as a constitutive element of Christian spirituality? I see *three primary strategies:* development of skill in contemplative eco-hermeneutics, increased attention to the natural sciences, and attention to indigenous and Earth-centered spiritualities in our interfaith work.

Spiritual or Contemplative Eco-Hermeneutics

The language of "eco-hermeneutics" is used in various ways today.[29] Rather than the biblical or philosophical uses of this language, I am here engaging the work of Douglas Christie, who traces an eco-hermeneutics distinctive to Christian spiritual practice. Christie's 2013 book, *The*

Intimacies and Biodicy."

28. For more on attending to the Book of Nature, see my expanded development in "Into Local Waters," as well as Clingerman, "Reading the Book of Nature."

29. See the essays by Norman C. Habel, Barbara R. Rossing, and David M. Rhoads in this volume for attention to biblical eco-hermeneutics; for more on philosophical eco-hermeneutics, see among others Clingerman et al., eds, *Interpreting Nature.*

Blue Sapphire of the Mind: Notes for a Contemplative Ecology, brings together resources of the Christian contemplative tradition—particularly
the earliest monastic immersions in Word and silence, desert and the
heart—*and* the contemporary moral and spiritual urgency of learning
to attend today with just such disciplined and devoted spiritual presence to the natural world as a place of divine encounter. In his chapter
titled "*Logos:* The Song of the World,"[30] Christie traces the contours of
sustained Christian contemplative attention to the living Word through
whom all things were made, from early philosophical grounding of
desert monastics' understanding of *Logos* into the practice of presence
to this Word precisely in and through the particular faces, sounds, and
movements of the creatures and forces of creation everywhere around
them. Showing how for these Christians the distinctive logic manifest in
each creature—hummingbird or lichen or cicada—embodies in a fundamentally trustworthy way a revelation of this divine Word, Christie
calls contemporary pray-ers too into deeply contemplative attention to
the creatures and larger forces of creation, precisely as means of divine
encounter. He writes: "There is a strong and recurring appreciation in
Christian contemplative thought and practice for the revelatory power
of the Word . . . as the enlivening force behind and within every living
being . . . [In attending to the world itself] One finds vivid traces . . . of an
incarnate Word. To listen to this Word is to become aware of a language
arising from the shape and texture of the living world, a Word as old as
the world itself."[31]

Such attention requires time in conscious awareness of this world
and its creatures in order to begin to get to know the patterns of their
sounds and movements, to learn to hear, or read, or sense them: the language of the spiritual senses returned to actual physical connection with
the creatures around us.[32] Surely the minimum hermeneutical attention
we need to give the Book of Nature is simply to get outdoors in a regular
and sustained way and begin listening: deepening relationship with that
wild *Logos* permeating all that is.

---

30. Christie, *Blue Sapphire of the Mind,* 179–222.

31. Ibid., 193, 208.

32. I develop this proposal at more length in my essay, "Bio-Theoacoustics."

Natural Sciences as Dialogue Partners

Part of contemporary alienation from ecological reality and need is that (as many have noted) at least since the Enlightenment the split between the worlds of "science" and "religion" has increasingly separated these two interwoven Books of divine revelation, to the conceptual impoverishment of both. Science can lose touch with the sacredness of all that is and participate in increasingly destructive forms of technology and exploitation of the biosphere, while religion—even the sacramental Christian imagination—is too often cut off from the vast weird mystery and beauty inherent in scientific insight: the emergence of new forms of life itself, the most intricate cell-biological processes, the scope of cosmic grandeur. Thus a second dimension of attention to the Book of Nature involves learning our way into natural-scientific fields and into scientific literacy generally. Systematic and constructive theologians have been engaging in dialogue with the natural sciences for decades in ways that have transformed the face of Christian theological reflection.[33] It's no easy task of course to become fluent in the technical, arcane, often mathematically-based sciences at the depth needed for them to inform our thinking. Yet surely all Christians must continue to deepen our listening from whatever point of scientific engagement we now have. If we are to contribute in vital ways toward the Great Work of our time, we need to hear what scientists are telling us. Only in this way can we discern where our gifts might make the most important difference, where our expertise can help Christians and humans and other species negotiate what is certain to be an agonizing, catastrophic set of transitions ahead, and how our distinctive voices best contribute to the much larger project of the world's life.

Indigenous Listening

We learn to listen to the natural world itself as a primary contemplative and mysteriously hermeneutical practice; we learn to listen to scientists who help us live into our world's life and death; we need to learn to listen also to indigenous leaders in particular and those who practice non-dualistic religions and spiritualities. Pope Francis too urges this priority of attention: "it is essential to show special care for indigenous communities

33. Those interested in listening into these conversations might begin with the work published in *Zygon: Journal of Religion and Science*. http://www.zygonjournal.org/.

and their cultural traditions. They are not merely one minority among others, but should be the principal dialogue partners."[34] Yet the unfortunate historical relationships between European Christians' "exploration," colonizing, dominating, and evangelizing of the rest of the world means that European-descended Christians do not have a good history of respectful listening to those who know the land best, let alone learning from them. As Tink Tinker writes, "[W]e need to step back and notice that Indian peoples and their cultures were some of the first victims of the eco-destructive machine that invaded this continent from Europe . . . Parked on so-called reservations, Indian people are [still] largely absent from American consciousness, erased even as we continue to live—in desperate poverty."[35]

Tinker's warning reminds us that learning from and with indigenous dialogue partners—like any truly transforming encounter—is not first a matter of books and study but a long-term, in-person, first-person process. Who are the indigenous inhabitants of your watershed? Do any members of this community live nearby? What resources will help us all listen more deeply to the past and present insights of non-dualistic spiritual communities toward cherishing together the places and planet we inhabit?[36]

CONCLUSION: WILD CHRISTIAN LIFE

I have asserted that outdoor Christian practices of Word and sacrament can help recast the meaning of Christian life toward encountering the *wild Logos* incarnate and filling all that is: a rewilded Christian *spirit*-uality.[37] Here Jesus Christ is not a mark of separation—Christians on one

34. Pope Francis, *Laudato Si'*, para.146. Francis continues, "For them, land is not a commodity but rather a gift from God and from their ancestors who rest there, a sacred space with which they need to interact if they are to maintain their identity and values. When they remain on their land, they themselves care for it best."

35 Tinker, "American Indians and Ecotheology," 71–72.

36. Because written insights also matter, one might look to the work collected in Grim, ed., *Indigenous Traditions and Ecology*, along with resources particular to a given place or project.

37. In "Into Local Waters," I expand questions of the Spirit: "What Spirit animates a baptismal practice and life outdoors, in full immersion into the natural world on its own terms? Do we have new contributions toward naming the experience of those who sense the Spirit alive in our *spirit*-ualities in more comprehensively ecological terms? From John Muir's ecstatically mountain- and rock-centered Spirit and spirituality, to

side, non-Christians elsewhere. Here Christ is the one who brings Christians and our best wisdom, faith, and practice back into restored unity in our *shared* waters with all people and all creatures. In a time of so many religious divisions, and of increasing interfaith or multi-religious collaboration, such baptismal Earth-belonging can help create truly shared *religious* space: namely this water, this creation we all love.[38] For people of all religions breathe the same air, drink the same water, are creatures of the same biosphere with one another and trillions of other kin, beyond our species. To all these Christians too are joined in the literal baptismal waters and watersheds of our place.

I am also curious about conceiving of forms of *interspecies* faith out here in the water. Does the Body of Christ into whom we are baptized—that *wild Logos*—include the fish, plants, birds, insects, animals, shellfish, and microbes alive in these waters as well? Can a Christian spirituality include I/Thou relations with creatures beyond the human? St. Francis thought so—but there haven't been many serious calls for interspecies spirituality since.[39] What kinds of prayer and practice will test, probe, and celebrate a rewilding baptism, new rites and renunciations, new forms of community, new watershed spiritualities?

At the outset of this essay I used the language of "perpendicularity" to describe the perception of radically *cross-wise* orientation from my usual fast-pace, technologically driven forms of life: an immersion in a world much thicker and slower and relationally diverse than that of the interstate highway far above. I find this image continuing to echo in me, as I still ponder the shape of the baptismal and intellectual Christian life. In whatever ways I can, I want to get off the freeway and back to the bike path, all the way into the river. I want to learn from those who live "way below" our destructive economic systems how life looks from their perspective. With all those contributing to this volume, and countless others around the world today, I want an Eco-Reformation for the life of the world.

Teilhard de Chardin's luminous vision of the universe encompassed fully in Christ, to contemporary eco-feminist and eco-liberation thinkers, Christians are expanding what we mean by 'Spirit' in many directions," 158.

38. The visionary collaboration between eco-philosopher Mary Evelyn Tucker and physicist Brian Swimme attempts, through a series of projects (book, film, curricula, web resources) to give vision and voice to this "Big Story" that is the universe itself, shared by all. See http://www.journeyoftheuniverse.org/.

39. My own work, "The View from *Way* Below," is an initial attempt in this direction, toward an interspecies Eucharistic spirituality.

How do climate change and the wild baptismal Spirit of life inter-
rupt our lives and call us into new leadership in the crises already unfolding on Earth? In small and large ways, with generosity and creativity,
we need all hands on deck. And we need a Christian spirituality for our
time, attentive to each endangered creature in our watersheds and across
the Earth—a spirituality courageous enough to name our complicity
with eco-erasure and climate injustice, to critique and turn from forms
of piety that no longer serve us well, and to invite all Christians into the
waters of life, for the life of the world. Grace calls us out into a much
larger communion, unpaved, unprivileged. The water's alive—let's go in.

BIBLIOGRAPHY

Abram, David. *Becoming Animal: An Earthly Cosmology.* New York: Vintage, 2010.
———. *The Spell of the Sensuous: Perception and Language in a More-than-Human World.* New York: Vintage, 1996.
Austin, Richard Cartwright. "Spirituality." In *Baptized into Wilderness: A Christian Perspective on John Muir,* 23–31. Abingdon, VA: Creekside, 1991.
Berry, Thomas. *The Great Work: Our Way Into the Future.* New York: Random, 1999.
Bradshaw, Paul. *Early Christian Worship: A Basic Introduction to Ideas and Practice,* second edition. Collegeville: Liturgical, 2010.
Christie, Douglas E. *Blue Sapphire of the Mind: Notes for a Contemplative Ecology.* New York: Oxford University Press, 2012.
Clingerman, Forrest. "Reading the Book of Nature: A Hermeneutical Account of Nature for Philosophical Theology." *Worldviews* 13 (2009) 72–91.
Clingerman, Forrest, et al., eds. *Interpreting Nature: The Emerging Field of Environmental Hermeneutics.* Groundworks: Ecological Issues in Philosophy and Theology. New York: Fordham University Press, 2014.
Dahill, Lisa E. "Bio-Theoacoustics: Prayer Outdoors and the Reality of the Natural World." *Dialog: A Journal of Theology* 52 (Winter 2013) 292–302.
———. "Indoors, Outdoors: Praying with the Earth." In *Eco-Lutheranism: Lutheran Perspectives on Ecology,* edited by Shauna Hannan and Karla Bohmbach, 113–24. Minneapolis: Lutheran University Press, 2013.
———. "Into Local Waters: Rewilding the Study of Christian Spirituality." *Spiritus: A Journal of Christian Spirituality* 16 (Fall 2016) 141-65.
———. "Life in All Its Fullness: Christian Worship and the Natural World." *Liturgy* 31 (Fall 2016) 43-50.
———. "The View from *Way* Below: Inter-Species Encounter, Membranes, and the Reality of Christ." *Dialog: A Journal of Theology* 53 (Fall 2014) 250–58.
Denysenko, Nicholas E. *The Blessing of the Waters and Epiphany: The Eastern Liturgical Tradition.* Burlington: Ashgate, 2012.
Francis. *Laudato Si': On Care for Our Common Home.* Rome: Libreria Editrice Vaticana, 2015.
Gibler, Linda. *From the Beginning to Baptism: Scientific and Sacred Stories of Water, Oil, and Fire.* Collegeville: Liturgical, 2010.

Grim, John A., ed. *Indigenous Traditions and Ecology: The Interbeing of Cosmology and Community.* Religions of the World and Ecology Series 6. Cambridge: Harvard University Press, 2001.

Haberman, David L. "River of Love in an Age of Pollution." In *Hinduism and Ecology: The Intersection of Earth, Sky, and Water,* edited by Christopher Key Chapple and Mary Evelyn Tucker, 339–55. Cambridge: Harvard University Press, 2000.

Hamilton, Clive, et al., eds. *The Anthropocene and the Global Climate Crisis: Rethinking Modernity in a New Epoch.* Routledge Environmental Humanities Series. New York: Routledge, 2015.

Hatley, James. "Blood Intimacies and Biodicy: Keeping Faith with Ticks." *Australian Humanities Review* 50, May 2011. http://www.australianhumanitiesreview.org.

———. "The Uncanny Goodness of Being Edible to Bears." In *Rethinking Nature: Essays in Environmental Philosophy,* edited by Bruce V. Foltz and Robert Frodeman, 13–31. Bloomington: Indiana University Press, 2004.

Hofstad, Lynn. "Murky Symbols: How Contamination Affects the Symbolic Meaning of Water in Religious Rituals." Unpublished paper, Lutheran Women in Theology and Religious Studies/American Academy of Religion, November 20, 2015.

IPCC. *Climate Change 2014 Synthesis Report: Contribution of Working Groups I, II and III to the Fifth Assessment Report of the Intergovernmental Panel on Climate Change,* edited by The Core Writing Team, Rajendra K. Pachauri, and Leo Meyer. Geneva: Intergovernmental Panel on Climate Change, 2014. http://ar5-syr.ipcc.ch.

Johnson, Elizabeth. "Deep Christology: Ecological Soundings." In *From Logos to Christos: Essays on Christology in Honour of Joanne McWilliam,* edited by Ellen M. Leonard and Kate Merriman, 163–79. Waterloo: Wilfrid Laurier University Press, 2010.

Lathrop, Gordon W. *Holy Ground: A Liturgical Cosmology.* Minneapolis: Fortress, 2009.

Louv, Richard. *Last Child in the Woods: Saving Our Children from Nature-Deficit Disorder.* Chapel Hill: Algonquin, 2008.

Marty, Martin. *Baptism.* Philadelphia: Fortress, 1977.

McFague, Sallie. *The Body of God: An Ecological Theology.* Minneapolis: Fortress, 1993.

McGann, Mary E. "A Theopolitics of Water: Celebrating Baptism in a Time of Global Water Crisis." Unpublished paper presented to the Ecology and Liturgy Seminar of the North American Academy of Liturgy, January 2012.

McKibben, Bill. *The Comforting Whirlwind: God, Job, and the Scale of Creation.* Cambridge: Cowley, 2005.

———. *Eaarth: Making a Life on a Tough New Planet.* New York: Henry Holt & Co., 2011.

Monbiot, George. *Feral: Rewilding the Land, the Sea, and Human Life.* Chicago: University of Chicago Press, 2014.

Myers, Ched. "From 'Creation Care' to 'Watershed Discipleship': Re-Placing Ecological Theology and Practice." *Conrad Grebel Review* 32 (Fall 2014) 250–75.

Price, Jennifer. *Flight Maps: Adventures with Nature in Modern America.* New York: Basic, 1999.

Santmire, H. Paul. *Before Nature: A Christian Spirituality.* Minneapolis: Fortress, 2014.

Schifferdecker, Kathryn. "Of Stars and Sea Monsters: Creation Theology in the Whirlwind Speeches." *Word & World* 31 (Fall 2011) 357–66.

Shepard, Paul. "The Domesticators." In *Nature and Madness,* 19–46. Athens, GA: University of Georgia Press, 1982.

Snyder, Gary. *The Practice of the Wild.* Berkeley: Counterpoint, 1990/2010.

Stewart, Benjamin J. *The Role of Baptismal Water at the Vigil of Easter in the Liturgical Generation of Eco-Theology.* Ph.D. diss., Emory University, 2009.

Tinker, Tink. "American Indians and Ecotheology: Alterity and Worldview." In *Eco-Lutheranism: Lutheran Perspectives on Ecology,* edited by Karla Bohmbach and Shauna Hannan, 69–84. Minneapolis: Lutheran University Press, 2013.

Tucker, Mary Evelyn, and Brian Swimme. *Journey of the Universe.* New Haven: Yale University Press, 2011.

White, Lynn. "The Historical Roots of Our Ecologic Crisis." *Science* 155 (March 10, 1967) 1203–07.

Zoloth, Laurie. "2014 AAR Presidential Address: Interrupting Your Life: An Ethics for the Coming Storm." *Journal of the American Academy of Religion* 84 (March 2016) 3–24.

12

Liberal Arts for Sustainability

Lutheran Higher Education in the Anthropocene[1]

—ERNEST L. SIMMONS

I believe that God has created me together with all that exists.

MARTIN LUTHER, *SMALL CATECHISM*

A constituency able and willing to fight for the long-term human prospect must be educated into existence.

DAVID ORR, *EARTH IN MIND*

"THE HUMAN IMPRINT ON the global environment has now become so large and active that it rivals some of the great forces of Nature in its impact on the functioning of the Earth system."[2] So begins an article co-authored by several of the world's leading geologists and climatologists as they begin to assess the appropriateness of naming our current geological

1. Some material in this chapter draws upon my shorter article, Simmons, "Lutheran Education in the Anthropocene," 6–9, and is reprinted here with permission by the publisher.

2. Steffen, et al., "The Anthropocene," 842–67.

epoch the "Anthropocene" to signify the impact of *homo sapiens* on Earth. What could be the role of Lutheran higher education in such a changed context and what resources in the Lutheran tradition can contribute to preparing students to be more effective sustainability[3] leaders? These are the two questions this brief chapter will focus on. *The thesis of this chapter is that Lutheran liberal arts education should become environmental and sustainability education in addition to whatever major a student selects. Through the theological and ethical exploration of vocation, colleges and universities can help prepare students to become sustainability leaders in the critical areas of Society, Ethics, Ecology, and Economics in this changing world of the Anthropocene.* As Leslie Paul Thiele observes, "The word 'sustainability' derives from the Latin *sustinere*, which literally means to *hold up*. Something is sustainable if it endures, persists or holds up over time."[4] Lutheran liberal arts education can become education for the long term to hold up society and creation for mutual benefit.

For Luther the purpose of education was the preserving of the Gospel and the equipping of the priesthood of all believers for their vocation of serving others within the world. Today this understanding of vocation must be enlarged to also include the natural environment, which fits well with Luther's appreciation of and wonder at creation. First we will look at Luther's understanding of creation and then consider its implications for the relation of theology and science as well as for sustainability. Second, we will explore Lutheran liberal arts education as expressed in questions of legacy, leadership, and vocation. Finally we will pull these elements together to call for Lutheran liberal arts education to become education for vocation in sustainability leadership to help foster life in the Anthropocene. We are empowered to save only that which we have come to love, and love begins in wonder. As Rachel Carson once said, "The more clearly we can focus our attention on the wonders and reality of the universe around us, the less taste we shall have for destruction."[5] Sustainability education at its best begins with the cultivation of a sense of wonder at the natural world and reverence for one's place within it.

---

3. For purposes of this chapter I will be using the definition of sustainability developed by Leslie Paul Thiele in his book *Sustainability*: "Sustainability is an adaptive art wedded to science in service to ethical vision. It entails satisfying current needs without sacrificing future well-being through the balanced pursuit of ecological health, economic welfare, social empowerment, and cultural creativity," 4–5.

4. Ibid., 7.

5. Carson, *The Sense of Wonder*, 163.

CREATION, SCIENCE, AND SUSTAINABILITY

When I first read the statement quoted above by Martin Luther in his *Small Catechism*, I was taken aback. "How arrogant," I thought. He places himself before all of creation and is concerned first and foremost about himself. As I studied more about Luther, however, I realized this was far from the truth; indeed, the truth was quite the opposite. In his explanation of the first article of the Apostles' Creed, what he was getting at is that our own existence, our own creation, body, mind, and spirit, is the most intimate experience of creation that we will ever have. It is through our own experience of being created that we have a window into the rest of creation and to the creator God to be found "in, with, and under" it. Luther got it right.

Luther on Creation

We are of God's creation and intimately connected with it. Our bodies are our little corner of the cosmos, from which we are enabled to perceive the rest of the universe and all that it contains. The heavy elements in our bodies, like copper and zinc, were forged in the thermonuclear reactions of stars that later exploded as supernovae spewing out their material into the vastness of space. We are quite literally star children, made from stardust. It is from within the intimate experience of wonder at our own creation that we can begin to consider the nature of creation itself. Wonder always drives us back to the questions of faith. Luther understood this very well.

Luther was deeply influenced by German creation mysticism, particularly as expressed in the *Theologia Germanica*.[6] The experiencing of God in all things runs throughout this short treatise and forms its mystical groundwork.[7] Heiko Oberman clarifies, however, that this is not "absorption mysticism."[8] It is not a mysticism of being merged or united into one being with God-in-nature, but actually rejects such an understanding. Bengt Hoffman explains that the *Theologia Gemanica* knows nothing of abnormal or unusual experiences, of absorption or merging. On the contrary, it involves the apprehension of the divine in

---

6. Hoffman, *The Theologia Germanica of Martin Luther*.

7. Ibid., 6. See also *Luther and the Mystics*.

8. Oberman, "*Simul gemitus et raptus*," 225, 232.

the everyday, which influences Luther's understanding of the presence of divine grace. Hoffman writes: "The theological term for experience of divine presence is *sapientia experimentalis* [experiential wisdom]. Martin Luther used this term as part of what 'justification' is."[9] Philip Watson puts it this way, "For Luther, God is not to be sought behind His [*sic*] creation by inference from it, but is rather to be apprehended in and through it."[10] Niels Henrik Gregersen further explicates: "Creation is a mystery, not because it is esoteric, not because it forces us to believe in a variety of supernatural truths, but because the mystery of creation takes place in the midst of everyday existence."[11] God is in all things, even though God is also more than the creation as well. There is a normalcy in Luther's nature mysticism that has him affirm the wonder, beauty, and grace of God in the everyday. Luther calls us to do the same. Steven Churchill writes, "Martin Luther is a *normal* creation mystic. This modified claim is good news for us: nature-mystical experiences—ordinary, daily, available-to-all, wonder-filled sightings of God in all creatures, neither more nor less—is open to you, me, all people. Truly Luther is trying to wake us up to the amazing spiritual truth that we are all creation mystics, through Christ's redemptive act."[12]

The Incarnation for Luther is the most intimate presence of God within the world and demonstrates that God is truly capable of entering into the reality of the finite: *infinitum capax finitum* (the infinite bears the finite). Gregersen further explains, "From this premise Luther proceeds to the logical conclusion that also the world of creation must be able to host the infinite God: *finitum capax infinitum*" (the finite bears the infinite).[13] Truly the finite can contain the infinite in the Incarnation. Just as God in Christ is incarnate within the finite natural world, so too is Christ transcendent and everywhere present by being at the right hand of God. For Luther there is an intrinsic connection between creation and salvation because it is the same God present in both. In some ways one could say that Luther reads the creation christologically. This is the basis for Luther's sacramental theology.[14]

9. Hoffman, *Theologia Germanica*, 6.
10. Watson, *Let God Be God!*, 78.
11. Gregersen, "Grace in Nature and History," 23.
12. Churchill, "The Lovely Music of Nature," 192.
13. Gregersen, "Grace in Nature and History," 24.
14. Rasmussen, "Luther and a Gospel of Earth," 2.

In his major work from 1527, "That These Words, 'This is My Body,' Still Stand Firm against the Fanatics," Luther interprets what it means for Christ to sit at the right hand of the Father. He de-literalizes the notion of the heavenly throne, for God is not sitting at a specific place, but is operative all over: "the almighty power of God can be nowhere and yet must be everywhere."[15] So too is Christ and this is why he had so much difficulty with Zwingli's symbolic approach to the Eucharist at the Marburg Colloquy in 1529. God did not have to be "made" present in the bread and wine; God was already there as God is in all of creation. However, through the Word and the Holy Spirit, God in Christ promises to be present in a specific, forgiving, "Real Presence" way, as the means of grace in the Eucharist. Luther charts a middle way between the Roman Catholic position of transubstantiation on the one hand and the Zwinglian symbolic or sacred metaphor on the other. God does not need to transubstantiate bread and wine into the body and blood of Christ, changing its very essence, but rather the body and blood of Jesus Christ is consubstantially present, "in, with and under" the natural elements of bread and wine. Christ's presence in the Eucharist is a particular example, for the forgiveness of sins, of the general presence of God in all creation.

As Luther so clearly pointed out nearly five hundred years ago, we are of the creation and know it intimately through our own existence. To see just how intimate it is, please use your finger to take your pulse. As you feel the pulse of life surging through your body say the word grace with each heartbeat. Grace . . . Grace . . . Grace. It is the grace of creation; it is the grace of life. It is the grace of our own createdness. It is the grace of wonder at life itself. Given this intimate Divine connection with creation and our own embeddedness within it, we have the theological basis for a creative and constructive relationship between theology and science as well as the potential for a faith-based commitment for the care of the creation.

Theology and Science

When we look up and gaze at the approximately three thousand stars that the naked eye can see on a moonless night, the questions inevitably come. Who are we? What is it all about? Where did it or we come from? And, of course, what is the meaning of it all? These are quintessential

15. *LW* 37:57.

human questions. They are at the heart of what constitutes the humanities in liberal arts education. They are the questions that inevitably arise as we contemplate our origins and become aware of our own finitude and mortality, the concrete awareness that we need not be. We are always pilgrims in this life and this wonder at existence has impelled philosophy and theology for millennia. It is with this same sense of human wonder at life and existence that science also pursues its quest to understand the creation.

From a theological point of view, God's *creatio continua* (continual, sustaining grace of creation) runs "in, with and under" the processes of nature such that science and theology need not be in conflict but rather in dialogue or even consonance, for they involve different levels of explanation of the same realities. Science and theology both begin in wonder at the natural world with its complexity and its beauty. But by intention they try to answer two different types of questions: how and why? By design, scientific methods in general self-restrict themselves to "how" questions: what can be observed, measured, quantified, repeated and, ideally, expressed in a mathematical formalism. Newtonian physics is the paradigmatic example of such an approach. Science is concerned with what philosophically is called secondary causation. It assumes something already exists. Theology (and philosophy) on the other hand, ask the "why" questions. Why does something exist, where did it come from, and what is its purpose? This is known as primary, originating, or foundational causation. When observing the appropriate boundaries of analysis, science and theology can together contribute to deeper understanding of the creation and be seen as complementary. This is critical if we are to formulate a meaningful joint response for sustainability.

Sustainability

As Genesis 2 points out, we are part of the "dust of the earth" and are intimately connected with the rest of the natural world. But we are also created with "the breath of God" and so in the image of God and called to be caretakers of the creation as creatures within it. Environmental science has increasingly pointed to our intimate connection to everything on this planet. But as St. Paul and the nightly news remind us, "We know that the whole creation has been groaning in labor pains until now" (Rom 8:22). All is not well with the creation. It is groaning, it is suffering, and much of that suffering is due to the human impact upon the planet. We have even succeeded in lighting up the planet at night. But human planetary impact goes much deeper, even when invisible, in such areas as species extinction or chemical genetic mutation. It is here in the intersection of humanity and the environment that science and faith must join forces. *Creation theology provides a theological justification for environmental science and sustainability.* It is the reconnection of fact and value that can empower us not only to reach out to other human beings but to seek sustainability for the systems of Earth that make our lives possible. To seek to sustain the environment is to seek to sustain the human species. This interconnection is clearly articulated in the guiding principles of the Earth Charter:

1. Respect Earth and life in all its diversity.

2. Care for the community of life with understanding, compassion and love.

3. Build democratic societies that are just, participatory, sustainable, and peaceful.

4. Secure Earth's bounty and beauty for present and future generations.[16]

The Earth Charter's ethical vision affirms that environmental protection, human rights, equitable human development, and peace are interdependent and indivisible.[17] These principles are key to formulating a sustainable world and also guide the expression of education for vocation and sustainability.

David Orr, who has thought about sustainability and education for decades, offers six suggestions:

1. All education is environmental education.

2. The goal of education is not mastery of subject matter, but of one's person.

3. Knowledge carries with it the responsibility to see that it is well used in the world.

4. We cannot say that we know something until we understand the effects of this knowledge on real people and their communities.

16. The Earth Charter, 2.

17. Earth Charter, *Wikipedia.*

5. Education has to stress the importance of "minute particulars" and the power of example over words.

6. The way learning occurs is as important as the content of particular courses.[18]

To incorporate such educational principles into liberal arts education empowers students not only to see the wider picture but also to begin to understand the multivalent and interdependent character of sustainability. Doing so would restore wonder at nature back into the curriculum. As Lisa Sideris argues, "Loss of direct contact with nature and immersion in overly specialized and balkanized disciplines creates a narrowness of vision that is the antithesis of wonder. Thus, depending on how education is designed, wonder can be cultivated or deadened through learning."[19] How then should these principles influence Lutheran higher education?

LUTHERAN LIBERAL ARTS EDUCATION[20]

Luther had a deep love for the natural world and understood the sustaining activity of the Creator Spirit to be present within it. Accordingly, education informed by such creational thinking must contain within it concern for the sustainability of the natural world. *Lutheran liberal arts education should become environmental and sustainability education in addition to whatever major a student selects.* One of the gifts of Christian faith is hope in the face of suffering and death, so this environmental education must center itself in religious and ethical education that can ground human and ecological possibility in the face of impending cultural and climatological change.

Luther was a relational thinker. For him one relates to God through faith and to the neighbor through love. This is the inner and the outer person referred to in "The Freedom of a Christian."[21] *The Lutheran sensibility is that life is a paradox, a dialectical tension, in the midst of which one must act and live.* Life need not be simple and clear in order to be livable and intelligible. Drawing upon Luther's model of simultaneity for the

---

18. Orr, "What is Education For?," 10–16. See also Orr, *Earth in Mind.*

19. Sideris, "Environmental Literacy and the Lifelong Cultivation of Wonder," 91.

20. Some of the material in this section comes from my article, "A Lutheran Dialectical Model of Higher Education."

21. *LW* 31:327–77.

Christian life (e.g., *simul justus et peccator*, simultaneously justified and sinner), such a dialectic, a movement between contrasting positions, can offer both affirmation and critique as it supports dialogue involving multiple points of view, contributing to mutual understanding and constructive change. Such a theology can inform a dynamic interaction between Christian freedom and academic freedom and assist in constructively critiquing the emerging global society in which we are immersed. We must argue neither for a faith so detached from the surrounding culture as to lack intellectual credibility nor for a faith so accommodated to a particular culture as to sanctify its idolatry and hubris. The Lutheran tradition rather informs an open and dialectical educational model that encourages the dynamic interaction of faith and learning supporting a vocational understanding of leadership for sustainability. In this section, I will turn first to a brief discussion of legacy, then to leadership, and finally vocation considering particularly the Lutheran dialectical model of higher education and its usefulness for preparing sustainability leaders for our time.

Legacy

Valuing the liberal arts, Luther viewed the fundamental purpose of education as preserving the evangelical message and equipping the priesthood of all believers for service in the church and the world. For Luther and his colleague, Philip Melanchthon, one of the direct results of the theological doctrine of justification by grace through faith was public education. In his treatise of 1524, "To the Councilmen of All Cities in Germany That They Establish and Maintain Christian Schools," Luther states this in a very practical manner:

> Now the welfare of a city does not consist solely in accumulating vast treasures, building mighty walls and magnificent buildings, and producing a goodly supply of guns and armor. Indeed, where such things are plentiful, and reckless fools get control of them, it is so much the worse and the city suffers even greater loss. A city's best and greatest welfare, safety, and strength consist rather in its having many able, learned, wise, honorable, and well-educated citizens. They can then readily gather, protect, and properly use treasure and all manner of property.[22]

22. *LW* 45:355.

For Lutheran higher education that purpose has not changed but the context has. The task now is to bring into creative interaction relationships of faith and learning in an increasingly global and multicultural society. In her recent book *Not for Profit: Why Democracy Needs the Humanities,* Martha Nussbaum argues forcefully for the value of liberal arts education to prepare future leaders to think critically and creatively for our time of global transition. She says there is a "silent crisis" at hand in education because so much of the arts and humanities is being dropped in American higher education in favor of emphasizing quantitative and technical skills.[23] At a time when critical thinking is needed the most, a time of rapid global change and adaptation, we are deemphasizing it in many of our educational institutions. For Nussbaum, nothing less than the survival of a democratic society is at stake.[24] Lutheran higher education has retained the arts and humanities, actually reveled in them as in our music programs, while not neglecting the applied sciences and practical skills. Nussbaum's "manifesto" supports exactly what most Lutheran colleges and universities in the United States are about. The challenge is to preserve this legacy of liberal arts education at our institutions so that they can continue to provide critical thinkers for our time. This would mean "educating into existence"[25] a constituency committed to sustaining the human prospect in all its diversity and complexity, involving the natural and life sciences as well as the arts, languages, and humanities. It would mean educating leadership that can see things in their entirety. David Orr concludes, "The great ecological issues of our time have to do in one way or another with our failure to see things in their entirety. That failure occurs when minds are taught to think in boxes and not taught to transcend those boxes or to question overly much how they fit with other boxes."[26] If liberal arts education is to remain true to its legacy it must not lose its originating purpose of cultivating informed, civil leaders but find creative ways to express this purpose today in a holistic and integrated way.

---

23. Nussbaum, *Not For Profit,* chapter 1.

24. Ibid., chapter 7.

25. Orr, *Earth in Mind,* 126.

26. Ibid., 94–95.

Leadership

Dialectic stands at the heart of the Lutheran tradition precisely because Luther refused to separate the life of faith from life in the world. Luther insisted on the Christian life being lived right in the midst of the world so that the resources of faith might be brought to bear on daily work and life, not in some separated, ostensibly (in the sixteenth century) more holy or religious sphere such as a church vocation. This simultaneity gives rise to a creative tension in Luther's thought. The Christian lives in the interface, the overlap, between the present world and the world to come; that is, the Christian lives in both worlds simultaneously. Richard Hughes summarizes: "The authentic Lutheran vision, therefore, never calls for Lutherans to superimpose the Kingdom of God on the world as the Reformed tradition seeks to do. Nor does it call for Lutherans to separate from the world as the heirs of the Anabaptists often seek to do. Instead, the Christian must reside in two worlds at one and the same time: the world of nature and of grace. The Christian in Luther's view, therefore, is free to take seriously *both* the world *and* the Kingdom of God."[27]

This dynamic "withness" sustains dialogue and does not fear a slippery slope into secularity. Rather, all of life, including that labeled secular, is part of God's creation and must be brought into dynamic relationship with faith and the potentially transforming grace of God. This dialectical interaction between nature and grace was demonstrated by Joseph Sittler to lie at the very heart of the Lutheran tradition, forming the basis for a Lutheran ecological theology.[28]

This very dynamic sustains openness and academic freedom in higher education while at the same time insisting on bringing this world of knowledge into dynamic relationship with the Christian faith, by means of Christian freedom. The result can often be messy, paradoxical, and ambiguous but that is where faith thrives. *Faith frees the mind for open inquiry and creative reflection, for we are saved not by our own understanding but by the grace of God.* Hughes observes, "The task of the Christian scholar, therefore, is not to impose on the world—or on the material that he or she studies—a distinctly 'Christian worldview.' Rather, the Christian scholar's task is to study the world as it is and then to bring that world into dialogue with the Christian vision of redemption and

27. Hughes, *Models for Christian Higher Education*, 6.

28. Sittler, *Essays on Nature and Grace*. See also *Evocations of Grace*, as well as the essay by Robert C. Saler in this volume.

grace."[29] To conduct open interdisciplinary reflection on reality in all its
thickness and complexity in dialogue with transcendence is clearly one
of the most important contributions Lutheran colleges and universities
can make to the church's mission of enlightened understanding of the
faith, empowering service to society. In a culture where public discourse,
especially about matters of religion, is not encouraged or even welcome,
colleges of the church may offer one of the most effective venues for such
deliberations. Our students, our society, and our religious institutions
need such reflection for we live in a time of significant spiritual searching.

Historically, individuals found personal meaning through the received religious and cultural explanations of their time, but no longer.
Renate Schacht speaking from a German perspective refers to the formation of what she calls a "collage identity" among many persons, especially
the young, today. She observes: "Modern man [sic] has no fixed roots.
Mobility, flexibility, plurality of standpoints, and freedom of opinion
development are key characteristics of modern life. These truly positive
characteristics, however, bring a dark side of insecurity and disorienta-
tion with them, which can retreat behind fundamentally secured walls or
vegetate into a 'nothing matters' position. The task of education then is to
make other paths visible and accessible."[30]

It seems to me that it is exactly the role of Lutheran higher education
to offer such identity forming alternatives.[31] Identity is a process, not a pos-
session; moreover, environment forms identity. Lutheran, as well as other
religiously oriented, colleges and universities may assist this meaning-
seeking, identity-forming process by cultivating an environment in
which faith and learning can be kept in dynamic relationship, cultivating
the possibility of an integrated vision of vocation for sustainability.

Vocation

The Lutheran tradition's emphasis upon vocation is one way to give theological grounding for responsible leadership. It centers upon one basic
question that has two fundamental dimensions. The question is, "Why
are you here?" The first dimension is the practical: Why are you *here*?
This question asks, what are you doing now and why are you doing it

---

29. Hughes, *Models*, 6.

30. Schacht, "Christian Education in Unstable Times," 68.

31. Simmons, *Lutheran Higher Education*, chap. 1.

there? This is the realm of practical engagement with life on a daily basis. This first dimension of the question is of the here and now variety. The second dimension cuts more deeply, however: Why are *you* here? That is, why do you exist? This is the existential dimension of the question, the dimension that focuses on the nature and challenges of human life. Why are *you* here and not someone else? Why did you come into life or existence at all? Where did you come from and to where are you going? The practical is composed of the necessary factors of place, history, resources (both physical and human), and structure. The existential is composed of the philosophical and theological dimensions of human existence. In a rather simplified manner, one could say that the practical dimension addresses instrumental questions of value (means), while the existential dimension addresses questions of intrinsic value (ends) for human life. *The point is: vocation occurs at the intersection of these two dimensions of the why question.* Vocation, in the Lutheran understanding, addresses the practical from the context of the existential. It seeks to connect purposes and practices, ends and means, and does not allow them to fall apart into separate realms. Why are we here? Luther's answer was vocation. It is through our work in the world that we incarnate faith and by so doing help sustain the creation. It is in fact *vocation for sustainability.* Vocation rejects the separation of the material from the spiritual, of nature from grace, insisting that they be kept together.

The Lutheran understanding of vocation empowering for public service is meant to serve the common good.[32] Certainly Luther's proposal of the "common chest" is a clear sixteenth-century example of such a pursuit.[33] He was concerned to provide for the poor and needy as monasteries and convents, the historic sources for such care, were being closed. Not only public education but also social service organizations were a direct result of the Lutheran Reformation. Our educational systems, accordingly, were organized to offer instruction for leadership in such programs and institutions. It is education for the common good, which today must also include sustainability.[34] A dialectically informed education will empower students to be more discerning in their employment

32. For an informative discussion of the common good for today see Daly and Cobb, *For the Common Good.*

33. Lindberg, "Luther on Poverty," 141.

34. For examples of colleges and universities working for sustainability, see the Association for the Advancement of Sustainability in Higher Education (AASHE) website at www.aashe.org.

choices, seeking work that will nurture the common good. The late historian and environmental studies professor James Farrell put it this way, "If the vocation of college students now includes citizenship and sustainability, then the vocation of college teachers changes, too . . . Today, the mission of every responsible college should be to teach students to avert and/or adapt to the vicissitudes of global weirding [McKibben] and to restore and respect the rich diversity of the earth's ecosystems. Students still have disciplinary responsibilities, of course, but they need to know that all disciplines are relevant to responsible in-habit-ation of the earth."[35] Lutheran higher education carries within it critical principles for ecological justice such as participation, solidarity, sufficiency, and sustainability[36] to ground an informed sense of vocation which can empower students to discern occupations supportive of the ecological common good. As always, the common good for any given situation must be discerned through dialogue and mutual participation by all parties involved. Vocationally inspired leadership for sustainability will seek such dialogue and is absolutely critical as we enter the age of the Anthropocene.

EDUCATION IN THE ANTHROPOCENE

What place does Lutheran liberal arts education have in such a changed social and environmental context as the Anthropocene? Here I think re-envisioning the classical purpose of liberal arts education will serve us well.

Classical Resources

As we may recall, in the Greek city-state the purpose of education was to prepare a person for thoughtful and responsible citizenship in the *polis* (city). This meant among other things having knowledge of the fundamental "liberating" arts of Grammar, Logic, and Rhetoric, what during the middle ages became known as the *Trivium*: literally "where the three roads meet." The classical descriptions are that: "Grammar teaches the mechanics of language to the student . . . Logic or dialectic is the 'mechanics' of thought and analysis; the process of identifying fallacious

35. Farrell, "Good Work and the Good Life," 42.

36. See the ELCA Social Statement, "Caring for Creation: Vision, Hope and Justice."

arguments and statements, . . . Finally Rhetoric is the application of language in order to instruct and to persuade the listener and the reader. It is the knowledge (grammar) now understood (logic) being transmitted outwards, as wisdom (rhetoric)."[37] While this is later supplemented by the *Quadrivium* of arithmetic, geometry, music, and astronomy, for our purposes these three basic "liberating arts" are the most important. One need only look at recent dissembling discussions about climate change to see the importance of these three arts. To be able to name something clearly and to ferret out the illogical and fallacious arguments that have been made are today survival skills for society. We have to prepare our students to be able to critique and dismantle such obstructionist thinking and call out the powers that have a vested interest in promoting such arguments.

Naomi Oreskes and Erik Conway in their book, *Merchants of Doubt*,[38] indicate that by supporting fringe scientific research, the fossil-fuel industry has engaged in the same tactics of sowing doubt or uncertainty about climate change that the cigarette industry did for decades concerning the carcinogenic character of cigarette smoking and nicotine addiction. As horrible as that loss of life was (and still is), smoking was (primarily) a personal decision. Climate change, however, is not and whole cultures and nations are at stake as well as the viability of human civilization. We no longer have time for such distracting and fallacious arguments. We must prepare our students to think clearly and critically about the matters at hand as well as creatively to formulate viable responses and then communicate them clearly, effectively, and persuasively to their social context. The art of Rhetoric is as needed today as in the ancient *polis*. Thus a liberal arts education is one of the best ways to prepare our students for sustainability leadership in the coming decades of this century. *As the liberating arts were once used to prepare persons for citizenship in the Greek polis, we must now prepare our students for citizenship on the planet: that is, for planetary citizenship.* What resources from within the Lutheran tradition can be of service to our students beyond these basic functions of the liberal arts?

---

37. "Trivium," *Wikipedia*.
38. Oreskes and Conway, *Merchants of Doubt*.

Lutheran Resources

As mentioned earlier, Luther had a deep love for creation. Such an understanding provides an excellent theological foundation for the development of an ecological and sustainable understanding of vocation on our
campuses. While the Lutheran tradition tended to emphasize justification
in terms of human salvation, particularly during the period of Lutheran
scholasticism and the Thirty Years War, Luther himself saw the justifying grace of God as acting to also restore nature and the human/nature
relationship. Just as human relationships are subject to distortion, curved
in upon oneself (*incurvatus in se*), leading to one's own destruction, so
too can humanity's relation with nature also be so distorted. Human attitudes toward nature have too often seen it merely as a natural resource
for human use, curving ourselves away from nature into our own sinful
self-preoccupation. Nature has been victimized by human sin and turned
into an object for exploitation rather than nurture and stewardship.

Divine Entanglement

In Christian faith, human hope along with salvation ultimately rest upon
the grace of God alone. This places human response and action in a
transcendent context that does not rely upon human motivation alone.
Indeed, as I have argued in my recent book, *The Entangled Trinity: Quantum Physics and Theology*,[39] God is "entangled" with creation in general
and humanity in particular through the work of Christ and the animating power of the Holy Spirit. In quantum physics, research has demonstrated that two particles (such as paired photons) are entangled once
they have interacted. When one is measured the condition of the other is
immediately known. Particles are still connected at the level of the quantum vacuum no matter how far apart they are separated in the physical
universe. This means that at a deep ontological level interrelationality
and connectivity permeate the universe. Metaphorically appropriating
this understanding for theology can affirm that God is interrelated to everything in the cosmos and that a reciprocity of effect exists. What we do
affects God as well as God affecting us. We are in a reciprocal, if unequal,
ontological relationship with God, where the divine is present in everything and everything is present in the divine, embodying a panentheistic

39. Simmons, *The Entangled Trinity*.

relationship. There is divine immanence but also transcendence, for God is more than the cosmos.[40] Theologically, Luther would surely affirm such a dynamic interrelationship. It is this entangled intimacy that can be the ground for hope, providing a more inclusive vision as well as animated action for constructive change. Such mutual relationality can also ground an "entangled" education that emphasizes the interconnectivity of all fields of study and their expression in an interrelational world. *Entangled education is sustainability education.* It does not condone the isolation of academic fields from one another or suffer from idolatrous devotion to one's own discipline (disciplinolatry).[41] Isolated academic study, like isolated individuality, denies the intrinsic connectivity of all existence and its entanglement with the Creator God who is its foundation. If all physical existence is entangled starting at the quantum level, then education must reflect this entanglement and open students to the beauty and wonder of such interrelationality. Grounded in the entanglement of God with the creation, such education would work to see that. "All education is environmental education."[42] *Lutheran higher education should seek to become such ecologically entangled education.*

CONCLUSION

The human question of why always hangs suspended between the finite and the infinite. Juxtaposed between time and eternity, humanity seeks meaning before its own beginnings and after its demise. Between *ethos* and *logos* we exercise our *pathos.* Part of the grandeur of being created in the image of God, humus becoming spirit-breathed and self-conscious, is the ability to ask "why?" The study of the liberal arts assists one in opening up to the transcendent dimensions of life and thus equips people of faith for meaningful expression in service to others of many varieties and species. The close historical connection between liberal arts education and the Christian faith expands today into service of the common good in countless contexts and ecosystems.

The Lutheran model of such an education is particularly helpful here because of its dialectical openness to alternative viewpoints and their dynamic interaction. This form of education critiques contemporary

40. Ibid., chapter 7.
41. Daly and Cobb, *For the Common Good,* 34.
42. Orr, *Earth in Mind,* 12.

society by bringing it into dialectical engagement with Christ and the Gospel. Such a model avoids what Tom Christenson has termed the "fallacy of exclusive disjunction."[43] There are middle positions between exclusion and accommodation in higher education, and the Lutheran dialectical model is one. The theology of the cross encourages humility both in terms of one's own thought and also in evaluating the claims of others. Such a theological perspective can and should confront any claim to absoluteness or finality (Tillich's "Protestant Principle") in both religious and secular expressions.

We need a grace that can open us out of ourselves and empower an education that helps us see and experience the wonder in nature and our intimate relationship with it. Only then will we come to care about it, for only then will we come to love it. The Christian tradition, among others, can provide such grace-filled change. The challenge today is to translate the spirit of the Reformation into an Eco-Reformation. *Lutheran higher education must take its place at the forefront of this process, fostering a realistic but open and hopeful attitude towards the future and the systemic changes we are facing. By publicly and comprehensively embracing the environmental dimension of its mission today, it must provide an education for vocational service that connects the practical and the existential in relation to sustainability for humanity and the rest of the natural world.*

BIBLIOGRAPHY

Association for the Advancement of Sustainability in Higher Education. www.aashe. org.

Carson, Rachel. *The Sense of Wonder*. San Francisco: HarperCollins, 1965 [1998].

Christenson, Thomas. *The Gift and Task of Lutheran Higher Education*. Minneapolis: Fortress, 2004.

Churchill, Steven. "'This Lovely Music of Nature': Grounding an Ecological Ethics in Martin Luther's Creation Mysticism." *Currents in Theology and Mission* 26 (1999) 183–95.

Cobb, John B., Jr. *The Structure of Christian Existence*. Philadelphia: Westminster, 1967.

Daly, Herman E., and John B. Cobb, Jr. *For the Common Good: Redirecting the Economy Toward Community, the Environment and a Sustainable Future*. Boston: Beacon, 1989.

Diamond, Jared. *Collapse: How Societies Choose to Fail or Succeed*. New York: Penguin, 2011.

Earth Charter Commission. *The Earth Charter*, 2000. www.EarthCharter.org.

ELCA. "Caring for Creation: Vision, Hope and Justice." 1993. www.elca.org.

43. Christenson, *The Gift and Task of Lutheran Higher Education*, 12.

Farrell, James J. "Good Work and the Good Life: Vocation as What We Do." In *Claiming Our Callings: Toward a New Understanding of Vocation in the Liberal Arts,* edited by Kaethe Schwehn and L. DeAne Lagerquist, 29–47. Oxford: Oxford University Press, 2014.

Frankl, Viktor. *Man's Search for Meaning.* Boston: Beacon, 2006.

Ferre, Frederick. *Hellfire and Lightening Rods.* Maryknoll, NY: Orbis, 1994.

Gilkey, Langdon. *Shantung Compound.* New York: Harper & Row, 1966.

Gregersen, Niels Henrik. "Grace in Nature and History: Luther's Doctrine of Creation Revisited." *Dialog: A Journal of Theology* 44 (2005) 19–29.

Gore, Albert. *Earth in the Balance.* New York: Houghton Mifflin, 1992.

Hoffman, Bengt. *Luther and the Mystics.* Minneapolis: Augsburg, 1976.

———. *The Theologia Germanica of Martin Luther.* Classics of Western Spirituality. Mahwah, NJ: Paulist, 1980.

Hughes, Richard T. *Models for Christian Higher Education.* Grand Rapids: Eerdmans, 1997.

Lindberg, Carter. "Luther on Poverty." In *Harvesting Martin Luther's Reflections on Theology, Ethics and the Church,* edited by Timothy Wengert, 134–51. Grand Rapids: Eerdmans, 2004.

Luther, Martin. "The Freedom of a Christian." In *Career of the Reformer I,* edited by Harold J. Grimm. *LW* 31:327–77. Philadelphia: Fortress, 1961.

———. "That These Words of Christ, 'This is my Body,' etc., Still Stand Firm against the Fanatics." In *Word and Sacrament III,* edited by Robert H. Fischer, 3–150. *LW* 37. Philadelphia: Muhlenberg, 1961.

———. "To the Councilmen of All Cities in Germany That They Establish and Maintain Christian Schools." In *The Christian in Society II,* edited by James Atkinson, 347–78. *LW* 45. Philadelphia: Fortress, 1961.

Nussbaum, Martha. *Not for Profit: Why Democracy Needs the Humanities.* Princeton: Princeton University Press, 2012.

Oberman, Heiko. "*Simul gemitus et raptus*: Luther and Mysticism." In *The Reformation in Medieval Perspective,* edited by Steven E. Ozment, 219–51. Chicago: Quadrangle, 1971.

Oreskes, Naomi, and Erik Conway. *Merchants of Doubt.* New York: Bloomsbury, 2010.

Orr, David. *Earth in Mind: On Education, Environment, and the Human Prospect.* Washington, DC: Island, 2004.

———. "What Is Education For?" *In Context: A Quarterly of Humane Sustainable Education* 27 (Winter 1991). http://www.context.org.

Prensky, Marc. "Digital Natives, Digital Immigrants." *On the Horizon* 9 (2001) 1–6.

Rasmussen, Larry. "Luther and a Gospel of Earth." *Union Seminary Quarterly Review* 51 (1997) 1–28.

Schacht, Renate. "Christian Education in Unstable Times." In *Luther and Melanchthon in the Educational Thought in Central and Eastern Europe,* edited by Reinhold Golz and Wolfgang Mayrhofer, 68–76. Munster: Lit Verlag, 1998.

Schwehn, Mark. *Exiles from Eden.* New York: Oxford University Press 1993.

Sideris, Lisa. "Environmental Literacy and the Lifelong Cultivation of Wonder." In *Teaching Environmental Literacy: Across Campus and Across the Curriculum,* edited by Heather L. Reynolds, et al., 85–97. Bloomington: Indiana University Press, 2010.

Simmons, Ernest. *The Entangled Trinity: Quantum Physics and Theology.* Minneapolis: Fortress 2014.

———. "A Lutheran Dialectical Model of Higher Education." *Intersections* 37 (2013) 27–31.

———. "Lutheran Education in the Anthropocene." *Dialog: A Journal of Theology* 55 (2016) 6–9.

———. *Lutheran Higher Education: An Introduction.* Minneapolis: Augsburg Fortress, 1998.

Sittler, Joseph. "Church Colleges and the Truth." In *Faith, Learning and the Church College: Addresses by Joseph Sittler,* edited by Connie Gengenbach, 27–28. Northfield, MN: St. Olaf College, 1989.

———. *Essays on Nature and Grace.* Philadelphia: Fortress, 1972.

———. *Evocations of Grace: The Writings of Joseph Sittler on Ecology, Theology and Ethics.* Grand Rapids: Eerdmans, 2000.

Steffen, Will, et al. "The Anthropocene: Conceptual and Historical Perspectives." *Philosophical Transactions of the Royal Society* 369 (March 2011) 842–67.

Thiele, Leslie Paul. *Sustainability.* Cambridge, UK: Polity, 2013.

Watson, Philip. *Let God Be God! An Interpretation of the Theology of Martin Luther.* Philadelphia: Muhlenberg, 1950.

13

Religion, Forestry, and Democracy in Rwanda after Genocide

—VICTOR THASIAH

Recognizing that sustainable development, democracy and peace are indivisible is an idea whose time has come.

Wangari Maathai, 2004 Nobel Peace Prize Laureate

Our well-being as a species depends on the mutually-supportive relationships between the natural and social worlds we inhabit. Christians have not always appreciated the significance of these connections. Combining environmental responsibility with substantive democracy and sustainable development, John Rutsindintwarane—Deputy Bishop of the Lutheran Church in Rwanda and Executive Director of PICO Rwanda (People Improving Communities through Organizing)[1]—rehabilitates a postcolonial Christianity complicit in political violence, mass atrocity, and ecological devastation. This essay sets out the integration of reforestation in his ministry and organizing as responsive to the call for environmental responsibility, while linking the latter to grassroots democ-

1. PICO Rwanda is affiliated with PICO International, which is affiliated with the PICO National Network in the United States. See PICO National Network at http://www.piconetwork.org and PICO International at http://www.picointernational.org.

racy and community development. The links Rutsindintwarane makes between ecology, politics, and progress, as we will see, confirm fellow East African Nobel Laureate Wangari Maathai's perspective concerning their indivisibility for peace. The call to environmental responsibility we consider in this essay is the Protestant Council of Churches of Rwanda's (CPR) 2011 "Theological Charter for the Environment" and its corresponding 2012 action plan "Role of Church Parishes in Protecting, Rehabilitating the Environment and Fighting against Climate Change in Rwanda."[2] What follows is based on field research conducted in Rwanda in 2013 and 2014.[3] On methodology, David Graeber captures the intention:

> When one carries out an ethnography, one observes what people do, and then tries to tease out the hidden symbolic, moral, or pragmatic logics that underlie their actions; one tries to get at the way people's habits and actions make sense in ways that they are not themselves completely aware of. One obvious role for a radical intellectual is to do precisely that: to look at those who are creating viable alternatives, try to figure out what might be the larger implications of what they are (already) doing, and then offer those ideas back, not as prescriptions, but as contributions, possibilities—as gifts.[4]

Many Rwandans helped me tease out the hidden logics—religious, ecological, political, and developmental—that underlie Rutsindintwarane's actions and figure out what the larger implications of what he does might be. He and his collaborators, those he has organized and trained

---

2. On the Protestant Council of Churches of Rwanda, see http://www.cpr-rwanda.org. These two statements are the most important and representative contemporary Rwandan Christian commitments on the environment.

3. The research involved observation of adults and youth participating in organizing in rural and urban settings; attendance at meetings with PICO Rwanda staff, community leaders, various constituencies, and public officials; participation in organizing and leadership training sessions; reading project reports from 2006 to the present; and interviewing either formally or informally an estimated fifty Rwandans associated with one or more of Rutsindintwarane's projects. The informants comprised people from rural and urban contexts either participating in or affected by community organizing; local, regional, and national-level public officials; field staff and executives of local and global, faith-based, non-governmental organizations (NGOs) working in development; and lay, clergy, and national leaders from several different Christian denominations. My approach is that of a committed, critical, participant observer of the theological, ecological, and political dimensions of Rutsindintwarane's organizing practices.

4. Graeber, *Fragments of an Anarchist Anthropology*, 12.

as leaders, are too modest, however, to have spoken about what they do as rehabilitating Christianity. Even when I witnessed them enacting the "prophetic church" they insisted Rwanda needs after political violence, civil war, and ethnic cleansing, they did not seem to regard themselves as exemplifying it. I see this essay as a way of "offer[ing] these ideas back" to them and to the larger church to focus our attention on the mutually-supportive relationships between our natural and social worlds for the flourishing of all life.

An estimated 800,000 Rwandans—as many as three quarters of the Tutsi population and thousands of moderate Hutu—were killed in thirteen weeks in 1994.[5] Alison Des Forges recounts what happened:

> The Hutu, vastly superior in number, remembered past years of oppressive Tutsi rule, and many of them not only resented but feared the minority. The government, run by Hutu, was at war with the Rwandan Patriotic Front (RPF), rebels who were predominantly Tutsi. In addition, Rwanda was one of the poorest nations in the world and growing poorer, with too little land for its many people and falling prices for its products on the world market. Food production had diminished because of drought and the disruptions of war: it was estimated that 800,000 people would need food aid to survive in 1994 . . . [The] genocide resulted from the deliberate choice of a modern elite to foster hatred and fear to keep itself in power. This small, privileged group first set the majority against the minority to counter a growing political opposition within Rwanda. Then, faced with RPF success on the battlefield and at the negotiating table, these few powerholders transformed the strategy of ethnic division into genocide. They believed that the extermination campaign would restore the solidarity of the Hutu under their leadership and help them win the war, or at least improve their chances of negotiating a favorable peace. They seized control of the state and used its machinery and its authority to carry out the slaughter.[6]

The genocide demonstrated that one could not rely on Christians to resist either active or passive support of mass murder. "Churches played an important role," according to Timothy Longman, "in helping to make participation in the killing morally acceptable. While Tutsi were never defined as heretics or infidels, the churches were extremely powerful and

5. See Des Forges, *Leave None to Tell the Story*, and Prunier, *The Rwanda Crisis*.

6. Des Forges, *Leave None to Tell the Story*, 6.

influential institutions in Rwanda, and their majority voice gave moral sanction to the killings as an acceptable form of political engagement."[7] What took place, Emmanuel Katongole recalled, "shattered any naiveté [he] had about the church and Christianity in Africa. For the Rwanda genocide not only happened in one of the most Christianized nations in Africa; the churches themselves often became killing fields, with Christians killing fellow Christians in the same places they had worshipped together."[8]

While some Christians overcame fear and crossed ethnic and political lines to protect people's lives, the majority did not. The ground for popular support had been prepared decades in advance. Longman maintains: "An analysis of the historical role of Christianity in Rwanda reveals that, far from simply adapting to and reflecting Rwandan society, the churches actively shaped ethnic and political realities that made genocide possible by acting to define and politicize ethnicity, legitimizing authoritarian regimes, and encouraging public obedience to political authorities."[9] This Christianity, consistently accommodating the regime in power, whether colonialist, nationalist, genocidal, or republican, some contend, still stands in need of interrogation and rehabilitation.[10]

Though the genocide was essentially a political conflict, Peter Uvin argues that Rwanda—the "small, landlocked, predominantly agricultural country with the highest population density in Africa"—is also "a prime example of the disastrous consequences of ecological resources scarcity."[11] Drought; the destruction of land, agriculture, and livelihoods by war; and the precipitous fall in food production and availability resulted in, among other things, mass hunger, high unemployment, internal displacement, and prolonged hopelessness.[12] "History demonstrates," Uvin observes, "that such situations are excellent breeding grounds for radicalism and violence against minorities, and the Rwanda experience certainly bears out the truth of that lesson."[13] The ecological consequences of the mass

7. Longman, *Christianity and Genocide in Rwanda*, 306–7.

8. Katongole, *The Sacrifice of Africa*, 8–9.

9. Longman, *Christianity and Genocide*, 10.

10. See, for example, Aguilar, *Theology, Liberation and Genocide*; and Carney, *Rwanda before the Genocide*.

11. Uvin, "Tragedy in Rwanda," 7.

12. See Moodley, Gahima, and Munien, "Environmental Causes and Impacts of the Genocide in Rwanda."

13. Uvin, "Tragedy in Rwanda," 14.

atrocity are also critical to examine. Moodley, Gahima, and Munien claim: "Severe environmental damage was caused during and after the genocide by the mass movement of refugees and the internal displacement of people. However, the most pressing environmental impact in Rwanda is increased deforestation for the purposes of housing construction, building of new facilities, the use of wood for energy and most importantly, the clearing of forested areas for agricultural purposes."[14]

Uvin adds: "By May 1995, more than 700,000 old caseload refugees (i.e., the children of the largely Tutsi refugees from 1959–63) had returned to Rwanda, mainly to the eastern plains their parents had abandoned, bringing with them at least as many cattle. This influx has had immediate ecological consequences, creating serious risks of overgrazing and the potential for sociopolitical conflict between refugees and the largely Hutu homesteaders."[15] These refugees included thousands of Lutherans returning from Tanzania, who established the Lutheran Church in Rwanda (LCR) that same year. Disturbed by and responsive to their both justifiable and oblivious clear-cutting of forests, compounding environmental damages from the war and genocide, Rutsindintwarane, one of the LCR's founders and early leaders, integrated reforestation into his post-genocide ministry of resettlement and reconstruction from the start. Integrating grassroots democracy through community organizing would follow a decade later. As we will see, his trajectory corroborates what Uvin concluded shortly after the genocide, namely: "[I]n the future, ecological and political dynamics need to be confronted simultaneously to promote sustainable development and social reconciliation. Rwanda's ecological problems cannot be addressed without resolving its political problems and vice versa. Any solution that addresses only one aspect of the dynamic is bound to fail."[16] The history of Christian complicity in ethnic division and political violence in Rwanda, and the environmental drivers and results of each, inform and motivate Rutsindintwarane's organizing today.[17] His ministry at the intersection of the natural and social worlds he inhabits in the context of ecological and political crises presents an example religious communities on every continent facing similar challenges can learn from. Before turning to his work, we examine the

---

14. Moodley, Gahima, and Munien, "Environmental Causes and Impacts," 115.

15. Uvin, 15. See also, "Role of Church Parishes," cited in note 18.

16. Uvin, "Tragedy in Rwanda," 15. See also Uvin, *Aiding Violence*.

17. See Thasiah, "Reconfiguring Church-State Relations."

most important and representative contemporary set of public, Rwandan Christian positions concerning the environment and climate change.

THE CALL FOR ENVIRONMENTAL RESPONSIBILITY IN RWANDA

The Protestant Council of Churches of Rwanda (CPR) publicly declared its "fight against the deterioration of human life due to climate change" in 2012.[18] The fight is based on a set of commitments titled "Theological Charter of the Environment" and a seven-year project to actualize them. The "negative signs of climate change" they observed included: longer periods of drought; demographic densities and pressures destroying ecosystems; intensive flooding and land loss; "natural disasters and the degradation of natural resources such as water, forests and biological diversity compromising the people's living conditions; loss of nutritive elements of the soil during the landslides causing acidification estimated to [comprise] 45% of cultivated space; and diarrheic diseases and high respiratory infection rate."[19] The biggest concern, however, was "the deforestation related to the intensive and uncontrolled cutting of trees without a well-planned programme of planting more trees by stakeholders in Rwanda."[20] Data cited indicated "the majority of Rwandan households (92.6%) of the rural and urban areas use trees as [a] source of energy and more than 60% of urban population use charcoal as [a] source of energy in Rwanda."[21] The CPR thus makes planting trees central to its seven-year project to protect the environment and fight climate change. "Based on the importance of trees and given the degradation of the environment in Rwanda in general and that of the forest in particular, churches have a big role to play in rehabilitating the forests to improve the quality of life of the people."[22]

The "Theological Charter of the Environment," comprising twelve commitments, calls Rwandan Christians to environmental responsibility. During a conference on "the promotion and protection of the environment" in September 2011, heads of Rwandan Protestant churches and

18. Protestant Council of Churches in Rwanda, "Role of Church Parishes."
19. Ibid.
20. Ibid.
21. Ibid.
22. Ibid.

CPR members representing every district in Rwanda drafted the document after discussing their views on Rwandan culture, the Bible, and the environment, and consultation with Rwandan Environment Management Authority (REMA) staff.[23] They adopted the charter, and the CPR's General Assembly approved it in December 2011.[24] Conference attendees considered the twelve commitments that materialized "as a sign of their gratitude to God the Creator, the Provider and Sustainer of Life." They read as follows, quoted in their entirety, in literal English translation:

1. We commit to mobilise Christians from CPR member churches to value more the land, to protect and manage it in a proper manner because we, human beings were created out of the land, the soil; we live on it, get our livelihood from it and will return to the land as we depart from our present day existence (Gen 2:7; 3:19).

2. We value more everything that God created for when the work was done, God found it good. Therefore, we should protect the integrity of the creation and take care of it (Gen 1:26–27; 2:15).

3. We call to the people of God, Christians, in particular to be aware of their role, as people chosen by God; we ought to take up our responsibility of leading and protecting the environment; we should be aware that we will have to account for how we have fulfilled that mission of protecting it (Gen 1:26; 2:15).

4. We commit ourselves to be advocates of the environment, protecting it and undertaking concrete actions in our respective churches like planting the trees of all species (food trees, trees that protect the land, medicinal plants and alike).

5. We commit ourselves to familiarise and live in harmony with the ecosystem because one [aspect] of Jesus' mission has been to reconcile us with God and the environment (Gen 1:28; Col 1:15–20; Rom 8:28).

6. We commit to doing our best so that our residential areas look like a new Eden and we commit to teach this culture to our children. By so doing, our children will inherit a good country to hand to the future generations.

23. See Rwandan Environmental Management Authority, "Rwanda: State of the Environment and Outlook Report."

24. Protestant Council of Churches in Rwanda, "Theological Charter for the Environment."

7. We commit to integrate the program of protecting the environment in our strategic plans of all CPR member churches by taking into account the national policy of the government of Rwanda in protecting the environment.

8. We commit to support and promote Rwandan values that do not conflict with the Gospel on the protection of the environment.

9. As we participants were trained, we commit to set up youth clubs and to sensitize them on the urgency and imperatives of protecting the environment.

10. We, trained pastors, commit to organise competitions around the protection of the environment calling from Rwandan culture in aspects like poems, songs, dances, proverbs, tales . . . and from the Bible.

11. We commit to inform Christians that mankind is the leader of all creation and that God has given them such a big responsibility.

12. We particularly commit to remind human beings that the environment existed before them, henceforth it is the existence of the environment that makes human being's existence possible. Therefore, whoever destroys the environment destroys themselves.

The commitments juxtapose a utilitarian, anthropocentric environmentalism and recognition of creation's integrity and intrinsic goodness. They present the God-given, leading role Christians should play in the exercise of environmental responsibility, involving advocacy and practices such as planting trees, for which Christians will be held accountable. The commitments call for environmental education, theological and ecological, and the instilling of a culture of harmony and reconciliation between humans and ecosystems among children and youth. The protection of the environment, informed by relevant national policy, should be integrated into CPR member churches' respective strategic plans and promoted as a broader, Rwandan cultural value. Finally, they acknowledge the shared fate of the natural world and human beings. While the charter contains much that would be expected from a Christian, consensus statement, it seems to ignore: deeply related Rwandan social, political, and economic conditions such as the ongoing recovery from genocide; challenges in transitioning from old political-ethnic identities to a new political-Rwandan one; critically engaging authoritarian, top-down planning and control with community-based organizing and development; and, of course, poverty and extreme poverty.[25] If the CPR were to at least name these issues in relation to ecological conditions, it would find much support in contemporary African biblical and theological interpretation on the environment.[26]

The CPR launched its seven-year project to implement the commitments titled "Role of Church Parishes in Protecting, Rehabilitating the Environment and Fighting against Climate Change in Rwanda" at the Alliance of Religions and Conservation (ARC) "Many Heavens, One Earth, Our Continent" celebration in Nairobi, Kenya, in September 2012. The project's overall objective is the "mobilization and involvement of pastors and Christians within parishes in the process of protecting the environment and fighting against climate change for sustainable development in Rwanda. It also establishes a vigorous action of parishes in tree planting."[27] The project focuses on raising awareness in churches concerning environmental degradation and conservation; climate change; food security; and the reduction of pollution, specifically due to pesticides and chemical fertilizer use. Other than being "advocates of the environment" and "taking into account the national policy of the government of Rwanda in protecting the environment" when CPR member churches determine their respective strategic plans, neither the charter nor the project mentions the relationship between ecological conditions on the one hand and political or economic conditions on the other. This failure is not unique to either the CPR or Rwanda. Global justice movements continue to address this oversight.[28]

What happens, for example, when (not if) state and/or business interests concerning the environment run counter to ordinary Rwandans' preferences, especially to the preferences of those who live most directly "off of the land"?[29] How would the CPR respond to Uvin's conclusion cited above that unless ecological and political conditions are confronted

25. See, for example, Mamdani, *When Victims Become Killers*; and Gaynor, *Decentralisation, Conflict and Peacebuilding in Rwanda*.

26. See, for example, the numerous references to African sources in Conradie, *Christianity and Ecological Theology*.

27. "Role of Church Parishes in Protecting."

28. See Klein, *This Changes Everything*.

29. See, for example, Newbury, "High Modernism at the Ground Level," 223–39; Ansoms, "Rwanda's Post-Genocide Economic Reconstruction," 240–51; and Huggins, "The Presidential Land Commission," 252–65; all three in Straus and Waldorf, eds., *Remaking Rwanda*.

simultaneously to promote sustainable development and social reconciliation, Rwandans are bound to fail?[30] The CPR and member churches should consider questions like these given contemporary African biblical and theological interpretation connecting ecology and politics, and lessons learned after the genocide.[31] Probing connections as theologian Kalemba Mwambazami does between environmental concerns on the one hand and politics, economics, technology, and urbanization on the other is vital to fighting climate change.[32] If the CPR engages these matters in relation, John Rutsindintwarane, who did not participate in construction of either the charter or the project, would be helpful to consult.

JOHN RUTSINDINTWARANE: PLANTING TREES AND ORGANIZING

Rutsindintwarane, raised by his Rwandan mother Kabasinga Beltilde, grew up among Rwandan refugees in the Nkwenda/Kimuli Refugee Settlement in Tanzania. The degradations and vulnerabilities he experienced as a refugee continue to determine his priorities in ministry and organizing. He can often be found today among people living in a similar precarity. Ordained and stationed as a Lutheran pastor in the Tanzania-Rwanda border town of Ngara on the eve of the 1994 Rwanda genocide—this region would receive hundreds of thousands of refugees escaping the massacre—he went on to settle in Rwanda, co-found the Lutheran Church in Rwanda (LCR) during his second year of ministry, and serve as the LCR's General Secretary and thought leader from 1995 to 2011. Reflecting on the extreme challenges of resettlement, reconstruction, and reconciliation people faced after Rwanda imploded, Rutsindintwarane wrote: "Thirty-two years of country divisionism, more than eight years of economic collapse, and four years of civil war and 90 days of savage genocide had left one million people dead, a collapsed nation and economy, and infrastructure destroyed. The violent legacy of genocide, civil war and of an authoritarian state has caused poverty, political instability, and social and spiritual fragility."[33]

30. Uvin, "Tragedy in Rwanda," 15.

31. See *Remaking Rwanda*. On contemporary biblical and theological interpretation connecting ecology and politics, see Daneel, *African Earthkeepers*.

32. Mwambazambi, "Environmental Problems in Africa."

33. Rutsindintwarane, "An Appreciative Inquiry," 16.

After completing two masters degrees abroad—one in Conflict Transformation at Eastern Mennonite University in Harrisonburg, Virginia, and the other in Theology, Evangelism, and Development at Wartburg Theological Seminary in Dubuque, Iowa—and a community organizing internship at the PICO National Network office in Oakland, California, Rutsindintwarane returned to Rwanda, founded PICO Rwanda, and began organizing in communities and congregations in 2006. The PICO National Network is a broad assembly of faith-based, community organizations established in the United States in 1972 to achieve ongoing, progressive social change. For a decade, as PICO Rwanda's executive director, Rutsindintwarane pursued his vision of a more prophetic church and a more united, democratic country. In 2011, he was elected Bishop of the Lutheran Church in Rwanda, but declined to further expand his organizing across the country. In 2014, though, he accepted an appointment as Deputy Bishop.

Settling in Rwanda in 1995, Rutsindintwarane witnessed other former refugees return and, for survival and their livelihoods, rapidly destroy the environment through deforestation. Uncontrolled and unsustainable tree cutting for land and energy, grazing and cultivating, and construction and commerce left places barren. He immediately encouraged Rwandan returnees to plant trees to replace what they removed, first teaching this practice as a form of peacemaking. Rutsindintwarane noted: "Wood is a source of life, useful for cooking, and when easily available allows women to do other productive things and children to go to school. It helps people get out of poverty, and reduces pressure and conflict at home. Trees are the first step to peacebuilding, contributing first to peace in the home."[34] Incorporating reforestation into his ministry, he acquired property in the Kanombe neighborhood directly adjacent to Kigali International Airport, "offsetting its pollution," and started a tree farm. Rutsindintwarane, his friends, and volunteers have since planted and managed a small forest there, and regularly distribute its seedlings to Lutheran parishes across the country. In addition to peacemaking, he presented the practice of planting trees to communities and congregations as exercising environmental responsibility. Wangari Maathai summarizes the implications of this reforestation: "In fact, scientists are only now beginning to understand the vast range of services—natural, social, psychological, ecological, and economic—that forests perform: the water

34. Notes on file, 2013.

they clean and retain; the climate patterns they regulate; the medicines they contain; the food they supply; the soil they enrich; the carbon they entrap; the oxygen they emit; the species of flora and fauna they conserve; and the peoples whose very physical existence depends on them."[35]

Since his mother died in 2013, Rutsindintwarane has planted more than 40,000 trees on his land on Rusumo Hill, named Kabanyana Forest after his aunt, overlooking the Rusumo Bridge border crossing where his mother and thousands of other Rwandans fled as refugees to Tanzania and/or returned home to Rwanda. The trees were planted to memorialize his mother, and "as a sign of hope for the future for not only Rwandans but for the global community."[36] Integrated into his ministry as "faith in action," reforestation would also be incorporated into his organizing, combining environmental responsibility with substantive democracy and sustainable development.

Much like PICO organizers in the United States, Rutsindintwarane believes people can best shape their futures by developing themselves as leaders and building powerful, locally-controlled, community organizations that directly engage political authorities, economic interests, and environmental concerns. Holding oneself, one's family, social groups, the broader community, civil society organizations, religious leaders, public officials, and local to national political institutions accountable in a predominantly Christian country to reconstruct Rwanda and rehabilitate Christianity are thus central to his efforts. Framed by faith, structured by grassroots democratic practices, and recognized for its effectiveness in mobilizing people to address their own social and material needs, Rutsindintwarane's organizing in Mumeya, Nyange, Matimba, Rusumo, and the capitol Kigali has involved thousands of Rwandans, including youth, in collective action ranging from building a regional health center in a remote, rural community, to forming urban women's associations helping people leave prostitution for legal forms of employment, to planting forests. These initiatives have established PICO Rwanda as both a national and global model for community organizing and leadership development.[37]

---

35. Maathai, *Replenishing the Earth*, 86.

36. PICO International, "In memory of John Rutsindintwarane's mother, Kabasinga Beltilde."

37. See Thasiah, "The Right to Freedom of Association."

Rutsindintwarane started PICO Rwanda in 2006 by organizing in the almost unreachable, mountainous region of Mumeya, Rwanda.[38] *The New Times*, a leading Rwandan English-language newspaper, described life in Mumeya at the time as desperate. "This close proximity to those [Tanzanian and Burundian] borders therefore means that most of the area inhabitants are returnee refugees who are struggling to cope with the serious business of survival, and so their existence is mostly characterized by a frustrated sense of hopelessness. The nearest hospital, [in] Kirehe, is 30 kilometers away. There was no school in a radius of 10 kilometers by 2006. The place itself is inaccessible, with only a rugged track serving for the road that they use to take in some supplies. They have to trudge five kilometers to the Akagera River to get a jerrycan of water for home use. What this actually translates into is a life of extreme hardship for the people living it; deaths, be they maternal or children, are a common occurrence, when most of them would have been preventable."[39] Rutsindintwarane organized people from various congregations—Roman Catholic, Anglican, Baptist, Seventh-day Adventist, and Lutheran—facing extreme poverty, ecological devastation, and genocide-related challenges such as the co-existence of victims, perpetrators, and, more generally, survivors and returnees. Together, they conducted several hundred one-to-one interviews throughout their villages, learned much about people's survival strategies given the scarcity of natural resources and the environmental degradation, and identified Mumeya's most pressing issue: access to health care, particularly maternal and neonatal care. Convening community meetings under what came to be called the "Jesus tree" on account of the "faith in action"—togetherness, reconciliation, healing, reflection, deliberation, judgments, and self-governance—taking place there, Rutsindintwarane helped emerging leaders consider what they heard from others, research possible responses, role-play interactions with public officials and religious leaders, and conduct evaluations on their own actions. Mobilizing thousands of Mumeyans, these leaders managed the laying of the foundation for the health center; researched complicated, construction-related issues; and held planning meetings with religious leaders and public officials—from local civil servants to the President of the Rwanda Senate in Parliament—to gain the necessary financial and technical support.

38. Mumeya is near Rwantonde in the Gatore Sector of the Kirehe District.
39. Gusongoirye, "Kirehe: Building and Healing Together as a Community."

In the one-to-one interviews throughout the villages, Rutsindint-warane and the emerging community leaders learned from village residents, the majority of whom are subsistence farmers, what environmental responsibility and sustainability means to them. The residents, sustained by, and the primary custodians and beneficiaries of the environment, spoke of "the stress of not enough natural resources and the need for more trees."[40] The added forest cover would "regulate rainfall," reduce soil erosion and damaging landslides, and provide wood and timber for fuel, cooking, building, and other income-generating activities.[41] Their perceptions are comparable to the perceptions of those viewed as experts working for the Rwanda Environmental Management Authority. In the latter's first state of the environment report in 2009, the authors explain: "Forests provide ecosystem services and products such as protection of water catchments, regulation of water flow, influencing climate, protection against soil erosion, water purification, food, wood for fuel and construction, tourism, non-timber forest products including medicine plants, honey and handcrafts. The role of forests in preserving ecological balance is particularly important in Rwanda. They contribute greatly to watershed protection against erosion, thus making agriculture viable and covering the daily basic needs for wood for more than 96 per cent of the country's population."[42]

The Mumeya community responded to its own ecological assessment by learning from Rutsindintwarane how to plant a forest. They combined their community organizing with tree planting, using seedlings from their mentor's tree farm, and now have both a health center and a small forest of fifteen hundred trees.

The health center—including a clinic, laboratory, and pharmacy—is fully staffed and functional. Another building on site houses a store, restaurant, meeting space, and crop storage facilities. The thirty-eight-room center is connected to Kirehe, the nearest city, by road, increasing availability of medical supplies and personnel. Since 2006, Rutsindintwarane has trained over one hundred Mumeyan men, women, and youth in organizing, leadership, and, more specifically, in holding religious leaders and public officials accountable to their constituencies. As a result, over thirty thousand area residents, including thirteen thousand children,

40. Notes on file, 2013.

41. Ibid.

42. Rwanda Environmental Management Authority, "Rwanda State of Environment and Outlook," 8.

have access to healthcare, and women in labor neither have to be carried by stretcher across miles of rugged terrain to reach a hospital nor fear death in childbirth. Moreover, Mumeyans now have clout. Religious leaders and public officials from all levels of Rwandan society have witnessed them working together across class, gender, denomination, and, most significantly, ethnic lines to establish a strong, grassroots, democratic organization, exert political power, develop their community, and practice environmental responsibility. Finally, Mumeyans have turned into trainers themselves, travelling across Rwanda and East Africa to share their stories of faith in action. Presentations of their work in Europe, the United States, Central America, and Haiti by members of the PICO International network confirm their global reputation.[43]

CONCLUSION

John Rutsindintwarane's ministry and organizing intuitively combine and integrate environmental responsibility, substantive democracy, and sustainable development. In doing so, he rehabilitates a Christianity complicit in political violence, mass atrocity, and ecological devastation. In the opening remarks of her Nobel Lecture delivered in Oslo's City Hall on December 10, 2004, just after she was awarded the Nobel Peace Prize, Wangari Maathai introduced one of her most powerful contributions to African and global development. "In this year's prize, the Norwegian Nobel Committee has placed the critical issue of environment and its linkage to democracy and peace before the world. For their visionary action, I am profoundly grateful. Recognizing that sustainable development, democracy, and peace are indivisible is an idea whose time has come. Our work over the past 30 years has always appreciated and engaged these linkages."[44] Otherwise put, "there can be no peace without equitable development; and there can be no development without sustainable management of the environment in a democratic and peaceful space."[45] For Rutsindintwarane, there can be no Lutheranism in Rwanda without eco-reformation: no faith without environmental responsibility, substantive democracy, and sustainable development; they are indivis-

---

43. See the PICO International website, http://www.picointernational.org, for reports on comparable work in Central America and Haiti.

44. Maathai, "Nobel Lecture."

45. Ibid.

ible for faith. This is how he reimagines Christianity for a post-genocide generation still in transition from recovery to resilience.

BIBLIOGRAPHY

Aguilar, Mario I. *Theology, Liberation and Genocide: A Theology of the Periphery.* London: SCM, 2012.

Conradie, Ernst. *Christianity and Ecological Theology: Resources for Further Research.* Study Guide in Religion and Theology. Stellenbosch: University of Western Cape, 2006.

Daneel, Marthinus L. *African Earthkeepers: Wholistic Interfaith Mission.* Maryknoll, NY: Orbis, 2001.

Des Forges, Alison. *Leave None to Tell the Story: Genocide in Rwanda.* New York: Human Rights Watch, 1999.

Carney, J. J. *Rwanda before the Genocide: Catholic Politics and Ethnic Discourse in the Late Colonial Era.* Oxford: Oxford University Press, 2014.

Gaynor, Niamh. *Decentralisation, Conflict and Peacebuilding in Rwanda.* Dublin: Dublin City University, 2013.

Graeber, David. *Fragments of an Anarchist Anthropology.* Chicago: Prickly Paradigm, 2004.

Gusongoirye, D. "Kirehe: Building and Healing Together as a Community." *The New Times* (November 1, 2009). http://www.piconetwork.org/news-media/coverage/2009/0323.

Katongole, Emmanuel. *The Sacrifice of Africa: A Political Theology for Africa.* Grand Rapids: Eerdmans, 2010.

Klein, Naomi. *This Changes Everything: Capitalism vs. the Climate.* New York: Simon & Schuster, 2015.

Longman, Timothy. *Christianity and Genocide in Rwanda.* African Studies. Cambridge: Cambridge University Press, 2010.

Maathai, Wangari. *The Challenge of Africa.* New York: Anchor, 2009.

———. "Nobel Lecture." December 10, 2004, Oslo City Hall, Oslo, Norway. http://www.nobelprize.org.

———. *Replenishing the Earth: Spiritual Values for Healing Ourselves and the World.* New York: Doubleday, 2010.

Mamdani, Mahmood. *When Victims Become Killers: Colonialism, Nativism, and the Genocide in Rwanda.* Princeton: Princeton University Press, 2002.

Mwambazambi, Kalemba, "Environmental Problems in Africa: A Theological Response." *Ethiopian Journal of Environmental Studies and Management* 3 (2010) 54–64.

Moodley, Vadi, Alphonse Gahima, and Suveshnee Munien. "Environmental Causes and Impacts of the Genocide in Rwanda: Case Studies of the Towns of Butare and Cyangugu." *African Journal on Conflict Resolution* 10 (2010) 103–19.

National Forestry Policy, Republic of Rwanda, Ministry of Forestry and Mines, May 2010.

PICO International. "In Memory of John Rutsindintwarane's Mother Kabasinga Beltilde." Press Release, February 12, 2013. http://www.picointernational.org.

Protestant Council of Churches in Rwanda. "Role of Church Parishes in Protecting, Rehabilitating the Environment and Fighting Against Climate Change in Rwanda," 2012. http://www.arcworld.org.

———. "Theological Charter for the Environment." 2011. http://www.arcworld.org.

Prunier, Gerard. *The Rwanda Crisis: History of a Genocide.* New York: Columbia University Press, 1997.

Rutsindintwarane, John. "An Appreciative Inquiry in Rusumo and Rukira Districts, Kibungo Province of Rwanda: A Study of the Perceptions, Challenges and Needs for Empowering the Lutheran Church of Rwanda." M.A.T.D.E., Wartburg Theological Seminary, 2005.

Rwandan Environmental Management Authority. "Rwanda State of the Environment and Outlook Report." 2009. http://www.rema.gov.rw.

———. "Rwanda State of Environment and Outlook: Summary for Decision Makers." 2009. http://www.rema.gov.rw.

Straus, Scott, and Lars Waldorf, eds. *Remaking Rwanda: State Building and Human Rights after Mass Violence.* Madison: University of Wisconsin Press, 2011.

Thasiah, Victor. "Reconfiguring Church-State Relations: Toward a Rwandan Political Theology." In *Lutheran Identity and Political Theology,* edited by Carl Henric-Grenholm and Göran Gunner, 190–207. Church of Sweden Research Series 9. Eugene, OR: Pickwick Publications, 2014.

———. "The Right to Freedom of Association: Organizing in Rwanda after Genocide." In *On Secular Governance: Lutheran Perspectives on Contemporary Legal Issues,* edited by Marie A. Failinger and Ronald W. Duty, 285–304. Grand Rapids: Eerdmans, 2016.

Uvin, Peter. *Aiding Violence: The Development Enterprise in Rwanda.* Sterling, VA: Kumarian, 1998.

———. "Tragedy in Rwanda: The Political Ecology of Conflict." *Environment* 38 (April 1996) 6–15.

14

Living Advent and Lent

A Call to Embody Reformation
for the Sake of Human and Planetary Health

—AANA MARIE VIGEN

Healer of our every ill, light of each tomorrow, give us peace beyond our fear, and hope beyond our sorrow.

MARTY HAUGEN[1]

INTRODUCTION

As I BEGIN THIS introduction, it is Advent in Chicago. Still early morning, the thermometer registers over fifty degree Fahrenheit outside. My eight-year-old son grouses his exasperation over the absence of snow. I watch him head to school and sigh, knowing that it is the warmest December, and year, on record.[2]

1. Haugen, "Healer of Our Every Ill."
2. It was seventy-two degrees in New York City on Christmas Eve. See Rathbun, "Warm Christmas Eve Shatters Records Across Eastern U.S." See also weather.com, "Record-Breaking Christmas Heat." According to two separate analyses, 2015

Such "anomalies" are actually characteristic of the new normal. Recently, we reached the foreboding milestone of raising the planet's average surface temperature by one degree Celsius,[3] resulting in increasingly severe and varied consequences (e.g. acidifying oceans, melting of ancient glaciers, accelerating mass extinctions, rising sea levels, prolonged periods of extreme heat and drought).[4] The arrival and intensity of such palpable, measureable effects have shattered the earlier and more conservative projections of likely consequences anticipated by the world's leading scientists.

It is all rather unsettling for this Midwesterner and parent. I feel the weight of guilt—knowing my generation is passing on serious problems to my son's generation that we created well before their birth, and that they (and those that come after them) will pay dearly-high prices for the varied failures and shortsightedness of their parents and grandparents. As I grapple with the high stakes before us, I find myself ruminating over a famous phrase not from Martin Luther, but from the Rev. Dr. Martin Luther King Jr. who, in a 1967 sermon critiquing the U.S. war in Vietnam, evocatively called us all to awaken to "the fierce urgency of now."[5]

Isn't such an impulse to "wake up" integral to the way Christians mark time? Indeed, Advent is a season of quiet but strong hope and of earnest preparation for the coming of Immanuel. And as I now finish this chapter, the church calendar is moving through Lent. For me, Advent and Lent have always been bound up together—hope and repentance; thanksgiving and lament; divine grace and human confession. Each season calls us to prepare our hearts and minds—to make room for divine love, to account for our actions and inactions, to reflect on what we want to change and how we might be changed by this radical love. Both Advent and Lent invite Christians to take stock of the acute and specific forms of suffering and injustice that invariably diminish the shiny reflections of our progress and achievements that we like to project to others.

Throughout this volume, we are chipping away at a tough question: In the face of pervasive and heart-breaking climate change, how

---

temperatures shattered every known meteorological high in 136 years of record-keeping. See NASA, "NOAA Analyses Reveal Record-Shattering Global Warm Temperatures in 2015."

3. See ScienceDaily.com, "2015 Likely to be Warmest on Record."

4. See Kolbert, *The Sixth Extinction*; and Brodwin, "Earth is on the Edge of a 'Sixth Extinction.'"

5. King, "Beyond Vietnam."

are we—as Lutheran Christians, as students, as educators, as pastors, as
healthcare providers, as citizens—to respond? Put differently, how do
we live—*embody*—Advent and Lent, creatively and intentionally? Such
questions are not an intellectual exercise; they are urgent. For too long,
we—especially those of us in affluent, industrialized, first world contexts—have failed to appreciate the full scope, implications, and origins
of the present health and ecological crisis.

In attempting to respond to such questions, I suggest that Christians need to reconnect not simply with the 1517 Reformation, but with a
dynamic, *reforming impulse* for our own particular moment in time and
space. We need to *live* lives of reformation more than simply rehash the
landmark historical and theological event of the Reformation. In particular, I contend that Lutheran Christians need to relate (more boldly
than we often do) our distinctive theological inheritance to the concrete,
agonizing groans of our planet in great peril.

Three central topics focus my discussion: First, I underscore two
fundamental conceptual shifts needed in how we understand the terms
"climate change" and "human health." Second, taking a cue from Luther's
distinctive methodological approach, I offer an honest assessment of how
climate change magnifies a nest of massive public health concerns. Third,
I point to facets of Luther's theological and moral vision that help us to
embody eco-reformation, to enact a hopeful and justice-filled response
to the climate and health challenges before us.

REFRAMING HOW WE THINK ABOUT
THE CLIMATE CRISIS AND HUMAN HEALTH

Reconceiving "Climate Crisis"

Climate change came home to roost in 2015. Its effects are viscerally felt
both in the United States and across the globe. 2015 is also the year that it
became (finally) untenable to ignore or deny outright the fact of climate
change. The strong testimony from international leaders and communities has broken through many news/social media barriers. Prominent
international leaders, from Pope Francis and President Obama to UN
Secretary-General Ban Ki-moon and World Bank President Jim Yong
Kim, speak frequently and forcefully about the gravity of the situation.
So too have various Hollywood stars: Matt Damon, Jessica Alba, Don
Cheadle, Leonardo DiCaprio, Harrison Ford, to name a few. Yet, even

with such hope-inspiring and powerful shifts in public attention and rhetoric, and even as we start to come to grips with how unhealthy the planet increasingly is becoming, what too many still fail to understand is that *we too are ill*—and that this illness is biological, social, and conceptual all at once. Thus, I want to highlight two basic ways we need to shift how we think about climate change so that we are able to grasp fully the profound changes in individual and collective behaviors, formal policies, public health infrastructures, and conceptual frameworks needed.

First, by "conceptual" I mean to say that *how* we as a society generally think about the problem is in itself a core part of the problem. Specifically, climate change is about much more than the careless overconsumption of fossil fuels. Indeed, it is a symptom of a much more pernicious, existential problem: the reigning psychological, spiritual, and moral disconnect between human beings and the rest of creation. Since the mid-late 1800s, we (especially Christians and secular humanists in the Western, northern hemisphere) have, wittingly and unwittingly, crafted a self-centered worldview in which humanity is set apart from and above nature: understood as its ruler, rather than as an interdependent facet within it.

Of course, it only takes a significant illness or other life crisis (loss of a job or home, a tragic accident) to expose the folly of this myth on personal levels. No one feels self-sufficient after a hurricane demolishes everything he/she owns. Or consider more ordinary moments in life: Given the inevitability of fragility and illness, no infant and few elders can carry off the image of a "self-made, independent" master of his/her universe. We may put up smoke screens during our youth and middle adulthood to avoid this truth of radical *inter*dependence; but at a minimum, around the times of both our beginnings and departures, we come face to face with our limits and utter mortality. Indeed, such encounters are integral to what makes us human.

Thus, at this most critical juncture in history (human and planetary), along with developing sufficient, renewable energy infrastructures and technologies, we need to own the truth that even as we are inventive and capable creatures, we never truly grow out of our radical dependence—on God, on Earth's ecosystems, *and* on one another—for our individual and collective well-being and futures. This is not a novel or revolutionary idea. Martin Luther knew it well in sixteenth century Saxony.

A second needed shift is this: For too long, climate change has been cast as a narrow topic pertinent to "nerdy" scientists, "tree-hugging" environmentalists, and "animal lovers." Thus, when some hear "global warming," images of polar bears immediately pop up in the mind's eye. A primary goal of this chapter is to widen what we see at stake. At the risk of sounding anthropocentric, when we think about the ecological crisis we also need to see the faces of hungry, impoverished, sickly children and adults. Climate change is the largest public health crisis we have ever faced as a species, as a planet. National and international research centers have begun to demonstrate such connections.[6]

Think of it this way: Earth—and *all* of its inhabitants—has a fever, even as some feel it more acutely than others. We have *all* contracted a chronic, life-threatening condition. And perhaps the hardest part to accept is that *we human beings*—through our combined reliance on fossil fuels, large-scale, industrialized ways of producing food, and sweeping deforestation—*are the primary cause* of the infection.

Actually, we are a "double whammy" of an infection agent. While releasing unprecedented amounts of carbon dioxide and methane into the air, we have simultaneously—gravely—compromised Earth's *arteries* (ocean acidification, fresh and salt water pollution, overfishing), *tissues* (desertification, soil degradation, overflowing trash landfills and other contaminating toxins), and *respiratory systems* (massive losses of forests which constitute Earth's lungs, intensifying air pollution and toxins produced by vehicles and industry). Overall, the prognosis for many living beings/species is grim. Perhaps most embarrassing is the fact that the world's most prominent and senior "physicians" (e.g., international specialists on climate and other related natural sciences)[7] first alerted us to the diagnosis and probable outcomes back in the 1970s. Yet, akin to the heavily-addicted smoker, we have waited a dangerously long time to begin to kick the carbon habit.

Thus, what is called for—theologically and morally—is a profound and vibrant *Eco-Reformation*—a radical *conversion* of minds, hearts, and habits. As Luther puts, it, we need to turn away from being self-absorbed and preoccupied (whether out of egocentric arrogance or anxious fear/insecurity)—turned in upon ourselves (*incurvatus in se*)—and turn toward God's grace. For Luther, in such a conversion, we (re)discover who we most truly are at the very core of our being as children of God. Even more, we (re)connect with our capacity to respond to the visceral needs and hurts of our neighbors. On this theme, Pope Francis is a kindred

6. See, for example, online resources from the Harvard Center for Health and the Global Environment, and The Center for Climate Change & Health.

7. See the work of the Intergovernmental Panel on Climate Change.

spirit. In his path-breaking 2015 encyclical, *Laudato Si*, the Pope issues a prophetic call to a holistic—and profoundly *ecological*—conversion. Ironically, as we celebrate this five hundredth anniversary of the Protestant Reformation, Pope Francis is just the kind of reforming papacy presence that Luther was looking for back in 1517!

Focusing on the moral life, the "fierce urgency" of our "now" means we need an authentic and robust re-making of personal and societal habits. And we need to seek out these new ways of living and being to save *both* polar bears and indigenous Alaskans; to salvage what we can of cultural *and* bio-diversity; to protect people and other endangered species gasping on the front lines of climate change; to feed hungry children and to shore up honey bees on the brink of colony collapse. In sum, making profound changes in energy, agriculture, industry, and consumer consumption patterns and policies is not simply an altruistic thing to do. Such conversions are vital to the recovery and renewal of our own spiritual, moral, and relational well-being. In short, this multi-textured Eco-Reformation is integral to our self-interest and survival; it is essential to *our individual and collective* health, future, and yes, *salvation.*

Three Contextual Notes on the Meaning of the Term "Health"

When some think of the terms "health" and "illness" they think in the specific biological/physiological sense: the absence/presence of a pathogen or other physical impairment that causes a disease or limits human functioning—whether from an injury, an infection, a genetic trait/defect, or atypical cells that invade healthy, host cells. In other words, we think of diseases, disabilities, and accidents that affect the level of our physical and cognitive functioning.

However, many experts across disciplines as diverse as public health and pastoral care urge us to think of health more holistically as something that is at once biological, social, psychological, environmental, and spiritual. For our collective understanding of the term "health," I draw upon a definition offered by a Protestant womanist ethicist, Emilie M. Townes:

> Health is not simply the absence of disease—it comprises a wide range of activities that foster healing and wholeness . . . [It] is a cultural production in that health and illness alike are social constructs and dependent on social networks, biology, and

environment. As it is embedded in our social realities, health also includes the integration of the spiritual (how we relate to God), the mental (who we are as thinking and feeling people) and the physical (who we are biologically) aspects of our lives.[8]

In short, national health/illness statistics speak to much more than the degree to which persons suffer from any given medical diagnosis. At its heart, the term "health" is not about the absence of disease; *it is about relationship*—biological, mental, social, even economic and political. "Health" speaks to the quality of our relationships—to our bodies and minds, to other people, and—for people of faith—to God.

This particular understanding of health resonates strongly with Lutheran theology. Luther's biblical commentaries, along with his more occasional writings, often show the depth of his concern for the physical and social welfare of people alongside the spiritual. Interestingly, the Latin noun *salus* originally meant "safety, welfare, health" before it came to denote "salvation." Similarly, the German word for "salvation," *Heil*, shares the same root as the word for "healing," *Heilung*. These ancient and medieval theological strands run deep in modern Lutheran theology. For example, they strongly shape the theo-ethical insights in the ELCA Social Statement, "Caring for Health: Our Shared Endeavor."[9] The point is that in Reformation theology, *Heil*/salvation is intrinsically bound up with healing. Even more, no call to reformation is sufficient without *eco*-reformation—without strong attention to the health, healing, and renewal of *all* creation.

Second, and in a related vein, we must move beyond an individualistic understanding of health. Undeniably, individual choices and behaviors matter: diet, exercise, sufficient sleep, taking necessary medications, not smoking, etc. Every year, many New Year's resolutions and Lenten disciplines focus on precisely these dimensions of our lives. Yet, this line of thinking presumes access to healthy food and to safe/affordable places to exercise (not to mention sufficient time and child care). Moreover, access to prescribed medications can be complicated by limited financial and insurance resources, both in the U.S. and around the globe.[10]

---

8. Townes, *Breaking the Fine Rain of Death*, 2.

9. ELCA, "Health Care."

10. As just one example, the World Health Organization (WHO) reports "one-third of the developing world's people are unable to receive or purchase essential medicines on a regular basis." WHO, "Access to Medicine."

Thus, we need to attend more to the "social determinants of health," which are missed when we focus too narrowly on the lifestyle, genetic, and biological causes of disease. That is to say, our relative individual and collective health is strongly affected by the environments and institutions in which we grow up and live. The World Health Organization (WHO) defines the social determinants of health as "the conditions in which people are born, grow, work, live, and age, and the wider set of forces and systems shaping the conditions of daily life."[11] Simply put: education policy is health policy; economic and social policy are health policy. How much a society invests in public health and other social safety nets can have dramatic effects on its national health outcomes. What is new in our time is that varied consequences of climate change also put a crippling stress on public health infrastructures.

Undeniably, facing climate change head-on can disrupt a good night's sleep (which, health experts routinely emphasize, is a basic ingredient needed for good health!). Yet, as much as many of us are tempted to minimize the scope of the climate challenge for the sake of a more peaceful conscience, doing so is even more hazardous to our individual and collective health. Thus, with Luther and all the saints, we will bravely face what is so difficult, yet vital, to understand.

"WARNING: CLIMATE CHANGE IS HAZARDOUS TO YOUR HEALTH"

A Note on Luther's Method

Before exploring the ways human health is harmed by climate change, a quick word on Luther's theological and ethical method may offer insight into ways to do helpful and relevant theological and ethical reflection today. Specifically, Luther brought Scripture and his own contextual situation together in original and visionary ways. He made creative use of the printing press and nailed ninety-five arguments against the overreach of religious authority to the door of the most visible place in his town for the sake of public knowledge and debate. Luther translated the Bible for the first time into vernacular German so that it could be read by common folk. He printed a series of pamphlets and commissioned woodblock cuts

11. "These forces and systems include economic policies and systems, development agendas, social norms, social policies and political systems." WHO, "Social Determinants of Health."

by Lucas Cranach to spread his ideas for those who couldn't read. Basically, he was using the Facebook, Instagram, Twitter, Snapchat, and YouTube of his day. And because Luther was so audacious and popular, he was called before an official tribunal and ordered to recant. He refused. That took guts. Luther was then excommunicated from the Church while some plotted his death. We may call Luther a lot of things, but "bland" or "complacent" cannot be among them.

Thus, I believe Luther matters for us today not *only* because of the music, scriptural commentaries, and theology he wrote, *but also because of how he lived and what he did.* Long before the term was coined, Luther *embodied* civil disobedience. What we stand to learn from him is *not only* a way of thinking about our relationship to God, but also a way of engaging in the world—*in our own particular moment.*

Three Basic Ways the Changing Climate Threatens Human Health

When many, perhaps most, U.S. inhabitants think about threats to human health, several disquieting "C's" come to mind: cancer, congestive heart failure, coronary heart disease, and cholesterol. It is true that heart disease and cancer are, by far, the top two causes of death in the United States.[12] Most likely, the "C" of climate change does not make our mental lists of dreaded health concerns.

And yet, back in 2009 a prestigious British medical journal, *The Lancet,* identified climate change as "the biggest global health threat in the 21st century."[13] Five years later, Margaret Chan, the Director-General of the WHO, called climate change "the defining issue of the 21st century," noting that it "is already causing tens of thousands of deaths every year." Chan noted "[t]hese deaths arise from more frequent epidemics of diseases like cholera, the vastly expanded geographical distribution of diseases like dengue, and from extreme weather events, like heat waves and floods. Climate change degrades air quality, reduces food security, and compromises water supplies and sanitation."[14]

To illustrate the connections, I will chart three of the most striking ways climate change and the extraction and use of fossil fuels pose grave

12. Centers for Disease Control, "Leading Causes of Death."
13. Costello, "Managing the Health Effects of Climate Change," 1728.
14. Chan, "WHO Director-General Addresses Event on Climate Change and Health."

public health threats in terms of "thirst," "hunger," and "bugs." Woven throughout this analysis is attention to systemic injustice. Succinctly put: Those who contribute the least to causing climate change—predominately black- and brown-skinned peoples living in resource-poor contexts in the United States and around the world—are paying the highest prices for it. They did not cause this global, public health crisis; yet they suffer the most severe symptoms, while having the fewest resources for mitigating them.

Thirst

Among the most fundamental building blocks for human health is access to sufficient clean water. For millennia, the ability to draw ample, seemingly unlimited, supplies of fresh water for drinking, agricultural irrigation, and industrial production was taken as a given. Climate change is radically disrupting this reality with respect to Earth's ability to regenerate sufficient fresh water supplies. It also contributes to the loss of tremendous amounts of fertile land due to surging waters, soil degradation, and excessive droughts and desertification, all of which complicate efforts to combat hunger and thirst.[15]

Clean water is essential for life; contaminated water is lethal. Around the world, an alarming number of children die each year (predominately in resource-stressed contexts) due to a lack of clean water. Contaminated water contributes to water-borne diseases taking up residence in vulnerable bodies. These children are then confronted with a lack of available/affordable medicine and adequate healthcare. It is perhaps unthinkable to some of us in affluent contexts that a child would die from diarrhea, yet it is all too common in parts of India, Sub-Saharan Africa, and East Asia. Nevertheless, as revelations of widespread drinking water contaminations in Flint, Michigan (lead poisoning), and along the Ohio River (algae blooms from toxic runoff) remind us, we are foolish if we think we are insulated from such public health failures.[16]

15. Undeniably, heavy uses of chemical pesticides and fertilizers also degrade soils and water and various other kinds of pollution contribute to their contamination. These factors also inhibit the production of sufficient amounts of safe and healthy food.

16. Arenschield, "Toxic Algae Bloom Now Stretches 650 Miles Along Ohio River." See also Rodrick, "Who Poisoned Flint, Michigan?"

In short, when societies are not equipped with sufficient, strong public works and public health infrastructure, storms demolish both homes and health systems. A storm's health effects are often felt for months, even years. Floodwaters often wipe out sanitation and waste facilities along with roads. Thus, they sully clean water sources with various toxins (building and machine debris, pesticides, lead and other toxins, feces, dead animals and people, etc.) Cholera is caused by the consumption of water or food that has been contaminated by a bacterium that flourishes when sanitation and public health systems flounder.

Over the globe, water is the site of thorny problems. In some places, rising seas lead to salt water fouling potable water supplies. In others, the urgent problem is the rapid depletion of fresh water reserves due to overuse and to increasingly hot climates. For others the most urgent problem is pollution and/or ocean acidification. Water is everywhere; yet human thirst intensifies. As many aptly note, in the twenty-first century, "water is the new oil" and we will likely see major battles to control "water rights."

Hunger

Now, let's turn briefly to consider the present health of the land. Climate change magnifies hunger challenges more than it expands the amount of arable land suitable for food production. Earth is losing arable land at alarming rates, not only to seas, but also to overdevelopment, to soil impoverishment, and to extreme droughts. A heating planet (especially one in which massive hectares of forests are burned or slashed every year) dramatically affects both the quality of the soil and the expanse of dry deserts.[17] The following statistics from the United Nations (UN) give a strong sense of the severity of land/soil degradation:

- 2.6 billion people depend directly on agriculture, but 52% of the land used for agriculture is moderately or severely affected by soil degradation.

- Land degradation affects 1.5 billion people globally.

- Arable land loss is estimated at 30 to 35 times the historical rate.

17. The United Nations defines desertification as "persistent degradation of dryland ecosystems by human activities—including unsustainable farming, mining, overgrazing and clear-cutting of land—and by climate change." United Nations, "Desertification." See also, *Deutsche Welle*, "Loss of Fertile Soils: A Food Security Risk."

- Due to drought and desertification each year 12 million hectares are lost (23 hectares/minute!), where 20 million tons of grain could have been grown.

- 74% of the poor (42% of the very poor and 32% of the moderately poor) are directly affected by land degradation globally.[18]

Taken together, what was once fertile land is in many places either being swallowed up by encroaching salt waters or is being turned into massive deserts or impoverished, sterile soil. Thus, from three distinct angles—overall loss of land, less fertile land, and less plentiful fish stocks (due to both over-fishing and ocean acidification)—we face striking food shortages.

Consequently, there is much concern over how to feed the world's swelling population. According to 2015 data, globally 795 million people are undernourished (about one in every nine people), which means they have insufficient food for achieving "healthy active" lives.[19] Changes across the world's microclimates are exacerbating two distinct hunger issues: an overall lack of sufficient food available in terms of calories *and* a lack of nutritious food/food diversity. Chronic hunger means far more than an ache in the belly. It means stunted growth and underweight children, diminished performance in school and work, and bodies that are more susceptible to disease and infection.[20] U.S. inhabitants are not invulnerable. In 2014, over forty-eight million Americans (including over fifteen million children) "lived in food insecure households."[21] In all, communities of color suffer more from hunger than their white counterparts in the U.S. and around the world.

One of the clearest examples is the heart-breaking and horrific Syrian Civil War (2011–) in which at least two hundred thousand people

18. United Nations, "Desertification." See also, United Nations Convention to Combat Desertification (UNCCD), "Desertification Land Degradation & Drought—Some Global Facts and Figures."

19. See United Nations Food and Agriculture Organization (FAO), "The State of Food Insecurity in the World 2015." See also United Nations World Food Programme (WFP), "World Hunger Falls to Under 800 Million, Eradication is Next Goal."

20. "In many situations, nutritional supplements may be needed to improve the nutritional status of the population in the short term. A range of food security and other nutrition-enhancing interventions in agriculture, health, hygiene, water supply and education, particularly targeting women, are necessary in the medium and longer term." See FAO, "The State of Food Insecurity in the World 2015."

21. *Feeding America,* "Hunger and Poverty Facts and Statistics."

have died[22] (a conservative estimate) and, according to 2015 UN data, another four million or more have become refugees.[23] While it is not accurate to say that the crippling four-year drought in the country (or climate change) *caused* the Syrian Civil War outright, it is fair to say that both are significant contributing factors. Syria is not an isolated case. According to 2015 UN data: "Extreme weather events, natural disasters, political instability and civil strife have all impeded progress—24 African countries currently face food crises, twice as many as in 1990; around one of every five of the world's undernourished lives in crisis environments characterized by weak governance and acute vulnerability to death and disease."[24] The combination of chronic hunger, minimal public health systems, and inept government is deadly.

Given these challenges and informed by his extensive work with people in resource-stressed contexts, philanthropist and Microsoft founder, Bill Gates, pointedly makes the case why the world's impoverished farmers need strong help in adapting now:

> [F]or the world's poorest farmers, life is a high-wire act—without safety nets. They don't have access to improved seeds, fertilizer, irrigation systems and other beneficial technologies, as farmers in rich countries do—and no crop insurance, either, to protect themselves against losses. Just one stroke of bad fortune—a drought, a flood, or an illness—is enough for them to tumble deeper into poverty and hunger. Now, climate change is set to add a fresh layer of risk to their lives. Rising temperatures in the decades ahead will lead to major disruptions in agriculture, particularly in tropical zones. Crops won't grow because of too little rain or too much rain. Pests will thrive in the warmer climate and destroy crops.[25]

Food and water: both are fundamental for life. Even more, both are sacramental elements in Christianity and are considered sacred in many other religious traditions. Luther extolls us to remember our baptism every day when we wash our faces. Jesus asks his disciples to remember him in the breaking of bread and sharing of wine. If bread and water

22. See Yourish, et al., "Death in Syria."

23. See UNHCR, "Total Number of Syrian Refugees Exceeds Four Million for First Time."

24. FAO, "World Hunger Falls to Under 800 Million, Eradication is Next Goal."

25. Gates, "We Need to Help Poor Farmers Prepare for Climate Change—Starting Now."

are so integral to religious rites, what does that mean for our everyday practices and patterns? How are we—as individuals and as communities—accountable to neighbors in need? What do our rites of baptism and communion mean for our accountability to those who viscerally hunger and thirst? How do we embody Advent and Lent in our everyday lives and in the world?

Bugs

In the context of climate change, global and US health/disease inequities intensify in numerous ways.[26] As Paul Farmer, MD, co-founder of Partners in Health, has remarked: "diseases themselves make a preferential option for the poor."[27] Consequently, he calls on healthcare providers, policymakers and public health officials to prioritize the poor in allotting medical treatments and prevention strategies. A variety of infectious diseases—tuberculosis, malaria, cholera, HIV-AIDS, Ebola, the Zika virus—flourish in weak public health systems in the United States and elsewhere. Indeed, there is a resurgence of tuberculosis in impoverished parts of Alabama.[28] Climate change adds one more factor with which these overloaded infrastructures must contend. A couple of crisp illustrations must suffice.

Compelling research has shown that dormant cholera bacteria become active when water temperatures rise.[29] Similarly, warmer land temperatures mean that malaria-carrying (and Zika virus-carrying) mosquitoes are extending into regions once too cold for them to survive. Thus, villages that had never before seen malaria cases have been caught off guard without necessary preventative and treatment plans in place.[30] Again, we would do well to remember that the U.S. is not im-

---

26. See WHO,"Protecting Health from Climate Change"; Environmental Health Perspective and National Institute of Environmental Health Science, "A Human Health Perspective on Climate Change"; 1 Million Women Blog, "Five Ways Climate Change Threatens Health"; Peeples, "Climate Change Threatens the Newest Prescription for Children"; Tavernise, "Unraveling the Relationship Between Climate Change and Health"; Peterson and Wirft-Brock, "Inside Energy."

27. Farmer, *Pathologies of Power*, 140.

28. See Lucas, "In Alabama's Poorest County, Tuberculosis is Far From Eradicated"; and CDC, "Trends in Tuberculosis, 2014."

29. Epstein and Ferber, *Changing Planet, Changing Health*, 25–28.

30. Ibid., 29–61.

mune. While the U.S. once eradicated malaria, there are now between one and two thousand cases per year.[31] And consider another disease at home in the United States: Lyme disease. It too is expanding as the ticks that carry it survive more winters and spread across wider areas given milder temperatures.[32]

Taking the above facts and realities together, in 2014 the World Health Organization (WHO) pointedly explained the myriad connections between climate change and human health and made startlingly projections: "Climate change affects the social and environmental determinants of health—clean air, safe drinking water, sufficient food and secure shelter . . . Between 2030 and 2050, climate change is expected to cause approximately 250,000 additional deaths per year, from malnutrition, malaria, diarrhea and heat stress . . . The direct damage costs to health (i.e. excluding costs in health-determining sectors such as agriculture and water and sanitation), is estimated to be between US$ 2–4 billion/year by 2030."[33] The likely costs of climate change—both in financial and health terms—are tangible and dear.

BLACK AND BROWN LIVES MATTER IN THE AGE OF CLIMATE CHANGE

I see climate change as the most pervasive site of socio-economic, racial-ethnic, gender, and postcolonial injustice in the twenty-first century. Black- and brown-skinned peoples face severe and disproportionate risks as compared with their white and relatively affluent neighbors. Moreover, in some respects, the public and scholarly conversation on climate change has not focused enough on the threats posed to communities of color, indigenous peoples, women, and to those living in poverty.

To illustrate, when trees are cut, not only are wildlife and wilderness spaces affected, but air quality suffers for every species. Trees are the planet's lungs. Trees also absorb carbon and release it when cut or burned. Thus, deforestation is a major contributor to rising surface temperatures. And the people and varied animal species who live on the front lines of forest losses (often indigenous populations) pay the most immediate

31. CDC, "Malaria Facts."
32. Epstein and Ferber, *Changing Planet, Changing Health*, 75–79.
33. WHO, "Climate Change and Health."

prices in terms of their cultures, their livelihoods, loss of habitat, and their health.

Similarly, burning fossil fuels disproportionately and negatively affects the quality of air, water, and living conditions for communities of color along with others living at or near poverty levels. These communities disproportionately live and/or work in environments with the most industrial plants, the largest commercial roads, the most toxic waste dumps, the most industrial and agricultural run runoff, the most pet coke, and the most methane released. The fact that, nationwide, black children in the U.S. suffer from far higher asthma rates than their white peers is no accident.[34] Burning fossil fuels is a public health dilemma that unjustly cripples people with the fewest options and the least insulation from the effects of climate change.

CONCLUSION: LUTHERAN RESOURCES FOR EMBODYING HOPE & REFORMATION

God of grace and God of glory . . . grant us wisdom, grant us courage, for the living of these days, for the living of these days.

HARRY EMERSON FOSDICK, "GOD OF GRACE AND GOD OF GLORY"

Climate change is the ultimate "game changer." Certainly the stakes and challenges are overwhelming. Yet, I take solace from remembering that others—Martin Luther, Sojourner Truth, Mahatma Gandhi, Dietrich Bonhoeffer, Martin Luther King, Jr., Dorothy Day, Cesar Chavez—have lived in critical moments of history. Each, along with a host of others, bears witness to the value of working hard for justice and love in the face of daunting odds and obstacles.

Lutherans and other Christians need to *live* the distinctive inheritance we take from Martin Luther, and not only because it is time to commemorate the five-hundredth anniversary of the Protestant Reformation. We need to remember Luther because his insight into the human person reminds us who we are in the deepest sense. When we remember who we are and to whom we belong, we have a better chance at creatively and meaningfully responding to the challenges of our own moments in

---

34. U.S. Department of Health and Human Services Office of Minority Health, "Asthma and African Americans."

history. I firmly believe that Luther's witness can embolden us to seek and enact "game-changing" reforms with respect to human and planetary health.

As I conclude this chapter, we are moving quickly through Lent. I often think how intimately and inextricably bound together are the seasons of Advent and Lent, as are repentance and redemption; as are hope and lament; as are confession and conversion; as are waiting and acting; as are introspection and outward analysis; as are love and grief. In fact, I think we are perpetually living simultaneously in both seasons. Advent reminds Christians that we worship a God who comes to the world as a vulnerable, brand new infant. But be careful not to romanticize this image. Newborns require tremendous care. They—like most people at the end of life—depend heavily on others for warmth, food, security, continuing health, and medicine when sick. God-with-us is also wholly "one of us" in our most intensely fragile moments. And we are *so* fragile now, as is the whole of planet Earth.

For its part, Lent calls us to turn our hearts yet again away from folly and back to God and to fervent love of God's creation. Our Earth—for all its awesome majesty—is in peril. It is vulnerable to human carelessness and shortsightedness. Our human fate is bound up with the planet's future. We remember God's solidarity with human fragility by venerating the cross, especially as part of Lenten liturgies. What we need to see now is not only a broken human body on the cross, but also with it, a broken, abused Earth.

Luther might begin by suggesting we remember where we begin and where we end: *With God.* He might whisper courage—inviting us to cling with every fiber of our being to the promise that God has our backs. Indeed, knowing in one's own bones that one is truly beloved—and that our being is bound up with divine love and grace—is basic sustenance for creative moral action. Such enfleshed knowledge is needed as much as air, food, and water. Moreover, a Lutheran vision of justice reminds us that it is not sufficient to think in the individualistic terms often found in rights and entitlement language in the United States. Nor is it sufficient to think in abstract terms. Instead, to understand what it means to be human and to live responsibly, one has to think concretely, relationally, and contextually.

At its best, a Lutheran sensibility emphasizes that we, by virtue of the *very structures of our being*, are accountable to one another. Relationality is not an elective to be chosen or not. We are hard-wired for relationship; thus doggedly seeking right relationship is a fundamental and shared responsibility. The only question is whether we will honor the relationships and responsibilities that already connect us to one another and to all of creation. A Lutheran worldview reminds us that God's grace has the power to embolden us to take real risks—to "sin boldly"—for sake of a more just world.

Put bluntly: the Reformation's not over and justice is never abstract.

BIBLIOGRAPHY

Arenschield, Laura. "Toxic Algae Bloom Now Stretches 650 Miles Along Ohio River." *The Columbus Dispatch*, October 3, 2015. http://www.dispatch.com.

Brodwin, Erin. "Earth Is on the Edge of a 'Sixth Extinction.'" *Business Insider*, April 27, 2015. http://www.businessinsider.com.

Centers for Disease Control (CDC). "Leading Causes of Death." April 27, 2016. http://www.cdc.gov.

———. "Trends in Tuberculosis, 2014." September 24, 2015. http://www.cdc.gov.

———. "Malaria Facts." April 15, 2016. http://www.cdc.gov.

The Center for Climate Change & Health. http://climatehealthconnect.org.

Chan, Margaret. "WHO Director-General Addresses Event on Climate Change and Health." World Health Organization (WHO), December 8, 2015. http://www.who.int.

Costello, Anthony, et al. "Managing the Health Effects of Climate Change." *The Lancet* 373 (2009) 1693–733.

Deutsche Welle. "Loss of Fertile Soils: A Food Security Risk." April 21, 2015. http://www.dw.com.

Environmental Health Perspective and National Institute of Environmental Health Science. "A Human Health Perspective on Climate Change." NIEHS, April 22, 2015. https://www.niehs.nih.gov.

Epstein, Paul R. and Dan Ferber. *Changing Planet, Changing Health: How the Climate Crisis Threatens Our Health and What We Can Do about It.* Berkeley: University of California Press, 2012.

ELCA. "Health Care." Adopted August 15, 2003. http://www.elca.org.

Farmer, Paul. *Pathologies of Power: Health, Human Rights, and the New War on the Poor.* Berkeley: University of California Press, 2005.

Feeding America. "Hunger and Poverty Facts and Statistics." 2015. http://www.feedingamerica.org.

Gates, Bill. "We Need to Help Poor Farmers Prepare for Climate Change—Starting Now." *The World Post*, September 2, 2015. http://www.huffingtonpost.com.

The Harvard Center for Health and the Global Environment. http://www.chgeharvard.org.

Haugen, Marty. "Healer of Our Every Ill." *ELW,* Hymn #612. Minneapolis: Augsburg Fortress, 2006.

Intergovernmental Panel on Climate Change. http://www.ipcc.ch/.

King, Martin L., Jr. "Beyond Vietnam." Sermon, Riverside Church, New York City, April 4, 1967. In *A Call to Conscience: The Landmark Speeches of Dr. Martin Luther*

King, Jr., edited by Clayborne Carson and Kris Shepard, 133–63. New York: Grand Central, 2002.

Kolbert, Elizabeth. *The Sixth Extinction: An Unnatural History.* New York: Holt, 2015.

Lucas, Phillip. "In Alabama's Poorest County, Tuberculosis is Far From Eradicated." *The Huffington Post*, updated January 22, 2016. http://www.huffingtonpost.com.

1 Million Women Blog. "Five Ways Climate Change Threatens Health." September 1, 2014. http://www.1millionwomen.com.

National Aeronautics and Space Administration. "NASA, NOAA Analyses Reveal Record-Shattering Global Warm Temperatures in 2015." January 20, 2016. http://www.nasa.gov.

Peeples, Lynne. "Climate Change Threatens the Newest Prescription for Children: Time Outdoors." *The Huffington Post*, September 6, 2014. http://www.huffingtonpost.com.

Peterson, Leigh, et al. "Inside Energy: If You Read One Story On Health And Fracking, Read This One." *Wyoming Public Radio*, September 5, 2014. http://wyomingpublicmedia.org.

Rathbun, Brett. "Warm Christmas Eve Shatters Records Across Eastern U.S." *AccuWeather.com*, December 26, 2015. http://www.accuweather.com.

Rodrick, Stephen. "Who Poisoned Flint, Michigan?" *Rolling Stone*, January 22, 2016. http://www.rollingstone.com.

Science Daily. "2015 Likely to Be Warmest on Record, 2011–2015 Warmest Five Year Period," November 25, 2015. https://www.sciencedaily.com.

Tavernise, Sabrina. "Unraveling the Relationship Between Climate Change and Health." *The New York Times*, July 13, 2015. http://www.nytimes.com.

Townes, Emilie M. *Breaking the Fine Rain of Death: African American Health Issues and a Womanist Ethic of Care.* New York: Continuum, 1998.

United Nations. "Desertification." http://www.un.org.

United Nations Convention to Combat Desertification. "Desertification Land Degradation & Drought—Some Global Facts and Figures." http://www.unccd.int.

United Nations Food and Agriculture Organization (FAO). "The State of Food Insecurity in the World 2015." http://www.fao.org.

United Nations World Food Programme. "World Hunger Falls to Under 800 Million, Eradication is Next Goal," May 27, 2015. https://www.wfp.org.

United Nations High Commissioner for Refugees (UNHCR). "Total Number of Syrian Refugees Exceeds Four Million for First Time." July 6, 2015. http://www.unhcr.org.

U.S. Department of Health and Human Services Office of Minority Health. "Asthma and African Americans." http://minorityhealth.hhs.gov.

World Health Organization (WHO). "Protecting Health from Climate Change." 2008. http://www.who.int.

———. "Climate Change and Health." Updated September, 2015. http://www.who.int

———. "Access to Medicine." http://www.who.int.

———. "Social Determinants of Health." Updated December, 2015. http://www.who.int.

Weather.com. "Record-Breaking Christmas Heat Clinches Record Warm December for Hundreds of Cities." January 2, 2016. https://weather.com.

Yourish, Karen, et al. "Death in Syria." *The New York Times*, September 14, 2015. http://www.nytimes.com.

15

Grace and Climate Change

The Free Gift in Capitalism and Protestantism

—TERRA S. ROWE

> We have no ontological status prior to and apart from communion. Communion is our being; the being we participate in is communion, and we derive our concrete selves from our communion.

JOSEPH HAROUTUNIAN[1]

AT A REMARKABLY EARLY moment in the rise of global environmental consciousness, Lutheran pastor and theologian Joseph Sittler identified the important and ambiguous role the Protestant doctrine of grace has played with regard to ecological concerns. Sittler criticized a doctrine of grace that focused merely on human redemption even as he maintained its importance for addressing ecological concerns.[2] In describing the ecological flux of reality he described the human self as profoundly graced—as fully dependent on the gifts of others, both divine and

---

1. Haroutunian, *God with Us*, 148, quoted in Sittler, "Essays on Nature and Grace," 174.

2. See, for example, Sittler, *Essays on Nature and Grace*, and "Called to Unity." For further development of Sittler's ecological theology, see the essay in this volume by Robert Saler.

creaturely. Rather than a substantial or essential self, Sittler's ecological self is held up and even constructed at the nexus of a multiplicity of gifts.[3] Think, for example, of the gift of breath. Even when we don't recognize it, the oxygen we inhale is a gift of trees, and in exchange for this gift we return carbon dioxide—tree breath. Or, think of what we now know as the microbiome, that ecosystem of bacteria that constitute our human bodies, helping us maintain basic functions like metabolism and immunity.[4] Such discoveries only increase awareness that, as Sittler affirms, "communion is our being" and our being only takes place in the midst of a continual exchange of interspecies gifts.

In suggesting that grace and selfhood are so closely connected Sittler seems to intuit a key insight from twentieth-century gift theory that who we conceive ourselves to be is intimately tied to the kinds of gifts we give and receive. Gift discourse was initiated in 1923 by socio-anthropologist Marcel Mauss in his now famous and still influential text, *The Gift: The Form and Reason for Exchange in Archaic Societies.*[5] While Mauss focused on connections between human gift practices, social connectivity, and economics, more recently ecotheologian Anne Primavesi has shifted gift theory from its anthropocentric focus to describe ecological reality. From Primavesi's perspective, life itself, and not just human society, emerges through a continual flow of gift exchanges. Emphasizing the network of gift exchanges that constitute life in the world, Primavesi describes the "essential contributions to present gift events made by 'more than' those participating in them now. They include antecedent generations of living beings: all those who, by their lives, their labor, their deaths, their vision, and their patient endeavors have made such events presently possible."[6] Echoing Sittler's remarkable vision of ecological grace, Primavesi emphasizes that the mode of the world and our being in the world is and emerges through a continuous flow of gift exchange.

Today Sittler might find our current climate concerns both disturbingly familiar and wholly unprecedented. It has become increasingly clear that any ecotheology must also engage economics since our relation

---

3. Sittler, *Gravity and Grace*, 44.

4. Indeed, new research reveals that our human bodies are not purely human—less than thirty percent of the cells in our bodies have human DNA so that ninety-nine percent of the genes in our bodies are bacterial and not human. See DeSalle and Perkins, *Welcome to the Microbiome*.

5. Mauss, *The Gift*.

6. Primavesi, "The Preoriginal Gift." See also Primavesi, *Gaia's Gift*.

to climate and nature is so determined by economic systems beyond the control of any one person or nation.[7] Even in current conversations regarding economics and theology the doctrinal focus seems not to have changed from Sittler's time, but where Sittler focused mainly on grace and ecology, current conversations regarding the Protestant tradition and the emergence and perpetuation of capitalism continually return to a critical focus on the Protestant doctrine of grace.

In 1905, long before scientists had established a key connection between fossil fuels and climate change or before arguments, such as Naomi Klein's, explicitly linking climate change and neoliberal capitalism,[8] German sociologist Max Weber may have been the first to link Reformation social and economic shifts with the exploitation of fossilized fuels: "[W] hen asceticism moved out of the monastic cells and into working life, and began to dominate innerworldly morality, it helped to build that mighty cosmos of the modern economic order . . . Today this mighty cosmos determines with overwhelming coercion, the style of life *not only* of those directly involved in business but of every individual who is born into this mechanism, *and may well continue to do so until the day that the last ton of fossil fuel has been consumed.*"[9] More recently, new voices recall a certain spirit of Weber's argument linking the Protestant tradition—particularly the doctrine of grace—to a fossil-fuel-dependent capitalism.[10]

---

7. Theologians John Cobb and Sallie McFague have been early advocates of this shift to consider economic issues alongside ecological concerns. See Daly and Cobb, *For the Common Good*; and McFague, *Life Abundant*.

8. Klein, *This Changes Everything*. Klein, an American journalist, advised Pope Francis as he was writing his encyclical on climate change, *Laudato Si'*; see Klein, "A Radical Vatican?" My argument is not that *any* form of capitalism would be destructive, nor is it that socialism *necessarily* provides an agreeable alternative. In large part, I would agree with theologian John Cobb and economist (and former member of the World Bank) Herman Daly, who argue that one of the most pressing challenges facing us today is to find an alternative to the capitalism/socialism binary since both systems "are fully committed to large-scale, factory-style energy and capital-intense, specialized production units that are hierarchically managed"; *For the Common Good*, 2. I emphasize capitalism in this essay because it is the predominant economic model in the world today.

9. Weber, *The Protestant Ethic*, 120–21; emphasis added.

10. It is clear the Reformers did not intend most of what we find in capitalism today. What's more, recent Lutheran theo-ethicists persuasively argue that capitalist practices were already emerging by the time Luther and Calvin inspired their theological movements. German theo-ethicist Ulrich Duchrow, for instance, argues that Luther and Calvin were already early critics of capitalist practices; Duchrow, *Alternatives to Global Capitalism*.

Anglo-Catholic John Milbank and others associating with the theological movement Radical Orthodoxy engage Mauss's gift theory, arguing that the Protestant articulation of grace created a new gift/exchange dualism by idealizing the gift as free of exchange. This dualism, and the nominalist philosophy on which they argue it was built, contributed to the conceptual foundations of neoliberal capitalism, namely individualism and commodification.

In a context where neoliberal capitalism is increasingly aligned with the pernicious effects of climate change and increasing global economic inequality, such arguments deserve serious analysis and critical, creative, and gracious responses worthy of an Eco-Reformation. In this essay we will submerse ourselves in these current tensions, challenges, and opportunities for Protestant theology with assistance from a proliferation of Protestant theologians responding to gift theory, especially those who align with the Finnish interpretation of Luther. However, where these responses rarely acknowledge the profound economic and climate implications of these debates, this essay will engage gift theory by focusing on the ecological and economic issues at stake in the way we define God's grace today.

GRACE AS FREE GIFT

The Lutheran understanding of grace is commonly—some might say even ubiquitously—characterized as a "free gift." Berndt Hamm's recent essay, "Martin Luther's Revolutionary Theology of Pure Gift without Reciprocation," powerfully captures this characteristic flavor of Lutheran conceptions of the gift by engaging Mauss's *The Gift*.[11] Hamm argues Mauss demonstrates a primary religious tendency to assume every gift deserves a return, and that a heightened use of this principle arose in the Middle Ages to the point where God and creatures were bound by relations of debt and obligation so there remained "no such thing as an unconditional gift or grace, no behavior without punishment and no pardon without reparation and atonement."[12] In this context Hamm argues, Luther "developed new criteria for what a gift in its absolute sense really is: a pure giving without the least reciprocal gift."[13]

---

11. Hamm, "Martin Luther's Revolutionary Theology," 134.

12. Ibid., 128.

13. Ibid., 150.

Not only did Luther's theology of grace oppose the medieval theologies that compared relation to God with commercial exchange by explicitly employing economic metaphors of "purchasing" merit and obtaining "eternal profit and interest,"[14] he also rejected any remnant of exchange in the theological tradition that most closely influenced him. This latter type of medieval piety—associated with the Franciscan Bonaventure and nominalists like Duns Scotus—already resisted crass comparisons to economic practices by emphasizing the radical difference between God and creation. And yet Luther went further than these as well, Hamm explains, excising all remaining elements of reciprocity or exchange from his concept of grace. Even Luther's "happy exchange" Hamm characterizes as actually "anti-exchange" in that it "runs counter to every sense of an earthly economic exchange as well as of religious logic of an exchange relationship between God and human beings."[15] Hamm's point is clear: Luther's theology initiated a previously "unforeseeable and unimaginable" break from economy and exchange.[16]

ECONOMIC AND ECOLOGICAL IMPLICATIONS OF THE FREE GIFT

Where Hamm clearly establishes the concept of free gift as a central and unique contribution of the Reformation tradition, John Milbank similarly argues that the Protestant movement introduced a new concept of gift. However, Milbank emphasizes that this new concept of gift created an unprecedented dualism between gift and exchange that has become a particularly pernicious expression of modernity. Milbank claims Mauss as an ally in his opposition to the pervasive impact of the free gift in society. Indeed, the impact of Mauss's thinking on the gift is difficult to understate. With it, Mauss inaugurated the discipline of socio-anthropology. Most significant for current theo-economic debates, Milbank and sociologist Mary Douglas highlight gift-exchange as one of the few alternatives to both capitalism and Marxism.[17] Mauss's study of the gift is a meta-analysis of premodern economies and a fundamental critique of the "free gift." Mauss argues that instead of the gift idealized as

14. Ibid., 132.

15. Ibid., 148–49.

16. Ibid., 137.

17. Douglas, forward to *The Gift*, xiv, xvi.

altruistic without expectation of a return gift, in pre-modern societies gift-exchange was the ideal. In these societies any idea of a gift as "free" was not only impossible but a contradiction, because it undermined social connectivity.

Rather than barter—the utilitarian precursor of capitalism—Mauss found that premodern societies and economies are more accurately characterized by gift exchange. More than just a guiding economic principle, gift exchange constituted *the society itself*.[18] Milbank identifies this as one of Mauss's critical insights: that "gift-giving is a mode (the mode in fact) of social being."[19] For Mauss, more than just objects, gifts include acts, practices, and traditions that transcend economic value and individual meaning.[20] These exchanges remain foundational to the society because they are practices that bind people together, even over generations.[21] According to Mauss, relationships are not established first and followed by gifts. Rather, gift-exchange creates relationship.[22]

Mauss explains that modern societies "draw a strict distinction . . . [between] things and persons. Such a separation is basic: it constitutes the essential conditions for a part of our system of property, transfer and exchange." This detachment, however, is "foreign" to a system of gift exchange.[23] Later gift theorists identified this detachment as the "alienable" quality of the free gift.[24] A person could give a gift without expectation of return because the gift was an object, a separable "thing." But in a society of gift exchange a gift was seen as inseparable or "inalienable" from its

18. Mauss, *The Gift*, 46.

19. Milbank, *Being Reconciled*, 156.

20. "What they exchange is not solely property and wealth, movable and immovable goods, and things economically useful. In particular such exchanges are acts of politeness: banquets, rituals, military services, women, children, dances, festivals, and fairs, in which economic transaction is only one element, and in which the passing of wealth is only one feature of a much more general and enduring contract" (Mauss, *The Gift*, 5).

21. Socio-anthropologist Mary Douglas explains: "Just the rule that every gift has to be returned in some specified way sets up a perpetual cycle of exchanges within and between generations" (Douglas, forward to *The Gift*, viii–ix).

22. "The gift is not prior to but coincident with relation such that they are inseparable—interlinked on horizontal and vertical planes, so to speak. As such, 'reciprocity' is inseparable from receiving a gift" (Milbank, "Can a Gift Be Given?," 136).

23. Mauss, *The Gift*, 47.

24. Mauss does not use the terms "alienable" and "inalienable." These developed in a later wave of gift theory aligned with the work of C. A. Gregory and Annette Weiner. See Gregory, *Gifts and Commodities*; and Weiner, *Inalienable Possessions*.

donor because, as Mauss explains, these gifts were imbued in a mysterious or magical way with the personhood of the donor.[25] A gift, therefore, was an extension of the giver so that in giving a gift one was not merely giving an object but a part of oneself. In this sense, the gift participated in the personhood of the giver so that exchange resulted in the interweaving not only of the giver and receiver, but the givers and receivers with their gifts as well.

Consequently, where reciprocity and exchange are commonly associated today with a crass kind of tit for tat or *quid pro quo,* Mauss demonstrates there are other forms of exchange where the expectation was not merely for the return of the gift itself, but of relationship because the gift embodied the giver. "By giving," Mauss explains, "one is giving oneself, and if one gives oneself, it is because one 'owes' oneself—one's person and one's goods—to others."[26] Once given, the gift did not shuttle between discrete individuals. Rather, such exchanges resulted in lives "mingled together" since this is, as Mauss explains, "precisely what contract and exchange are."[27]

In mingling subject and object Milbank argues that Mauss "wrote a meditation against Descartes."[28] According to Milbank, the gift/exchange dualism has its roots in significant metaphysical and cosmological shifts associated with nominalism, particularly the philosophical trajectory from Duns Scotus to William of Ockham that "abandoned a metaphysically participatory framework."[29] Before nominalism, the relation between God and world could be seen as mingled or interwoven together by creation's participation in a continuous Trinitarian gift exchange.[30] Pre-modern gift exchange was viewed "not [as] merely social or cultural at all but [as] an aspect of a cosmic ecology: a vast circulation encompassing natural beings, the gods and the ancestors."[31] But with nominalism a strong divide emerged between God and creation that Milbank sees functioning in the Reformation emphasis on grace as a unilateral gift

---

25. Mauss, *The Gift,* 24.
26. Ibid., 46.
27. Ibid., 20.
28. Milbank, "Can a Gift Be Given?," 133.
29. Milbank, *Beyond Secular Order,* 36.
30. Milbank, *Being Reconciled,* x.
31. Milbank, "The Gift and the Given," 444.

from active giver to passive recipient.[32] Without a participatory sense of exchange a gift could be given from a god increasingly pushed outside the world, ruling with autonomous and sovereign power over the world which could only passively receive from a divine wholly other. A loss of participation and exchange also allowed forgiveness to be opposed to justice and expressed as a "counterpart of Creation" or as "de-creational" since forgiveness simply uncreated or erased a transgression without simultaneously insisting on reciprocal justice to make right what was put wrong.[33] As modernity progressed a divine ideal of external rather than participatory relations increasingly became a model for human subjectivity in autonomy, self-sufficiency, and human beings' assertion of *their* will over a passive and inert nature.[34] This development becomes typified in Descartes's modern subject wherein he defined human consciousness over and against an objectified, unconscious material world. By removing human consciousness from the realm of material nature Descartes's subject/object dualism created the possibility for humans to see nature as object and potential resource rather than something in which they were inherently participants.[35]

32. Milbank describes this gift as "strictly formalist and unilateral . . . as not expecting a return" (Milbank, "Can a Gift Be Given?," 123).

33. Milbank, *Being Reconciled*, 45. Milbank draws on an example from Søren Kierkegaard here.

34. See also Michael Northcott who explains that this nominalist division between God's absolute, arbitrary power and creation set in motion "a new politics, first of the 'divine right' of kings apart from the consent of the governed, and then in the modern era of the social contract according to which the individual is autonomous of the body politic into which she is born until she *contracts* some of her autonomous power by an act of will. This split also gave rise to a new religion in which the individual soul exists as an independent entity within the body, drawn by piety to a life of Puritan self-denial and a related quest for the inner feeling of divine presence. And the split gave rise to a new science in which the body of the earth and the human body become available for investigation and reordering by empirical science, free through nominalist logic from the theologic symbolism of medieval cosmology"; *A Political Theology of Climate Change*, 43.

35. The question of Luther's connection to nominalism is complex. Historians Heiko Oberman and Steven Ozment emphasize Luther's clear alignment with nominalism and also point out that Luther resisted the nominalist formula to "do what is within you" to receive God's grace. However, as Ozment argues, while rejecting this formula he also retained a key structural influence from Ockham, emphasizing that God's grace as well as any church institution could no longer rely on a metaphysical connection to or participation in the divine life. Instead, they became contingent on a "divine act," that "from an infinite number of theoretical possibilities God" had chosen them to be the instruments of the divine will in time (Ozment, *The Age of*

THE DISENCHANTMENT OF THE WORLD
AND ISOLATED INDIVIDUALISM

In spite of Milbank's polemics, his anti-feminism, and his lack of explicit attention to environmental concerns, I find the critique of Protestant grace as a popularization of gift/exchange dualism unavoidable for addressing an Eco-Reformation in our current climate.[36] Milbank's claim that the free gift has become pervasive in modern society is especially difficult to deny. Even after all traces of religious thought have been erased or forgotten the gift/exchange binary has taken on a life of its own. For example, Milbank identifies ways that the free gift functions in the ethics of philosophers Emmanuel Levinas and Jacques Derrida. Milbank argues that in Derrida's gift the altruistic posture of the free gift finds its extreme, but *logical*, conclusion in nihilism. In *Given Time*, Derrida suggests that despite the fact that Mauss said he was writing about the gift, he only arrives at reciprocity and exchange since "[f]or there to be a gift, there must be no reciprocity, return, exchange, countergift, or debt."[37] Yet he also admits this gift is impossible because even knowledge of having given a gift can be a reward of its own. Consequently, the conditions of the gift purified of reciprocity and exchange mean that such giving remains impossible. Milbank argues that in spite of the fact that Derrida, a Jewish-born "rightly passing as an atheist"[38] philosopher, would have no conscious intention of upholding Protestant doctrine, he assumes the modern gift/exchange dualism and demonstrates its logical conclusion in impossibility and nihilism. Milbank's claim also gains support from a far less-sophisticated source that seems bent on inserting itself into this essay. The grammar checker on my word processor indefatigably objects to

---

Reform, 1250–1550, 244). Thus, salvation and authorities of institutions came to rely on God's unilateral declaration. Like Ockham's view of the relation between God and the world, such declaration of worth was not inherent but arbitrary; it depended on the free will of God. Similarly, Graham White and John Montag argue that Luther was both influenced by and resisted nominalism. Montag argues that "Luther recognized the inadequacy of this nominalist restriction, and . . . tried to reinvent—or at least re-invoke—the lush kind of *communicatio/partipatio* between God and creation allowed by the pre-Scotist hierarchy of being"; Montag, "Revelation," 50.

36. See important responses to Milbank in Ruether and Grau, eds., *Interpreting the Postmodern*; and see Rowe, "'A Better Worldliness,'" for a reciprocal critique of Milbank's own capitalizing tendencies.

37. Derrida, *Given Time*, 12.

38. Derrida and Bennington, *Circumfession*, 155.

the phrase "free gift," underscoring the phrase in red with the explanation that this is a "redundant expression." Apparently, the gift *by definition* is free: free of debt, reciprocity, and exchange.

More significant for our current concerns, though, are the implications of the gift/exchange dualism evident in commodification and individualism. Where Max Weber regretted a certain "disenchantment" of the world, Mauss similarly indicates that inalienable gifts were, in a way, enchanted by the giver so that the receiver not only receives an object, but relational participation in the giver. Milbank also takes up the question of the Christian trajectory toward disenchantment, arguing that this "crucial theological issue today" involves the theological constructs that underwrite commodification.[39] "In ancient times," he explains, "objects were not yet commodities, and so were seen as specific things with specific characteristics liable to achieve specific but not quite predictable effects."[40] Gift exchange was possible "in part because of a certain belief in the animation of objects."[41] When presents lost their inalienable qualities, gifts that were once extensions of the giver became mere objects, commodities. Where gifts once wove the fabric of an interconnected society, commodification designates passive objects awaiting human inscription of meaning. Commodities shuttle between separative parties with no enduring relational ties over time.

An alienable or free gift, for example, makes it possible for me to go to a grocery store to purchase milk without any prior, nor continued, relationship to the grocer, the farmers, the cows, or the land on which they were raised. I can enter the building, purchase my commodified cow product and leave without any debts, further obligations, or responsibilities to any of these providers. The shadow side of such purchasing practices becomes evident when we consider our relationship to something less wholesome than milk. Waste, for example, functions by this same logic since it involves rendering something separable from a continuous cycle of rights and responsibilities. I can throw some thing out as "waste" or excess only by unconsciously assuming that this object is alienable from my person.

39. He argues that this tendency to "disenchant" cosmologies is not "entirely loyal to its own nature," but that in actuality Christianity "at its liturgical and sacramental heart, propose[s] a heightened enchantment"; Milbank, *Beyond Secular Order*, 17.

40. Milbank, "The Gift and the Given," 446. See also Gregory, *Gifts and Commodities*, on the connection between alienable gifts and commodification.

41. Ibid., referencing Godbout and Caillé, *The World of the Gift*.

While the gift/exchange dualism lies at the root of the alienation of property, the alienable gift of commodification also implies isolated individualism since the exchange of property involves cutting the ties between giver and receiver that, according to Mauss, create community. As William Cavanaugh explains in his Milbank-influenced critique of Luther's eucharistic theology, the alienable gift marks a "radical differentiation between what is mine and what is thine"[42] because exchange becomes a "spacial transfer of goods between individuals."[43] Rather than a gift tying together members of a community the alienable gift shuttles between isolated individuals leaving no necessary obligation to other members of a body. Milbank argues that when Western society shifted from a cosmology of continual gift exchange wherein creation participated in divine reality to a gift/exchange dualism the groundwork was laid for commodification, isolated individualism, and ultimately neoliberal capitalism. He polemically identifies capitalism as "a mode of Protestant religion" that, because it relies on the free gift which Mauss declared anti-social, offers a "theological legitimation of a new sort of 'amoral' economic practice."[44]

Milbank's main concerns seem to be economic, social, and ecclesial so he does not focus on ecological implications. Christian environmental ethicist Michael Northcott agrees with Milbank's assessment of the destructive influence of nominalism in Western modernity and adds that the nominalist turn marked a decisive shift in the church's previous prohibition of mining. When nominalism removed a perceptible correlation between God's will and the Earth the church no longer felt mining was a sacred violation of the Earth: "If, as Ockham argued, there is only an arbitrary relationship between physical created order and divine moral will, there are no theological grounds for restraining the reordering of the earth by miners and in the forges and metal works that coal fed."[45] As a result, coal mining began, creating the "material base of the emergent capitalism of Germany."[46] At a time when we are realizing, as Northcott explains, that "the fossil fuel economy was not possible without capitalism" and furthermore, that it seems impossible to conceive of a capitalism

---

42. Cavanaugh, "Eucharistic Sacrifice and the Social Imagination," 592.

43. Ibid.

44. Milbank in Žižek and Milbank, *The Monstrosity of Christ*, 127 and 129; cited in Robbins, "The Monstrosity of Protestantism," 93.

45. Northcott, *A Political Theology of Climate Change*, 55.

46. Ibid.

that is not wholly dependent on fossil fuels,[47] an ecotheology that aims
to be eco-reformational is pressed to address some key questions about
its doctrine of grace and corresponding concept of the ideal gift. One of
the most pressing questions appears to be whether a Lutheran theology
of grace can faithfully, accurately, and exclusively be described, as Berndt
Hamm insists, as a free gift exclusive of participation and exchange.

PROTESTANT RESPONSES TO GIFT THEORY

Perhaps the most sustained engagement with gift discourse has been
among Scandinavian Lutherans—particularly those aligning with the
Finnish interpretation of Luther. The Finns offer a crucial counterar-
gument to Milbank's characterization of Protestant theology as fully
nominalist by emphasizing a profound sense of participation in Luther's
theology of grace. Yet even for some scholars affirming the Finnish interpretation the question of the relation between grace and exchange
remains in play.

Tuomo Mannermaa, the instigator of the Finnish interpretation,
first became suspicious that something of Luther's understanding of
grace had been neglected when he was reading Luther's lecture on Gala-
tians and came across the phrase *in ipsa fide Christus adest*, which [Man-
nermaa] retranslates literally as "in faith itself Christ is really present."[48]
Expanding on this emphasis on the indwelling presence of Christ in
faith, the Finns emphasize that grace is not just God's declared favor *extra nos* (outside us), but also includes union with Christ. Finnish scholar
Veli-Matti Kärkkäinen explains, "It is highly significant that Luther himself—in contradistinction to later Lutheranism—does not differentiate
between the person and work of Christ. Christ himself, his person and
his work is the righteousness of man [*sic*]. In the language of the doctrine
of justification it means that Christ is both *donum* and favor (not only favor as subsequent Lutheranism teaches)."[49] Where God's gift is no longer
just a declaration only from outside the human but is now also a gift of
communion with Christ, Christ is no longer just *means* of grace, but *is*
grace as well. Here Christ both *is* and *gives* the gift, indicating a shift from
an alienable to the inalienable gift.

47. Ibid.
48. Braaten and Jenson, eds., *Union with Christ*, viii.
49. Kärkkäinen, "'Christian as Christ to the Neighbor,'" 107.

Consequently, the Finns are critical of the definition of grace in the *Formula of Concord* that ruled out indwelling grace *intra nos* (Christ's presence in us).[50] As we have seen, an emphasis only on the external presence and work of God creates a unilateral gift dynamic where the giver (God) is active and wholly separate from the passive (human) receiver. As Danish scholar Bo Holm explains, "If the divine gift and the divine giver are separated, an emphasis on the forensic dimension of justification and the unilateral direction of it seem to be the necessary consequence . . . On the other hand, if the divine gift and the divine giver are identified, as in the concept of divine self-giving, then there seems to be more room for mutuality between giver and receiver, since the receiver, by participating in the divine self-giving, him/herself becomes a giver."[51] So rather than just emphasizing forensic justification and God's action as purely exterior, the Finns suggest that in generations following Luther an important sense of God's grace as indwelling presence was lost.

Danish theologian Niels Henrik Gregersen agrees that such an emphasis on the redeeming power of love, creating union in gifting relationships, is just what has been underemphasized in Reformation soteriologies. Echoing the Finnish interpretation Gregersen insists, "God not only forgives something but actually gives [Godself], gives shares in [the] divine nature so that human beings become 'participants of divine nature' (2 Peter 1:4)."[52]

The significant shifts in the ideal form of gift proposed by the Finnish interpretation of Luther have also inspired some theologians to suggest that Luther's theology of grace is more like Milbank's participatory ontology of gift-exchange than its opposite. Danish scholar Bo Kristian Holm, for example, does not spend time defending the free gift, since he is convinced that Milbank's "purified gift exchange" is actually a better description of Luther's doctrines of grace and justification than "pure gift." He even argues that from a certain perspective Luther is more exchangist than Milbank himself.[53] Both Holm and American scholar Piotr Malysz point to the "happy exchange" at the heart of Luther's articulation of grace. Responding to William Cavanaugh's critique of Luther's

50. See Mannermaa, "Justification and *Theosis* in Lutheran–Orthodox Perspective," 27–28.

51. Holm, "Nordic Luther Research in Motion," 100.

52. Ibid., 142.

53. See Holm, "Justification and Reciprocity," 89, 100.

eucharistic theology, Malysz agrees with Cavanaugh, arguing as outlined above, that

> Luther's harsh criticism of the commercialized piety and the profit-driven ecclesial establishment of his day—deserved as it was—'led him to the dualism of exchange and gift', which, ironically, only formalized and legitimized contractual exchange by making gift into an idealised exception to, and an interruption within, social transactionality. This dualism lies at the root of the commoditisation and alienation of property in modernity. Because the exchange of property is no longer a process intimately involving the giver and the recipient, modernity is individualistic.[54]

Malysz sets out to demonstrate, however, that in Luther's happy exchange "there are no individualistic 'boundaries between what is mine and what is thine'" for Luther.[55] Both Holm and Malysz argue that on account of the union formed between Christ and the sinner, the gift of grace is inalienable rather than unilateral or purified of exchange. Consequently, in the happy exchange the gift is not merely a transfer of goods but communion between Christ and the sinner.

While Holm, Malysz, and Gregersen embrace participatory union in Luther's understanding of grace, others, like Finnish scholar Risto Saarinen, remain skeptical about any kind of exchange that would blur the lines between giver and receiver. Here again the influence of nominalist dualistic relations seems to emerge when Saarinen argues that "Luther probably could not call agape a 'purified gift-exchange', since his interpretation of God's love is permeated by the fundamental distinction between the giver and the receiver."[56] While Saarinen argues this does not necessarily mean that Luther's gift is "completely unilateralist,"[57] for him, Luther's ideal gift remains free: "A pure love would require a person who is not seeking his own profit but would act altruistically. Giving a completely free gift would be an example of pure love and altruism."[58]

Building off Saarinen's description of Luther's gift, American theologian Ted Peters affirms that according to Luther the gift is free of

---

54. Malysz, "Exchange and Ecstasy," 297.

55. Malysz, 301, citing Cavanaugh, 597.

56. Saarinen, *God and the Gift*, 57.

57. Ibid., 57–58.

58. Ibid., 52.

reciprocity.[59] Peters seems to follow Derrida's logic here, arguing that this kind of pure giving is, in the end, impossible "in the human economy of exchange" where there "are no gifts without strings attached."[60] So, Peters asks, "Are we being asked to do the impossible?"[61] He suggests we move past the aporia of the mandated but impossible gift and see that our gift definitions are abstractions, removed from the concrete world, our concrete experiences with gifts, and the concrete event of God's entering the world and forgiving our sins: "I would like to suggest this is not a real problem . . . there is a confusion here between what is abstract and what is concrete."[62] So according to Peters, the search to find and define a pure gift is not only impossible but unnecessary.

In the significant current conversations about the nature of God's gift and the definition of grace there is not sufficient acknowledgment of the key ecological, economic, and climate issues at stake. I sympathize with Peters's exasperation with gift theory and the search for a pure gift selflessly given without any reciprocity. But as I have demonstrated, there are other ways of articulating the Lutheran concept of gift that embrace interdependent forms of exchange. Where certain Finns shift toward a more participatory ontology and the inalienable gift this also implies a shift from transaction and commodification to communion. So perhaps the issue is not with abstracting as such, but with the *particular* abstraction of gift as free of reciprocity or exchange—in essence, a gift free of interdependent relationship. As Peters notes, the free gift is an abstraction; I suggest this is precisely why it *is* a real problem. The abstract, especially when idealized, has a way of becoming concrete. Our ideal concept of gift and the human self in relation to God and creation matters; they will come to materialize in the ways we interact with humans and all creation.

OUR BEING IS COMMUNION

The doctrine of grace remains one of the most urgent areas in need of ecotheological engagement. In current conversations about the nature of God's grace the stakes are not merely theological, but economic and ecological as well. It is difficult to see how the doctrine of grace would

59. Peters, *Sin Boldly!*, 376.

60. Ibid., 377.

61. Ibid., 378.

62. Ibid., 378–79.

be able to provide a life-giving alternative to and not unwittingly under-write foundational modes of a socially and ecologically degrading form of capitalism if we exclusively insist on grace as a function of God's active work on us *extra nos* (outside ourselves), with no indwelling, participa-tory sense of communion with Christ *intra nos* (among ourselves). Lu-ther's own sense that Christ both *gives* and *is* the gift in reciprocity and interdependence may function today as a corrective to a pervasive and ecologically perilous articulation of grace as a gift free of exchange.

We live in an interdependent world of continual ecological and economic gift exchange. If we take this vision of reality as a given, so to speak, what then is the relation of the particular articulation of Lutheran grace to this reality? Do we talk about grace from the pulpit, at the font, and around the table in a way that seems to have anything to do with the way we view nature? Protestants are now pressed to reflect seriously on the way we envision divine redemption in relation to this interdependent world sustained by creaturely exchanges. Is divine grace truly separate from—merely an interruption of—the systems of creation that sustain life in the world? How do we reconcile such views with a God who is both creator and redeemer? Bill McKibben has persuasively argued in his reflections on the book of Job that in this age of global climate cri-sis humans have become decreators.[63] In this context do we really want to profess that the work of redemption is anti-exchangist and thus de-creational?[64] Can we live with the consequences? Can we survive them?

Sittler strove to articulate a concept of grace where the human self emerged as fully embedded in and dependent on a multiplicity of divine and human gifts—where we have no self prior to communion. Sittler's poetic prose tied grace and nature together with seeming ease—a remarkable achievement given the challenges. Even more today it is im-perative that our concepts of grace affirm—or even confront us with—a sense that we are embedded in a delicately balanced and interdependent relationship with the rest of creation. This task is imperative for the sake of clearly and coherently articulating a doctrine of grace worthy of an Eco-Reformation.

The practical implications of this articulation of gift are signifi-cant and widely untapped in contemporary American expressions of

63. McKibben, *The Comforting Whirlwind*, 8. See also Cynthia Moe-Lobeda's essay in this volume on humans as "un-creators."

64. See Milbank, "Forgiveness," in *Being Reconciled*, 44–60, where he argues Prot-estant forgiveness essentially does the work of "decreation."

the Lutheran tradition. If God's mode of saving and life-giving activity emerges primarily in exchanges that create community with Christ's body, then our churches can no longer theologically or ethically afford to limit grace to the forgiveness of human sins. If God's work appears not as anti-exchange but in community-building exchanges with the human and other-than-human world, then our congregations are not just called to engage these communities in acts of philanthropy and charity. They are also called to engage global economic systems and envision alternative local economies that work toward practices to build up community rather than exclude, alienate, or degrade the natural world—including other humans. Saving grace provides an alternative to alienating human economies with a life-giving economy built on participation in the wider biotic community and the divine life itself.

As we stand at an historical moment looking back on five hundred years of the Reformation and forward for the next five hundred we may justifiably wonder what shape the Reformation tradition will take in that time—and the shape of Earth as well. I have suggested that these two questions and concerns are intimately related. This movement inspired massive social, economic, political, and religious shifts five hundred years ago. Today the world needs shifts on this same scale and even broader. As we look to the next five hundred years the doctrine of grace may again emerge as an indispensable resource for reimagining social, economic, political, divine, and now ecological relations.

BIBLIOGRAPHY

Billings, J. Todd. "John Milbank's Theology of the 'Gift' and Calvin's Theology of Grace: A Critical Comparison." *Modern Theology* 21 (2005) 87–105.

Braaten, Carl E., and Robert W. Jenson, eds. *Union with Christ: The New Finnish Interpretation of Luther.* Grand Rapids: Eerdmans, 1998.

Cavanaugh, William T. "Eucharistic Sacrifice and the Social Imagination in Early Modern Europe." *Journal of Medieval and Early Modern Studies* 31 (2001) 585–605.

Connolly, William E. *Capitalism and Christianity, American Style.* Durham: Duke University Press, 2008.

Daly, Herman E., and John B. Cobb, Jr. *For the Common Good: Redirecting the Economy toward Community, the Environment, and a Sustainable Future.* 2nd ed. Boston: Beacon, 1994.

Derrida, Jacques. *The Animal That Therefore I Am.* Edited by Marie-Louise Mallet. Translated by David Wood. New York: Fordham University Press, 2008.

———. *Given Time: I. Counterfeit Money.* Translated by Peggy Kamuf. Chicago: University of Chicago Press, 1994.

Derrida, Jacques, and Geoffrey Bennington. *Circumfession*. In *Jacques Derrida*. Translated by Geoffrey Bennington. Chicago: University of Chicago Press, 1993.

DeSalle, Rob, and Susan L. Perkins. *Welcome to the Microbiome: Getting to Know the Trillions of Bacteria In, On, and Around You*. New Haven: Yale University Press, 2015.

Douglas, Mary. Foreword to *The Gift: The Form and Reason for Exchange in Archaic Societies*, by Marcel Mauss, vii–xviii. New York: Norton, 1990.

Duchrow, Ulrich. *Alternatives to Global Capitalism: Drawn from Biblical History, Designed for Political Action*. Utrecht: International Books, 1996.

Godbout, Jacques T., and Alain Caillé. *The World of the Gift*. Translated by Donald Winkler. Montreal: McGill/Queen's University Press, 1998.

Gregory, C. A. *Gifts and Commodities*. Studies in Political Economy. London: Academic Press, 1982.

Hamm, Berndt. "Martin Luther's Revolutionary Theology of Pure Gift without Reciprocation." Translated by Timothy J. Wengert. *Lutheran Quarterly* 29 (2015) 125–61.

Haroutunian, Joseph. *God with Us: A Theology of Transpersonal Life*. Philadelphia: Westminster, 1965.

Holm, Bo Kristian. "Justification and Reciprocity: 'Purified Gift-exchange' in Luther and Milbank.'" In *Word—Gift—Being: Justification—Economy—Ontology*, edited by Bo Kristian Holm and Peter Widmann, 87–116. Religion in Philosophy and Theology 37. Tübingen: Mohr/Siebeck, 2009.

———. "Luther's Theology of the Gift." In *The Gift of Grace: The Future of Lutheran Theology*, edited by Niels Henrik Gregersen, Bo Holm, Ted Peters, and Peter Widmann, 78–86. Minneapolis: Fortress, 2005.

———. "Nordic Luther Research in Motion." *Dialog* 47 (2008) 93–104.

Kärkkäinen, Veli-Matti. "'Christian as Christ to the Neighbor': On Luther's Theology of Love." *International Journal of Systematic Theology* 6 (2004) 101–17.

Klein, Naomi. *This Changes Everything: Capitalism vs. the Climate*. New York: Simon & Schuster, 2014.

Malysz, Piotr J. "Exchange and Ecstasy: Luther's Eucharistic Theology in Light of Radical Orthodoxy's Critique of Gift and Sacrifice." *Scottish Journal of Theology* 60 (2007) 294–308.

Mauss, Marcel. *The Gift: The Form and Reason for Exchange in Archaic Societies*, translated by W. D. Halls. New York: W. W. Norton, 1990.

McFague, Sallie. *Life Abundant: Theology and Economy for a Planet in Peril*. Minneapolis: Fortress, 2001.

McKibben, Bill. *The Comforting Whirlwind: God, Job, and the Scale of Creation*. Cambridge, MA: Cowley, 2005.

Milbank, John. *Being Reconciled: Ontology and Pardon*. Radical Orthodoxy Series. New York: Routledge, 2003.

———. *Beyond Secular Order: The Representation of Being and the Representation of the People*. Hoboken, NY: Wiley-Blackwell, 2013.

———. "Can a Gift Be Given?: Prolegomena to a Future Trinitarian Metaphysic." *Modern Theology* 11 (1995) 119–61.

———. "The Gift and the Given." *Theory, Culture & Society* 23 (2006) 444–47.

Montag, John. "Revelation: The False Legacy of Suárez." In *Radical Orthodoxy: A New Theology*, edited by John Milbank, Catherine Pickstock, and Graham Ward, 38–63. New York: Routledge, 1999.

Northcott, Michael. *A Political Theology of Climate Change*. Grand Rapids: Eerdmans, 2013.

Oberman, Heiko A. *The Dawn of the Reformation: Essays in Late Medieval and Early Reformation Thought*. Grand Rapids: Eerdmans, 1992.

———. *Luther: Man between God and the Devil*. Translated by Eileen Walliser-Schwarzbart. New York: Doubleday, 1992.

Ozment, Steven. *The Age of Reform, 1250–1550: An Intellectual and Religious History of Late Medieval and Reformation Europe*. New Haven: Yale University Press, 1980.

Peters, Ted. *Sin Boldly!: Justifying Faith for Fragile and Broken Souls*. Minneapolis: Fortress, 2015.

Primavesi, Anne. *Gaia's Gift: Earth, Ourselves and God after Copernicus*. New York: Routledge, 2004.

———. "The Preoriginal Gift—and Our Response to It." In *Ecospirit: Religions and Philosophies for the Earth*, edited by Laurel Kerns and Catherine Keller, 217–32. Transdisciplinary Theological Colloquia. New York: Fordham University Press, 2007.

Risto Saarinen, *God and the Gift: An Ecumenical Theology of Giving*. Collegeville, MN: Liturgical, 2005.

Robbins, Jeffrey. "The Monstrosity of Protestantism." *Expositions* 4 (2010) 89–94.

Rowe, Terra S. "'A Better Worldliness': Economy, Ecology and the Protestant Tradition." PhD diss., Drew University, 2016.

Ruether, Rosemary Radford, and Marion Grau, eds. *Interpreting the Postmodern: Responses to "Radical Orthodoxy."* New York: T. & T. Clark, 2006.

Sittler, Joseph. "Called to Unity" *Ecumenical Review* 14 (1962) 177–87.

———. *Essays on Nature and Grace*. Philadelphia: Fortress, 1972.

———. *Gravity and Grace: Reflections and Provocations*. Edited by Thomas S. Hanson. Minneapolis: Fortress, 2005.

Walter, Gregory. *Being Promised: Theology, Gift, and Practice*. Grand Rapids: Eerdmans, 2013.

Weber, Max. *The Protestant Ethic and the 'Spirit' of Capitalism and Other Writings*. Translated and edited by Peter Baehr and Gordon C. Wells. New York: Penguin, 2002.

Weiner, Annette B. *Inalienable Possessions: The Paradox of Keeping-While-Giving*. Berkeley: University of California Press, 1992.

Žižek, Slavoj, and John Milbank. *The Monstrosity of Christ: Paradox or Dialectic?* Cambridge: MIT Press, 2009.

16

Ninety-Five Eco-Theses

A Call for Churches to Care for Earth

—NORMAN C. HABEL

PREFACE

THE FOLLOWING "NINETY-FIVE ECO-THESES" have been formulated on the basis of insights and writings of concerned Christians across the globe who have been exploring the role of the church in the context of the current ecological crisis. These Eco-Theses announce that the time has come to call the church to account and to engage in Earth care. Earth care is a serious mission of the church grounded in the principles outlined in these theses.

I have long been involved personally in exploring the interconnections between Lutheran theology, ecology and biblical interpretation. *The Earth Bible Series*, first published in 2000, articulates principles for an ecological reading of the Bible, principles that have been developed in later publications. I was also involved in the formulation and promotion of *The Season of Creation*, a discrete season of the church year designed to focus on worship with, and care for, creation. This season also enables the church to integrate theology, ecology, and liturgy in the context of the current environmental crisis.

More recently I have developed an *Earth-Care Charter* in collaboration with Lutheran Education Australia as a basis for making Earth Care an integral part of the curriculum of Lutheran schools in Australia. This charter commences with a principle designed to make students aware they are living in a "cosmic sanctuary" called planet Earth, a sanctuary that needs to be sustained and celebrated, not polluted or degraded.

Taking into account this background, the current ecological crisis, the anniversary of the Lutheran Reformation, and the urgent need for the church to take Earth Care seriously, I have formulated the following theses that I believe are consistent with the Lutheran heritage and sensitive to the cries of our wounded planet.

THESES 1–10:
THE PRINCIPLE OF CONTINUING REFORMATION

1. *Ecclesia semper reformanda* (the church is always reforming) is an axiom from the Lutheran tradition that supports future reformation of the church.

2. An Eco-Reformation is a crucial reformation that the church must face as its members become aware of the current environmental crisis.

3. An Eco-Reformation is a challenge the church needs to face today as it remains true to its history precisely as a church of the sixteenth century Reformation.

4. An Eco-Reformation must take into account the Gospel principle of *deus crucifixus* (the crucified God), our earlier Reformation heritage, Biblical voices, the cries of creation, and ecological insights.

5. An Eco-Reformation must also take into account theologies, traditions, practices and biblical readings that have hindered positive relations with creation and made us heaven-oriented or overtly anthropocentric.

6. An Eco-Reformation needs to confront Lutheran traditions that have viewed the earlier Reformation as a *fait accompli* of the sixteenth century, and re-examine traditional doctrines to discern whether they are relevant in the current environmental crisis.

7. An Eco-Reformation is necessary if the church is to have a voice that is relevant in a contemporary society where the ideology of economic progress tends to govern our relationship to planet Earth.

8. An Eco-Reformation must develop a world-wide eco-mission and eco-ministry program that works toward the restoration of creation.

9. An Eco-Reformation requires that the worship life of the church be transformed to embrace the suffering of, and celebration with, creation.

10. An Eco-Reformation ought to be a positive extension of the original Reformation, giving thanks to God for the past, as we face the environmental crisis and the future.

THESES 11–20:
THE PRINCIPLE OF COSMIC ECOLOGY

11. The universe is an integrated cosmos designed by the Creator Spirit employing Wisdom as the primal blueprint (Prov 8) and *Logos* (John 1) as the primal creative force.

12. The various domains in the universe are not only primal expressions of the Creator Spirit, but also interrelated forces, laws and realms that form an integrated cosmos.

13. This interrelationship of realms and laws of creation was discerned by Job during his tour of the cosmos under the tutelage of God, the Sage (Job 38–39).

14. Contemporary ecology explores the cosmos and its interrelated components in a scientific way comparable to that of ancient Wisdom thinkers.

15. The findings of ecology are, in fact, tantamount to a contemporary revelation of the cosmos as the integrated web of God's creation.

16. Ecology has demonstrated that there is a single integrated community called Earth that includes all its members, whether human or other than human. Every member of that community is an integral part of the cosmos.

17. Ecology has made it clear that Earth is a living planet with a delicate lifeline that demands our constant care and attention, if we are to survive.

18. Ecology emphasises that Earth is a fragile web of interconnected forces and domains of existence that require the loving care of everyone living on the planet.

19. The preservation of biodiversity—everything from seeds to species—is crucial for the survival of life on our planetary home.

20. The church, in its eco-reformation mandate, needs to make cosmic ecology an integral part of its theology, mission and ministry.

THESES 21–30:
THE PRINCIPLE OF EARTH AS SANCTUARY

21. Earth is a sanctuary, a sacred site in the cosmos, a holy place chosen by God.

22. The Sanctus of Isa 6:3 makes it clear that the whole Earth is "filled" with the "presence" of God, making our planet a divine sanctuary like the tabernacle of ancient Israel.

23. To celebrate Earth as a sanctuary we are invited to worship in God's presence at sacred places across the planet, everywhere from rainforests to beaches, from green gardens to red deserts.

24. Worshiping in Earth as a sanctuary involves joining with the domains of creation in celebrating God's presence as the Psalmist does in Ps 148.

25. The church has too frequently given thanks *for* the gifts of creation without giving thanks *with or to* creation. It is time to sing with the trees, the birds and the bees in thanking the God of creation, and to give thanks also to the creation.

26. By celebrating *The Season of Creation*, churches could dedicate a period of the church year to celebrate their relationship with God's creation.

27. Since God is present in this sanctuary called Earth, this planet is also sacramental, imparting blessing and healing to all animate beings and inanimate domains.

28. To pollute planet Earth is to defile God's sanctuary, an action the church should oppose openly and publicly.

29. The church is called to affirm publicly the sacred dimension of our planetary home and find ways to create a conscious awareness of God's presence on Earth in all its worship and witness.

30. The church, in terms of its eco-reformation mandate, needs to relate to Earth as a vibrant sanctuary rather than a lifeless mass of matter.

THESES 31–40:
THE PRINCIPLE OF NATURE AS REVELATION

31. Luther's recognition of the domains of creation as *larvae dei* (masks of God) challenges us to revere creation and its eco-systems as media of divine revelation rather than resources to be exploited.

32. Indigenous peoples, like the Australian Aborigines, have long read the landscape and discerned the presence and the work of the Creator Spirit in natural phenomena.

33. Whether we recognize it or not, scientists have also long been reading the natural world and discovering mysteries that reveal to Christians an even greater mystery, the Creator Spirit.

34. One of the greatest recent discoveries of scientists is ecology, a revelation that highlights the primal design of the universe as an integrated cosmos.

35. In Job 28 we are confronted with God, functioning as a scientist, searching creation to locate the mystery of Wisdom innate in nature; God finds that mystery located in the laws of nature (Job 28:23–27).

36. Another profound revelation is evolution, the primal creative impulse from the Creator continuing through time. As Lutherans, we can recognize this revelation in nature as *creatio continua* (continual creation).

37. We can also recognize all these mysteries in nature as expressions of the Spirit embedded in the *larvae dei*, the masks of God's dynamic presence and continuing revelation via creation.

38. After his tour of the cosmos and his discernment of Wisdom throughout the domains of creation, Job confesses that creation reveals God's presence; Job observes/sees God in the cosmos (Job 42:2–5).

39. *Creatio continua* (continual creation) is evident also in the life-giving presence (face) and animating spirit (breath) of God that renews the "face of the ground" every day (Ps 104:27–30).

40. The church, in the context of an Eco-Reformation, needs to focus on the numerous revelations of God's presence through nature as inspirations and directives for reading the cosmos as a sacred text.

THESES 41–50:
THE PRINCIPLE OF ECO-HERMENEUTICS

41. It is time for the church to read the Scriptures not only from the perspective of humans (anthropocentric hermeneutics), but also from the perspective of God's Earth and all domains of creation (eco-hermeneutics).

42. An ecological reading of the Scriptures reveals a long tradition of Earth suffering at the hands of humans and of creation groaning in resistance to human exploitation.

43. By identifying with all creatures and domains in the text, it is possible to discern whether Earth and Earth creatures are affirmed as realms of value and worth or devalued as dispensable.

44. Reading from an ecological perspective, we can encounter texts that explicitly value creation and the domains of creation as green texts, and passages that devalue creation as grey texts.

45. A green reading of the text is also grounded in the recognition that, as an Earth being, the reader ought to have empathy for Earth and Earth beings found in the text.

46. One goal of reading the text from an ecological perspective is to retrieve the suppressed voice of Earth creatures and desecrated domains of creation.

47. In the beginning of the flood narrative (read as a grey text), for example, we could hear Earth asking why Earth and all the creatures of Earth must die because of the sins of one species—human beings (Gen 6:5–7, 13).

48. At the end of the larger flood story (read as a green text) we can hear Earth's cry of relief when God makes a covenant never again to destroy Earth with a flood (Gen 9:9–17).

49. A challenge for the church is to come to terms with texts that seem to indicate that Earth is disposable or of little value when the Creator originally declared all creation to be "very good" (Gen 1:25).

50. The church, in the context of an Eco-Reformation, needs to question whether its readings of the Scripture have been sensitive to the valued presence of Earth, or whether its anthropocentric readings have tolerated the de-valuing of creation and domains of creation resulting in the current environmental crisis.

THESES 51–60:
THE PRINCIPLE OF RESTORATIVE JUSTICE

51. The church needs to promote restorative justice as a fitting model of eco-justice to face the current crisis for our planet home.

52. Restorative justice recognizes that the abuse of God's creation is unjust and cruel.

53. In this context the church needs to hear the cries from Earth and the creatures of Earth as did the prophets of old (Jer 4:28; Joel 1:10).

54. The church needs to recognize that these laments of creation are cries for justice addressed to God (Jer 12:11; Joel 1:17–20).

55. Hearing the cries of Earth and other Earth beings requires that we listen with a consciousness that we humans are also Earth beings who strive for the restoration of Earth.

56. For restorative justice and reconciliation to be genuine, the church needs to confess its role and the role of humanity in the abuse of creation as the church promotes a public policy of eco-ministry.

57. The church also needs to hear the groaning of creation as cries of hope—labor pains—for the restoration of all humans and all creation (Rom 8:18–21).

58. The church needs to assure those who hear Earth's cries that the Wounded Healer is with God's people in the task of healing and restoration.

59. Pursuit of restorative justice for Earth and Earth creatures ultimately requires an eco-ethics policy that embraces the rights of Earth and the domains of Earth.

60. An Eco-Reformation calls on those in tune with the voices of Earth to be outspoken advocates on behalf of Earth and the creatures of Earth.

THESES 61–70:
THE PRINCIPLE OF BEING EARTH BEINGS

61. The church needs to face the fact that popular theology has often focused on heaven as our true home, viewing Earth as "this barren" land where humans travel as pilgrims.

62. The time has come for us to acknowledge that we are not only human beings but also Earth beings and that Earth is our God-given home, a home to be loved and protected.

63. The reality that we are Earth beings is not only revealed in the creation of the first human being from the humus of Earth (*adam* from *adamah*), but also from the confession of the Psalmist that we are formed secretly by the Creator in "the depths of Earth" (Ps 139:13–15).

64. Ecology also reveals that we have emerged from Earth, that we are Earth beings composed of the same matter as the planet—soil, air, fire, water and minerals.

65. Being born of Earth, we can view Earth as a parent whom we not only love and support, but also from whom we can learn how to live in this community called planet Earth.

66. As Earth beings we are kin with all other Earth beings—everything from worms to whales, from lizards to lilacs—and have a responsibility to care for our kin.

67. The Gospel of John reveals that God, the Word, became flesh, a living being who was an Earth being like each of us humans (John 1:14).

68. As an Earth being, the very presence of God in Jesus Christ is an integral part of the cosmos where we live and move and have our being as Earth beings.

69. It is incumbent on the church to proclaim a Gospel that links us humans as Earth beings, the Earth being called Jesus and all Earth beings, as part of God's Earth, a sacred domain in the cosmos.

70. An Eco-Reformation can affirm the Gospel principle that *sola gratia* (grace alone) relates not only to the free gift of human salvation but also to the free gift of creation which we are so privileged to enjoy by our very existence as Earth beings.

THESES 71–80:
THE PRINCIPLE OF ECO-MISSION

71. The mission of the church is to announce the good news of the Gospel to all peoples (Matt 28:18–20).

72. The mission of the church is to follow the way of Jesus Christ and announce the good news to the poor, oppressed, and broken (Luke 4:18).

73. The mission of the church is eco-mission or a mission to care for creation that God has entrusted to us.

74. This encompassing mission is first announced to the first humans in Eden, a mission to nurture and preserve the primal forest of planet Earth (Gen 2:15).

75. This mission is also found in the early church who remembered Jesus saying, "go and preach the Gospel to all creation" (Mark 16:15).

76. The commission to "serve and preserve" (Gen 2:15) is more than a biblical reference; it is a call to change our dominating ways and relate to creation as custodians who love and care for creation as a precious gift from God.

77. As committed custodians of creation we also need to recognize and learn from Aboriginal custodians of past generations who preserved their environment before the advent of the industrial eras.

78. The church needs to face the harsh reality that humanity has committed crimes against creation by its exploitation of planet Earth believing such actions were justified in the light of the mandate to dominate Earth creatures and "subdue the Earth" in Gen 1:28.

79. The church ought to proclaim the Gospel message Jesus articulates when he claims the Son of Man has some to "serve" and not to dominate, like the rulers of his day (Mark 10:42–45).

80. The eco-mission of the church demands an eco-ministry, which involves actual programs of Earth-care that demonstrate our commitment to the principles of an Eco-Reformation.

THESES 81–90:
THE PRINCIPLE OF *DEUS CRUCIFIXUS*

81. The traditional teaching of *deus crucifixus* (God crucified) is pivotal to our faith in a God who suffers not only with and for humanity, but also with and for the entire cosmos.

82. Central to our understanding of the Gospel is our faith in a God whose true nature is revealed on the cross of Jesus Christ.

83. This God on the cross is the God who suffers for and with all creation in the Earth being we know as Jesus Christ.

84. This God is also the God of creation and ecology "in whom all things hold together" (Col 1:15–17) and who unites "all things" (all creation) in Christ (Eph 1:10).

85. This God is the divine presence in the cosmic Christ through whom "all things are reconciled" in the cosmos (Col 1:19–20).

86. This reconciliation of the forces in nature is grounded in the "blood of the cross," the human presence of the crucified God (Col 1:20).

87. The empathetic involvement of creation in the death of Christ is revealed when "Earth quakes and rocks split" as Jesus breathes his last (Matt 27:51–52).

88. In response to the compassion of the Creator revealed in *deus crucifixus*, the church needs to respond with empathy for the suffering domains of nature.

89. The compassion of the Creator is a cosmic reality known to the Psalmists of old who declared that Earth is filled not only with the presence of God (Isa 6:3) but also with the compassion of the Lord (Ps 33:5).

90. The church, in the context of an Eco-Reformation, needs to proclaim the good news that our compassionate God suffers for and sustains not only human beings on Earth, but also the suffering domains of the cosmos.

THESES 91–95:
THE ECO-REFORMATION MANDATE

91. The Church should give thanks for five hundred years of Reformation history and embark on an Eco-Reformation as recognition of its commitment to continuing Reformation as a necessity for creation.

92. The Church should teach and preach a theology of creation that incorporates the principles of these Ninety-Five Eco-Theses and focuses on the Gospel principle of God suffering for and with all the cosmos.

93. The Church should pursue an eco-mission and an eco-ministry that involves explicit ecological practices designed to heal our wounded planet and restore creation.

94. The Church should be in tune with creation as it worships, responding to the laments of Earth and celebrating with the diverse domains of the cosmos.

95. The Church should take the initiative to proclaim to the world the good news that the Creator Spirit continues to breathe in and restore all places of suffering and brokenness on Earth, a resurrection begun in Christ and continuing through the church's own life and ongoing eco-reformation.

POSTSCRIPT

As I indicated in Thesis 77, we can learn much from the Aboriginal custodians of our lands on Earth. If we listen, we can also hear their empathy for the wounding of our planet mother. One poem by an Aboriginal Australian, Mary Duroux, illustrates this empathy:

> My mother, my Mother,
>   what have they done?
> Crucified you
>   like the Only Son!
> Murder committed
>   by mortal hand.
> I weep my mother,
>   my mother, the land.

BIBLIOGRAPHY

Duroux, Mary. *Dirge for Hidden Art.* Moruya, NSW: Heritage, 1992.

CPSIA information can be obtained
at www.ICGtesting.com
Printed in the USA
LVHW052255161220
674393LV00005B/478